W9-BXC-435

LYRIC POETRY

LYRIC POETRY

BEYOND NEW CRITICISM

EDITED BY CHAVIVA HOŠEK

AND PATRICIA PARKER

CORNELL UNIVERSITY PRESS

ITHACA AND LONDON

First published 1985 by Cornell University Press.

International Standard Book Number 0-8014-1647-7 (cloth)
International Standard Book Number 0-8014-9301-3 (paper)
Library of Congress Catalog Card Number 84-20000
Printed in the United States of America

Library of Congress Cataloging in Publication Data

Main entry under title
Lyric poetry.

Bibliography: p.
Includes index.
1. Lyric poetry—History and criticism—Addresses, essays, lectures. I. Hošek, Chaviva, 1946– II. Parker, Patricia, 1945–
PN1356.L97 1985 809.1'4'09 84-20000
ISBN 0-8014-1647-7 (alk. paper)
ISBN 0-8014-9301-3 (pbk. : alk. paper)

The paper in this book is acid-free and meets the guidelines for permanence and durability of the Committee on Production Guidelines for Book Longevity of the Council on Library Resources.

CONTENTS

Contents

PART THREE

PART FOUR

PREFACE

This book is designed to serve as an introduction to the varieties of criticism and theory which have transformed literary interpretation in recent years—structuralist and poststructuralist, feminist, psychoanalytic, Marxist, semiotic, reader-response. It is intended to appeal to students, critics, and teachers of poetry, as well as to those interested in the application of literary theory to the study of texts from several historical periods.

Many of the newer criticisms have arisen since, and in opposition to, New Criticism, which greatly influenced the interpretation of poetry from the 1930s to the 1950s and whose influence still persists in the classroom, long after multiple pronouncements of its demise. The essays in this volume bring together a variety of recent critical practices and introduce their assumptions and strategies to the reader on New Criticism's chosen ground, the analysis of poetic texts. Rather than raise issues and conflicts of theory at a purely abstract level, the essays bring contemporary critical questions to bear on actual readings of specific lyric poems and traditions.

Drawing on a wide range of influences on contemporary theory—from Saussure, Lacan, Derrida, and Cixous to Adorno, Benjamin, Foucault, and others—the essays as a whole both exemplify and provide perspectives on several central issues within current critical debate: the conflict between an emphasis on rhetorical tropes and the analysis of speech acts; the impact of feminism and Marxism on literary inquiry; the interest in "intertextuality" or the "anxiety of influence"; the possibility of bringing history, politics, and biography back into the interpretation of poetry; the relation of deconstructive and other formalisms to the formalism of New Criticism itself. The poetic texts and forms addressed range from classical and medieval to contemporary lyric, from epitaph and elegy to sonnet and ode, from the relation between the lyric and the dramatic monologue or longer poem to the workings of parody, allusion, and pastiche.

The book, therefore, seeks to bring the reader the best of two worlds—the close analysis of poetry which was the greatest achievement of New Criticism and the theoretical speculation of more recent criticism—in a way that makes the latter readily accessible.

A volume of this range inevitably runs many debts. We thank Jennifer Levine and C. Anderson Silber for their helpful reading of drafts of the introduction; Jean Wilson and Joseph Adamson for assistance with the bibliography; Ann McCarthy, Karen Schucher, and Rea Wilmshurst for their typing of various portions of the manuscript and Karen Schucher for her cheerful help in countless other ways; and Bernhard Kendler for his unfailing patience and support. For help with imagining, planning, and executing the symposium "Lyric Poetry and the New New Criticism" (October 1982), which occasioned the first appearance of thirteen of these essays, we are grateful to Jonathan Arac, H. Jennifer Brady, Cyrus Hamlin, Mary Nyquist, Julian Patrick, and C. Anderson Silber. And for financial support that made the symposium possible, we thank the Alumni of Victoria College; the Departments of English and French, the Graduate Centre for Comparative Literature, and the Dean of Arts and Science (The Snider Bequest) at the University of Toronto; Goethe House (Toronto); the British Council; and the Social Sciences and Humanities Research Council of Canada.

Illness prevented Paul de Man from reading his own paper at this symposium; it was read in his absence by John Hollander and played a major role in the subsequent debate. Professor de Man died while this volume was in preparation. Many of the essays in it could not have been written without his thought and work, which remain a provocative presence both in this book and in the continuing investigation of poetry and theory of which it forms a part.

We express our thanks to the publishers and individuals who have granted permission to quote passages from the following works: Permission to quote from "Autumnal," "The Death of Lovers," and "Alchemy of Suffering" from *Les Fleurs du Mal* by Charles Baudelaire, translated by Richard Howard (Boston: David R. Godine Inc., 1981); translation copyright © 1981 by Richard Howard, reprinted by permission of David R. Godine, Publisher, Boston. Permission to quote from Daryl Hine, "The Double-Goer," in *The Devil's Picture Book,* copyright © 1960 by Daryl Hine, reprinted with the permission of Atheneum Publishers from *Selected Poems,* copyright © 1980 by Daryl Hine. Permission to quote from Jay Macpherson, "No Man's Nightingale" and "O Fenix Culpa" from *Poems Twice Told* (1981), © Oxford University Press Canada. Permission to quote from "Aubade" by William Empson in *Collected Poems,* copyright 1949, renewed 1977 by William Empson, reprinted by permission of Harcourt Brace Jovanovich, Inc., the author's Literary Estate, and Chatto & Windus. Permission to quote from "Peter Quince at the Clavier" and "An Ordinary Evening in New Haven" by Wallace Stevens from *The Collected Poems of Wallace Stevens* (New York: Alfred A. Knopf, 1954), copyright © 1954 by Wallace Stevens; from "In the South" by Wallace Stevens from *Opus Posthumous,* edited by Samuel French Morse (New York: Alfred A. Knopf, 1957), copyright © 1957 by Elsie Stevens and Holly Stevens; from a letter of 3 May 1939 in *Letters of Wallace Stevens,* edited by Holly Stevens (New York: Alfred A. Knopf, 1972), copyright © 1972 by Holly Stevens; from *The Necessary Angel: Essays on Reality and the Imagination* (New York: Alfred A. Knopf, 1951), copyright © 1951 by Wallace Stevens.

Permission to quote from a letter of Wallace Stevens of 20 December 1949 that is now in the Dartmouth College Library has been kindly granted by Holly Stevens. Permission to quote from manuscript material by Wallace Stevens described as "An Ordinary Evening in New Haven" has been given by the Collection of American Literature, the Beinecke Rare Book and Manuscript Library, Yale University. Permission to quote from "Our Bias," "Words," "The Composer," and "Lullaby" by W. H. Auden from *W. H. Auden: Collected Poems,* edited by Edward Mendelson (New York: Alfred A. Knopf Inc., 1976) has been granted by Alfred A. Knopf Inc. and also by Faber and Faber Ltd. from *Collected Poems* by W. H. Auden.

Permission to use all or part of some essays in this book has been granted by the following periodicals and publishers: *Diacritics* for Paul de Man, "Hypogram and Inscription: Michael Riffaterre's Poetics of Reading," from *Diacritics,* 11:4 (Winter 1981), 17–35. *ELH* for Sheldon P. Zitner, "Truth and Mourning in a Sonnet by Surrey" (Fall 1983), 509–29; permission granted by The Johns Hopkins University Press. *Michigan Romance Studies* for Barbara Johnson, "Les fleurs du mal armé: Reflections sur l'intertextualité," *Discours et Pouvoir,* Michigan Romance Studies, vol. 2 (1982), 87–99. The University of Minnesota Press for parts of Paul de Man's "Introduction" to *Toward an Aesthetic of Reception,* by Hans Robert Jauss, translated by Timothy Bahti (Minneapolis: University of Minnesota Press, 1982), pp. vii–

xxv. *Representations* for Stanley Fish, "Authors-Readers: Jonson's Community of the Same," *Representations,* vol. 7 (Summer 1984); and for Joel Fineman, "Shakespeare's Perjured Eye," *Representations,* vol. 8 (Fall 1984).

Chaviva Hošek
Patricia Parker

Toronto, Canada

Patricia Parker

Introduction

Oliver: . . . What's the new news at the new court?
Charles: There's no news at the court sir, but the old news.
That is, the old Duke is banished by his younger brother
the new Duke. . . .

I

The play on "new news" in these lines from *As You Like It* might seem appropriate to recent developments in literary theory, as a series of new approaches to literature has challenged and displaced the "New Criticism." This label, derived from the title of a book published by John Crowe Ransom in 1941, grouped together the work of such poets and critics as Ransom himself, Robert Penn Warren, Allen Tate, Randall Jarrell, R. P. Blackmur, W. K. Wimsatt, Monroe Beardsley, Maynard Mack, and Cleanth Brooks, who produced a host of books and essays massively influential in North American criticism and pedagogy from the 1930s to the 1950s and beyond.[1] Though any definition of a critical movement risks treating a diverse body of writing as a monolith, two principles might be said to be among the most influential legacies of the New Critics' work: the program of treating

1. The major writings of these critics are listed under their names in Suggestions for Further Reading, together with the work of their English counterparts I. A. Richards and William Empson, of early dissenters such as R. S. Crane, Northrop Frye, and E. D. Hirsch, and of other figures mentioned in this Introduction. William Wimsatt and Monroe Beardsley's strictures against the "Intentional" and "Affective" fallacies appear in Wimsatt's *The Verbal Icon* (Lexington, Ky., 1954).

the literary text as an isolated artifact or object, dismissing concern with author's intention and reader's response, and the tenet of the text's organic wholeness, its reconciliation of tension or diversity into unity. New Criticism has also been defined by its place within the outlines of a larger poetic and critical history. M. H. Abrams, Murray Krieger, and others early on described it as a particular modern version of the need to mount a "Defence of Poetry," this time against the encroachments of science and technology. In the present volume, the discussions of New Criticism by Northrop Frye, Jonathan Arac, and others situate it variously: within the history that leads from Poe's *Poetic Principle,* through the French Symbolists, to the generation of T. S. Eliot, who exerted such a powerful influence on New Critical conceptions of poetry; and, more pragmatically, within the developments in postwar American education which made its emphasis on treating the text in isolation a theory and practice eminently suited to its time.

New Criticism itself has been chronicled both in its rise and in its decline or, perhaps more accurately, its Cheshire Cat dispersal into the forms of its successors—in accounts such as Murray Krieger's *The New Apologists for Poetry* and Frank Kermode's *Romantic Image* (1956), Gerald Graff's *Poetic Statement and Critical Dogma* (1970) and Frank Lentricchia's *After the New Criticism* (1980). Among the several forms of criticism and theory which have arisen to fill the gap is that French *nouvelle critique* whose differences from American New Criticism have been lucidly outlined by Edward Wasiolek in his introduction to the translation of Serge Doubrovsky's *The New Criticism in France.* Associated with writers such as Roland Barthes, Michel Foucault, and Jacques Derrida, this Continental import, increasingly available in English translation, has yielded the compound "new new criticism," a term whose very awkwardness has the virtue not only of distinguishing this newer foreign influence from that of the New Critics but also of allowing the perception that the forms it has assumed, in North America at least, may be themselves a continuation and refinement of the formalist legacy of New Criticism.

Making it new in any area often involves proclamations of discontinuity, which in turn almost inevitably provoke the perception of continuities—even apart from the familiar charge of the American talent for disarming anything radical, foreign, or new by assimilating it. Jonathan Culler's survey here starts from the premise that recent criticism has produced not a radically different theory of the lyric but rather "changes in the study of the lyric," though the differences he outlines between the "new new criticism" of a critic such as Paul de

Man and the New Criticism of a Cleanth Brooks may seem to others less important than their similarities. Jonathan Arac's polemical Afterword, therefore, like the recent analyses of American *nouvelle critique* by Edward Said and others,[2] argues for the need to step outside this particular critical line, as other contributors here suggest alternatives to formalism in any future study of poetry.

The volume as a whole, then, presents no single "armed vision," unlike collections that bring together representatives of reader-response criticism, deconstructive criticism, or other particular approaches to the text. What unites the present essays is the focus, throughout, on poetry itself. In this, the book reflects its own beginnings, in the series of questions that informed the symposium at which many of the essays were first presented.[3] Why did so much of recent theory—structuralist and poststructuralist, feminist, Marxist, psychoanalytic—tend to concentrate (with some notable exceptions, discussed by Culler here) primarily on narrative or on poetry with a marked narrative element? What might these newer approaches, whose own "return to narrative" was in part a reaction to New Criticism, teach us about lyric poetry in particular? And what, in turn, might this "return to lyric" reveal about the biases or limitations of certain kinds of critical practice and theory?

The lyric was chosen for practical as well as for more strictly theoretical reasons. In their comments here on the difficulty of actually defining what constitutes a lyric, both Northrop Frye and David Bromwich come to rest on the single indisputable feature of its relatively short length, a feature that both serves to distinguish it from more obviously narrative poetry and allows the reader to hold it more easily in mind. The claim that theory and practical criticism have in recent years increasingly parted company, that debates between different theoretical positions rarely descend to discussions of particular texts—or, more to the point for some, to readings that (like those of the New Critics) might be useful in presenting both literature and theory in the classroom—also prompted the decision to focus attention on a single lyric or group of lyrics. New Criticism was in its pedagogical aspect a vigorously North American phenomenon, and the demand that theories prove themselves upon the lectern a reflec-

2. Said's argument that American new new criticism both domesticates radical European theory and continues the preoccupations of New Criticism despite the rhetoric of opposition appears in his recent study, *The World, the Text and the Critic* (Cambridge, Mass., 1983).

3. "Lyric Poetry and the New New Criticism," initiated by Chaviva Hošek and held at the University of Toronto in October 1982.

tion of the educational context that led to its rise and to its continuing influence as a method for teaching poetry. At the Toronto symposium, which included not only teachers and critics but students both graduate and undergraduate, the lyric was chosen both so that newer forms of criticism and theory might confront New Criticism on the latter's chosen ground and so that each participant might have a short text in hand while a particular paper was being read—serving as a means of testing a theory against the text it chose as primary exhibit, stimulating debate and gauging theoretical differences. In this volume likewise, where a poem treated in detail is not easily available to most readers, it is provided along with the essay, in order to enable precisely such readerly answering back. Paul de Man's essay, for example, effects its critique of Riffaterre and Jauss by suggesting what each leaves out in analyses of particular poems by Hugo and Baudelaire. Readers might, in turn, begin from those poems as a way of gauging the differences among all three of these contemporary approaches to the lyric, and then move from de Man and Jauss on Baudelaire to the readings of Fredric Jameson, Jonathan Culler, or Barbara Johnson, who have their own reasons for evoking the example of this poet.

Rather than raising issues and conflicts of critical theory at a purely abstract level, then, the essays that follow bring contemporary theoretical questions to bear on the interpretation of specific lyric traditions and poems—John Hollander (after a magisterial survey of poetic refrains from Theocritus, Catullus, and Villon to Campion, Swinburne, and Rossetti) on Hardy's "During Wind and Rain" and Trumbull Stickney's "Mnemosyne"; Jonathan Arac on a fragment from Sappho; Stanley Fish and Annabel Patterson on lyrics from Ben Jonson's *Under-wood;* Cynthia Chase on Keats's "Ode to a Nightingale"; Barbara Johnson on Mallarmé's "L'Azur," "Swan" sonnet, and "Don du poème"; Herbert F. Tucker on Browning's "Fra Lippo Lippi" and "My Last Duchess"; Mary Nyquist on Stevens's "Peter Quince at the Clavier"; Joel Fineman on Shakespeare's *Sonnets;* Tilottama Rajan on poems by Wordsworth, Blake, and Shelley; Fredric Jameson on Baudelaire's "Chant d'automne" and "La Mort des amants"; David Bromwich on poetry from Hogg to T. S. Eliot to Daryl Hine; John Brenkman on Blake's "A Poison Tree"; Eleanor Cook on Stevens's "An Ordinary Evening in New Haven"; Julian Patrick on Auden's "Our Bias"; Eugene Vance on a lyric by Gace Brulé, and so on. The range of poems reflects the comparatist outlook of recent theory in contrast to the New Critics' more exclusively English canon, as a glance at the Index will quickly reveal, just as the range of theories brought to bear in these discussions reflects the New Pantheon of names associated with a criticism increasingly cosmopolitan in its affiliations: Heidegger, Sartre, Adorno, Benjamin, Bloch, Marcuse, Gramsci, Jakobson, Saussure, Riffaterre, Iser, Jauss, Freud, Lacan, Derrida, Greimas, Cixous, Irigaray, Bakhtin, Foucault.

After the introductory section, the essays in this volume are arranged for the most part chronologically, to suggest newer perspectives on a number of the traditional periods of lyric and to make the volume easier to use. But the multiple links between the essays crisscross this ordering, raising problems common both to the lyric in general and to the preoccupations of contemporary critical theory: the difficulty of defining a form that defies neat generic categorization; the relation between lyric and other discursive forms (from Culler on riddles, through Vance, Rajan, Jacobus, Tucker, and Nyquist on the tension between lyric and narrative, or lyric and dramatic); the connection between lyric poetry and music (Frye, Jacobus), and between lyric and epitaph or inscription (de Man, Frye, Zitner, Jacobus, Chase); the role in lyric of particular technical devices (Hollander, Frye); the problem of subjectivity and voice (Fineman, Rajan, Nyquist, Frye, Tucker) or, more specifically, of the alignment of apostrophe and ode (Culler, de Man, Jacobus, Chase); the phenomenon of "intertextuality" as distinct from both deliberate allusion and what Harold Bloom has termed the "anxiety of influence" (Johnson, Culler, de Man, Chase, Arac); the identification, in lyric, of "I" and "eye" (Fish, Fineman, Cook); the disappearance of the referent, which de Man treats in his critique of Riffaterre and which Jameson argues can be located historically, in the movement from high modernism to postmodernism; the place of biographical and historical context in the interpretation of a poem or poet's career (Patterson, Zitner, Brenkman, Jameson, Patrick); the bearings of developments in feminist critical theory on the reading of poems and the formation of assumptions about poetry (Johnson, Nyquist); and the bringing of the new Marxism—influenced by the Frankfurt School and Althusser—into contact with a genre that traditional Marxist criticism has tended to bypass in favor of narrative (Jameson, Brenkman).[4]

4. Some of these concerns also link the essays here with other recent work on lyric. Frye's discussion of the problem of defining the lyric, Rajan's description of Shelley's lyricized drama, and Tucker's comments on the dramatic monologue might be read with W. R. Johnson's *The Idea of Lyric* (Berkeley, 1982), which discusses lyric as "the most unstable of generic impulses," the lyricizing of drama in Euripides, and classical examples of the monologue; the several discussions of subjectivity and voice, with Sharon Cameron's *Lyric Time* (Baltimore, 1979); Culler's consideration of lyric and

The volume as a whole, then, is meant to raise a series of questions, just as its subtitle might be understood as ending in a question mark. What *would* enable future work on the lyric, or on poetry more generally, to go "beyond" New Criticism rather than simply following "after" it? This question, posed by Patterson in the course of her essay on Jonson and renewed by Tucker in his closing discussion of the limits of both New Criticism and *nouvelle critique,* still remains open at the end, as Jonathan Arac's Afterword points to other kinds of work the reader might consult and alternative directions that still remain to be explored. Patterson herself suggests the limitations of structuralist, deconstructive, and Marxist criticism in turn, in a way the reader might want to assess by turning from her account to the essays by Culler, de Man, Jameson, Vance, Johnson, and others. The volume has as its primary aim the raising of precisely such questions, and the divergence of perspectives within it is intended to provoke debate both within and beyond its covers.

II

Viewed together, the essays suggest a number of larger concerns which have surfaced both in the debate over New Criticism and in the context of newer forms of criticism. Space allows only three of these issues to be singled out here: the vexed issue, in lyric, of subjectivity and speaking voice; the problem of canon-formation and of theories which themselves become canonical, preventing other kinds of work from being done or getting heard; and the reciprocal, though not necessarily complementary, relation between poetic practice and critical theory, or between the writing of poetry and the criticism of it.

First, the questions surrounding subjectivity and voice. Tucker observes here that the oral convention in poetry is so strong that, in the absence of contrary indications, we infer a voice even though we know that we are reading words on a page. This itself may be a remnant of the long history of the separation of written lyric from lyric as sung or performed utterance—a separation that poets frequently present as a fall from the plenitude or communal function of song and a history

riddle, with Andrew Welsh's *The Roots of Lyric* (Princeton, 1978) and Eleanor Cook's "Riddles, Charms and Fictions in Wallace Stevens" (in her *Centre and Labyrinth* [Toronto, 1983]). These and other writings on lyric which might be consulted along with the present volume are cited in the Suggestions for Further Reading, in the notes to individual essays, and in section III of this Introduction.

that Jacobus evokes here through the importance in the eighteenth century of the revived Pindaric ode. The lyrical, as Frye remarks apropos of Pindar and the Psalms, cannot simply be identified with the subjective; indeed, Fineman's discussion of Shakespeare implies that the very notion of subjectivity is historically produced. But critical discussions of subject and of voice have been intimately related at least as far back as the Romantics. Certainly the fiction of a speaker has been a powerful one in post-Romantic interpretation of lyric, whether this speaker is assumed to be the poet or that lyric "persona" which the New Critics made a major part of our critical vocabulary, so major indeed that it is often adopted in readings that might otherwise call attention to their quarrels with New Criticism.[5] Culler begins his essay here with Frye's definition of lyric as "utterance . . . overheard," itself a paraphrase of John Stuart Mill's influential definition, which several other essays return to. Culler's description of the New Critics' tendency to read all poems as if they were implied dramatic monologues (which as a general characterization of New Criticism, rather than as a revealing fissure within it, is called into question by Arac) might thus be read together with Tucker's situating of the New Critical "persona" against the background of both the rise of the dramatic monologue and the subjectivist convention that governed the reading of Romanticism after Mill.

Much of the post–New Critical rewriting of Romanticism has centered on the problem of poetic voice and what threatens or undermines it—a preoccupation that has appeared to make much of this recent theory compatible with Derrida's investigations of the relation of writing and speech. The essays here by Rajan, Jacobus, Tucker, and Chase continue this interest in the invasion of voice by inscription or writing, in the haunting of the apparently autonomous lyric voice by other voices, and in the implications of both for the critical stereotype of Romantic lyric subjectivity. This phenomenon of the haunting or inhabiting of an apparently autonomous voice by traces of alien voices or texts suggests another link between Romantic lyric and later lyric or dramatic monologue. The gothic terror of a monologue such as Browning's "The Bishop Orders His Tomb" may involve not only its fictive speaker's fear of an invasion of the self but also the threat of

5. For the New Critical doctrine of a speaker distinct from the poet, see "The Intentional Fallacy" in Wimsatt's *Verbal Icon,* Maynard Mack's "The Muse of Satire" (*Yale Review,* 41 [1951], 80–92), and Reuben Brower's *The Fields of Light* (New York, 1951); Irvin Ehrenpreis's "Personae" (1963), reprinted in his *Literary Meaning and Augustan Values* (Charlottesville, Va., 1974), provoked an influential debate by its dissenting view.

incursions into his single, dominant speaking voice—whose "order" includes a willed summoning of particular allusions—by texts beyond this speaking subject's ordering or control. This, in turn, might lead us to reflect on Pound's disciplining of Eliot's *Waste Land* through the decorum of acknowledgment and allusion described by Bromwich here, and to a comparision of such apparently controlled allusion with the uncanny pastiche of a poem such as "Gerontion," a poetic house in terror of its own inhabitants.

Subjectivity and lyric voice also remain important in a debate whose wider coordinates can only be suggested here—as a conflict between an interest in rhetoric as trope, or in apostrophe as the *figure* of voicing, and an interest in rhetoric as persuasion, in the analysis of speech acts, and in apostrophe itself as at least potentially contextualizable address; or between that "intertextuality" which Barbara Johnson here describes as an invasion of poetic "property" and an insistence, as in Bromwich, that techniques such as pastiche, though they undo the New Critical assumption of the inviolability of the single text, do not necessarily lead to the conclusion that such intrusions are "an act without an agent" or the work of language itself.

The second major issue, implicit in much of the volume itself—including the contributors' own choice of poets and poems—is the problem of canon-formation, shared by New Criticism and newer criticisms alike. This problem, discussed by Arac in his Afterword, has recently sparked studies of the process by which literary canons are produced and of the ways in which such choices affect what gets printed, anthologized, and taught, though they rest on assumptions that often become evident only on closer inspection.[6] Can we really be certain, for example, that of the two poems Browning himself thought of as a pair, "My Last Duchess"—which is amenable to New Critical techniques of analysis—is a "better" poem and thus more worthy of inclusion in the curriculum than "Count Gismond," whose inconsistencies more immediately frustrate the translation of its written characters into the characters of a psychologically coherent utterance? What important historical or political issues get left out in the evaluative polarity that places the poetry of Shelley, say, down in the context of New Critical formalism or up in the theories represented in *Deconstruction and Criticism?* And what does it reveal about the *ideology*

6. See, for example, the issue on "Canons" of *Critical Inquiry,* 10:1 (September 1983); Leslie Fiedler and Houston A. Baker, eds., *English Literature: Opening up the Canon* (Baltimore, 1981); and Alastair Fowler's *Kinds of Literature* (Cambridge, Mass., 1982).

of canon-formation that a poem such as Whitman's ode to the Paris Commune—well known to students in the socialist bloc—is rarely encountered in North American classrooms?

Critical theories of the lyric also frequently slight or reduce crucial aspects of even the poetry they canonize. Ralph Rader and others have suggested that the New Critics' valuing of certain eighteenth-century poetry over the Romantics was a mixed blessing for the former, since the New Critical doctrine of poetic impersonality necessarily slighted the dimension of biographical, historical, and social context crucial in the interpretation of poets such as Dryden and Pope.[7] Julian Patrick, here, suggests that something similar happened to the political Auden at the hands of Cleanth Brooks. Recent criticism has called attention to elements in the poetry of Donne and Eliot which the New Critical elevation of these poets left out. In a reading of Donne's "Canonization" which could be placed alongside his essay in this collection, Culler points to aspects of that poem which might undermine its status as the exemplary self-contained artifact of Brooks's *The Well Wrought Urn* or indeed of the whole New Critical project of reading other poems "as one has learned to read Donne and the moderns."[8] And Bromwich's essay reminds us that poets themselves frequently provide such de-canonizing readings of privileged poems, as Jay Macpherson's "O Fenix Culpa" might be seen to place itself as subversive companion to Shakespeare's "The Phoenix and the Turtle" or Daryl Hine's "The Double-Goer" to become an idiot questioner of "The Canonization" itself.

The centrality of Eliot and Donne for the New Critics and of Romantic poetry for deconstruction raises, finally, the question of the influence of literary texts themselves—including poetry—on the practices of criticism and theory. What happens to the contours of Leopold Bloom or Stephen Daedalus in the course of Joyce's *Ulysses* clearly anticipates much subsequent structuralist discussion of the "disappearance of the subject," just as a good deal of more recent theory takes its clues from Pater, James, and *Finnegans Wake.* And a single poet—Mallarmé—has exerted a profound influence not only on the avant-garde poetry of this century but also on its literary theory, a phenomenon that Arac, invoking Foucault, suggests may itself be understood as part of a history nearing its ending. As one way of raising this issue, the symposium that led to this volume included not

7. See Phillip Harth, "The New Criticism and Eighteenth-Century Poetry," *Critical Inquiry*, 7:3 (Spring 1981), 521–37.

8. See Culler, *On Deconstruction* (Ithaca, 1982), p. 204.

only critics but poets—Anthony Hecht, John Hollander, Richard Howard, and Jay Macpherson—in a juxtaposition that posed in still different ways the questions of authorial intention, poetic subjectivity and voice, and the relation between the practice of poetry and the criticism of it. Hollander suggests at the end of his essay a possible relation between the newer criticism and the writing of poetry, though some may feel that this relation is chiefly revealing of the kinship of certain kinds of poetry with certain kinds of theory and leads back, once again, to the problem of canon-formation.

Contemporary theory also frequently involves or presents itself as a rediscovery of elements of poetry and language obscured by earlier critical doctrines and literary practice. Much of French *nouvelle critique,* for example, starts from the revolt of Mallarmé against the hegemony of Classicisme in France and the influence of nineteenth-century Realism. But Mallarmé himself not only returned to classical Greek and Latin lyric but also evoked Renaissance instances of linguistic play, a fact which suggests that any theory that attempts to date such awareness of language as beginning with the Symbolists has to ignore what the Symbolists themselves recalled and revived. Many of the essays in this volume suggest, similarly, that much of what interests contemporary critical theory can be found in the poetry itself. Vance justifies his invocation of semiotics and psychoanalysis by citing the affinities of both with the highly formal nature of trouvère lyric. Fish suggests ways in which the problem of beginning—central to the contemporary speculation brought together in Said's *Beginnings*—is already prominent in the structure of the poems of Ben Jonson, and calls into question the whole tradition of criticism which has labeled Jonson a poet of the "plain style" when the poetry itself so insistently proclaims the difficulty of representation. Fineman argues in the conclusion to his essay that many of the issues currently engaging philosophy and theory—including the theories of Derrida and Lacan—might be seen as anticipated by the poetics of Shakespeare's *Sonnets.* Cook suggests that Stevens's own anti-apocalyptic strain might enable us to perceive the apocalyptic language persisting in both logocentric and deconstructive criticism.

The persistence of such "apocalyptic" tendencies—including the claim to be able finally to see what earlier forms of criticism had obscured—might well be endemic to the language of all criticism. Rajan's argument, for example, that "the movement from lyrical to interdiscursive reading is something which happened in the history of Romantic poetry and its perception of itself, and not just something which is happening now in the history of criticism about Romantic poetry" is a reflection of the more recent critical practice that, Culler observes, has "quite altered the image suggested by literary history, of a mystified Romanticism demystified by a modernist reaction." And yet here, as with other kinds of criticism, including New Criticism, one form of revelation or unveiling may simply give way to another. And this raises, as with any coupling of modern theory and past poetry, the difficult problem of assigning significant starting points in literary history, or of claiming to be closer to a particular poetry's understanding of itself than the criticism of other periods in the variable history of a poem's reception.

III

One feature distinguishing the scene of recent criticism from that of New Criticism is the often baffling plurality of contemporary theories and critical schools. A short introduction does not allow an adequate treatment of this variety, but a brief sketch of some of the most important areas for the study of lyric may be useful here, both as a way of placing the essays included in this volume and as a prospectus for reading beyond its covers. The following outline is organized informally into categories—structuralism and semiotics; the role of the reader; lyric and society; feminism and the lyric; and rhythm and meter—but the passages between them reflect the fact that such categories in modern criticism and theory are frequently anything but watertight. Both Culler's introduction to developments within recent criticism and Arac's concluding critique provide supplementary extensions of this map.

Structuralism and Semiotics: Structuralism's primary engagement with the lyric, as Culler points out, was in the linguistic analyses of Roman Jakobson, and its primary modification has been the semiotics of Michael Riffaterre, whose work, from *Essais de stylistique structurale* (1971) to *Semiotics of Poetry* (1978) and *La Production du texte* (1979), provides the best introduction to the application of semiotics to the reading of a wide range of poems. One of Riffaterre's most important early essays, "Describing Poetic Structures: Two Approaches to Baudelaire's 'Les Chats,'" raises the question, in its critique of Jakobson and Lévi-Strauss, of how it might be possible to pass from the techniques of structural analysis to a study of the role of a poem's reader. A tangentially related problem—of how it might be possible to move from identifying the various codes at work in a poem to interpreting it—was raised in turn in the exchange between Riffaterre and Geoffrey Hartman over Wordsworth's "Yew-Trees," a useful exemplary instance of the points at issue between a semiotic analysis and a more phenomenological one, concerned with issues of speaker and voice.[9]

Riffaterre's interest in the passage from structural analysis to the role of the reader may be, as Paul de Man suggests, partly the result of "the feeling of liberation felt by any European-trained interpreter of literature transposed to America in the late forties" and encountering the pedagogical context of New Criticism. For New Criticism itself, by its placing of the individual reader before an isolated text, may paradoxically have opened up this passage out of formalism, despite its strictures against the Affective Fallacy. In this volume, de Man's study of Riffaterre on Hugo attempts to trace the complications involved when "a formalist like Riffaterre feels compelled to integrate the hermeneutic activity of the reader within his enterprise," thus potentially undoing "the postulate of self-referentiality which defines and delimits for him the specificity of literature."[10]

The Role of the Reader: Riffaterre's incorporation of the reader into semiotic analysis reflects the wider interest in the reception of literature which has arisen since the New Criticism, precisely in opposition to the doctrine of the Affective Fallacy. Recent anthologies of reader-oriented studies, such as Jane P. Tompkins's *Reader-Response Criticism* and Susan R. Suleiman and Inge Crosman's *The Reader in the Text,* give some idea, both in their contents and in their comprehensive bibliographies, of the highly divergent character of this common interest—crossing as it does the boundaries between semiotic, psychoanalytic, deconstructionist, sociological, hermeneutic, phenomenological, and historical approaches.

One particular European version of this interest is the "Aesthetics of Reception" (*Rezeptionsästhetik*) of Hans Robert Jauss and the

9. See Riffaterre's essay, "Les Chats," reprinted in Jane P. Tompkins, ed., *Reader-Response Criticism* (Baltimore, 1980), pp. 26–40, together with Roman Jakobson and Claude Lévi-Strauss, "Charles Baudelaire's 'Les Chats,'" in R. T. De George and F. M. De George, eds., *The Structuralists* (New York, 1972), pp. 124–46; and Riffaterre's "Interpretation and Descriptive Poetry: A Reading of Wordsworth's 'Yew-Trees,'" *New Literary History,* 4 (1973), 229–56, together with Hartman's "The Use and Abuse of Structural Analysis: Riffaterre's Interpretation of Wordsworth's 'Yew-Trees,'" *NLH,* 7:1 (1975), 165–89.

10. Paul de Man, "Hypogram and Inscription: Michael Riffaterre's Poetics of Reading," *Diacritics,* 11:4 (Winter 1981), 19–21. Part I of de Man's essay in this volume is taken from the same source.

Konstanz school of literary studies, whose combination of the linguistic analyses of Prague-school poetics with a hermeneutic concern for the production of meaning might be seen in the title of their main publication series *Poetik und Hermeneutik.* Jauss has repeatedly argued that the formal and aesthetic aspects of a text must not be separated from an investigation of its historical reception, a combination that de Man's critique of Jauss here suggests may involve some of the same risks as the passage from semiotics to reader response in the poetic analyses of Riffaterre.[11]

Reader-response criticism in North America has been associated largely with the work of Stanley Fish, whose essay in this volume both continues this interest and, in its incorporation of the insights of Stephen Orgel and others, gestures toward a more historical concern with the social contexts of reading. Jane Tompkins, in her conclusion to *Reader-Response Criticism,* argues that such criticism needs to become less tied to the legacy of New Critical formalism—the mere proliferation of readings of texts—and more overtly political in the questions it asks about reading. Feminist criticism, in this regard, has recently directed attention to the importance of the gender of the reader, a question that New Criticism and much of reader-oriented criticism have tended to ignore but one that is crucial to the experience of poems such as Yeats's "Leda and the Swan," Sylvia Plath's "Daddy," and Mallarmé's "Don du poème," or arguably of any literary text. An interest in reading also leads to questions of ideology: Tony Bennett, in *Formalism and Marxism,* argues for a theory that might elucidate the historical production of texts by readers whose institutional and class interests inform their readings, while Jameson and Brenkman, in the present volume, both discuss the historical constraints that shape the reading of a given poem or poet, suggesting possibilities for a Marxist approach to reception different from the traditional European Marxism that Jauss and *Rezeptionsästhetik* have defined themselves against.

Lyric and Society: Both the work of Walter Benjamin and Theodor Adorno's "Rede über Lyrik und Gesellschaft," discussed in several essays here, raise historical and social questions about lyric which American criticism after decades of formalism—New Critical, struc-

11. For a more comprehensive discussion and examples of the work of Jauss and the Konstanz school, see de Man's Introduction to Hans Robert Jauss, *Toward an Aesthetic of Reception* (Minneapolis, 1982), the text from which part II of his essay in this volume is taken; Rainer Warning, ed., *Rezeptionsästhetik* (Munich, 1975); and R. E. Amacher and V. Lange, eds., *New Perspectives in German Literary Criticism* (Princeton, 1979).

turalist, and poststructuralist—has just begun to explore. This recent return to history, in books such as Lentricchia's *After the New Criticism* and Said's *The World, the Text and the Critic,* itself raises the question of how what Geoffrey Hartman over ten years ago projected as the move "beyond formalism" might in practice be effected. De Man's analysis of Jauss's attempts to combine history and poetics as "particularly instructive for American readers whose legitimate impatience with the techniques of formal analysis sends them in search of models for historical understanding" here offers one perspective on the potential complications of such a recourse to history in the study of lyric.[12]

In very different ways, however, the essays by Patterson, Zitner, Jameson, Brenkman, and Patrick bring biographical, political, and historical considerations into play. Zitner's reading of Surrey's "Epitaph" combines the resources of pre–New Critical historical scholarship with an interest in both formal analysis and sociological context: it questions ahistorical strategies of reading by presenting us with a poem that cannot even be construed without historical study, but also reveals that, in the various commentaries on "Epitaph," a whole history has been *invented* in order to make its proper names refer to a theme with a particular kind of pathos. Patrick suggests the ways in which Auden's turn away from "history" to the more existential category "time" may itself be the product of the historical pressures on a poet writing in the era that gave rise to Existentialism. Patterson's claim that lyricism in Jonson's *Under-wood* is a socio-political construct, "especially in its declarations of independence, and especially in its silences," suggests that what Fish here describes as Jonson's ideal "community of the same" might profitably be viewed as an example of Gramsci's characterization of the "traditional" intellectual and thus itself be placed within a particular political and historical context.

Marxist criticism has tended not only to ignore the lyric but to assume a purely extratextual relation between literature and society, though, as Tucker notes here, it offers potentially the most comprehensive explanation of the social functions of poetry. In his recent *Poetry as Discourse,* Antony Easthope has argued that history must be seen not as outside but rather as inscribed within a poem. And Brenkman's assertion here that the poetry of Blake "encourages us to counter the habits of Marxist and non-Marxist criticism alike by recognizing that society and politics shape the very project of a poet's work and the inner dynamics of poetic language itself" leads to a

12. See de Man, Introduction to Jauss, p. x.

reading that, in Brenkman's words, "owes as much to hermeneutics and poststructuralism as it does to the aesthetic writings of the Frankfurt School." In Brenkman's analysis, the history of a poem such as "A Poison Tree" also includes its future, in ways that readers of this essay might want to compare with more traditional, prophetic readings of Blake. Jameson, similarly, sees Baudelaire as contemporary with the developments of a future history, including the decentering poetics of postmodern theory itself.

Feminism and the Lyric: Among the most recent of theoretical approaches, feminist criticism directs attention to many of the concerns raised so far—to biographical context, in its interest in the relation of a poet's art to her or his life; to reception, in its stress on the gender of the reader and on the gender-constraints on interpretation in different historical periods; to voice, in its concern with the conditions permitting the subject of lyric to speak; to structure, in its explorations of the function of female figures in lyric, from Catullus's Lesbia and Petrarch's Laura to Keats's "Belle Dame" and her sisterhood; to language and figure, in its investigations of the language a woman poet must both work within and work against; and to canon-formation, in its eliciting of the often invisible assumptions behind the view that a course ranging from the Brontës, Barrett Browning, and Dickinson to Moore, Plath, Levertov, and Atwood is narrowly gender-based, unlike one moving from Keats, Browning, and Tennyson to Frost, Stevens, Ammons, and Dorn. Poet-critic Adrienne Rich's story of having been taught early on that "poetry should be 'universal,' which meant, of course, non-female" calls attention to the often suppressed factor of gender in the criticism of poetry, whether New Critical or new new critical, though more recent feminist studies that draw upon both have begun to alter this history. Sandra Gilbert and Susan Gubar, in *The Madwoman in the Attic,* invoke Harold Bloom's oedipal model of poetic interrelation but stress the problematic status of the woman poet within the struggle of poetic fathers and sons, while anthologies such as their *Shakespeare's Sisters* and Suzanne Juhasz's *Feminist Critics Read Emily Dickinson,* along with studies such as Margaret Homans's *Women Writers and Poetic Identity,* signal a movement toward feminist readings of women poets which seems destined to prove one of the most challenging to past thinking about poetry.[13]

13. For related work in feminist criticism, see *inter alia* Elizabeth Abel, ed., *Writing and Sexual Difference* (Chicago, 1982); Mary Jacobus, ed., *Women Writing and Writing about Women* (New York, 1979); Sally McConnell-Ginet, Ruth Borker, and Nelly Fur-

Several essays in this volume suggest, both explicitly and implicitly, possibilities for feminist reading of the lyric. Barbara Johnson, invoking the analogy of pen and penis at least as ancient as the *Romance of the Rose,* suggests that Mallarmé's critique of logocentrism—an insistent preoccupation of poststructuralist theory—may also include a critique of phallocentrism, a possibility that has inspired the writing of Hélène Cixous, Luce Irigaray, and others. Mary Nyquist implies that, for all his multiple ironies, Stevens proffers no such critique, and gestures in her own concluding remarks toward the possible conjunction of feminism and Marxism in future interpretation of the lyric. Nyquist's assertion that "the female muse is, in Stevens's poetry as in the tradition he inherits, always to some degree represented as the other who makes possible the creative articulateness of the male voice" points, like Johnson's study, to the obsession of much of Symbolist poetry with the figure of the mute, dead, or silent female; and this element of female muteness, or of potentially subversive voice, emerges in other essays as well. Tucker cites the "lyric woman" of Browning's "Cleon," who bears a gift from male tyrant to male poet, and relates the silencing of female voice in "My Last Duchess" to the partial overruling of lyric in dramatic monologue. Fineman argues that it is the introduction of the "Dark Lady" into Shakespeare's *Sonnets* which disrupts what we might call (borrowing from Fish on Jonson) their ideal "community of the same" and introduces a complicating difference into their economy of reciprocation. A similar complication arises when the Dark Lady in question is the poet herself. Fineman describes the Dark Lady sonnets as a parodic undoing of the poetics of "two distincts, division none" in "The Phoenix and the Turtle," whose "phoenix riddle" of union enters Donne's "Canonization" and through it the New Critics' emphasis on the resolution of tension as of difference. Bromwich's analysis of Jay Macpherson's "O Fenix Culpa" and its opening up of division within the perfect "twain

man, *Women and Language in Literature and Society* (New York, 1980); Jonathan Culler, "Reading as a Woman," *On Deconstruction,* pp. 43–64; Elaine Marks and Isabelle de Courtivron, eds., *New French Feminisms* (Amherst, Mass., 1980); *Yale French Studies,* 62 (1981) ["Feminist Readings: French Texts/American Contexts"]; *Diacritics,* 12:2 (Summer 1982) ["Cherchez La Femme: Feminist Critique/Feminine Text"]. For comments by Adrienne Rich on poetic "universality," see her "When We Dead Awaken: Writing as Re-Vision," reprinted in the Norton Critical Edition of *Adrienne Rich's Poetry* (New York, 1975). It is important to note that one strain of current feminist criticism resurrects the notions of author, subject, and reader suppressed by the New Critics while feminist theory influenced by poststructuralism locates the "feminine" within writing itself.

made one" of Shakespeare's poem argues that such a marginal and potentially subversive poetic might be explained by the fact that this poet is neither British nor American but Canadian. But it must also be observed that in this case (especially since her title recalls the *felix culpa* ambivalently associated with Eve), the poet cannot for other reasons entirely fit into the line of Shakespeare and Donne.

Rhythm and Meter: The essays by Hollander, Frye, Zitner, and Patrick suggest in varying degrees the importance of technical devices in the writing and interpretation of a poem, a concern often conspicuously absent from contemporary theoretical treatments of the lyric. In contrast to the earlier Russian formalists and Prague linguists, much of poststructuralist criticism of the lyric has paid remarkably little attention to prosodic analysis, despite its own theoretical insistence on the uncanny autonomy of language and its invocation of Mallarmé, who repeatedly returned to the magic of rhythm, sound, and rhyme. A similar omission characterizes much of the criticism interested in wider social or historical questions. Some recent work in this area, however, suggests possibilities for linking prosodic analysis with contemporary theoretical concerns. Veronica Forrest-Thomson's *Poetic Artifice* (1978) directs its discussion of a broad range of poetic effects against any interpretation that in its concern for the meaning behind the words all too readily bypasses the words themselves. Donald Wesling's *The Chances of Rhyme* (1980) includes reflections on the New Critics' concept of organic form, while his more recent work on "grammetrics" draws on the insights of poststructuralist theory. Charles O. Hartman's *Free Verse* (1980) counters New Critical strictures against the Intentional Fallacy and Affective Fallacy in its remarks on "the discovery of form" and on the role of the reader. Derek Attridge's *The Rhythms of English Poetry* (1982) brings the resources of linguistic and literary theory into a revision of traditional prosodic analysis and, with John Hollander's *Vision and Resonance* (1975) and lucidly witty *Rhyme's Reason* (1981), provides an excellent introduction to the subject for the uninitiated. Antony Easthope's *Poetry as Discourse* (1983), finally, in its discussion of iambic pentameter, suggests how one kind of Marxist analysis of lyric might approach the ideological and historical implications of a particular metrical form.

Derrida remarks that introductions are always preposterous, written after what they purport to come before. This introduction has been necessarily brief and schematic as well as preposterous. The links it suggests will emerge clearly only in a reading of the essays themselves; and the issues it sketches only in the continuing debate over poetry and theory both within and beyond the confines of this book.

PART ONE

NORTHROP FRYE

Approaching the Lyric

Some people believe that literary terms can be defined: there was a purist in the Greek Anthology who maintained that an epigram is a poem two lines long, and that if you venture on a third line you're already into epic. But that seems a trifle inflexible. At the other extreme, there is a popular tendency to call anything in verse a lyric that is not actually divided into twelve books. Perhaps a more practicable approach would be to say that a lyric is anything you can reasonably get uncut into an anthology. Or perhaps we can at least limit the subject by saying what the lyric is not.

The kind of formulaic, half-improvised poetry that, we are told, lies close behind the Homeric poems is poetry of pure continuity. Like motion in Newton, there is nothing to stop it except some external factor, such as the end of the story it tells or the beginning of the occasion it was composed for. If the poet does not read or write, the poem exists only in the one dimension of pure continuity in time, because such a poet is not thinking of lines on a page. If the poem is written, it appears in two spatial dimensions, across and down a page, as well as in time, and the crucial term "verse," with its associations of turning around or turning back, becomes functional. The poem may still be continuous, but in "verse," where we keep coming to the end of a line and then starting another, there is a germ of discontinuity. The more this sense of the discontinuous increases, the more closely we approach the lyrical area.

In the lyric, then, we turn away from our ordinary continuous experience in space or time, or rather from a verbal mimesis of it. But we cannot simply identify the lyrical with the subjective. Continuous poetry may also be subjective, like the *Prelude* or *Childe Harold,* and lyrical poetry may be a communal enterprise, like the Old Testament Psalms or the odes of Pindar. As these examples show, the discontinuous element in poetry is often linked to a specific, usually ritual, occasion, and the element of occasion means that the poem revolves around that occasion, instead of continuing indefinitely. If there is no public occasion, what corresponds to it may be a private occasion like drinking or love-making, to cite two standard themes. But even in this kind of "occasional" verse there is still an identity of subject and object. Many years ago, when logical positivism was in vogue among philosophers, I picked up one of their books and read the following: "Many linguistic utterances are analogous to laughing in that they have only an expressive function, no representative function. Examples of this are cries like 'Oh, Oh,' or, on a higher level, lyrical verses." This remark put me off reading philosophy for some years, at least until philosophers stopped chasing these red herrings of expressive and representative functions.

The private poem often takes off from something that blocks normal activity, something a poet has to write poetry about instead of carrying on with ordinary experience. This block has traditionally been frustrated love, as in the Petrarchan poetry of Elizabethan England, where the frustration is normally symbolized by the cruelty and disdain of a mistress. Such a block has much to do with creating the sense of an individualized speaker. Something similar occurred in ancient Greece: in fact, Bruno Snell, in his book on the evolution of what he considers a unique type of individual consciousness in the period between Homer and the age of Socrates, associates the decisive turning point with the early lyrical poets, Archilochus, Sappho, Anacreon, and their contemporaries.[1]

Here the blocking point makes the lyrical poem part of what biologists call a displaced activity, as when a chimpanzee crossed in love starts digging holes in the ground instead. In another lyrical genre the block relates to the reader rather than the poet: this is what we find in the epitaph convention that we have had from Greek times on. Here the reader is assumed to be a traveler, pursuing his normal course through time and space, who is suddenly confronted with something he should stop and read. What he reads is the verbal essence of a life which has once had its own context in space and time but is now enclosed in a framework of words. He is often told, at the end, that he has been looking in a mirror: his own context is still in

1. Bruno Snell, *The Discovery of Mind: The Greek Origins of European Thought,* trans. T. G. Rosenmyer (Cambridge, 1953).

ordinary space and time, but it will eventually disappear, and the verbal essence of *his* life may make an equally short poem.

We notice in, for example, Mallarmé, a good many occasional pieces as well as poems called *Toast Funèbre* or thought of as inscribed on tombs. So we are not surprised that it is Mallarmé who gives us the best-known parable of the displacing operations of lyric in *L'après-midi d'un faune,* where a faun tries to pick up a nymph and finds that he has two nymphs stuck together, interested in each other but not in him. There is nothing for it but to retreat into the dream world where verbal creation begins, and where, as he says, he will see instead the shadows that they will turn into.

When the block ceases to be opaque and becomes transparent, the lyric of frustration expands into the lyric of mental focus. Gerard Manley Hopkins speaks of two kinds of poetic process: a transitional kind, which operates in narrative and story-telling, following the rhythm of the continuity of life in time, and a more meditative kind, which turns away from sequential experience and superimposes a different kind of experience on it. The superimposing provides an intense concentration of emotion and imagery, usually on some concrete image. It is on this level that we have Keats's contemplation of the Grecian urn, Hopkins's recognition of the presence of God in the windhover, Rossetti's remembering from a moment of anguish that "the woodspurge has a cup of three." In this kind of meditative intensity the mind is identified with what it contemplates.

In Oriental poetry the tradition of meditation is so well established that a poem can often simply give a few verbal clues and leave it to the reader to recreate the process. The meditative power of Japanese or Chinese lyric may have something to do with the nature of the written language, which seems to provide a visual supplement to the verbal intensity, so that the seventeen syllables of the haiku, for instance, can become a kind of exploding verbal atom. However much may be lost through ignorance of Japanese, no one can miss this exploding power that comes through a haiku of the poet Rippo, which must surely be one of the world's greatest death songs.

> Three lovely things . . .
> Moonlight . . . cherry blossoms . . .
> And now . . .
> The untrodden snow.

This hieroglyphic quality is mentioned by Hart Crane in one of his rare critical essays: "It is as though a poem gave the reader as he left it a single, new *word,* never before spoken and impossible to actually enunciate, but self-evident as an active principle in the reader's consciousness henceforward."[2]

So far I have touched mainly on the visual side of the lyric, but of course traditionally the lyric is primarily addressed to the ear. A good deal has been said about the deferring of written language to the spoken word: much less has been said about the deferring of written poetry to music, especially in lyrical poetry, where the very word lyric implies a musical instrument. For centuries poets refused to admit that their expression was verbal: they insisted that it was song, or even instrumental music. In pastoral poetry the instrument was often a flute or reed, like the "oat" of *Lycidas* or the pipe of Blake's *Songs of Innocence,* regardless of the fact that it is impossible to sing and play a wind instrument at the same time. The sixteenth century, more realistically, featured the lute: poets who do not think musically give us some curious musical images, such as Coleridge's damsel lugging a dulcimer across Abyssinia.

This association with music has two elements of importance. One is that the lyric turns away, not merely from ordinary space and time, but from the kind of language we use in coping with ordinary experience. Didactic or even descriptive language will hardly work in the lyric, which so often retreats from sense into sound, from reason into rhyme, from syntax into echo, assonance, refrain, even nonsense syllables. The strict forms of traditional lyric, villanelles, ballades, sonnets, and the like, form part of the same tendency. Many lyrics are written in stanzas, and the metaphor of "room" inherent in "stanza" suggests a small area complete in itself even though related to a larger context. So a stanza unit may impart a lyrical quality even to a long continuous poem: *The Faerie Queene* seems "lyrical" in a way that *Paradise Lost* does not. "We'll build in sonnets pretty rooms," as Donne says. If we start to read this poem of Wyatt:

> Process of time worketh such wonder,
> That water which is of kind so soft
> Doth pierce the marble stone asunder,
> By little drops falling from aloft

we can hear the imitative harmony in the rhythm that suggests a self-contained world where reality is verbal reality. Imitative harmony is

2. Hart Crane, "Appendix I: General Aims and Theories," in Philip Horton, *Hart Crane: The Life of an American Poet* (New York, 1957), p. 327.

sometimes called a trick of rhetoric, but in Wyatt, who is better at it than anyone else I know in English literature, it is certainly no trick. More important, we are circling around a defined theme instead of having our attention thrown forward to see what comes next. We hear, so to speak, the end in the beginning: we have stepped out of experience into something else, a world like the rose-garden in *Burnt Norton* from which we must soon return.

The second factor connecting lyric with music is that for the most part, musical sounds are in a special area, different from the sounds we hear in ordinary life. The poet, however, has to use much the same words that everyone else uses. In lyric the turning away from ordinary experience means that the words do not resonate against the things they describe, but against other words and sounds.

Sometimes this verbal resonance comes from allusiveness, from deliberate echoes of Classical and other myths, as in Swinburne:

> And the brown bright nightingale amorous
> Is half assuaged for Itylus,
> For the Thracian ships and the foreign faces,
> The tongueless vigil, and all the pain.[3]

Here we are psychologically close to magic, an invoking of names of specific and trusted power. At other times the resonance is not allusive but, more vaguely, or at least more indefinably, an evoking of some kind of mysterious world that seems to be concealed within ordinary time and space. Verbal magic of this kind has a curious power of summoning, like the proverbial Sirens' song. When Keats says that the nightingale's song has "Charmed magic casements, opening on the foam / Of perilous seas, in faery lands forlorn," half our brain closes down and says it doesn't know what Keats is talking about. The other half wakes up and recognizes a strange environment that still has something familiar in it. The poet, in the ancient phrase, unlocks the word-hoard, but the word-hoard is not a cupboard: it is something more like a world that our senses have filtered out, and that only poets can bring to awareness.

It is very common for a single line to possess this quality of resonant and summoning magic. There is the line from Thomas Nashe's elegy, "Brightness falls from the air," which many people know who know nothing else of Nashe. One critic has suggested that the line may be too good for Nashe, who perhaps wrote the more commonplace

3. In "Atalanta in Calydon," ll. 69–72.

"Brightness falls from the hair," the present version being a printing accident. I dislike the suggestion, but it is true that accident can play some part in verbal magic. There is a Newfoundland folksong with the original refrain: "I love my love but she'll love no more." Through a lucky short circuit in oral transmission, this turned into "I love my love and love is no more," a line that teases us out of thought like the Grecian urn.

So the frustrating or blocking point, the cruel mistress or whatever, becomes a focus for meditation rather than brooding, and thereby seems to be the entrance to another world of experience, "the fitful tracing of a portal," as Wallace Stevens calls it. This world is one of magic and mystery, one that we must soon leave if we are to retain our reputations as sober citizens of the ordinary one. But there is still a residual sense that something inexhaustible lies behind it, that it is good not merely to be there, but, as Ferdinand says at the masque in *The Tempest,* to remain there. Two highly cerebral poets, Mallarmé and Rilke, have said that the end and aim of lyrical poetry is praise. They did not say this in any sort of conventional religious context: they were not talking about a prefabricated heaven, but an earthly paradise we stumble on accidentally, like the castle of the Grail, a paradise we can bring to life for ourselves if we ask the right question, which is, according to Chrétien de Troyes: "Who is served by all this?"

For many centuries the lyric was content to be a relatively minor aspect of poetic experience, but Poe's essay "The Poetic Principle" reacted against this and identified the lyrical with the authentically poetic, dismissing all continuous poems as fragments of genuine lyric stuck together with versified prose. This essay had, as is well known, a tremendous influence on the French school that runs from Baudelaire to Valéry, and that influence made its way into English poetry in the generation of Eliot and Pound. I imagine that one reason for its influence was the belief that the standard meters of continuous verse had exhausted their possibilities, so that narrative shifted to prose, while long poems, even the poems of that master of the interminable, Victor Hugo, tended to become increasingly fragmented.

One of the by-products of this movement was the critical approach that developed two generations ago, which I suppose this volume would call "the old new criticism." This was a technique of explication that approached all literature, whatever the genre, in terms of its lyrical quality, and tended to place the great continuous poets, Milton, Goethe, Victor Hugo, below the poets of the greatest fragmented intensity, Hopkins, Hölderlin, Rimbaud. This movement in criticism seems to me essentially a practical one, excellent for classroom discussion but not well grounded in critical theory. Theoretical developments since then have tended to focus on continuous qualities and on narrative. I take it that the present book owes its existence to a feeling that it is high time for critical theory to come to firmer grips with the lyrical element in literature. I share this feeling, and I have therefore an additional reason for being interested in it.

Jonathan Culler

Changes in the Study of the Lyric

In the *Anatomy of Criticism* Northrop Frye writes that "the basis of generic distinctions in literature appears to be the radical of presentation" and that the lyric is "preeminently the utterance that is overheard."[1] Now when we overhear an utterance that engages our attention, what we characteristically do is to imagine or reconstruct a context: identifying a tone of voice, we infer the posture, situation, intention, concerns, and attitudes of a speaker. This is, roughly, the approach to the lyric expounded and exemplified by the New Criticism, and it remains the only theory of the lyric to gain wide currency and influence. In M. H. Abrams's *Glossary of Literary Terms* "lyric" is defined as "any fairly short, non-narrative poem presenting a single speaker who expresses a state of mind or a process of thought and feeling."[2]

The most precise and articulate statement of this theory of the lyric that I know is presented by Barbara Herrnstein Smith in *On the Margins of Discourse,* which treats literary works as "fictive utterances": fictional imitations of various sorts of nonfictional or "historical" utterances. "The various genres of literary art," Smith argues, "can to some extent be distinguished according to what types of discourse—for example, dialogues, anecdotes of past events, public speeches, and private declarations—they characteristically represent. Thus, lyric poems typically represent personal utterances . . ."[3] It is as if every

1. Northrop Frye, *Anatomy of Criticism* (New York, 1965), p. 249.
2. M. H. Abrams, *A Glossary of Literary Terms,* 4th ed. (New York, 1981), p. 99.
3. Barbara Herrnstein Smith, *On the Margins of Discourse* (Chicago, 1978), p. 8.

lyric began with the invisible words, "For example, I (or someone) could say . . .":[4] [For example, I (or someone) could say], "That's my last duchess hanging on the wall . . ." or [For example, I (or someone) could say], "Busie old fool, unruly sunne . . ."

Smith goes on to argue that since a poem is a fictional representation of an utterance, interpreting a poem is, in large measure, a process of working out, from the textual evidence and from our knowledge of speakers, the nature of the speaker's attitudes. To interpret Shakespeare's sonnet 87, "Farewell, thou art too dear for my possessing," is "to conceive of the kind of situation that might lead a man to feel thus and speak thus."[5] Study of the lyric seeks to identify the concerns to which the speaker is responding and the tone of the response. The methodological heritage of the New Criticism encourages us to focus above all on the complexities of the speaker's attitude revealed over the course of the overheard utterance and on the culmination of the poem in what Cleanth Brooks calls "the total and governing attitude."[6]

This has certainly been a productive approach to lyric, but if we turn to some of the most famous lyric openings—"Hail to thee, blithe Spirit / Bird thou never wert!" or "Thou still unravished bride of quietness," or "O Rose, thou art sick!"—problems immediately arise. It is difficult to see these apostrophes as fictional representations of plausible historical speech acts. This is one reason why apostrophes are awkward and embarrassing: it is difficult to find a tone in which to read them, and one declaims them with mildly embarrassed, self-conscious grandiloquence. We find it hard to imagine any nonpoetic or nonfictional utterance that would use them. If we try, as Smith says, to "conceive of the kind of situation that might lead a man to feel thus and to speak thus," we find ourselves suggesting, in an uncomfortably circular fashion, that these lyrics are fictional representations of utterances by speakers who are waxing poetical, indulging in bardic flights.

With a poem like "Tintern Abbey," on the other hand, we fare better if we treat the poem as the fictional representation of a nonfictional utterance, and ask what sort of speaker, situation, tone, and drama of attitudes are represented here. We draw inferences about the attitudes of a speaker who is meditating on the scene he is now revisiting. This procedure works well for "Tintern Abbey" precisely

4. Ibid., p. 142.
5. Ibid., p. 33.
6. Cleanth Brooks, *The Well Wrought Urn* (New York, 1947), p. 207.

because its tone and syntax of meditation preserves the fiction of a speaker's historical utterance and avoids flights and figures that might force us to read the poem as something else. We can treat this lyric as if it were a dramatic monologue, which is what the reigning New Critical theory of the lyric encourages us to do; but the theory creates difficulties both for lyrics whose voice is not individualized, such as songs, and for poems in the bardic tradition whose apostrophes to the wind, to nature, or to Canada do not belong to a recognizable attitude, a familiar tone of speech overheard. One can see why this New Critical theory of the lyric led, for example, to disparagement of Shelley: if to interpret a poem is to take it as a fictional imitation of a personal utterance and to imagine the circumstances, attitude, and tone in which someone would speak thus, then one is likely to look askance at a speaker who, in declaiming "I fall upon the thorns of life, I bleed!" makes a spectacle of himself, displaying a woeful insufficiency of irony. To ask when, why, and how one might say, for example, "O lift me as a wave, a leaf, a cloud" is not guaranteed to yield pertinent replies. The figure of apostrophe is critical, I think, because its empty "O," devoid of semantic reference, is the figure of voice, a sign of utterance, and yet, as a *figure* of voicing, quite resistant to attempts to treat the poem as a fictive representation of personal utterance. Apostrophes trouble attempts to read poems as dramatic monologues. The fact that the figure of voice is what resists reduction to utterance suggests that there is a confusion of rhetorical levels in our reigning theory of the lyric.

This theoretical orientation also leads to neglect of two important aspects of the lyric: what Frye calls its *melos* and its *opsis* or, in a translation for those of us without Greek, *babble* and *doodle.*[7] "In babble, rhyme, assonance, alliteration, and puns develop out of sound associations," as in Hopkins's line, "The flower of beauty, fleece of beauty, too too apt to, ah! to fleet . . ." There are many ways sound patterning and paranomasia can work in poetry—numerous incantatory effects, for example. The reigning theory of the lyric urges us to attend to sound patterning when it has a bearing on the attitude of the speaker; and it encourages us to interpret puns as *wit,* though that by no means exhausts the possible functions of the play of signifiers in lyric. Frye defines *doodle* as "elaboration of verbal design," as in shapes, stanzas, and conventional forms that create patterns for the eye; but later he identifies *riddle* as the "radical" or root form of *doodle:*

7. Frye, *Anatomy,* p. 275.

> The radical of *opsis* in the lyric is *riddle,* which is characteristically a fusion of sensation and reflection, the use of an object of sense experience to stimulate a mental activity in connection with it. Riddle was originally the cognate object of read, and the riddle seems intimately involved with the whole process of reducing language to visible form, a process which runs through such by-forms of riddle as hieroglyphic and ideogram. The actual riddle-poems of Old English include some of its finest lyrics, and belong to a culture in which such a phrase as "curiously inwrought" is a favorite aesthetic judgment.[8]

To think of lyrics as fictional representations of possible historical utterances makes it harder to explore them as ingenious artifacts that puzzle or riddle.

If the New Criticism's productive and influential theory of the lyric is insufficient, what has more recent criticism done to remedy this? It has not produced a new theory of the lyric. Indeed, it might be thought to have neglected lyric poetry in favor of narrative, or philosophical prose, or *The Prelude.*

Roland Barthes, for example, whom Wayne Booth calls "the man who may well be the strongest influence on American criticism today,"[9] has practically nothing to say about poetry, much less a convincing or innovatory encounter with lyric. Despite Barthes's broad literary tastes—he likes modern authors and old-fashioned authors, terse authors and exuberant authors—he takes no interest in poetry. With the exception of Racine, he never writes about verse, and Racine's verse scarcely detains him. No comprehensive Barthian theory of poetry explains his neglect, but various remarks suggest two explanations. On the one hand, in *Le Degré zéro de l'écriture* and occasionally elsewhere, Barthes speaks of modern poetry as an attempt to destroy language, to achieve a pre- or post-semiological state in which things are presented directly.[10] At the end of *Mythologies* he remarks, "by poetry I understand, in a very general way, the search for the inalienable meaning of things."[11] But since Barthes shows no inclination to believe that poetry does or could present an unmediated reality, one is led to suppose that there is something else at stake, that other forces in Barthes's critical practice work to produce this neglect of poetry. Indeed, Barthes also associates poetry with symbol, with plenitude of meaning, with attempts to create motivated rather than

8. Ibid., p. 280.
9. Wayne Booth, *Critical Understanding* (Chicago, 1979), p. 69.
10. Roland Barthes, *Le Degré zéro de l'écriture* (Paris, 1972), pp. 38–39.
11. Barthes, *Mythologies* (Paris, 1970), p. 247.

arbitrary signs, and thus sees it as the aspect of literariness that Brecht and Robbe-Grillet, for example, are trying to combat.[12]

By taking these two views of poetry, attributing these two projects to it, Barthes makes poetry a scapegoat: by banishing it from the realm of his critical practice he seems to exorcize the "natural" from the realm of literature, whether the natural takes the form of symbols said to fuse form and meaning in a natural unity, or that of a state prior to or beyond language. In *Qu'est-ce que la littérature?* Jean-Paul Sartre associates linguistic or semiotic experimentation with poetry in order to eliminate such aspects of literature by setting poetry aside. The terms of Barthes's distinction are quite different—for him it is *prose* that experiments with language while poetry attempts to transcend, naturalize, or destroy it—but structurally he is engaged in the same operation: by dubiously identifying some important general aspect of literature with poetry, he can ignore this quality or project by declining to discuss poetry. Other contemporary critics have not followed Barthes's lead, fortunately; they have questioned precisely these two notions that Barthes seems to accept: that poetry is the realm of the symbol—signs so motivated as to become natural and inevitable—and that modern poetry explores ways of transcending language so as allow things to present themselves directly.

Structuralism's primary engagement with the lyric was Roman Jakobson's linguistic analysis of a range of poems from different periods and languages. His success in describing an array of formal patterns that articulate interlocking poetic structures and bind a poem together was hailed by some as an important breakthrough, but the immense detail of Jakobson's analyses and the bewildering multiplicity of patterns that phonological, morphological, and syntactic categories could bring out led to an extreme reaction: one did not wish to be obliged to read or write this kind of thing. Faced with the disturbing prospect of endless Jakobsonian analyses, we had an interest in discovering some principle that might make them irrelevant, and thus were inclined to accept Michael Riffaterre's dubious argument that relevant poetic structures are distinguished from irrelevant linguistic structures by their perceptibility. Many of the patterns Jak-

12. In *L'Empire des signes* (Geneva, 1970), Barthes writes that for the Westerner *haiku* is a seductive form because it seems that you record an impression and "your sentence, whatever it may be, will articulate a lesson, release a symbol, you will be profound, effortlessly, your writing will be *full*" (p. 92). For Barthes, Western notions of poetry involve symbolic plenitude and lead us to read haiku accordingly, whereas in his imagined Japan they remain empty, asymbolic.

obson describes "make use of constituents that cannot possibly be perceived by the reader; these constituents must *therefore* remain alien to the poetic structure, which is supposed to emphasize the form of the message, to make it more 'visible,' more compelling."[13]

The notion that poetic patterns are distinguished from linguistic patterns by their perceptibility would be difficult to defend. I. A. Richards judiciously identified the problem when he noted, in his praise of Jakobson, that while patterns work subliminally to shape a response, not all of them are necessarily operative, but "that the separation of essential features from others is a very tricky undertaking. It is not easily paralleled in simpler tasks of analysis."[14] We have no models or reliable procedures for doing so. The idea that the poetically relevant might be simply identified with what the reader perceives is little more than a pragmatic restriction that permits critics to ignore exhausting formal analyses—analyses which, at the very least, had the virtue of drawing attention to aspects of babble, doodle, and riddle. The possibility of studying the language and the figures of lyric as formal structure rather than utterance to be interpreted was cut short by a rush into reader-response criticism, which urged critics to interpret what readers, informed readers, or superreaders had perceived.

Recent criticism has not developed an alternative theory of the lyric, but it has produced changes in the study of the lyric.[15] Rather than attempt a survey I shall outline some changes that have occurred since Reuben Brower, introducing the English Institute essays of

13. Michael Riffaterre, "Describing Poetic Structures: Two Approaches to Baudelaire's 'Les Chats,'" in *Reader-Response Criticism,* ed. Jane P. Tompkins (Baltimore, 1980), p. 31 (my italics). Jakobson's writings on poetry are most conveniently available in his *Questions de poétique* (Paris, 1973).

14. I. A. Richards, "Jakobson's Shakespeare: The Subliminal Structures of a Sonnet," *Times Literary Supplement,* 28 May 1970, p. 590.

15. In addition to works referred to elsewhere in this paper, one should mention at least the following: Hans Robert Jauss's essays on Baudelaire, included in the collections of his essays, *Toward an Aesthetic of Reception* (Minneapolis, 1982) and *Aesthetic Experience and Literary Hermeneutics* (Minneapolis, 1982); Michael Riffaterre's *La Production du texte* (Paris, 1979); and Stephen Booth's *An Essay on Shakespeare's Sonnets* (New Haven, 1969). Harold Bloom's *Wallace Stevens: Poems of Our Climate* (Ithaca, 1977) is his most sustained reflection on lyric. Joseph Riddel's pioneering study, *The Inverted Bell: Modernism and the Counterpoetics of William Carlos Williams* (Baton Rouge, 1974) was the first work to draw upon Derrida when discussing poetry. On the Romantic lyric, one might consult Geoffrey Hartman, *The Fate of Reading* (Chicago, 1975); Leslie Brisman, *Milton's Poetry of Choice and Its Romantic Heirs* (Ithaca, 1973), and *Romantic Origins* (Ithaca, 1978); Francis Ferguson, *Wordsworth: Language as Counter Spirit* (New Haven, 1977); and the essays by different hands collected in *Romanticism and Language,* ed. Arden Reed (Ithaca, 1984).

1970, *Forms of Lyric,* justly observed that Coleridge was "still the presiding genius of twentieth century criticism of poetry."[16]

Though Coleridgean notions still direct much of our reading of poetry, one can observe changes if one contrasts Cleanth Brooks's reading of Yeats's "Among School Children" in *The Well Wrought Urn* with Paul de Man's comments on the final stanza in *Allegories of Reading.* Brooks emphasizes that "the poem is a dramatization . . . a controlled experience which has to be *experienced,*" and he explores its complexity of attitude—"the tone of half-amused whimsy," for example—by following the movements of the speaker's mind as he engages with the "Presences / That passion, piety or affection knows."[17] De Man, on the other hand, is interested not in the speaker, his tone, or the complexities of his attitude toward love, mortality, his past, and the presences that break hearts, but in the relation between grammatical structure and rhetorical figure in the concluding stanza:

> O chestnut-tree, great-rooted blossomer,
> Are you the leaf, the blossom, or the bole?
> O body swayed to music, O brightening glance,
> How can we know the dancer from the dance?

Critics read these sentences as rhetorical questions asserting the impossibility of telling the dancer from the dance, or the inappropriateness of trying to divide a living unity into constituents. Brooks writes, "Certainly we ought to do no less here than to apply Yeats's doctrine to his own poem. The poem, like the 'great rooted blossomer' that it celebrates, is not to be isolated in the 'statement' made by Stanza V or by Stanza VII or by Stanza VIII."[18] Nor can we properly know the poet except in and through the poem: " 'How can we know the dancer from the dance?' " Brooks confidently takes the apostrophes as rhetorical questions. But "it is equally possible," de Man writes, "to read the last line literally rather than figuratively, as asking with some urgency the question . . . how can we possibly make the distinctions that would shelter us from the error of identifying what cannot be identified? . . . The figural reading, which assumes the question to be rhetorical, is perhaps naive, whereas the literal reading leads to greater complication of theme and statement."[19]

16. Reuben A. Brower, ed., *Forms of Lyric* (New York, 1970), p. vii.
17. Brooks, *The Well Wrought Urn,* p. 190.
18. Ibid., p. 185.
19. Paul de Man, *Allegories of Reading* (New Haven, 1979), p. 11.

Faced with this suggestion, the critic may be included to ask which reading better accords with the rest of the poem, but it is precisely this move that is in question: our inclinations to use notions of unity and thematic coherence to exclude possibilities that are manifestly awakened by the language and that pose a problem. If a reader heard "bowl" in "bole," that might not engage with the interpretation that was developing, but the literal reading of Yeats's concluding question cannot be dismissed as irrelevant. "The two readings have to engage each other in direct confrontation," de Man notes, "for the one reading is precisely the error denounced by the other and has to be undone by it. . . . the authority of the meaning engendered by the grammatical structure is fully obscured by the duplicity of a figure that cries out for the differentiation that it conceals." The question of the relation between the dancer and the dance, or between the chestnut tree and its manifestations, is similar to and entangled with the problem of the relation between the literal, grammatical structure and its rhetorical use. To interpret "How can we know the dancer from the dance?" as a rhetorical question is to take for granted the possibility of distinguishing accurately between the form of an utterance (the grammatical structure of the question) and the rhetorical performance of that structure here; it is to assume that we can tell the question from the questioning (or nonquestioning), the question itself from its rhetorical performance. But to read the question as a rhetorical question is precisely to assume the *impossibility* of distinguishing between an entity (the dancer) and its performance (the dance). The claim that Brooks and others have interpreted the poem as making—the affirmation of fusion or continuity (of the impossibility of making a distinction)—is subverted by the discontinuity that must be assumed in order to infer that claim (the discontinuity between the interrogative grammatical structure and the noninterrogative figure of the rhetorical question).

This is a useful example because it enables us to identify differences while preventing us from reducing the New Criticism to caricature. In summing up, Brooks asks whether Yeats embraces idealism or materialism, and he replies, in a way that reminds us of J. Hillis Miller, that "Yeats chooses both and neither. One cannot know the world of being save through the world of becoming (though one must remember that the world of becoming is a meaningless flux apart from the world of being which it implies)."[20] Brooks's reading does not seem *thematically* simpler than, say, deconstructive readings, but when one con-

20. Brooks, *The Well Wrought Urn*, p. 187.

trasts it with de Man's remarks, one can identify three differences. First, de Man is not elucidating the utterance of a speaker, exploring tone, posture, and attitude, but investigating problematical aspects of language, such as the relation between performative and constative functioning of language, or between grammatical forms and rhetorical structures, or between linguistic entities and the self-referential claims they contain or imply. Second, one can detect here a different understanding of the functioning of self-referentiality: not as an organic, unifying force that closes off interpretation by making the poem account for itself and stand free as a self-contained fusion of being and doing, but as a turn that opens gaps and generates contradiction. Third, there is a different view of symbol implicitly at work in the two discussions: for Brooks, the symbol, as exemplified in the figures of the chestnut tree and the dancer, is the culmination of lyric. Concrete embodiments of complex ideas, these fusions of the sensuous and the spiritual are the acme of poetic language and poetic knowledge, as opposed to the language and knowledge of science. De Man, on the other hand, encourages a questioning of the notion of symbol and can lead us to rethink its role in poetry and in critical discourse. I shall take up these three changes again shortly.

Frye speaks of babble and doodle as the two poles of lyric, and the new new criticism has taken renewed interest in what are two aspects of poetic language rather than features of dramatic monologue. One might say that de Man's chapter on Rilke in *Allegories of Reading* reads Rilke as babble: as poetry wagering all on mastery of sound. But at the moment of greatest success, as the play of sound seems mimetically to overcome contingency and the masterful parallelism, as sound reinforces and determines meaning, seems the very model of unity, the poems lead one to ask, de Man argues, whether this parallelism "really signifies the unity that it constitutes." "Is it not rather a play of language, an illusion, as arbitrary as the shape of the constellations which share a common plane only as the result of an optical appearance?"[21] The most resolute exploration I know, of modern poetry as manipulation of sound and rhythm, is Veronica Forrest-Thomson's *Poetic Artifice: A Theory of Twentieth Century Poetry,* which vigorously rejects referential and thematic reading as "bad naturalization" and finds the best modern poetry working through sound patterns to limit the relevance of external contexts and to function as parody and pastoral.[22]

21. De Man, *Allegories,* p. 55.

22. Veronica Forrest-Thomson, *Poetic Artifice: A Theory of Twentieth-Century Poetry* (New York, 1978).

Michael Riffaterre, whose *Semiotics of Poetry* is certainly one of the most interesting books on poetry in recent years, treats lyrics not as babble, nor as dramatic monologues of speakers with complex attitudes, but as riddles, formed by the periphrastic transformation of clichés. A poem is a riddle that "says one thing and means another." If read as a representation of an action or a statement about objects and situations, it contains nonsensical or contradictory elements and displays organization that cannot be interpreted. These difficulties provide clues by which a second reading can identify a hidden, unifying source. "Then suddenly the puzzle is solved, everything falls into place, indeed, the whole poem ceases to be descriptive, ceases to be a sequence of mimetic signs, and becomes a single sign, perceived from the end back to its given as a harmonious whole, wherein nothing is loose, wherein every word refers to one symbolic focus."[23]

This focus is the *matrix* or kernel out of which the poem has been constructed. "The poem results from the transformation of the *matrix,* a minimal and literal sentence, into a longer, complex, and nonliteral periphrasis."[24] Each of the "poetic signs" of the text is a variant of this matrix and of "a preexistent word group" which Riffaterre calls a "hypogram." A hypogram may be a cliché, a quotation, or a group of conventionalized associations which he calls a "descriptive system." Thus in Baudelaire's first Spleen poem, "Pluviôse, irrité contre la ville entière," the matrix is identified as the thematic kernel "all-pervading gloom," and the poem is seen as an expansion of this matrix into a text through the application of the matrix to the descriptive system associated with *maison*—the clichés of "home sweet home." Elements of this descriptive system, brought into contact with the matrix "all-pervading gloom," are transformed into negative images: the fireside is inhospitable, the sleek household cat napping on a rug becomes a thin and mangy creature uncomfortably seeking repose on the cold tiles, and homey knickknacks have turned sinister, taking on a life of their own.[25]

Riffaterre treats poems as riddles, intricate constructions that can be described without reference to the attitudes of a speaker. De Man sums up Riffaterre's conception as "All verse is nonsense verse but nonsense verse that knows itself to be such."[26] More important, perhaps, Riffaterre describes poems as intertextual constructs which re-

23. Michael Riffaterre, *Semiotics of Poetry* (Bloomington, 1978), pp. 1, 12. For discussion see Jonathan Culler, *The Pursuit of Signs* (Ithaca, 1981), chap. 4.

24. Riffaterre, *Semiotics of Poetry,* p. 19.

25. Ibid., pp. 69–70.

26. Paul de Man, "Hypogram and Inscription: Michael Riffaterre's Poetics of Reading," *Diacritics,* 11:4 (Winter 1981), p. 26.

fer primarily to prior discourse of various sorts. Riffaterre has a superb grasp of the commonplaces of the nineteenth-century French poetic discourse, which enables him to open up poems by identifying their transformations of other texts—from the Virgilian lines used as grammatical examples in French textbooks to the distinctive epithets of recent poetic diction. Though he sees poems primarily as puzzles concealing clichés, this is by no means the only possible account of intertextual relations. Indeed, recent criticism of the lyric, from Jauss's reconstructions of horizons of expectation to Bloom's teasing out of deadly oedipal struggles, can be seen as a wide-ranging exploration of intertextuality.

The result is, above all, a criticism no longer devoted to demonstrating the unity of the poem by explaining how each part contributes to a harmonious synthesis. One can, for example, focus on portions of poems to describe the figures by which one passage reads or assimilates another. The study of Romanticism, drawing upon Harold Bloom's lurid accounts of poetic influence, has recently concentrated on interpreting poems as readings of prior poems, but Bloom has opened new lines of thought for students of the lyric in all periods. His understanding of intertextuality is quite different from Riffaterre's: for Bloom a poem is not a puzzle but a psychic battlefield where the poet wages a struggle against oblivion.[27] Bloom directs our attention not to the periphrastic transformation of clichés but to the ways poems create a space for themselves in the tradition by misinterpreting—limiting and troping upon—the central poems of a major precursor. In reading poems as moments of an oedipal struggle, Bloom portrays the tradition of post-Renaissance poetry as "a history of anxiety and self-saving caricature, of distortion, of perverse, wilful revisionism, without which modern poetry could not exist."[28]

Bloom's intertextuality brings the poet back into studies of the lyric. The New Criticism urged us to focus on the speaker rather than the poet because it wished to substitute for the empirical poet an ideal poet who could sanction and be credited with the complex ironies at work in his verse. Its modes of critical interpretation required a principle that would forestall any objection that a given poet would not have thought thus and such or would not have conceived the elaborate structures elucidated by the critic. Instead of developing a conception of the unconscious that would allow empirical poets to write better than they knew, or instead of identifying the ironic structures

27. Harold Bloom, *Poetry and Repression* (New Haven, 1976), p. 2.
28. Harold Bloom, *The Anxiety of Influence* (New York, 1973), p. 30.

of poetic discourse with a poetic unconscious that might serve as the basis for the tradition, New Critics opted to replace the empirical poet with an ideal poet responsible for all the complexities he had created. When Brooks writes in his discussion of the "Ode on a Grecian Urn" that "the poet knows precisely what he is doing," he is not relying on information about John Keats and his intentions in this poem but rather articulating a general principle of considerable importance for the New Criticism.[29] For recent criticism this remains a major issue of critical decorum: Does one treat the author as a function rather than a person? Does one deem empirical authors responsible for what is discovered in their texts? Does one allow oneself the possibility of treating authors as blind to the forces operating in and through their language? Different decisions on these issues produce great variations in critical rhetoric, but one can hazard a structural rule: the more a critical discourse attempts to restore empirical authors to a place of honor, the more it opens the possibility of analyzing authors as victims of the forces they seek to control. Bloom's criticism is exemplary here: his celebrations of the struggles of strong poets identify structures in poetic discourse—in the relations between poems—that can lead to description of poets as products of intertextuality. The most brilliant and resourceful modern explorations of intertextuality, such as Barbara Johnson's "Les Fleurs du mal armé: Réflexions sur l'intertextualité," which appears for the first time in English in this volume, take us beyond Bloom's oedipal model to a space in which critical distinctions between poems or poets may be a way of attempting to overcome divisions within poems or poetic discourse. Studying the sequence Hugo–Baudelaire–Mallarmé, Johnson shows how the father survives by his way of claiming to be dead, so that the son always arrives too late to kill him. "What the son suffers from is not the desire to kill the father but his powerlessness to kill him whose power consists precisely in articulating his own death."[30]

Let me turn now from these two changes—increased interest in babble and doodle and the major reorientations associated with intertextuality—to the three changes I earlier elicited from a comparison of Brooks and de Man. First, there is the shift from utterance to trope. Frye and others have argued that the lyric is utterance overheard. "The lyric poet," Frye writes, "normally pretends to be talking

29. Brooks, *The Well Wrought Urn,* p. 159.

30. Barbara Johnson, "Les Fleurs du mal armé: Réflexions sur l'intertextualité," in *Discours et pouvoir,* ed. Ross Chambers (Ann Arbor: Michigan Romance Studies, 1982), p. 99. For an English version of this article, see the present volume.

to himself or to someone else: a spirit of nature, a Muse, a personal friend, a lover, a god, a personified abstraction, or a natural object. . . . The poet, so to speak, turns his back on his listeners."[31] If this is so, then apostrophes—"O wild west wind," "O Canada," "Thou still unravished bride of quietness"—are central; but as I noted earlier, they are precisely the elements of lyric that the New Critical orientation finds it most awkward to treat. Critics either ignore them or transform apostrophe into description, treating "O Rose, thou art sick" as nothing more than an emotionally intensifying way of describing the rose as sick.[32] We also have tended to think of apostrophic poetry as bad poetry—while making an exception for poems we like by ignoring the apostrophes—and we have been inclined to treat personification in general as a stale poetic device, a banal feature of an outmoded rhetoric.

There are signs, however, that this is changing: critics are beginning to consider the fact that voice in lyric is a *figure* and to explore the role of this figure of voicing. In "Hypogram and Inscription: Michael Riffaterre's Poetics of Reading," de Man selects, as the point on which to take issue with Riffaterre, his neglect of apostrophe in Hugo's lyric "Ecrit sur le vitre d'une fenêtre flammande." Riffaterre designates as a purely conventional personification the figure of address on which the poem depends, and de Man shows this to be a mark of his erroneous reliance on perceptual models. The figures of apostrophe and prosopopoeia, which give a face to nonperceptual entities such as time and the hour, are the defining features of a mode which, de Man writes, "can be seen as paradigmatic for poetry in general."[33] In neglecting apostrophe to take the poem as description rather than address, Riffaterre misses the fundamental aspect of lyric writing, which is to produce an apparently phenomenal world through the figure of voice. In another article, "Autobiography as Defacement," de Man reflects on the intimate relation between apostrophes to inanimate objects or to the dead and the figure of prosopopoeia, which gives the dead or inanimate a voice. He notes "the latent threat that inhabits prosopopoeia, namely that by making the dead speak, the symmetrical structure of the trope implies, by the same token, that the living are struck dumb, frozen in their own death." The fiction of address, as in the "Stay, traveller" of an epi-

31. Frye, *Anatomy*, pp. 249–50.

32. For discussion see Jonathan Culler, "Apostrophe," in *The Pursuit of Signs*. An earlier version of this paper appeared in *Diacritics*, 7:4 (1977), 59–69.

33. De Man, "Hypogram and Inscription," p. 32.

taph, "thus acquires a sinister connotation that is not only the prefiguration of one's own mortality but of our actual entry into the frozen world of the dead."[34]

There is a close relation in lyric between apostrophe and the threat of becoming inanimate: elegies, for example, are highly apostrophic poems which take an irreversible temporal disjunction, the passage from life to death, and displace it into a reversible alternation of apostrophic movements, as in Shelley's "Adonais":

> O weep for Adonais—he is dead!
> Wake melancholy Mother, wake and weep!
> Yet wherefore? Quench within their burning bed
> Thy fiery tears . . .
>
> Most musical of mourners, weep again!
> Lament anew, Urania!
>
> Mourn not for Adonais . . .
> Ye caverns and ye forests, cease to moan![35]

The tension between narrative and apostrophic movements, and the roles of apostrophe in lyrics, are important topics for criticism to explore in the coming years.

Recent criticism has also produced a change in our understanding of self-referentiality. One important function of the notion of self-referentiality, especially in the New Criticism, has been to make masterable a situation of potential excess and proliferation. If a poem might give rise to an unchecked series of interpretations, one can move to block that series by asking what the poem *itself* has to say about its own nature or the process of interpretation, granting special authority to the answer one discovers. This function of rounding off the poem by closing off interpretation helps to explain how self-reflexivity could be associated with a poem's organic unity—otherwise a bizarre connection. For Brooks, the application of "Yeats's doctrine to his own poem" instructs us to treat it as a self-enclosed unity, like the "great-rooted blossomer": in reading the poem, he writes, we must avoid the temptation "to take the root or the blossoms of the tree for the tree itself."[36] What de Man's reading does is to display poten-

34. Paul de Man, "Autobiography as De-facement," *Modern Language Notes,* 94 (1979), 928.

35. Percy Bysshe Shelley, *Complete Poetical Works,* ed. Thomas Hutchinson (Oxford, 1964), pp. 432–41.

36. Brooks, *The Well Wrought Urn,* p. 191.

tial self-reference as self-deconstruction: whichever reading one gives the final stanza, the poem practices the opposite of what it preaches. This emerges when one applies to its own rhetorical procedures the alternative assumptions on which its persuasive effects depend.

Self-referentiality opens a gap, between the enunciating *I* and the *I* of the statement (as in "I am lying") or between the enunciating poem and the poem described. This is most evident in the logical paradoxes generated by self-reference: the paradox of the barber who shaves all the men in the regiment who do not shave themselves, or Epimenides' paradox, better known as the paradox of the Cretan liar. These have precise literary analogues: when a poem describes poetry as lies, if it speaks true it lies and vice versa. In general, self-referentiality does not create a self-enclosed organic unity where a work accounts for itself or becomes the thing that it describes but rather produces paradoxical relations between inside and outside and brings out the impossibility for a discourse to account for itself. A work's self-descriptions do not produce closure or self-possession but an impossible and therefore open-ended process of self-framing.[37]

Finally, let me turn to the question of the symbol. For the New Criticism, the lyric is the domain of the symbol par excellence: its quintessential achievement is to bring about a fusion of the concrete and the abstract, the particular and the general, the physical or sensuous and the spiritual or intellectual. In lyrics, moments or objects of the phenomenal world are revealed as invested with significance.

Coleridge is the source of the basic opposition between *symbol*, in which inner and outer, particular and general, are organically fused, and *allegory*, which is a mechanical yoking together of object and meaning. The symbol is a motivated sign; "it always partakes of the Reality which it renders intelligible; and while it enunciates the whole, abides itself as a living part in that Unity, of which it is the representative," while allegorical signs are "but empty echoes which the fancy arbitrarily associates with the apparitions of matter."[38] This hierarchical opposition, which brings with it fundamental metaphysical oppositions, has been questioned in several ways, which I shall sketchily indicate.

First, in discovering the importance of allegory for modernist poetry, recent criticism has disputed the association of symbol with lyric

37. For further discussion of the problem of self-reference, see Jonathan Culler, *On Deconstruction: Theory and Criticism after Structuralism* (Ithaca, 1982), pp. 200–205.

38. Samuel Taylor Coleridge, *The Statesman's Manual*, in *Lay Sermons*, vol. 6 of *The Collected Works of Samuel Taylor Coleridge*, ed. R. J. White (London, 1972), p. 30.

excellence. Walter Benjamin's discussions of Baudelaire identify allegory as the semiotic mode of modern consciousness: objects of the world have become commodities that can be invested only with contingent meaning, and poetic discourse, or the poetic imagination, becomes an exploration of allegorical significations generated by an unhappy consciousness.[39] One might cite Baudelaire's "Voyage à Cythère," which narrates a poetic subject's entrapment in allegory when seeking a land of symbol:

> Le ciel était charmant, la mer était unie;
> Pour moi tout était noir et sanglant désormais,
> Hélas, et j'avais, comme en un suaire épais,
> Le coeur enseveli dans cette allégorie.
>
> Dans ton île, O Vénus! je n'ai trouvé debout
> Qu'un gibet symbolique où pendait mon image . . .

[The sky was beautiful; the sea was calm; for me henceforth everything was dark and bloody, alas, and I had my heart buried in an allegory, as in a thick shroud.
In your island, O Venus, I found standing only a symbolic gallows on which my image hung . . .]

The lyric becomes an exploration of the allegorical significations generated by the poetic consciousness.

However, investigation of the role of allegory in so-called modernist poetry has led critics to question whether Romantic poetry was in fact an art of the symbol, as the critical tradition would have us believe. Recent readings of Romantic verse, particularly of Wordsworth, have quite altered the image suggested by literary history, of a mystified Romanticism demystified by a modernist reaction. The most important agent of this change has doubtless been de Man's essay "The Rhetoric of Temporality," which identified in the work of major Romantics an allegorical mode of figuration, where temporal patterns or minimal narratives are generated out of language itself—either prior texts and typologies, or the play of signifiers. De Man cites as an example Wordsworth's "A Slumber Did My Spirit Seal," where the word *thing* helps to produce an allegorical narrative of mystification and demystification: in the first stanza "She seemed a thing that could not feel / The touch of earthly years." In the second stanza, what

39. Walter Benjamin, *Charles Baudelaire: A Lyric Poet in the Era of High Capitalism* (London, 1973).

might have been a "lighthearted compliment has turned into a grim awareness of the demystifying power of death." She has become a *thing* in the full sense of the word, "Rolled round in earth's diurnal course, / With rocks, and stones, and trees."[40] "The fundmental structure of allegory reappears [in this poem]," de Man argues, "in the tendency of the language toward narrative"—or perhaps one should say, in the way in which a narrative that captures an aspect of temporality emerges from the ambiguity of *thing*. This obscure notion has been made more plausible by later discussions, such as Maureen Quilligan's *The Language of Allegory,* which demonstrates that allegory is fundamentally narrative generated by word play, and Barbara Johnson's descriptions of Baudelaire's prose poems as allegorical narratives produced by the literalizing of figure or cliché.[41]

Finally, to conclude this schematic summary, recent work on allegory now permits us to see that what critics such as Brooks celebrate as symbols are in fact elements in an allegorical narrative. Their centrality comes from their allegorical functioning in generating critical readings. The magnificent tree, great-rooted blossomer, and the dancer in motion are two powerful symbols—so representative that Frank Kermode's *The Romantic Image* derives from them the title of its first section, "The Dancer and the Tree." They initiate a narrative of the poetic imagination. In Brooks's discussion, they give rise to an account of how criticism should proceed: not by attempting to identify root, blossom, or bole as the essence of the tree, nor by questioning the dancer about her life and loves, but by experiencing the dance. What these symbols articulate, then, is an allegory of reading, and though Brooks speaks as if he were propounding their significance as symbols, "which abide themselves as a living part in that unity of which they are the representative," he is in fact developing an allegorical narrative. Further exploration of this point might enable us to show that what we call "symbol" is only a special case of allegory.

The five changes in the study of the lyric I have described—attention to babble and doodle, exploration of intertextuality, interest in voice as figure, a new understanding of self-reflexivity, and the deconstruction of the hierarchical opposition of symbol and allegory—are not theories or methods of a school (there are numerous disagreements among the critics I have mentioned); but they do help to define a new discursive space for criticism of the lyric, a space in which such figures as "Hail to thee, blithe Spirit" are not beyond the pale.

40. Paul de Man, "The Rhetoric of Temporality," in *Interpretation: Theory and Practice,* ed. Charles Singleton (Baltimore, 1969), pp. 205–6.

41. Maureen Quilligan, *The Language of Allegory* (Ithaca, 1979); Barbara Johnson, *Défigurations du langage poétique* (Paris, 1979).

Paul de Man

Lyrical Voice in Contemporary Theory: Riffaterre and Jauss

The principle of intelligibility, in lyric poetry, depends on the phenomenalization of the poetic voice. Our claim to understand a lyric text coincides with the actualization of a speaking voice, be it (monologically) that of the poet or (dialogically) that of the exchange that takes place between author and reader in the process of comprehension.

Since this voice is in no circumstance immediately available as an actual, sensory experience, the poetic labor that is to make it manifest can take several forms and adopt a variety of strategies. No matter what approach is taken it is essential that the status of the voice not be reduced to being a mere figure of speech or play of the letter, for this would deprive it of the attribute of aesthetic presence that determines the hermeneutics of the lyric. In two eminent practitioners of the interpretation of lyric poetry in our time, one can see this anti- or metafigural strategy deployed with all desirable complexity. In both cases, the main emphasis falls on what is called actualization or concretization as a phenomenal aspect of the text. And in both cases, this actualization is linked to an act of reading, to an emphasis on the reception rather than on the production of the text. For Michael Riffaterre, intelligibility is achieved in a dialogue between text and reader which reveals a subtext (hypotext or hypogram) and a system of transformations between text and subtext susceptible of determined description. For Hans Robert Jauss, the process is historical rather than structural: the dialogue takes place within a temporal gap that opens up between the individual author and his collective, historically time-bound audience. Both instances lead to authoritative interpretations in which the poetic voice ultimately, on the far side of the reading, coincides with the phenomenality of its own discourse.

Our readings, here, of the poems by Hugo and Baudelaire used by Riffaterre and Jauss try to demonstrate that these concretizations depend on a repression of the figural and literal powers of the signifier. As a result, the claim for vocal presence made, however indirectly, by both of these theorists is challenged, in the practice of their reading as well as in the theoretical apparatus that sustains this practice. The consequences for a theory of the lyric and, more generally, for the relationship between genre and figure are far-reaching, but too complex for summary exposition. They can be elaborated, however, only by way of readings of this general type, in which the phenomenality of the form is critically examined in terms of figural substitutions or material inscriptions.[1]

I

First, Riffaterre.[2] Announced in a footnote to the article on the French formalists, the theory of the textual paragram and hypogram, concepts that stem from Saussure, will become the theoretical crux of Riffaterre's work from 1971 on.[3] It constitutes the theoretical substructure of *Semiotics of Poetry* and receives systematic treatment in several essays, up to the present. . . . In one of his tentative notes, Saussure discusses the various uses of the word hypogram in Greek.[4]

1. For another example of such a reading see "Anthropomorphism and Trope in the Lyric" in my *The Rhetoric of Romanticism* (New York, 1984). This paper, which deals with Baudelaire's "Correspondances," was read at the Toronto conference on the lyric but could not, for reasons having to do with copyright arrangements, be reproduced here.

2. [The following discussions combine parts of two previously published essays by de Man—"Hypogram and Inscription: Michael Riffaterre's Poetics of Reading," *Diacritics,* 11:4 (Winter 1981), 17–35, and his Introduction to Hans Robert Jauss, *Toward an Aesthetic of Reception,* trans. Timothy Bahti (Minneapolis, 1982). De Man's longer discussion of Jauss outlines the distinctions between "poetics" and "hermeneutics," and between poetics and history, drawn on here and sketched on pp. 22–23 of our Introduction. The works of Riffaterre referred to by de Man include *Essais de stylistique structurale* (Paris, 1971), *La Production du texte* (Paris, 1979), and *Semiotics of Poetry* (Bloomington, 1978). Those of Saussure include the *Cours de linguistique générale* (Paris, 1972), translated by Wade Baskin, *Course in General Linguistics* (London, 1960), and *Les Mots sous les mots: Les Anagrammes de Ferdinand de Saussure* (Paris, 1971), translated by Olivia Emmet as *Words upon Words* (New Haven, 1979). On Riffaterre and Jauss more generally, see our Introduction, pp. 21–24, and the discussion by Culler above, pp. 42–50.—Editors.]

3. Michael Riffaterre, *Essais de stylistique structurale,* p. 270–71, n. 25.

4. Ferdinand de Saussure, *Les Mots sous les mots: Les Anagrammes de Ferdinand de Saussure,* pp. 30–31 and n. 1, p. 31.

The very sketchy passage is as unclear as it is tantalizing. Saussure notes and seems to be disturbed by the meaning of *hypographein* as "signature," but he also mentions a "more special, though more widespread meaning as 'to underscore by means of makeup the features of a face' (souligner au moyen du fard les traits du visage)."[5] This usage is not incompatible with his own adoption of the term, which, by analogy, "underscores a name, a word, by trying to repeat its syllables, and thus giving it another, artificial, mode of being added, so to speak, to the original mode of being of the word." *Hypographein* is close in this meaning to *prosopon*, mask or face. Hypogram is close to prosopopoeia, the trope of apostrophe. This is indeed compatible with Saussure's use of "hypogram. But *prosopon-poiein* means to *give* a face and therefore implies that the original face can be missing or nonexistent. The trope which coins a name for a still-unnamed entity, which gives face to the faceless is, of course, catachresis. That a catachresis can be a prosopopoeia, in the etymological sense of "giving face," is clear from such ordinary instances as the *face* of a mountain or the *eye* of a hurricane. But it is possible that, instead of prosopopoeia being a subspecies of the generic type catachresis (or the reverse), the relationship between them is more disruptive than that between genus and species. And what would this imply for the textual model of the hypogram?

Such questions belong to the field of tropology, a part of rhetoric which Riffaterre acknowledges, albeit somewhat grudgingly. As a matter of fact, the very first sentence of the *Essais de stylistique structurale* denounces normative rhetoric as an obstacle to stylistic analysis—something which, in the context of French pedagogy, is certainly to the point. By the time of *Semiotics of Poetry,* after Jakobson, Barthes, and Genette (not to mention Derrida's "White Mythology"), the term rhetoric has evolved a great deal and can no longer be dismissed so casually. Riffaterre remains consistent, however, in keeping his distance from any suggestion that rhetorical categories might lead a life of their own that is not determined by grammatical structures. At the very outset of *Semiotics of Poetry,* in a rare dogmatic moment, he declares: "I am aware that many such descriptions (of the structure of meaning in a poem), often founded upon rhetoric, have already been put forward, and I do not deny the usefulness of notions like figure and trope. But whether these categories are well defined . . . or are catchalls . . . they can be arrived at independently of a theory of read-

5. Ibid., p. 31.

ing or the concept of text."[6] Since it can be and has been argued that no theory of reading can avoid being a theory of tropes, and since the notion of hypogram, from the start, is intertwined with a specific tropological function (namely catachresis by prosopopoeia),[7] Riffaterre's assertion stands or falls with the practical results of the readings it makes possible. Do these readings cope with the sheer strength of figuration, that is to say master their power to confer, to usurp, and to take away significance from grammatical universals? To some extent, the readings confront the interplay between tropes. They have no difficulty incorporating the Jakobsonian pair of metaphor and metonymy within their transformational logic;[8] they can account for various catachretic coinages.[9] But how do they confront the trope which threatens to dismember or to disfigure the lexicality and the grammaticality of the hypogram, namely prosopopoeia, which, as the trope of address, is the very figure of the reader and of reading? It is again a sign of Riffaterre's very sound philosophical and rhetorical instincts that, although the figure of prosopopoeia is downplayed or even avoided in his terminology, it reasserts itself as the central trope of the poetic corpus which, more than any other, is the model for the textual system he has so carefully worked out: the corpus of the poetry (and the prose) of Victor Hugo.[10]

For all too obvious reasons of economy, the demonstration of this point will have to be confined to one single instance, the reading of the Hugo poem "Ecrit sur la vitre d'une fenêtre flamande" in the paper entitled "Le poème comme représentation: une lecture de Hugo."[11] The text of the brief poem is as follows:

6. Michael Riffaterre, *Semiotics of Poetry,* p. 1.

7. See Saussure's comparable hesitation about the relationship between hypogram and trope: in his case, the trope under consideration is that of paronomasia (*Mots,* p. 32).

8. There are numerous examples throughout the work of the metonymization of apparently metaphorical structures, a technique of rhetorical analysis that Riffaterre shares with Gérard Genette. For one particularly striking instance, see *Semiotics,* p. 122 (on *ardoise* in Ponge).

9. See, for instance, "Poétique du néologisme," chap. 4 of *Production,* or the observations on a poem by Queneau in *Semiotics.*

10. The *Essais de stylistique structurale* could be said, without exaggeration, to be a book on Victor Hugo: the essays were originally destined, I believe, to be just that. *Semiotics of Poetry* deals primarily with symbolist and surrealist poets in the wake of Hugo. There is, of course, ample historical justification for this grouping, for the impact of Hugo on French nineteenth- and twentieth-century poetry is comparable only to that of Goethe on German poetry of the same period, or that of Milton and Spenser combined on English Romanticism. If so-called Symbolist and surrealist French poetry has a "face," it is that of Hugo.

11. Riffaterre, *Production,* pp. 175–98.

J'aime le carillon de tes cités antiques,
O vieux pays gardien de tes moeurs domestiques,
Noble Flandre, où le Nord se réchauffe engourdi
Au soleil de Castille et s'accouple au Midi!
Le carillon, c'est l'heure inattendue et folle,
Que l'oeil croit voir, vêtue en danseuse espagnole,
Apparaître soudain par le trou vif et clair
Que ferait en s'ouvrant une porte de l'air.
Elle vient, secouant sur les toits léthargiques
Son tablier d'argent plein de notes magiques,
Réveillant sans pitié les dormeurs ennuyeux,
Sautant à petits pas comme un oiseau joyeux,
Vibrant, ainsi qu'un dard qui tremble dans la cible;
Par un frêle escalier de cristal invisible,
Effarée et dansante, elle descend des cieux;
Et l'esprit, ce veilleur fait d'oreilles et d'yeux,
Tandis qu'elle va, vient, monte et descend encore,
Entend de marche en marche errer son pied sonore!

[In as literal a translation as is possible, without any attempt at poetic meter or effect: "I love the chimes of your ancient cities / O aged land, keeper of your domestic virtues, / Noble Flanders, where a chilled North warms itself / At a sun of Castille and mates with the South! / The carillon is the unexpected and crazy hour / That the eye thinks it sees, dressed up as a Spanish dancer / Appearing of a sudden through the lighted living hole / That an opening door of air would make. / She appears, scattering over lethargic roofs / Her silver apron filled with magic sounds / Awakening, pitiless, old bores from their sleep / Hopping with small steps like a joyous bird / Trembling like a dart that vibrates in the target; / By a frail staircase of invisible crystal, / Aghast and dancing, she descends from the skies; / And the mind, watchman made of ears and eyes / While she goes, comes, rises and falls again / Hears her sonorous feet wander from step to step!"]

Riffaterre analyzes the text as an example of descriptive poetry and uses it to demonstrate that the poetic representation, in the case of such a description, is not based on the reproduction or imitation of an external referent, but on the expansion of a hypogram, matrix, or cliché that functions in a purely verbal way: "it is not the external reality that is poetic but the manner in which it is described and in which it is 'seen' from the point of view of the words (à partir des mots)" (p. 178) or, even more forcefully: "Literary description only apparently returns us to things, to signifieds; in fact, poetic representation is founded on a reference to the signifiers" (p. 198). This not only allows him to avoid the usual platitudes about Hugo's travels and tastes but it also allows him to account for several of the details that organize the text and that have indeed little to do with the perceptual outline of the entity that is being described. It allows him, finally, to account for the *rightness* of the figural vehicles that were chosen, not in terms of the accuracy of actual observation (bound to be endless in its denotations and therefore always arbitrary and inconclusive) but in terms of the interplay between several verbal systems that restrict and define each other by mutual convergence or contrast. The representation of the clock as a Spanish dancer as well as a bird, of the chimed tune as an ascending and descending staircase as well as an overspilling apron, and several other apparently incompatible details, are shown to be generated by a common matrix. This matrix generates, by way of a set of clichés, its own system of hypograms. This "donnée sémantique" is identified as "carillon flamand," which produces by amplification the determining configurations of descriptive systems that make up the poem. One will find little room for disagreement in any of Riffaterre's descriptions of the description which the poem is supposed to perform.

The descriptive system "carillon flamand" can indeed be said to occur in the poem, but it begins only by line 5 and the three concluding lines are not, strictly speaking, a part of it. It is in fact not in the least certain that the poem is descriptive at all: a title such as "Le carillon," which would perhaps be suitable for Rilke's *New Poem* on the same topic, "Quai du rosaire," would not be fitting. The "description," if description there is, is embedded within a very different frame. The poem is a declaration of love addressed to something or someone, staged as an address of one subject to another in a *je-tu* situation which can hardly be called descriptive.

> J'aime le carillon de *tes* cités antiques
> O vieux pays gardien de tes moeurs domestiques . . .

The apostrophe, the address ("O vieux pays . . ."), frames the description it makes possible. It is indeed a prosopopoeia, a giving face to two entities, "l'heure" and "l'esprit," which are most certainly deprived of any literal face. Yet by the end of the poem, it is possible to identify without fail the *je* and the *tu* of line 1 as being time and mind. The figuration occurs by way of this address. Riffaterre notes this—it would indeed be difficult to overlook it—but does not seem to consider it as being in any way remarkable, stylistically or otherwise. He calls it personification and dismisses it from his commentary by stressing the banality of "describing, once again, a reality in terms of another, the inanimate by ways of the animated" (p. 177). Now it is certainly beyond question that the figure of address is recurrent in lyric poetry, to the point of constituting the generic definition of, at the very least, the ode (which can, in its turn, be seen as paradigmatic for poetry in general). And that it therefore occurs, like all figures, in the guise of a cliché or a convention is equally certain. None of this would allow one to discard or to ignore it as the main generative force that produces the poem in its entirety. For the singularity of "Ecrit sur la vitre d'une fenêtre flamande" does not primarily consist in the surprising details; these "descriptions" can only occur because a consciousness or a mind (l'esprit) is figurally said to relate to another abstraction (time) as male relates to female in a copulating couple (l. 5). The matrix, in other words, is not "carillon" but "j'aime le carillon," and this matrix is not a "donnée semantique" but is itself already a figure: it is not supposed to describe some peculiar sexual perversion, such as chronophilia, since the persons involved in this affair are persons only by dint of linguistic figuration. The description that follows is a mere expansion, in Riffaterre's sense of the term, of the original figure. It does not describe an entity, referential or textual, but sets up a rapport between concepts said to be structured like a sense perception: the sentence culminates in the verb *to hear*—"Le carillon, c'est l'heure . . . Et l'esprit *(l)'entend*"—which carries the full burden of dramatic resolution and of intelligibility. As in Hegel's first chapter of the *Phenomenology,* the figural enigma is that of a conscious cognition being, in some manner, akin to the certainty of a sense perception. This may be a classical philosopheme, but not a kernel of determined meaning. Riffaterre is certainly right in saying that what is presumably being described is not referential but verbal. The verbal entity, or function, is not, however, the signifier "carillon" but the figure *l'esprit entend* (as well as "voit" and, eventually, "aime") *le temps.*[12] The text is therefore not the mimesis of a signifier but of a specific figure, prosopopoeia. And since mimesis is itself a figure, it is the figure of a figure (the prosopopoeia of a prosopopoeia) and not in any respect, neither in appearance nor in reality, a description—as little as the alliterating bottles or the synecdochal churches in Proust's *Recherche* are descriptions. A proper title for Hugo's poem could be "Prosopopée" rather than "Le carillon," not just in the vague and general manner in which

12. See Riffaterre's justification of the use of verbs of perception (ibid., p. 191). The point is not how fictive persons ("des personnages") are being affected by time, since what is here being affected are not persons, real or fictional, but mind, in the most general sense conceivable.

any poem of address could be given this title,[13] but in the very specific way that the burden of understanding and of persuasion, in this poem, corresponds exactly to the epistemological tension that produced prosopopoeia, the master trope of poetic discourse. The actual title, however, is "Ecrit sur la vitre d'une fenêtre flamande," the "here" and the "now" of the poem which elicits no comment from Riffaterre and remains to be accounted for.

The relationship between the carillon and time should be of special interest to a semiotician, for it is analogous to the relationship between signifier and signified that constitutes the sign. The ringing of the bells (or the conventional tune that serves as the prelude to the actual chimes) is the material sign of an event (the passage of time) of which the phenomenality lacks certainty; just as it has been said that if it were not for novels no one would know for certain that he is in love, in the absence of chimes and clocks no one could be certain that such a thing as time exists, in the full ontological sense of that term. For as most philosophers well know, the very concept of certainty, which is the basis of all concepts, comes into being only in relation to sensory experience, be it, as in Hegel, as unmediated assurance or, as in Descartes, as reflected delusion. If there is to be consciousness (or experience, mind, subject, discourse, or face), it has to be susceptible of phenomenalization. But since the phenomenality of experience cannot be established *a priori,* it can only occur by a process of signification. The phenomenal and sensory properties of the signifier have to serve as guarantors for the certain existence of the signified and, ultimately, of the referent. The carillon's relationship to time has to be like the relationship of the mind to the senses: it is the sonorous face, the "masque aux yeux sonores" (Rilke) of cognition which, by metonymic substitution, links the sound of the bells to the face of the clock. Once the phenomenal intuition has been put in motion, all other substitutions follow as in a chain. But the starting, catachretic decree of signification is arbitrary. This text, like all texts, has to adhere to the program of these problematics, regardless of the philosophical knowledge or skill of its author. It accomplishes the trick by arbitrarily linking the mind to the semiotic relationship that connects the bells to the temporal motion they signify. The senses become the signs of the mind as the sound of the bells is the sign of time, because time and mind are linked, in the figure, as in the embrace of a couple. This declaration ("j'aime le carillon" or *l'esprit aime le temps*) is then

13. As they in fact often are, though preferably by the more euphonic and noble term "ode" or "Ode to X."

acted out, in the erotic mode of "mere" sense perception,[14] in the allegory of cognition that follows, a seduction scene that culminates in the extraordinary line, the prosopopoeia of prosopopoeia:

> Et l'esprit, ce veilleur fait d'oreilles et d'yeux . . .

This bizarre waking monster, made of eyes and ears as mud is made of earth and water, is so eminently visible that any attentive reader will have to respond to it. It is the visual shape of something that has no sensory existence: a hallucination. As any reader of Hugo or, for that matter, anyone who ever wondered about the *legs* of a table or, like Wordsworth, about the *faces* or the *backs* of mountains, knows, prosopopoeia is hallucinatory. To make the invisible visible is uncanny. A reader of Riffaterre's caliber can be counted on to respond in this fashion. One of his earliest essays, going back almost twenty years, collected in the *Essais de stylistique structurale* is entitled "La vision hallucinatoire chez Victor Hugo." The tone and the technique may appear quite "ideological," especially if compared to Riffaterre's later rigor, but the essay already struggles valiantly to keep literary effects and psychological experience apart. The analysis is stylistic in name only, since Riffaterre still uses thematic procedures which critics like Poulet or Bachelard had been using for nonstylistic aims. But the programmatic aim is clearly stated: what the poems give us is not a hallucination but a hallucinatory effect. The same clear distinction is stated in a footnote to the crucial word *invisible* in our present poem: "'veilleur fait d'oreilles et d'yeux' sharply distinguishes between two orders of sensation . . .; the transposition from the auditive to the visual is therefore not represented as a synesthesia, but as hallucination. Hallucination is poetically effective, but from the viewpoint of poetic mimesis, it is still an excuse, the avowal of a visionary reference to a rational context."[15] Once again, what should give one pause in statements such as these is not the assertion of nonreferentiality, which is obvious, but the implied assertion of semantic determination of which nonreferentiality is the specular negation. Descartes found it difficult to distinguish between waking and sleeping because, when one dreams, one always dreams that one is awake, just as Hugo's "mind" is awake ("l'esprit, ce veilleur . . ."). How then is one to decide

14. Rather than being a heightened version of sense experience, the erotic is a figure that makes such experience possible. We do not see what we love but we love in the hope of confirming the illusion that we are indeed seeing anything at all.

15. Riffaterre, *Production*, p. 186, n. 1.

on the distinction between hallucination and perception since, in hallucination, the difference between *I see* and *I think that I see* has been one-sidedly resolved in the direction of apperception? Consciousness has become consciousness only of itself. In that sense, any consciousness, including perception, is hallucinatory: one never "has" a hallucination the way one has a sore foot from kicking the proverbial stone. Just as the hypothesis of dreaming undoes the certainty of sleep, the hypothesis, or the figure, of hallucination undoes sense certainty. This means, in linguistic terms, that it is impossible to say whether prosopopoeia is plausible because of the empirical existence of dreams and hallucinations or whether one believes that such things as dreams and hallucinations exist because language permits the figure of prosopopoeia. The question "Was it a vision or a waking dream?" is destined to remain unanswered. Prosopopoeia undoes the distinction between reference and signification on which all semiotic systems, including Riffaterre's, depend.

The claim of all poetry to make the invisible visible is a figure to the precise extent that it undoes the distinction between sign and trope. It smuggles the wiles of rhetoric back into the hygienic clarity of semiotics. This claim is overtly stated in Hugo's poem, and it puts a particularly heavy burden on the word "invisible" that appears in the text (line 14). Riffaterre comments on the line

> Par un frêle escalier de cristal invisible
> . . . elle (l'heure) descend des cieux

by stressing (1) the hyperbolic function of the tautology "cristal invisible" which makes the cristal even more cristalline and (2) the negative power of the epithet which replaces the architectural, spatial, and hence visible, staircase by an invisible one. It thus prepares the transfer from sight to sound in the concluding line. In the descriptive context to which Riffaterre has chosen to confine himself, the two observations, as well as their combined overdetermining effect, are entirely correct. These descriptive strategies of intra-sensory circulations are inscribed however within a wider scene, in which the interaction does not occur between one kind of sense experience and another but between, on the one side, the sensory as such and, on the other, the nonsensory mind. This is why, in the line "l'esprit, ce veilleur fait d'oreilles et d'yeux," as Riffaterre correctly observes, eyes and ears are treated as separate but equal, without dialectical tension between them. What in Baudelaire's "Correspondances" is achieved by infinite expansion, the confusion and unification of the various sensory faculties, is here achieved by the figure of the initial apostrophe;[16] therefore, it is the authority of that figure, and not of a synecdoche of totalization that does not appear in the poem, that has to be examined. Aside from the functions pointed out by Riffaterre, "cristal invisible" functions in still another register which carries, for the poem as a whole, the burden of a heavier investment. By way of the mediation of the scaled stairways time can be called an invisible crystal; the materiality of crystal, which is at least accessible to one of the senses, can serve the insistent strategy of the poem in helping to make the elusive passage of time accessible to sight and sound. But there is another "crystal" in the poem which is no longer invisible and which also achieves materiality, albeit in a very different manner: namely the window on which, according to the title, the poem is supposed to have been written. Because the poem is written on the transparent window, the window has indeed become visible, and one could consider this metamorphosis as one more figure for the linkage between mind and senses. By coining the prosopopoeia of address, Hugo has time and mind reflect each other in a couple as inseparable as Narcissus's eye is inseparable from his reflected face. But that is not all there is to the title. Unlike everything else in the poem, the title contains an element that is not hallucinatory. Every detail as well as every general proposition in the text is fantastic except for the assertion, in the title, that it is *écrit,* written. That it was supposed to be written, like Swift's love poem to Stella, as words upon a windowpane, is one more cliché to add to those Riffaterre has already collected. But that it, like Hegel's text from the *Phenomenology,* was written cannot be denied. The materiality (as distinct from the phenomenality) that is thus revealed, the unseen "cristal" whose existence thus becomes a certain *there* and a certain *then* which can become a *here* and a *now* in the reading "now" taking place, is not the materiality of the mind or of time or of the carillon—none of which exist, except in the figure of prosopopoeia—but the materiality of an inscription. Description, it appears, was a device to conceal inscription. Inscription is neither a figure, nor a sign, nor a cognition, nor a desire, nor a hypogram, nor a matrix, yet no theory of reading or of poetry can achieve consistency if, like Riffaterre's, it responds to its powers only by a figural evasion which, in this case, takes the subtly effective form of evading the figural.

16. This simplifies "Correspondances" in a manner that cannot be discussed here. The reference is to the canonical *idée reçue* of the poem, not to the poem read.

II

In the practice of his own textual interpretation, H. R. Jauss pays little attention to the semantic play of the signifier, and when, on rare occasions, he does so, the effect is quickly reaestheticized before anything unpleasant might occur—just as any word-play is so easily disarmed by assimilating it to the harmlessness of a mere pun or *calembour.* Thus, in a recent article that makes use of one of Baudelaire's Spleen poems as a textual example,[17] Jauss comments judiciously on the lines in which the name of eighteenth-century painter Boucher is made to pseudo-rhyme with the word "débouché" (uncorked).

. . . un vieux boudoir
Où les pastels plaintifs et les pâles Boucher,
Seuls, respirent l'odeur d'un flacon débouché.

[In as literal a translation as is possible, without any attempt at poetic meter or effect: ". . . an old boudoir / Where only sorrowful pastel drawings and (paintings by) Boucher / Breathe in the perfume of an uncorked flask."]

In a rare Lacanian moment, Jauss suggests that what he calls a "grotesque" effect of verbal play—the rhyme-pair Boucher/débouché—is also something more uncanny: "The still harmonious representation of the last perfume escaping from the uncorked bottle overturns [*kippt um*] into the dissonant connotation of a 'decapitated' rococo painter Boucher."[18] After having gone this far, it becomes very hard to stop. Should one not also notice that this bloody scene is made gorier still by the presence of a proper name (Boucher) which, as a common name, means butcher, thus making the "pâle Boucher" the agent of his own execution? This pale and white text of recollection (the first line of the poem is 'J'ai plus de souvenirs que si j'avais mille ans") turns red with a brutality that takes us out of the inwardness of memory, the ostensible *theme* of the poem, into a very threatening literality to which an innocent art-term such as "dissonance" hardly does justice. Much more apt is Jauss's very concrete and undecorous, almost colloquial, word *umkippen* (to overturn), which "overturns" the beheaded Boucher as if he were himself an uncorked "flacon" spilling his blood. That this would happen to the

17. H. R. Jauss, "The Poetic Text within the Change of Horizons of Reading: The Example of Baudelaire's 'Spleen II,'" chap. 5 of *Toward an Aesthetic of Reception.*
18. Ibid., p. 157.

proper name of a painter, and by means of a merely "grotesque" and frivolous play on words, tells us a great deal about the difficult-to-control borderline (or lack of it) between the aesthetics of *homo ludens* and the literal incisiveness of *Wortwitz.* For reasons of decorum, the gap that Jauss has opened, by his own observation, in the aesthetic texture of the language is at once reclosed, as if the commentator felt that he might betray the integrity of the text with which he is dealing.

This hesitation, this restraint before giving in to the coarseness and the potential violence of the signifier, is by no means to be condemned as a lack of boldness. After all, Baudelaire himself does not threaten us, or himself, directly, and by keeping the menace wrapped up, as it were, within a play of language, he does not actually draw blood. He seems to stop in time, to fence with a foil[19]—for how could anyone be hurt by a mere rhyme? Yet the poetic restraint exercised by Baudelaire differs entirely from the aesthetic restraint exercised by Jauss. For the play on words, as we all know from obscene jokes, far from preserving decorum dispenses with it quite easily, as Baudelaire dispensed with it to the point of attracting the attention of the *police des moeurs.* What it does not dispense with, unlike decorum (a classical and aesthetic concept), is the ambiguity of a statement that, because it is a verbal thrust and not an actual blow, allows itself to be taken figurally but, in so doing, opens up the way to the performance of what it only seems to feign or prefigure. The false rhyme on Boucher/débouché is a figure, a paronomasis. But only after we have, with the assistance of H. R. Jauss, noticed and recognized it as such does the actual threat inherent in the fiction produced by the actual hands of the painter (who is also a butcher) become manifest. This no longer describes an aesthetic but a poetic structure, a structure that has to do with what Benjamin identified as a nonconvergence of "meaning" with "the devices that produce meaning," or what Nietzsche has in mind when he insists that eudaemonic judgments are inadequate "means of expression" of a cognition. Since this poetic (as distinguished from aesthetic) structure has to do with the necessity of deciding whether a statement in a text is to be taken as a figure or *à la lettre,* it pertains to rhetoric. In this particular instance, Jauss has come upon the rhetorical dimension of language; it is significant that he has to draw back in the face of his own discovery.

19. In "Über einige Motive bei Baudelaire," *Illuminationen* (Frankfurt, 1961), p. 210, Benjamin quotes the lines from another of the *Fleurs du Mal* poems: "Je vais m'éxercer seul à ma fantasque escrime, / Flairant dans tous les coins les hasardes de la rime, . . ." (Le Soleil).

But how can it be said that Jauss swerves from the consideration of rhetoric where he has so many perceptive and relevant things to say about it, and does so without any trace of the restraint for which I am both praising and blaming him in his gloss on Baudelaire's poem? An extended study of his writings would show that something similar to what happens in the essay on Spleen occurs whenever rhetorical categories are at stake. One hint may suffice. In a polemical exchange with Gadamer about the rhetoric of classicism,[20] classical art is assimilated to a rhetoric of mimesis (the Aristotelian rhetorical category par excellence) and opposed to medieval and modern art, which are said to be nonmimetic and nonrepresentational. A rhetorical trope serves as the ground of a historical system of periodization that allows for the correct understanding of meaning; once again, a poetic and a hermeneutic category have been seamlessly articulated. But if this assertion seems so reasonable, is it not because it corresponds to a received idea of literary history rather than being the result of a rigorous linguistic analysis? The alternative to *mimesis* would be, one assumes, allegory, which all of us associate with medieval and, at least since Benjamin, with modern art. If we then ask whether Jauss's own model for reading, the horizon of expectation, is classical or modern, one would have to say that it is the former. For it is certainly, like all hermeneutic systems, overwhelmingly mimetic: if literary understanding involves a horizon of expectation it resembles a sense perception, and it will be correct to the precise extent that it "imitates" such a perception. The negativity inherent in the Husserlian model is a negativity within the sensory itself and not its negation, let alone its "other." It is impossible to conceive of a phenomenal experience that would not be mimetic, as it is impossible to conceive of an aesthetic judgment that would not be dependent on imitation as a constitutive category, also and especially when the judgment, as is the case in Kant, is interiorized as the consciousness of a subject. The concept of nonrepresentational art stems from painting and from a pictorial aesthetic that is firmly committed to the phenomenalism of art. The allegory, or allegoresis, which Jauss opposes to mimesis, remains firmly rooted in the classical phenomenalism of an aesthetic of representation.

"Allegory," however, is a loaded term that can have different implications. A reference to Walter Benjamin can be helpful, all the more so since Jauss alludes to him in the same essay on Baudelaire from which I have been quoting. In his treatment of allegory Ben-

20. Jauss, *Toward an Aesthetic of Reception*, p. 30.

jamin plays, by anticipation, the part of Hamann in a debate in which Jauss would be playing the part of Herder. For him, allegory is best compared to a commodity; it has, as he puts it in a term taken from Marx, *Warencharakter,* "matter that is death in a double sense and that is anorganic." The "anorganic" quality of allegory is, however, not equivalent, as Jauss's commentary seems to suggest, to the negation of the natural world;[21] the opposition between organic and anorganic, in Benjamin, is not like the opposition between *organisch* and *aorganisch,* familiar from the terminology of idealist philosophy in Schelling and also in Hölderlin. The commodity is anorganic because it exists as a mere piece of paper, as an inscription or a notation on a certificate. The opposition is not between nature and consciousness (or subject) but between what exists as language and what does not. Allegory is material or materialistic, in Benjamin's sense, because its dependence on the letter, on the literalism of the letter, cuts it off sharply from symbolic and aesthetic syntheses. "The subject of allegory can only be called a grammatical subject"; the quotation is not from Benjamin but from one of the least-valued sections of Hegel's *Lectures on Aesthetics,*[22] the canonical bible, still for Heidegger, of the phenomenalism of art. Allegory names the rhetorical process by which the literary text moves from a phenomenal, world-oriented to a grammatical, language-oriented direction. It thus also names the moment when aesthetic and poetic values part company. Everyone has always known that allegory, like the commodity and unlike aesthetic delight, is, as Hegel puts it, "icy and Barren."[23] If this is so, can one then still share Jauss's confidence that "the allegorical intention, pursued to the utmost of *rigor mortis,* can still reverse [*umschlagen*] this extreme alienation into an appearance of the beautiful"?[24] If the return to the aesthetic is a turning away from the language of allegory and of rhetoric, then it is also a turning away from literature, a breaking of the link between poetics and history.

The debate between Jauss and Benjamin on allegory is a debate between the classical position, here represented by Jauss, and a

21. Ibid., p. 179.

22. *Vorlesungen über die Ästhetik* (Werkausgabe), 1:512.

23. Ibid.

24. Jauss, *Toward an Aesthetic of Reception,* p. 179. *Erscheinnung des Schönen* is, of course, the traditional Hegelian vocabulary for the aesthetic experience. The "umkippen" of Jauss's earlier, corrosive observation on Baudelaire's play on *Boucher/débouché* (ibid., p. 157), which suggests the demolition of the aesthetic idol as if it were the *colonne Vendôme* or any monument honoring a tyrant, is now replaced by the more dignified "umschlagen." Taken literally, however, *schlagen* (to beat) in the cliché *umschlagen* is rather more threatening than *kippen* (to tilt).

tradition[25] that undoes it, and that includes, in the wake of Kant, among others Hamann, Friedrich Schlegel, Kierkegaard, and Nietzsche. The debate occurs in the course of interpreting Baudelaire's poem "Spleen II." The poem deals with history as recollection, *souvenir*, Hegel's *Erinnerung*. Jauss's precise and suggestive reading carefully traces the manner in which an inner state of mind (spleen) is first compared to an outside object (ll. 2 and 5), then is asserted to *be* such an object (l. 6), then becomes the voice of a speaking subject that declares itself to be an object (l. 8), and finally culminates in the dialogical relationship of an apostrophe by this subject to a material object that has itself acquired consciousness:

> —Désormais tu n'es plus, ô matière vivante!
> Qu'un granit entouré d'une vague épouvante, . . .
> (ll. 19–20)
>
> ["Henceforth, o living matter, you are
> Merely a granite rock, wrapped in shapeless terror, . . ."]

At the conclusion of the poem, the enigmatic figure of "Un vieux sphinx" appears and is said, however restrictively and negatively, to be singing

> Un vieux sphinx . . .
> Ne chante qu'aux rayons du soleil qui se couche.
> (ll. 22–24)
>
> ["An ancient sphinx . . .
> Sings only to the rays of a setting sun."]

Jauss convincingly identifies this sphinx as the figure of the poetic voice and his song as the production of the text of "Spleen II."[26] We rediscover the not unfamiliar, specular (that is to say solar and phenomenal) conception of a "poetry of poetry,"[27] the self-referential

25. The use of "tradition" in this context is one of the numerous occasions in which one can share Rousseau's naive regret that we have no diacritical mark at our disposal by which to indicate irony. It also indicates that, try as I may, when I seem to be reproaching Jauss for not freeing himself from classical constraints, I am not more liberated from them than he is.

26. Jauss, *Toward an Aesthetic of Reception*, pp. 169, 170.

27. "Poesie der Poesie" is a concept frequently developed in connection with Paul Valéry, whose authority as a poetician is, for various and complex reasons, overrated in Germany. The "Valérization" of Mallarmé and of Baudelaire is a case in which Harold Bloom's notion of belatedness would have a salutary effect.

text that thematizes its own invention, prefigures its own reception, and achieves, as aesthetic cognition and pleasure, the recovery from the most extreme of alienations, from the terror of encrypted death. "The dissonance of the statement is aesthetically harmonized by the assonance and the balance between the various textual layers."[28] "In a successfully elaborated form, the literary representation of terror and anxiety is always already, thanks to aesthetic sublimation, overcome."[29] The promise of aesthetic sublimation is powerfully argued, in a manner that leaves little room for further questioning.

The assurance that further questioning nevertheless should take place has little to do with one's own spleen, with pessimism, nihilism, or the historical necessity to overcome alienation. It depends on powers of poetic analysis, which it is in no one's power to evade. One of the thematic textual "layers" of "Spleen II" that remain constant throughout the text is that of the mind as a hollow container, box, or grave and the transformation of this container, or of the corpse contained in it, into a voice:

> mon triste cerveau.
> C'est une pyramide, un immense caveau,
> Qui contient plus de morts que la fosse commune.
> —Je suis un cimetière abhorré de la lune,
> . . . .
> —Désormais tu n'es plus, ô matière vivante!
> Qu'un granit entouré d'une vague épouvante,
> Assoupi dans le fond d'un Saharah brumeux;
> Un vieux sphinx ignoré du monde insoucieux,
> Oublié sur la carte, et dont l'humeur farouche
> Ne chante qu'aux rayons du soleil qui se couche.

["... my sad brain / Is a pyramid, an immense cave / Filled with more corpses than the pauper's grave, / —I am a graveyard that the moon abhors / ... / Henceforth, o living matter, you are / Merely a granite rock, wrapped in shapeless terror / Dozing at the bottom of a foggy desert; / An aged sphinx, ignored by a careless world / Forgotten on the map and whose somber mood / Sings only to the rays of a setting sun."]

The transformation occurs as one moves from mind (as recollection) to pyramid and to sphinx. It occurs, in other words, by an itinerary that travels by way of Egypt. Egypt, in Hegel's *Aesthetics*, is the birthplace of truly symbolic art, which is monumental and archi-

28. Jauss, *Toward an Aesthetic of Reception*, p. 182.
29. Ibid., p. 167.

tectural, not literary. It is the art of memory that remembers death, the art of history as *Erinnerung*. The emblem for interiorized memory, in Hegel, is that of the buried treasure or mine (*Schacht*), or, perhaps, a well.[30] Baudelaire, however, fond though he is of well-metaphors, uses "pyramid," which connotes, of course, Egypt, monument and crypt, but which also connotes, to a reader of Hegel, the emblem of the sign as opposed to the symbol.[31] The sign, which pertains specifically to language and to rhetoric, marks, in Hegel, the passage from sheer inward recollection and imagination to thought (*Denken*), which occurs by way of the deliberate forgetting of substantial, aesthetic, and pictorial symbols.[32] Baudelaire, who in all likelihood never heard of Hegel, happens to hit on the same emblematic sequence[33] to say something very similar. The decapitated painter lies, as a corpse, in the crypt of recollection and is replaced by the sphinx, who, since he has a head and a face, can be apostrophized in the poetic speech of rhetorical figuration. But the sphinx is not an emblem of recollection but, like Hegel's sign, an emblem of forgetting. In Baudelaire's poem he is not just "oublié" but "oublié sur la carte," inaccessible to memory because he is imprinted on paper, because he is himself the inscription of a sign. Contrary to Jauss's assertion—"for who could say with more right than the sphinx: j'ai plus de souvenirs que si j'avais mille ans"—the sphinx is the one least able to say anything of the sort. He is the grammatical subject cut off from its consciousness, the poetic analysis cut off from its hermeneutic function, the dismantling of the aesthetic and pictorial world of "le soleil qui se couche" by the advent of poetry as allegory. What he "sings" can never be the poem entitled "Spleen"; his song is not the sublimation but the forgetting, by inscription, of terror, the dismemberment of the aesthetic whole into the unpredictable play of the literary letter. We could not have reached this understanding without the assistance of Jauss's reading. His work confronts us with the enigma of the relationship between the aesthetic and the poetic, and, by so doing, it demonstrates the rigor of its theoretical questioning.

30. *Enzyklopädie der philosophischen Wissenschaften* (Werkausgabe), vol. 3, sec. 453, p. 260.

31. Ibid., sec. 458, p. 270.

32. Ibid., sec. 464, p. 282.

33. That the coincidence may be due to common occult sources in Hegel and Baudelaire obscures rather than explains the passage. It distracts the reader from wondering why the use of this particular emblematic code can be "right" in a lyric poem as well as in a philosophical treatise.

JOHN HOLLANDER

Breaking into Song: Some Notes on Refrain

Edgar Allan Poe, in "The Philosophy of Composition," told a fable of the genesis of "The Raven" which became Symbolist, and eventually modernist, scripture. He speaks of having to start with what he calls a "point" (we would say a device, or scheme, or formal structure—but not a trope) of a purely musical sort, a timing device for a short (and thus authentic) poem. Poe's "pivot upon which the whole structure might turn" proved to be a minimal refrain, a condensation of it, a synecdoche of a returning burden whose name—*refrain*—is etymologically *refractus,* broken back or rebroken: in short, a single word. We know how Poe—and with what mixed consequences in France—declared that the *o* and *r* of "Nevermore" (the most "sonorous" vowel and the most "producible" consonant) determined his choice of the word. This bit of visionary linguistics is phonetically nonsensical—the *o* and *r* he was characterizing are only those phonemes of the word "sonorous" itself. Moreover it represses a matter of allusive signification. Like the agent of a dream whose very sinews of meaning are woven on the warp of unacknowledgment, Poe's raven itself speaks deep and hidden truth (the author's account of the bird's utterance only stirs up the clouds). For Poe knew well that the squawk of the raven in the age of classical Rome's grandeur was rendered in Latin as "cras cras cras" (not "caw caw" as in English), and thus "tomorrow, tomorrow," thereby affirming the bird's prophetic powers. Poe's raven knows, in the dreary light of what Harold Bloom would call Romantic belatedness, that there is no poetic tomorrow ("a bird of ill-omen," Poe calls it), and so declares, albeit allusively. Perched on an emblem of wisdom washed out—not a beautiful, dark, haunted Pallas, but an anemic Athena—the poetic bird speaks of the limits of art for the man whose name is part "poe-t" only. It is the "lost Lenore" that is in the poem for alliteration and rhyme, not the word of the bird. "Nevermore" cancels and refigures "cras."

Poe went on to observe of his broken refrain that its "application"—as he called its syntactic, logical, and rhetorical role *in situ* of each strophe that it concluded—was to vary, even as the word itself remained unchanged. In practice, the whole refrain line varied, the fragment "-more" only remaining constant, the full clause ("Quoth the Raven, 'Nevermore'") occurring in only five out of eighteen instances. Poe's concern for his broken or refracted fragment as a device for breaking into an anxiety-ringed, hermeneutico-poetical circle of silence indicates a half-awareness that a formal element, or "point" previously used in song-texts, might itself be allegorized when employed in a true poem. In this case, the return of "Nevermore" denies the return of dead beauty to memory. In general, lyrics from the Renaissance on—poems whose relation to song-text is itself figurative—have tended more and more to trope the scheme of refrain, to propound a parable out of its structural role.

I am talking here of poetic, rather than merely schematic, refrain. This tradition starts perhaps with Theocritus, whose first idyll varies what Poe called the "application" of the repetend to signal phases of beginning, middle, and end of the whole poem itself.[1] Thyrsis's song commences with (and I quote from Daryl Hine's splendid recent translation)—"Start up the pastoral music, dear Muses, begin the performance" (*Archete buokolaikas Moisai philai, archet'aoidas*), which returns at intervals of from three to five lines, until it modulates, now avowing in the changed verb its own earlier form: "Muses, continue the pastoral music, on with the performance" (*archete boukolaikas Moisai, palin archet'aoidas*) and, finally, to "Muses, come finish the pastoral music, conclude the performance" (*lêgete boukolaikas Moisai, ite lêget'aoidas*), which reiterates, and completes, the self-referential effect.

But modern lyrical refrain derives in good part from the medieval carol burden, whose reiterations have a literal quality: a leader-singer will sing the strophes, the choral dancers will each time respond with the frequently macaronic burden which punctuates the periods of varying, and unfolding, monophonic material. Each occurrence of

1. See the treatment of repetitive forms in pastoral by Thomas G. Rosenmeyer, *The Green Cabinet* (Berkeley and Los Angeles, 1969), pp. 93–95.

the danced-to burden increases its redundancy, and tends to collapse it into a univocal sign (*That was all full of meaning; now meaning stops for a while and we all dance again*). Poetic refrain, on the other hand, starts out by troping the literalness of the repetition, by raising a central parabolic question for all textual refrain: *Does repeating something at intervals make it important, or less so?* Does statistical over-determination—the criterion of redundancy-as-predictability—apply to such repetitions, or rather the interpreter's concept of over-determination as implying an increased weight of meaning? It would appear that gradations of signification can appear, and operate, in any single case. We might suggest at first that the more complex the poem, the more it becomes necessary for it to confront the dialectic of these two emblematic readings of, say, the strophic *fa-la-la.* Feelings of "O, *that* again," "*We* know," etc. war with the incremental pain of each rapped knuckle; as we know, the ultimate story of modern poetic refrain is "What is it to mean *this* time around?"

Refrain breaks into the unfolding or unrolling of any lyrical text. It partakes as well of that action of restraint invoked by our doublet word in English, "refrain" (Fr. *refréner,* for *se retenir,* literally "to bridle oneself"). But the major tradition of poetic (some might say "literary," some "self-conscious," some "writerly") refrain is rooted in a rhetorical self-consciousness. There is something allusive about all refrains, if only to their musical and conventionalized origins; and every attempt to make structures of permutation in what Poe called their application can only be a momentary confusion—as it were—against stay, a lie against repetition. We may perceive patterns of variation which are doomed from the outset to play themselves out, e.g., Algernon Charles Swinburne's anaphoristic refrain pattern beginning with the scriptural "Watchman, what of the night?" and continuing through "Prophet, what of the night?" "Mourners, what of the night?" and on through the sequence "Dead men . . . ," "Statesman . . . ," "Warrior," "Master," "Exile," "Captives," "Christian," "High priest," "Princes," "Martyrs," "England," "France," "Italy," "Germany," "Europe," and, finally, "Liberty, what of the night?" ("A Watch in the Night" from *Songs before Sunrise*).[2] Then there are those poems with paired refrains which depend upon a quasi-echoic rhyme; this is made a trope of decaying structure in Rossetti's "Troy Town" (of which I quote the first of fourteen stanzas):

2. Swinburne explores refrains as short as a single word in his *A Century of Roundels;* in one of these, he characterizes the roundel's refrain: "As a bird's quick song runs round, and the hearts in us hear / Pause answer to pause, and again the same strain caught."

Heavenborn Helen, Sparta's queen,
    (O Troy Town!)
Had two breasts of heavenly sheen,
The sun and moon of the heart's desire:
All Love's lordship lay between.
    (O Troy's down,
    Tall Troy's on fire!)

The word "desire" terminates the fourth line throughout the poem, although as a half-suppressed sub-refrain, unmarked by the formal position, the italicization, etc. of the other three lines. The effect is to have "desire" in the text lead to "*fire*" in the refrain; but aside from the growing significance of this in the narrative, the refrain's mode of application does not change.[3] It is the unvarying rhetoric of the Rossettian double-refrain (as in "Eden Bower," where it alternates in successive stanzas) which made it vulnerable to light-verse parody, as in Charles Stuart Calverley's "Ballad," the last stanza of which tweaks the nose of redundancy:

The farmer's daughter hath soft brown hair
(Butter and eggs and a pound of cheese)
And I met with a ballad, I can't say where,
Which wholly consisted of lines like these.

Aside from the matter of redundancy of application, there are questions of more specific allusiveness. Yeats, in many of his later lyrics, substitutes for the empty signaling of earlier poetical *fa-la-la*s, which signal only "refrain here, now," defiantly "unmusical" prosaic phrases ("*Daybreak and a candle-end*"). But allusive fragments can be turned into refrain in a similar way; this will sometimes constitute an initial interpretation of the nature of the fragment's canonical quality. Consider, for example, how Catullus's "nobis cum semel occidit brevis lux, / nox est perpetua una dormienda" (Ben Jonson gives it as "Suns that set may rise again; / But if once we lose this light, / 'Tis with us perpetual night") becomes for Thomas Campion a varying refrain in his far from mere translation, "My Sweetest Lesbia." It reinterprets the momentary *memento mori* that breaks into the argument for immediate bed:

But soon as once is set our little light,
Then must we sleep one ever-during night.

3. But see the dense and delicate variations of the refrain in Rossetti's "A Love-Parting."

The second variation refigures the "night" as a moral and spiritual benightedness:

> But fools do live and waste their little light,
> And seek with pain their ever-during night.

The third and final stanza ends with a re-literalizing of the "night," and collapses eternity into mere hyperbole:

> And, Lesbia, close up thou my little light,
> And crown with love my ever-during night.

There are many matters about refrains in poetry which I shall not take up in these remarks but which should at least be considered briefly. One of these is a spectrum or scale of lexical or syntactic variation, or of rhythm of recurrence (at regular or irregular intervals), along which particular applications of refrains in poems might be arrayed. Another is a sort of referential scale, with one pole at what used to be called the "purely musical"—the *fa-la-la* mentioned earlier, a univocal sign of music returning to embrace narrative or analytic information in the strophes. The other pole of such a spectrum would be one of optimum density of reference, in which each return accrued new meaning, not merely because of its relation to the preceding strophe (their glossing of each other), but as a function of the history of its previous occurrences in the poem. Such a mapping would reveal an interesting relation to the rhetoricity of the lyric form as such—the refrains of what Yeats called "words for music perhaps" have, as historical revisions of the burdens of song-texts, a special structural, or quasi-musical, "perhaps"-ness of their own. But in all these taxonomies, historically belated or locally troped refrains would seem to have the property of remembering: their own previous occurrence in the poem, their distant ancestry in song and dance and their more recent poetic parentage are recollected at each return.

Refrains can time a poem, tolling its strophic hours in the tongue of bells that may be wholly foreign to the noises of the stanzas' daily life. And poetic refrains can enact tropes, as well as schemes, of time and memory. Our English words "memory" and "remembrance" contain the meanings of both *la mémoire* and *un souvenir* (i.e., a phrase like "I have no memory of him" is ambiguous as to the nature of the verb's object). Thus we again observe that refrains *are,* and *have,* memories—of their prior strophes or stretches of text, of their own preoccurrences, and of their own genealogies in earlier texts as well.

The refrain lines of François Villon's ballades exhibit a range of syntactic and rhetorical modes of Poe's "application." But the whole of ballade structure seems almost to have been reinvented for, and by, the first of the ballades dispersed throughout *Le Testament* (it is also the foremost in the canon), the famous "Ballade des dames du temps jadis"; I quote the first stanza, together with Dante Gabriel Rossetti's version:

Dites moi où, n'en quel pays
Est Flora la belle Romaine,
Archipiades, ne Thais,
Qui fut sa cousine germaine,
Echo parlant quant bruit on maine
Dessus rivière ou sus estan,
Qui beauté eut trop plus qu'humaine.
Mais où sont les neiges d'antan?

[Tell me now in what hidden way is
Lady Flora, the lovely Roman?
Where's Hipparchia, and where is Thais,
Neither of them the fairer woman?
Where is Echo, beheld of no man,
Only heard on river and mere,—
She whose beauty was more than human? . . .
But where are the snows of yester-year?]

The pattern of *ubi sunt* catalogue proceeds forward in time from the dead ladies of antiquity toward Villon's own age, and the first refrain is introduced with the nymph Echo—"Echo parlant quant bruit on maine / Dessus rivière ou sus estan / Qui beauté eut trop plus qu'humaine"—who re-presents momentarily vanished voice (if we were to cry "jadis!" she would sigh "y" in return), and momentarily appears as a sort of muse of refrain herself. Then come "les neiges d'antan," melting like Echo's body, in the post-Ovidian textual history, into mere voice, or even "melting" like sound into silent air. This is the bottom line, itself to be re-echoed and remembered—even though in the poem-as-warhorse it is too easy to misremember the refrain as "*Et* où sont les neiges d'antan," an unstated but simple summary repetend, canceled by Villon's with its qualifying "but." Villon's line calls wonderful attention to the way in which the refrain can incorporate the rhetorical features of a "that's that for the moment" with those of an "and then . . ."

The dialectic of memory and anticipation enacted by the scheme of poetic refrain can become prominent when the scheme has become most fully troped, or, to put it another way, when the formal occasion of redeploying the conventional lyric device, of making the words for music even more "perhaps," enters the allegory of the poem's own making. A magnificent example of this is the beautiful, problematic refrain of Trumbull Stickney's "Mnemosyne," a poem written fairly close to 1900 (I should guess) by a remarkable poet who died in 1904 at the age of thirty. The handful of powerful lyrics he left behind include some sonnets which belatedly recapitulate an American romantic Hellenism—indeed, in a sonnet beginning with one of his favorite *mises-en-scène* ("The melancholy year is dead with rain"), his own diction speaks of itself: "So in the last autumn of a day / Summer and summer's memory returns. / So in a mountain desolation burns / Some rich belated flower." His major summoning up of what he elsewhere calls "memory's autumnal paradise" is the poem originally called (on the manuscript) "Song," but then retitled:

It's autumn in the country I remember

How warm a wind blew here about the ways!
And shadows on the hillside lay to slumber
During the long sun-sweetened summer-days.

It's cold abroad the country I remember.

The swallows veering skimmed the golden grain
At midday with a wing aslant and limber;
And yellow cattle browsed upon the plain.

It's empty down the country I remember.

I had a sister lovely in my sight:
Her hair was dark, her eyes were very sombre;
We sang together in the woods at night.

It's lonely in the country I remember.

The babble of our children fills my ears,
And on our hearth I stare the perished ember
To flames that show all starry thro' my tears.

It's dark about the country I remember.

There are the mountains where I lived. The path
Is slushed with cattle-tracks and fallen timber,
The stumps are twisted by the tempests' wrath.

But that I know these places are my own,
I'd ask how came such wretchedness to cumber
The earth, and I to people it alone.

It rains across the country I remember.

Structurally, the refrain here is complicated by the ambiguity of its role; starting out the poem, it seems more like a thematic, expository opening, immediately qualified (a) by the white space separating it from the tercet which it should else have joined to make a regular quatrain, and (b) by the implied opening-up of the syntax. In the exposition of autumn as the condition of remembering summer, the full stop is almost put back two words, and "I remember" enjambed to the tercet.[4] With one's realization, at the first repetition, that a varying refrain has indeed been thereby instituted, comes the further problem of the Janus-like line in its very liminal placement. We have to ask whether the *rentrement* introduces or concludes, whether the line in its paradigmatic recurrence is epistrophic to its proceeding tercet, or anaphoric to its following one. The meticulously shaded echoic quality of the half-rhymes with the middle lines of the tercets, not to speak of the deep, inner resonance of the white space surrounding the refrain lines, underscores their liminal role. In their very placement, they control the mode of crossing from one chamber of remembrance, from one *topos,* to another. The white spaces are full of ellipsis: *But* (after the first tercet) "It's cold" or "*But now* it's empty" or "*Yet now* it's lonely." and yet the last two returns are not governed by those *and yets*—"*You see,* it's dark . . ." then leads to the vision of a ruined landscape in the next tercet, and the ellipsis of the refrain itself before the final one. The poem has a bipartite structure, controlled by the pattern of variation of the refrain line. Not only do we have the sequential narrative which leads us through the five successive predicates *autumn, cold, empty, lonely, dark.*[5] In addition, there is the mode of attributing the adjectives, which we come to hear as a superimposed sequence of varied predication: *it's . . . in, it's . . . abroad, it's . . . down. It's . . . in* returns to open the second sequence

4. The syntactic ambiguity is threefold. (1) "It's autumn in the country that I remember." (2) "I remember that it's autumn in the (that) country." (3) "It's autumn in the country: I remember / How warm a wind," etc. Throughout most of the poem, (2) and (1) seem to combine in some way. Donald Wesling kindly pointed out to me that I had not emphasized the relation of (1) and (2) clearly enough.

5. We might schematize this repetitive pattern, R, as $R = f(r + x_1, r + x_2, r + x_3, \ldots)$, where x is the varying predicate and r the invariant material.

(followed by *it's dark about*) which concludes with the ellipsis of the last intermediate refrain, and its displacement to the end of the poem, where it forms a kind of sonnet-sestet of the last two tercets, replacing the predicatory sequence of adjectives in the previous ones with a verb. And so much is going on in those tercets: the introjection of the landscape cumbered by what has come to pass; the realization that "the ruin, or blank," as Emerson calls it, is in his own eye, which causes the speaker to reject the rhetorical posture of a Noah; and the rain of the *rentrement* which follows (I shall refrain from calling it, in the manner of my colleague Geoffrey Hartman, a ref-rain, despite its saturated allusiveness, of which more later) portends no new deluge. (For the "wretchedness" came to "cumber" the earth in an array of that word's senses: *overwhelm, destroy, trouble, fill or block up, benumb with cold.*)

The second section of the poem is also distinguished by the only full rhyme in the sequence. The "lonely in . . . remember" and the "dark about . . . remember" lines embrace the remarkable trope of "staring the perished ember / To flames," which itself revivifies the latent allusion to Shakespeare's "glowing of such fire / That on the ashes of his youth doth lie," a precursor text of belated, autumnal, not-yet-totally post-erotic mediation. The "ember" morpheme is elicited by punning analysis, from "remember." The emphasis of that analysis in the one perfect rhyme underscores an etymological trope of Mnemosyne's scene as one of flame reduced to its hotter spores, rather than one of re-collection or regathering. The poem organizes its own derivately autumnal quality (the late September of Stickney's almost Parnassian romanticism) in specific relation to Shakespeare and Keats (its swallows as yet ungathered, but like swift Camillas that "skim" the plain); to its scene of present hearth and wasted outdoors; to its autumnal time-scale, in which recent summer seems so very bygone (one of the effects of the biblical diction evoking the "sister lovely in my sight"); and, of course, to its own schematic form of threshold refrain, of the chant of the word "remember" itself.

The interwoven narratives of tercet and repetend here are also effective in allegorizing the poem's structure. The movement from summer's remembered "here" to autumn's present "there"; the extended meditative and moralizing moment of the last two tercets and the way in which the interposition of the refrain between them would seem a transgression of some more than structural line; the final avowal of the mythological nature of "these places"—they are the speaker's "own," fully possessed, fully, in Wallace Stevens's sense, "abstract"—this movement is played out against the refrain sequence noted before, which could be said to name autumn and then unpack some of its store of predicates. *Autumn in . . . cold abroad . . . empty down . . .* (where the preposition is troped with such plangency), then the repeated preposition starting out the second part, in *lonely in . . . dark about* (with its echoes of "empty down"); then the displacement, and, at the end (one wants to say, "in the end," for this is what it all *comes down to*), "It rains across the country I remember." The rain is out of sequence in that it is not one of the attributes of the scene, and the refrain is framing a very different kind of statement from the others. Whether projecting (again, echoically and thereby belatedly) an original introjection of Verlaine (as if to say: "Il pleut sur le pays / Comme il pleure dans ma mémoire"); or momentarily realizing again the visionary geography of the now rainy country, Baudelaire's "pays pluvieux," the falling rain now plunging the whole poem in "*l'eau* verte du Lethé"; or indubitably evoking the refrain of rain raining every day in Feste's song in *Twelfth Night,* the final return is most complex. Apparently turning from emotional moralizing to the plenitude of plain statement, it cannot help but be over-determined, both by virtue of, and in demarcation of, its terminal position. It is no longer liminal, save that on the other side of its threshold is the endless Lethean flood.

This remarkable poem by a rather young man fictionalizes his very youth as latecoming and therefore, figuratively, old enough to look—we cannot say, "back at," but rather "across"—such a long landscape. "Memory," said Swift, "is an old man's observation"; here, imagination is a young man's memory. And yet Walter Savage Landor's octogenarian observes, in a great poem called "Memory," that the names of his dearest surviving friends get lost to him. Specifically, they cumber like blocked river water the threshold between storage and retrieval: "To these, when I have written and besought / Remembrance of me, the word *Dear* alone / Hangs on the upper verge, and waits in vain." And then Landor concludes: "A blessing wert thou, O oblivion, / If thy stream carried only weeds away / But vernal and autumnal flowers alike / It hurries down to wither on the strand." (If not, as for Spenser, "Flowers + flow-ers, things that move in water," then at least the flow of what has been remembered into what is re-membered in the retrieval and articulation of it is seen as a flood that staves off the transverse flow of Lethe.) But for the young poet, there is no terror of a damming-up of the flow of eloquence. He is in sure control of the returning sequence of half-rhymes, and its own structural narrative (*slumber—limber—sombre—ember—timber—cumber*): framed by the *slumber* that comes to *cumber,* bracketed within that by the *limber* now felled to *timber,* mediated by the Janus faces of "remember."

Stickney's poem clearly tropes its scheme of refrain as a fable of memory, but less obviously, it makes refrain a matter of autumn. Wallace Stevens's not-quite-blank-verse sonnet, "Autumn Refrain," grapples directly with earlier voices (as if to say, "Where are the songs of autumn? Where are they?"), and picks its way through sun and moon and evening and song and nightingale, hearing in these Miltonic and Keatsian tropes not available refrains, but burdens of the past. The poem itself (which I have discussed in more detail elsewhere) employs only broken recurrences, true *refractions,* in its scattered repetitions of word and phrase.[6] The autumn in the poem is that of the poet's silent aftermath of eloquence, an autumn of stillness that is "all in the key of that desolate sound" that is the residuum of the voice of the fictions of the past. In a sense, Stevens's poem takes the trope of an autumn refrain and embodies it in an original scheme of belated structure—all the *tra-la-la*s, all the *forlorn*s, tolling like bells, lie about in bits of fractured echoic hearsay, in rumors of *rentrement.* In Stevens's sole poem of 1931, an aftermath of refrain makes for an extreme schematic pattern of a sort of *durchkomponiert* stuttering, or of an ungathering of the fragments which are collected into a full, line-terminal refrain in a passage from *Paradise Lost* (V., ll. 180–204).[7] But I should like to move back in time, to a poem with another kind of refrain structure, and another way in which autumn, memory, and schematic return enter into figurations of each other.

Composed sometime between 1913 and 1917 (almost midway between Stickney's and Stevens's poems), Thomas Hardy's "During Wind and Rain" presents a typically problematic Hardyian formal face: as always, we want to ask, with a kind of modernist (but perhaps callow) earnestness, how he ever allowed himself to get trapped in his singsong stanzas' awkward rooms. Frequently some marvellous lyric or short-story-in-verse of Hardy's will seem to have been composed by letting an opening take up a self-generated formal space, and then passively accepting the strophic fiat for the successive stanzas. But many do not, and the scheme of this poem, its pattern of minor and major variation, and its remarkable meta-refrain in the ultimate line of each stanza mark out the places of remembering and the moments

6. See "The Sound of the Music of Music and Sound," in *Wallace Stevens: A Celebration,* ed. Frank Doggett and Robert Buttel (Princeton, 1980), pp. 248–50.

7. This gradual accumulation of the varying refrain lines, all ending in "[some verb] his praise," I have discussed in detail in *The Figure of Echo* (Berkeley and Los Angeles, 1981), pp. 37–41.

of judgment of what has been summoned up in a way totally different from Stickney's.

They sing their dearest songs—
He, she, all of them—yea,
Treble and tenor and bass,
  And one to play;
With the candles mooning each face. . . .
  Ah, no; the years O!
How the sick leaves reel down in throngs!

They clear the creeping moss—
Elders and juniors—aye,
Making the pathways neat
  And the garden gay;
And they build a shady seat. . . .
  Ah, no; the years, the years;
See, the white storm-birds wing across!

They are blithely breakfasting all—
Men and maidens—yea,
Under the summer tree,
  With a glimpse of the bay,
While pet fowl come to the knee. . . .
  Ah, no; the years O!
And the rotten rose is ript from the wall.

They change to a high new house,
He, she, all of them—aye,
Clocks and carpets and chairs
  On the lawn all day,
And brightest things that are theirs. . . .
  Ah, no; the years, the years;
Down their carved names the rain-drop ploughs.

The four strophes of the poem frame four vignettes of an elliptical family novel, presented in strains interrupted by minimal, fragmentary refrains—"yea" and "aye" of ironic assent in alternating strophes, "Ah, no; the years O!" alternating with 'Ah, no; the years, the years," and the repetition of "He, she, all of them" in the last stanza bringing full rondure, albeit with the "aye" now replacing the initial "yea." The refrains seem to be uttered by almost antithetical voices, the second one recoiling with ironic dismay—even disgust—from the initial affirmations and particularly, in the even-numbered stanzas, from the punning reading of "aye" as "ever" (rather than "ay," perhaps from the "I" of voice-vote: "Ever, eh?—Ah, no; the years, the years"). And then the problematic closures, the terminal lines which, for each stanza, are summary, interpretive, offered by the second voice as if in evidence, or as cause, of its distaste. These four lines are like one-line poems in their own right. The novelistic vignettes—two indoors, two outdoors; the first set, possibly, in a cheerful winter evening, the other three in spring and summer—move chronologically toward greater wealth, the proliferation of generation, the sense of in-dwelling rather than merely inhabiting. The first refrain is merely schematic, merely an exercise of the rhetoric of verse rather than prose; the second refrain, as syntactic herald of the terminal line, is the voice of the poet reminding the novelist that he has suppressed exactly what his characters have. Seasonal cycle may unroll in strophes, as the providential cycle of the months unfolds its pageant of the working year in *Les Très Riches Heures du duc de Berry*, but such cycles are often rooted in spring or summer without knowing or avowing it. The chronicler in this poem purports to believe in the beneficience of cycle, of seasonal pattern, of unrolling, of (and here Hardy shudders) *developing* time. The poet reminds him, in the terminal lines, that it is always autumn and that, indeed, chronicle of the foregoing sort is always being recounted as a defense against the autumnal sense of the entropy of consequence. The poet of the terminal lines reads the genre-scenes in the brightly painted stanzas, and groans as he sees that each is an unwitting *memento mori.*

The first of these repudiating monostichs is emblematically autumnal, and at the same time merciless in its trope—via Shelley's "Ode to the West Wind"—of sick leaves ("Yellow, and black, and pale, and hectic red") in throngs ("pestilence-stricken multitudes") of dying generations. The terminal line sings for Hardy's poet the Shelleyan refrain. Formally considered, these terminals rhyme only with the stanzaic openings, six lines back, the effect being first to render them almost blank, but then, on reconsideration, to link them in a violent antithetical couplet with those openings ("They are blithely breakfasting all": "And the rotten rose is ript from the wall"). Rhetorically, each subsequent emblem of autumn and decay underlines its own mode of pseudo-refrain in that the expected return is, in each case, an autumnal emblem as the accountant's bottom line of a cheerful and hopeful scene, of "luxe" and "calme" ("volupté" not sorting well with the others in England, even in dream). And the bottom line of the emblem-sequence is the most self-aware, rhetorically: culminating the sequence of powerful verbs—*reel, wing, is ript*—comes the terrible *ploughs* of the terminating trope of rain. The rain, which conventionally weeps over tombstones, here plows down the already furrowed, text-blossoming stone, apparently to trace names out with a commemorative finger, but actually with the effect of eventually effacing them altogether. Here again, as in Stickney's poem, the falling rain sings the final refrain, and claims the role of autumn's ultimate emblem.

This resonant raining engulfs a welter of allusive streams. The wind and rain of the title are those of the poem's formal paradigmatic precursor, Feste's final song in *Twelfth Night.* There, the paired alternating refrains, "With hey, ho, the wind and the rain" and "For the rain it raineth every day," enact the trope of refrain as marking a redemptive cycle, and a reclamation of the generality of rain from autumnal and wintry claims to it. Feste's vignettes of the phases of life are framed by his music of rainfall. For Hardy, the usurpation by autumn of all scenes of remembrance has long been irreversible. In addition, the short refrains of "During Wind and Rain" echo those of a slightly earlier poem, "The Change," which similarly looks back grimly at moments of innocent pleasure and calm ("And who was the mocker, and who the mocked when two felt all was well?"), and similarly employs narrative material from the life of Hardy's first wife, Emma Gifford (a scene of candlelit singing, in this case, of duets with her sister). The sequence of refrains both modifies and alternates: "Who shall read the years O!"; "Who shall spell the years, the years!"; "Who shall unroll the years O!"; "Who shall bare the years, the years!", "who shall lift the years O!"; finally coming down to "Who shall unseal the years, the years!"—and thus framing the whole lyric in the textual tropes of reading and unsealing. Hardy echoed this refrain, and its very mode of alternation ("the years, O" and "the years, the years"), in the later poem, but he assigned it to the lyrical ironist of his final lines, rather than to his putative chronicler of the vignettes. The terminal, image-bearing lines of each stanza are, as has been observed, quasi-refrains in that they time, pace, and return to their mode of moralizing-by-riddling, as it were (rather than moralizingly interpreting the tropes they adduce). Their return is like a bell at the end of a line of manual typewriting, rather than Feste's wind and rain refrain, which tolls like a church bell in certain fictions of simple, organic village life finding a providential comfort in reminders of transience.

A glance at Hardy's revisions of his original text of the poem, by the way, shows how he came to realize the different schemes of the refrain sequence. Originally, the odd- and even-numbered stanzas were identical in their repetends—"aye" was "yea" throughout, as was "the years o." (These revisions may have accompanied, or followed by some time, those of "The Change," which likewise introduced the alternation of the two half-lines.) But more significantly, the rhythm of the terminal lines can be seen to have emerged from an earlier, more regular conception, notwithstanding the changes in diction. The terminal lines originally read: "How the sickened leaves dropped down in throngs!"; "See the webbed white storm-birds wing across"; "And the wind-whipt creeper lets go the wall"; and, at first, "On their chiselled names the lichen grows" (in manuscript), then, "Down their chiselled names the rain-drop ploughs." The acephalic pentameters yield to tetrameters with a starting dactyl or anapest, which catches up the bits of triple movement throughout the poem, and allows the monostich of the terminal lines to return an echo of these mingled with the sobs, in all but the third one, of spondee.

Hardy's and Stickney's unrolling patterns of refrain in their respective autumnal songs are ultimately descendents of Poe's in that his "Nevermore" was avowing the *poetic* impossibility of merely formal—others might have said merely "musical"—refrain. Nevermore can refrain be merely *tra-la-la,* stand for "now everybody sings," trope the turning of a page to a new chapter, allow the singer to rest. Poe claimed falsely that his refrain was a true *fa-la,* a true bit of verbal music, but his schematic arguments for its varying "application," the ways in which "Nevermore" continues to answer every question the speaker puts (and thereby reveals the rhetorical nature of each question), merely go back to the echo-device which descends from Ovid through the Renaissance. For Poe, refrain is the trope of reiteration of reiteration, of how "jadis!" is the only musical cry. For Stickney and Hardy, it is a much more complex matter. Memory, time, autumn, penultimateness, all enter into the structure of their fables of refrain. And the ultimate point is that for *poetry,* rather than mere verse, to employ a refrain, it must thereby, therein, therewith, propound its own parable of the device itself, its etiology or its effect, or its emblematic reading, or whatever.

I should like to conclude these observations in a somewhat unusual way, particularly for a theorist. Premonitory glimpses of much in the foregoing observations came to me in a poem of my own called "Refrains" (one of the sections of the long sequence entitled *Powers of Thirteen*). It is not trivial or merely decorative, I think, that four poets (congenial to each other, but radically different in their work) should have read their poems as part of this conference. Ordinarily, one would feel the concerns of the contemporary poet and of the literary historians were totally divergent (save, I suppose, for hagiographical longings, half-acknowledged wishes to be canonized by the same critical judgments the poets had affected to despise). But in a strange way, some of the areas intruded upon by the theoretically oriented critic—such as the larger question of the troping of what is schematic (a better way of coping with what was once called the matter of the "content" of "form" itself)—are just those in which the poet most privately dwells. It is those areas, too, which the poet withdraws from discussing overtly, either because of some kind of principled reticence or out of despair at being able to do so in any genuine way other than in, and by, the poems themselves. The thematizing and periodization of older forms of academic criticism mean little to the poet, whose very oeuvre—if it is genuine poetry—will somehow deconstruct such notions as "form," "content," "persona," "lyric voice," etc. But the attempt by sophisticated criticism to get below (and beyond) such notions is one the poet must recognize as being akin to his or her own imaginative work. (The poets at this conference all felt this to be true.)

But such "new new criticism" is in itself more aware of the critical dimensions in all poetry, even if—especially if—it is not didactic. (If anything, it is so aware to a fault.) My own meta-formal broodings over the poetics of refrain originated in the following poem, which started out with a willful misprision of the great refrain line of the late Latin *Pervigilium Veneris,* "cras amet qui numquam amavit, quiquam amavit cras amet" ("tomorrow those new to loving will love, those used to loving will love tomorrow"), and led me on through a play on the two etymologies of "refrain" discussed earlier, but by means not of philology, but of the homonyms *break* and *brake,* as the reader will observe. As for the poem's conclusion, it is also that of this entire paper.

Refrains[8]

Cras amet qui numquam amavit, quiquam amavit cras
Moriatur—"those who never loved before will love
Tomorrow, those used to loving will tomorrow come
To die"—The old refrains all come down to this: either
Reduced to *tra-la-la*s at whose regular return
Children look at each other and, smiling, mouth the words
And old people nod heads in time, or, if they retain
Meaning at all, they always end up in whispering
"*Death*" in the deep chambers hidden among their tones.

8. From *Powers of Thirteen* (New York, 1983).

That is how *Greensleeves,* her smock stained from love in the grass,
Outlasts all the boys who had a go at her. That is
How *nonny-nonny-no* etcetera can survive
The next stanza, and the next, and the next, and the next.

Breaking off the song of the refrain, putting the brakes
On the way that the ever-returning chorus tends
To run away with the whole song—well, that may well be
Breaking away from a frightening joyride before
The wrap-up of metal around some tree or other.
Yes, you say, *but something has to get out of hand so*
That we can go on: and, yes, I answer, but better
Let it be the new material in each stanza
That bridles at sense, reckless of disaster, and leaps
Up into the less and less trustworthy air. The same
Old phrase comes back anyway, waiting for what we say
To be over and done, marking its time, the heavy
Burden of the tune we carry, humming, to the grave.

PART TWO

Eugene Vance

Greimas, Freud, and the Story of Trouvère Lyric

Though it is probably safe to say that all cultures subsist to some degree by means of stories, much remains to be understood about how stories themselves may be said to subsist in culture. In the last several decades, much has been revealed about the morphology of narrative, yet little about the different modes of existence of stories. Does a story (for instance the "story" of nuclear holocaust) need to be actually narrated or written out to be called a story? Is a latent story the same story when it is narrated? If a story is *not* narrated, is the suppression of that story a part of the story? Or is it *another* story?

Nor have narratologists told us much about the psychodynamics of stories: what happens inside us when we tell them, what happens as we become their audience. To be sure, considerable effort has been made by Hans Robert Jauss, Wolfgang Iser, and others in the modern school of Hermeneutics in Germany to formalize models of identification that prevail in the relationship of audiences to heroes of different genres at different historical moments, but to my knowledge, few have tried to explore the yet more basic psychic conditions that make such identifications possible in the first place.[1]

In this paper I shall attempt to deal with two aspects of twelfth-century *trouvère* lyric, tht is, lyric poetry composed in the vernacular of northern France (*langue d'oïl*) beginning in the second half of the

1. Hans Robert Jauss, *Aesthetische Erfahrung und literarische Hermeneutik,* vol. 1 (Munich, 1977), trans. Michael Shaw, *Aesthetic Experience and Literary Hermeneutics* (Minneapolis, 1982); Wolfgang Iser, *Der implizite Leser—Kommunikationsformen des Romans von Bunyan bis Beckett* (Munich, 1972), trans. as *The Implied Reader: Patterns of Communication in Prose Fiction from Bunyan to Beckett* (Baltimore, 1977).

twelfth century. First, I shall try pragmatically to define what I shall call the underlying, "latent" story that subtends courtly lyric discourse, and I shall then try to explain what I believe to be the controlling psychodynamics of our response to this carefully *untold* story of trouvère lyric.[2] My procedures in doing so will perhaps seem unduly mechanical and old-fashioned, at least in the context of the present volume, for I shall take a specific lyric poem by the twelfth-century Champenois, Gace Brulé, and invoke Greimassian actantial theory to describe the roles that are evidenced in the grammatical, lexical, and illocutionary resources of trouvère lyric discourse. Although structural analysis as an end in itself has long since lost its appeal in modern critical thought, I would propose that in certain instances structuralist methods can still be useful as a kind of primary descriptive grammar that allows us to pass on to other, more interesting, questions involving the "why" and the "how" of stories. Moreover, the highly abstract and formal aspect of Greimassian theory is strangely appropriate to trouvère lyric, whose discourse is also highly formal, abstract, and uniform.

The second part of this paper will, I hope, redeem the obsolescence of the first. I shall try to explain the psychodynamics of the relationship between the figures of poet and audience in trouvère lyric by redefining the actantial model underlying its performance in accordance with a theory of repression developed by Freud in his treatise, *Jokes and Their Relation to the Unconscious.*[3] Once again, there is a remarkable compatibility between Freud's theory of jokes and trouvère lyric performance, all the more because jokes tend to exploit the same technical resources of language as trouvère lyric: replacement of object-association by word-association, discovery of what is familiar, faulty thinking, condensation, displacement, absurdity, representation of the opposite, and so on. My motive for passing from a Greimassian, or structural, articulation to a Freudian one corresponds to my conviction that, if structural analysis is no longer a

2. Several studies have been devoted to the "latent" story of lyric: Paul Zumthor, "Les Narrativités latentes dans le discours lyrique médiévale," in *The Nature of Medieval Narrative,* ed. Minnette-Grunmann-Gaudet and Robin F. Jones (Lexington, Ky., 1980); Rupert T. Pickens, "B(l)atant Narrativity and Textual Change in the Early Troubadour Lyric" (forthcoming); Peter Haidu, "Text and History: The Semiosis of Twelfth-Century Lyric as Sociohistorical Phenomenon (Chrétien de Troyes: 'D'amors qui m'a tolu,')" *Semiotica,* 33 (1981), 1–62.

3. Sigmund Freud, *Der Witz und seine Beziehung zum Unbewussten* (Leipzig and Vienna, 1905), trans. James Strachey, *Jokes and Their Relation to the Unconscious* (New York, 1963). See also Tzvetan Todorov, "Freud sur l'énonciation," *Langages,* 17 (1970), 34–41.

worthwhile objective in its own right, the challenge remains for critics to discover those conditions (whether historical, ideological, or psychic) in which this or that structure of verbal signification is manifested in the first place.

Before proceeding to the analyses that I have proposed to undertake, I should say a word about Gace Brulé, the poet himself, and I should provide the text of the poem (and its translation) that I have chosen as an example of trouvère lyric. Gace Brulé was one of the more important poets of the court of Champagne in the late twelfth or early thirteenth century, and hence was quite possibly a contemporary of Chrétien de Troyes. The literary court of Champagne had been established by Marie de Campagne, daughter of Eleanor of Aquitaine and wife of the great count of Champagne, Henri-le-libérale. Henri was largely responsible for the burst of commercial activity in his territory in the context of the *foires* de Champagne, which is to say that the flourishing of letters in the twelfth century was closely linked to the rise of commerce. Gace himself was a minor nobleman whose political identity was no doubt reinforced by his participation in the literary activities patronized by the Count and his wife. The most recent editor of Gace's poetry attributes sixty-nine lyric poems to his hand, of which the following poem is the first:[4]

Au renoviau de la douçor d'esté,
Que resclarcist la doiz en la fontaine
Et que sont vert bois et vergier et pré
Et li rosiers en mai florist et graine,
Lors chanterai, car trop m'avra grevé
Ire et esmai ki m'est al cuer prochaine;
Et fins amis, a tort achaisonez,
Est mout sovent de legier esfreëz.

Voir est qu'amors m'a estre loi mené,
Mes mout m'est bel qu'a son plesir me maine,
Car, se Dieu plet, encor me savra gré
De mon travail et de ma longue paine.
Mes paor ai que ne m'ait oublié
Par le conseil de fausse gent vilaine,
Dont li torz est coneüz et prouvez,
Qu'a poine sui sans morir eschapez.

4. *Chansons de Gace Brulé,* ed. G. Huet (Paris, 1902), pp. 1–3. See also H. P. Dyggve, *Gace Brulé* (Helsinki, 1951). Trans. mine.

III Tant ai d'amor mon fin cuer esprové
Que ja sans li n'avrai joie certaine;
Tant par sui mis tot a sa volenté
Que nus travaus mon desir ne refraine;
Quant plus me truis pensif et esgaré,
Plus me confort es biens dont elle est plain;
Et vos, seignor, qui priez et amez,
Fetes ensi se joïr en volez.

IV Douce dame, tant m'ont achesoné
Faus tricheor en lor parole vaine
Que lor dehet m'ont si desconforté
Pres ne m'ont mort; Dieus lor dont male estraine!
Mes, maugré aus, vos ai mon cuer doné,
Plein de l'amor ki ja n'en iert lointaine;
Tant s'est en vos finement esmerez
Que si loiaus n'iert ja quis ne trovez.

V Douce dame, car m'otroiez, por Dé,
Un douz regart de vous en la semaine;
Si atendrai par ceste seürté
Joie et merci, se bons eürs la maine.
Remembre vos que lede cruauté
Fet qui ocit son lige home demeine.
Douce dame, d'orgueil vos desfendez,
Ne traïssiez vos biens ne vos biautez.

VI Fuiez, chançons, ja ne me regardez,
Par mon seigneur Noblet vos en alez,
Et dites lui de male ore fu nez
Qui toz jors aime et ja nen iert amez.

[At the renewal of the sweetness of summer
When the flow of the fountain becomes clear
And when the woods and orchards and fields are green
And the rosebush flowers and the reproduces in May
Then I will sing, because for too long ire and distress
Will have afflicted me, present in my heart.
And the gentle lover, wrongly accused
Is very often easily troubled.

It is true that love has carried me out of the law,
But it delights me that he does with me what he pleases,
For, if it pleases God, yet will he reward me
For my travail and for my long suffering.
Yet I am afraid that he has forgotten me

Because of the counsel of false and villainous men,
Whose wrongdoing is recognized and proven,
From which I have barely escaped without dying.

So much have I felt gentle love in my heart
That surely without it I will not have certain joy;
So much have I given myself over to his will
That no labor can restrain my desire;
The more I find myself pensive and stunned [vacant]
The more I take comfort in the plenitude of her goodness;
And you, lords, who love and pray
Do as much if you wish to come into joy.

Sweet lady, so much have false cheaters
Slandered me with their vain speech,
And so much have their abuses put me out of comfort
That they have nearly slain me; may God give them painful rewards.
Yet, despite them, I have given you my heart,
Full of love which surely will never be distant from it;
So finely has it been purified in you
That a more loyal man will surely not be sought or found.

So grant me, sweet lady, for the sake of God,
One sweet glance of yours this week;
Then I will await with this assurance
Joy and reward, if happiness brings it to me.
Remember that he commits ugly cruelty
Who kills his own liege man.
Sweet lady, preserve yourself from pride,
And do not betray your goodness [possessions] nor your beauty.

Flee, song, look at me no longer,
Make your way to Lord Noblet
And tell him that he was born in an unhappy hour
Who loves each day and will never be loved.]

Since Greimas's actantial model is commonly familiar even to medievalists, I shall not describe it here in any detail.[5] Suffice it to say that Greimas proposes that all narrative is constituted by a restricted set of interdependent roles, even though these roles may be filled by a very large number of diverse individuals or things. Greimas calls these roles actants. There are only six actants: the *sujet,* the *objet,* the *adjuvant,* the *opposant,* the *destinateur,* and the *destinataire.* These actants

5. A. J. Greimas, *Sémantique structurale* (Paris, 1966), pp. 192–221.

are "classes of actors." The role of *sujet* tends to be filled by some person or thing manifesting a transitive force or need, often semanticized as desire, and resulting in a quest. Obviously, the object of this force, need, or desire assumes the actantial role of *objet.* The *adjuvant* "aids" the sujet as he fulfills his quest, while the *opposant* hinders or obstructs the sujet from doing so. The *destinateur* is a person or thing that assigns destinies or rewards to someone (the *destinataire*), or who communicates something. Although Greimas himself does not say so, we may suspect that the fundamentally tripartite structure of what Gerald Prince calls the "kernel story" reflects the interaction of the three actantial pairs that comprise a story.[6]

One particularly important aspect of Greimas's theory, at least for our purposes, is his allowance for the possibility that more than one actantial role may be assumed by a single figure. The example of this "syncretism" that Greimas furnishes is pertinent, moreover, to the "situation" of trouvère lyric. Greimas writes,

> For example, in a story which is only a banal tale of love, concluding with the intervention of the parents, in marriage, the subject is also the *destinataire,* while the object is also the *destinateur* of love:
>
> $$\frac{\text{He}}{\text{She}} \simeq \frac{\textit{Sujet, Destinataire}}{\textit{Objet, Destinateur}}$$
>
> The four actants are there, symmetrically inverted, but syncretized in the form of two actors.[7]

It is obvious that in this poem by Gace Brulé the situation of *je* crying out for mercy (that is, for the favor of love) to a lady who has the power both to provoke desire in him and to deny him her favor is similar to that in Greimas's example, except for these important differences: "she" does not love "him"; neither "he" nor "she" has the goal of marriage in mind; finally, no "story," whether banal or exquisite, is recounted in this poem. If we dispose the four actantial roles in a square (which is a modification of the Greimassian *carré sémiotique*), we may easily see how each role accounts for an aspect of the two persons *je* and *elle* of Gace's poem as these persons relate both to each other and to themselves:

6. Gerald Prince, *A Grammar of Stories* (The Hague and Paris, 1973), pp. 38–55.
7. Greimas, p. 177.

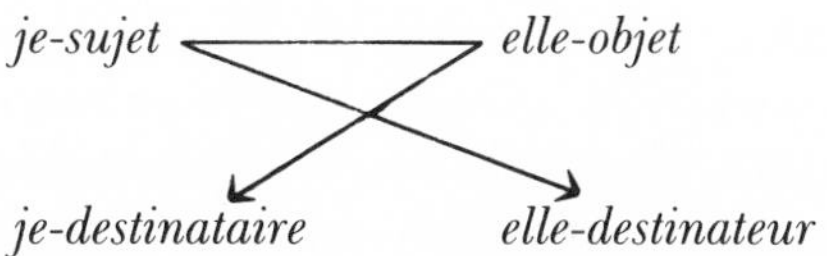

In other words, *je* loves the lady as objet, but despises himself because he is also the passive victim of her denial, that is, her destinataire. *Elle* despises *je* and loves herself as destinateur, which is to say that she is quite simply proud. Singing is the manifestation of desire in *je,* which is to say that the presence of the song is a sign of *joi d'amor* that is absent because it has been denied. That the song should have the capacity not only to mediate desire but to constitute itself as an object of desire which can become the rival of the lady is a problem of deferral that will call for special consideration later.

The actantial roles of adjuvant and opposant in this poem by Gace Brulé do not function as simply or as obviously as the four roles that I have described so far. In the vast majority of poems in the *troubadour* and trouvère traditions, the actantial role of opposant is occupied by a figure called the *lozengier* or médisant and not at all, surprisingly, by a rival suitor, or, much less, by a jealous spouse: the latter is an especially rare bird in this verbal habitant of the nightingale. The médisant and his band are above all those who turn the supreme powers of the human tongue against the supreme cause of love. Thus, they tell lies, they reveal secrets, they denounce lovers in public, they flatter, they boast, and (worst of all) they even dare mouth the language of true love. The role of the adjuvant in this poem is less simple, because it includes all of those people and things that are the poet's potential allies: God, all *fins amans* in the audience of the poem, and even the agency of the poem itself. What I find interesting is that the médisant, as a man of words and letters who is not a sexual rival of *je-sujet,* tends very clearly to displace a drama of sexual desire away from erotic provocation into the sphere of language: is the médisant not more the enemy of the lover as poet than of the poet as lover? We are dealing, here, with a fascinating and important presupposition of the courtly lyric register, yet one that is perhaps pertinent to the relationship between any erotic text and the process that it pretends to represent.

One may judge from the following list how well Grimas's actantial model serves the poem by Gace Brulé, for this list contains all of those utterances and terms in the poem that indicate an implicit role. Such a list is far from perfect, since it reflects with difficulty the illocutionary fuction of certain phrases: for instance, when *je* pleads with *elle* that she *grant* him a glance ("*car m'otroiez . . . / Un douz regart,*" ll 33–34), his plea by its form casts him in the role of destinataire and by its semantic content confers upon her the power of the destinateur, that is, the power to *grant* him a reward for his service in love. Here, then, is the distribution of actantial (and actorial) roles in Gace's poem in the grammatical form of their manifestation:

Sujet	*Objet*
je	Dame
fin cuer	douçor
fins amis	rosiers
Qui toz jors aime	amors
	joie
	ses biens
	bons eürs
	vos biautez
	douz regart

Destinataire	*Destinateur*
trop m'avra grevé/Ire et esmai	a son plesir me maine
de legier esfreëz	encor me savra gré
estre loi mené	m'ait oublié
mon travail et ma longue paine	otroiez (as action, not as imperative)
a poine sui sans morir eschapez	seürté
sui mis tot a sa volenté	led cruauté/Fet qui ocit
travaus	orgueil
me truis pensif et esgaré	
car m'otroiez/ün douz regart (as imperative)	
atendrai nen iert amez	
a tort achaisonez	
paor ai	
n'avrai joie	
si loiaus	
lige home	

Adjuvant	*Opposant*
si Dieu plet	conseil de fausse gent vilaine
Fetes ensi (audience as interlocutor)	li torz
chançons	faus tricheor en lor parole vaine
mon seigneur Noblet	lor dehet m'ont si desconforté
por Dé	pres ne m'ont mort

Quite clearly, Gace Brulé's lyric poem has all of the ingredients for uttering a complete story, but this story remains latent or repressed. This is a narrativity not of linear actions, but rather of substitutions and displacements of actors within a stable actantial configuration. This is a paradigmatic, rather than a syntagmatic, process of signification, one where our hermeneutic response consists in identifying a redundancy of actantial roles as they are refracted through the semantic and illocutionary processes of uttering. To understand trouvère lyric is to grasp its latent story—that is, to recognize the configuration of roles that subtends its discourse—but also to participate in that fiction. Before I may cast myself in the role of a frustrated *je* singing out my desire for *elle,* I must first constitute myself as reader or as audience of the trouvère text, hence as adjuvant who takes to heart both the lover's cause *and* his song. My opposant in this primal operation is the médisant: he is that abuser of speech, that transgressor of codes whose false and evil actions are as much instigators of the poem that I am now enjoying as the fictive lady is of my erotic desire. However, to the degree that I enjoy the trouvère text as an object of desire in its own right (I would not consent to become its reader or audience if I did not enjoy it), it is obvious that the injurious function of the médisant is an indispensable precondition of my pleasure in the poetic performance. A peculiar oscillation arises in me: as a creature of pure erotic desire, I hate the médisant as a spoiler of my pleasure; as a lover of pure poetry, I can only applaud him for causing the poem to exist, even at the expense of my joy in love. I love to hate him; I hate him to love. If it is true that an overwhelming desire to desire is a condition of *je* in his manifestations as both poet and lover, an interesting analogy arises:

lady:lover :: *médisant*:poet

To put it in other terms, I am suggesting that the fiction that "I am a lover" is an occultation of the reality of my being a reader or audience enjoying the poem: I must willingly restage my readerly desire as a frustration in love if I am to be textually satisfied. I must blind myself to my secret connivance with the médisant and blame the recalcitrant lady for begetting my fictive, unrequited love. Yet it is clear that if I were really to enjoy that lady (or any lady), the *je* of the singing poet and his audience would instantly die: semen and ink cannot flow in the same vein, if I may abuse a profoundly medieval analogy.

I am suggesting, then, that the process of enunciation or of uttering in the discursive terrain of the trouvère lyric not only entails the perception of a redundant paradigm of actantial roles, but also excites yet deeper oscillations within the actantial model constituting its latent story. Such oscillations may be described by linguists as semantic features of poetic language, yet it is safe to propose that they correspond to a set of motives which are extra- or pre-linguistic; hence, that they may be understood only if we pass to another level of analysis. Accordingly, I shall now proceed to explore an interesting homology between transformations in the actantial roles implicated in the enunciation of trouvère lyric and the psychodynamics that Freud believes to be at work (or in play) during the enunciation of what he calls tendentious sexual jokes.

For my purpose here, the chief value of Freud's analysis of sexual jokes is that it allows us to explain in a thorough way the relationships of interdependence and the transformations which simultaneously engage all six of the actantial roles manifested by trouvère lyric in the process of its utterance. In making recourse to Freud's theories of wit, I should specify from the outset two points that I am taking for granted in the discussion that follows. First, I shall assume that the performance of trouvère lyric, in all its elegance and refinement, is a source of enjoyment for its own sake, but that, like the performance of tendentious jokes where an expression of sexual (or even hostile) aggression is involved, this performance affords to both its performer and its audience some kind of "pleasure" over and beyond that provided by the indulgence in the purely formal aspects of lyric as a verbal artifact. Second, I shall assume that this pleasure arises from our participation in the dynamics of roles implied by the enunciation of lyric, and that this pleasure coincides with some kind of rebalancing of forces within our mental universe.

According to Freud, a tendentious joke usually requires for its performance three persons. First, there is the teller, and Freud says that his motivation to perform the joke originates in a circumstance where he has been an unsuccessful aggressor upon a woman that he desires. Secondly there is the woman who is the interlocutor in whom the teller desires, according to Freud, to instigate pleasure in the form of laughter. Thus, the performance of a sexual joke implicitly involves the following sequence of events: when a subject finds his libidinous impulses blocked by the woman who is the object of his aggression he then directs his attention to some third party, who has been perceived as a spoiler, an intruder, or a rival, and thus as some personification of the negative principle displayed by the woman. The teller employs the sexual joke to transform this third person into an ally or confederate by offering him, through verbal representation of the sexual act, easy gratification of his libido. The laughter produced in the listener also results in vicarious laughter in the teller as well, and this marks a pleasurable release of impulses (both libidinous and hostile) in the subject which, until now, have been repressed, but which now may be expressed because they have been transformed or sublimated into a semiological emission that is an acceptable aim in itself: "Since the sexual aggressiveness is held up in its advance toward the act, it pauses at the evocation of excitement and derives pleasure from the signs of it in the woman. In so doing the aggressiveness is no doubt altering its character as well, just as any libidinal impulse will if it is met by an obstacle."[8]

Freud says, however, that the demands of a refined culture act as a censorship that forbids the telling of raw sexual jokes, even in the absence of the woman, and in such conditions, pleasure can be obtained when the resources of verbal wit are brought into play. When our aggressive impulses are refined through techniques of wordplay, we lose our capacity to distinguish in the tendentious joke what part of our pleasure originates in the joke's technique and what part from the release of aggression. "Thus, strictly speaking," Freud says, "we do not know what we are laughing about."[9] To transform thwarted erotic desire into highly refined verbal art, as is the case in the art of *fin'amor,* does not mean, though, that innocence is being restored: indeed, Jeffrey Mehlman has proposed that already in Freud's writing the opposition between innocent and tendentious jokes is perfectly spurious, and that we may infer that even the seemingly innocent "pleasure from signs" in supposedly nontendentious human is really nothing other than a simulation, within the process of language, of the fundamentally autoerotic character of human sexual desire.[10]

Although the performance of courtly lyric (especially in the *langue d'oïl*) does not tend to elicit laughter from its audiences (nor, for that matter, do we always roar at Freud's examples of sexual jokes), I believe that a fundamentally humorous cast is implicit in the register of trouvère lyric, and that to pursue the complementarity of the processes of enunciation or uttering in trouvère lyric and in sexual wit is worthwhile. It is obvious that Freud's model implicates three persons,

8. Freud, *Jokes and Their Relation to the Unconscious,* p. 199.

9. Ibid., p. 102.

10. Jeffrey Mehlman, "How to Read Freud on Jokes: The Critic as *Schadchen,*" *NLH,* 5 (1973), p. 443.

but six distinct roles. These roles have almost exactly the same configuration as that of the actantial roles as they are invariably expressed in trouvère lyric. Thus, the teller of the joke is both the desiring subject *and* the victim of denial on the part of the woman; she, in turn, is both the object of desire *and* the bestower of disfavor. The audience as third party is both a rival *and* a potential ally, or opposant and adjuvant. Although the hearer of the joke can be perceived as a sexual rival by the teller, unlike the mèdisant, his participation in the processes of transformation is still restricted to the sphere of verbal action. Freud's theory of sexual wit allows us to grasp with more assurance how we the audience of the trouvère performance are related to the médisant: as audience, we are his transform. The médisant's evil verbal deeds, along with the cruelty of the lady, have provoked pain in the speaker, whose relief takes the form of the poem as gratification. However, to the extent that the médisant provokes the instance of poetic discourse that we as audience crave, we may say that there is a strongly autoerotic character to our readerly desire, even though the enactment of this performance requires the fiction that we are primarily lovers. The *je* of the erotic lover is a third party to that secret dialogue between our two natures as ally and adversary, just as we are the third party to his thwarted desire for sexual gratification with the woman. The médisant is not just a hostile third person: as a vitiator of verbal signs, he is the fictive incarnation of that absolute zero-person (Emile Benveniste)[11] over and against which the whole axis of interpersonal (and of intramental) communication constitutes itself. By his transgressions of the discourse of honest love, the médisant is nothing less than the guarantor of the code and the instance of lyric discourse. Hence, the médisant is just as indispensable to my status as audience enjoying a poem as the cruelty of the lady is to the deferred libidinous desire that makes *je* sing (to me). To perceive the latent story of trouvère lyric is less to perceive the fiction of thwarted desire as a motivation of the trouvère text than to perceive the actual *fictivization* of our libido as precisely the means by which we willingly occult—and thereby sustain—our autoerotic joy in the signs of the poetic text. Yet the fictiveness of unending erotic desire is also the truth of a textual libido, or a love of signs (and of signs of signs) which too can never be satisfied if only because of the dual nature of the sign itself: invested with a signification that is purely conventional and that belongs, therefore, to everyone and to no one, the body of the word may never be completely possessed by the enunciating individual

11. Emile Benveniste, *Problèmes de linguistique générale* (Paris, 1966–74), 2 vols.

without being destroyed. To the contrary, the domain of the verbal sign, even the verbal sign (of a sign) of love, is a public domain whose public convention must be sustained if the sign is to continue to signify. On the other hand, if the sign expresses *more* than what is merely conventional, its discourse becomes threatened. Thus, in trouvère lyric, the female body remains rigorously stereotyped. The woman must be perceived through a repertory of conventional signs, lest her presence become so amplified as to disturb those mechanisms of language which give rise to the joy of the text. For me, to utter the *je* of trouvère discourse is less to appropriate that discourse than to be appropriated *by* it, hence to be dispossessed of my individual phantasms. To utter my desire in the language of the other is to utter the alterity of my desire; and of my desire to desire. Even ordinary language can be both crueller to *homo ardens* than extraordinary ladies—and as desirable. All the more, then, is the trouvère text the inscription of unfulfilled *joi d'amor* in its most seductive and enduring form: no poetic convention in European literature has been more stable than that of the vernacular courtly lyric, nor more central to other literary discourses, including that of the novel—all of which suggests that the story of trouvère lyric is the hidden story of literature itself.

Sheldon Zitner

Surrey's "Epitaph on Thomas Clere": Lyric and History

Surrey's epitaph on Thomas Clere is not only language for a tomb, but words that try to justify both the tomb and the mourner. Its double impulse is bereavement and legalism, and one of its particular pleasures is the sudden outcropping of sorrow from argument. The poem's intensity of feeling is sometimes denied by critics who apparently mistake formality for enervation.[1] Perhaps they have failed to read aloud the loaded halts that resist easy utterance, and the interjections that sigh the cause. The end-stopping and emphatic caesura placement are not cut-and-dried, but expressions of the "formal feeling" that Emily Dickinson said comes "after great pain." Grief and argumentation are worked together, but not only on the technical level; like all lyric the sonnet is reflexive.

Norfolk sprang thee, Lambeth holds thee dead,
Clere of the County of Cleremont though hight;
Within the wombe of Ormondes race thou bread,
And sawest thy cosine crowned in thy sight.
Shelton for love, Surrey for Lord thou chase:
Ay me, while life did last that league was tender;
Tracing whose steps thou sawest Kelsall blaze,
Laundersey burnt, and battered Bullen render.

1. Henry Howard, Earl of Surrey, *Poems*, ed. Emrys Jones (Oxford, 1964), p. 32. Citations below are modernized. A longer version of this essay appears as "Truth and Mourning in a Sonnet by Surrey," *ELH*, 50 (1983), 509–29.

At Muttrell gates, hopeles of all recure,
Thine Earle halfe dead gave in thy hand his Will;
Which cause did thee this pining death procure,
Ere Sommers four times seaven thou couldest fulfill.
  Ah Clere, if love had booted, care, or cost,
  Heaven had not wonn, nor Earth so timely lost.

The argument of the poem is Surrey's attempt to justify the burial of Thomas Clere in the Howard family chapel of Lambeth parish church. Surrey claims him, though Clere is of the County Cleremont "hight." The elongated vowel and slightly dispersed accent call attention to the awkward fact of Clere's family origin, a fact that Surrey must counter. But the sonnet crushes the objection, which is preceded by the opening line, whose halves localize birth and death with the directness of a tombstone; Norfolk and Lambeth span the whole of life. Clere was born—as was Surrey—in Norfolk, whose Duke Surrey's father was and Surrey expected to be. Clere was buried in Lambeth, as Surrey should expect to be. The objection from Clere's lineage is followed by further counter-arguments. First, there is Clere's connection with the Ormondes. Ormondes, Howards, and Boleyns twined together on a trellis of lands, marriages, friendships, campaigns against the Irish and Scots, exchanges of title, and scuffles in alliance for place, and were also united through supreme occasions—such as the coronation of a cousin, both Clere's and Surrey's, Anne Boleyn. But relatedness and proximity are givens, accidents of birth. The second quatrain shows us Clere freely choosing what life imposed. The choice, like the necessity, is introduced with lapidary phrasing and rhythmic finality: "Shelton for love, Surrey for Lord"—again an exhaustion of categories, here love and war, the categories of epic. Like what they represent, the two chosen figures are related.

Mary Shelton was the daughter of Sir John Shelton of Shelton in Norfolk. Her maternal aunt married the brother of Anne Boleyn. One tracks her in the Devonshire MS (B.M. 17492) of the poems of Wyatt.[2] Her hand is a scrawl, and her bits of doggerel unimpressive. But she seems to have been a young woman of spirit, undergoing examination for evidence of Surrey's supposed treason, and standing by him until his execution. The Devonshire MS is not only a compilation of Wyatt's verse, but a commonplace book, passed from hand to hand through a small circle of friends. Through the poems entered in

2. See Richard Harrier, *The Canon of Sir Thomas Wyatt's Poetry* (Cambridge, 1975), pp. 17–21, 26.

it, it is a partial record of the tragic love of Lady Margaret Douglas and Surrey's half-uncle, Lord Thomas Howard, a secret alliance encouraged by Anne Boleyn. The MS implies a romantic but not mawkish circle of young aristocrats whose public and personal lives were intense and closely knit. The sigh for the tender "league" in Surrey's poem arises in an ambience one glimpses through the Devonshire MS.

In choosing Henry Howard, Clere also chose the Howard family part in the King's senseless wars. He was with Surrey—both of them about twenty-five—"pacifying" the Scottish border when an outbreak of Scots nationalism gave Henry VIII his chance to further plans for annexation. At his command, the Howards invaded, burning the stronghold of Kelso to the ground in 1542, and withdrawing only when the beer supply ran low.[3] Clere was also with Surrey at the burning of Landrecy and at the siege of Boulogne.

The sonnet preserves something of the difference between octave and sestet; not an Italian leap, but an English shift of focus. By the end of the second quatrain Surrey has demonstrated his case, and the focus narrows to a single incident during the siege of Montreuil.

The story goes that Surrey, anticipating French attempts to raise the siege, tried on 19 September 1544 to take the Abbeyville gate by storm, reached the gate, was seriously wounded, and was saved only by the efforts of Clere, who was himself wounded during the rescue and lingered on, dying on 14 April 1545.

At only one point in the sonnet's supposed recital of these events does the telling seem to falter—with the appearance of a typically cloudy sixteenth-century relative pronoun. To just *which* cause of Clere's pining death does the "which cause" in the eleventh line refer? Probably not to the taking or taking down of the will; perhaps to a sortie against the gate, but just as plausibly to "tracing" Surrey's steps, to the accidents of birth as well as the choices of service, to a life-pattern that further justifies claiming Clere for the Howards. For once, the gelatinous Renaissance pronoun seems to admit the too much one needs to see. Elsewhere the syntax is lucidly articulated, leaving no impression of word or construction stretched further than the mind or breath can gracefully reach. The poem wears its diction and syntax off the rack of common usage. This is, I suppose, what C. S. Lewis meant by Drab, but it is precisely Drab that gives the interrupting sighs of lines six and thirteen their power.

Yet lucid syntax is not always simple sense. There are two passages

3. Edwin Casady, *Henry Howard, Earl of Surrey* (New York, 1938), p. 93.

in which the poem seems less than forthcoming. The first and less obvious one is: "And saw thy cousin crownèd in thy sight." Is Anne Boleyn too well known to require naming? Or was it prudent to recall only a coronation and not a beheading? After all, Norfolk *had* presided over the judging peers, and Surrey himself *had* consequently deputized as Earl Marshal in his father's stead, this after Surrey had carried the fourth sword before the King at Anne's coronation. Yet prudence was hardly Surrey's virtue. For whatever reason, the coronation line tells less than it might, and, unlike adjacent lines, it is bland and uncircumstantial. It has, moreover, a coolness that comes from its centering on the naive wonder of simply being present at a great occasion, an attitude that may well have been less Clere's than Surrey's, since the latter had been so prominently placed. Mordantly, the suppressed name of the dead queen returns in the unintentionally appropriate words "battered Bullen."

Still more problematic are the events "At Muttrell gates." It is barely possible, but highly unlikely, that Surrey or anyone else went into battle carrying his will. That Surrey uses the word "will" rather than the admittedly less easily versified "testament" suggests dictation rather than a transfer of papers.[4] But why leave a muddle, however small? Why not

Thy earl, half dead, bade thee indite,
bade thee set down,
swore thee to guard,
bade thee keep safe
his will?

I suppose that the only line one doesn't want is: "Thy earl, half dead, bade thee probate his will." Short of that, any of these suggestions will do for prosody and patina. But none will do for the poem Surrey was writing. They lack the tactile immediacy and the ambiguity that permit us to read a literal surrender of the self into another's hands. The diction, freed of exclusive reference to a deposition, loads up with feeling that makes the gesture symbolic. The word "will" acquires overtones of "accord" and "desire."

A larger difficulty remains. What happened at Muttrell gates? We know what the historical annotations say. In effect it is this:

4. I am indebted for advice on these matters to Father Michael Sheehan of the Pontifical Institute for Medieval Studies (Toronto), who bears, of course, no responsibility for its possible misuse.

You saved your half-dead earl at Muttrell gate;
Yourself in pain, wrote out his breathless will;
Suffered six months and, not yet twenty-eight,
Died the next spring. Your earl is living still.

Fortunately, this Rupert Brookelet is not the quatrain Surrey gives us. In the poem, the earl's rescue is, at best, only to be inferred. Somehow Surrey, half dead, attends to his will, recovers, and writes an epitaph for Thomas Clere, who died—having done what? Surrey's quatrain seems to displace Clere from the heroic center of the supposed event. The half-dead earl is central, his will obscurely "procuring" the death of Thomas Clere. The two young men had been close companions in military service, in court life, and in the London high jinks for which they had both been imprisoned. Whatever prompted the curious vagueness of the third quatrain, it was not a simple egotism.

Surrey's attack on the Abbeyville gate and Clere's fatal rescue have been editors' and biographers' gospel from Nott through Padelford and Casady to the present. Almost alone among them, Casady fully acknowledges that in retelling the tale "I follow the reconstruction of this [incident] by Nott." Nott, however, states that the "anecdote is preserved in Surrey's epitaph." The dispatch of 19 September 1544, to which Nott alludes for validation, does nothing whatever to substantiate his romantic "re-construction."[5] No extant document known to me supports it, and the military circumstances preclude it.[6] There were no heroics: no raid, no rescue, no wounds—certainly not on the 19th and, in all likelihood, at no other time during the siege. Surrey was, we know, on duty on the 26th. Nott misread the poem and misread the dispatch in shoring up the first misreading, and the twin blunders have been augmented and certified by subsequent scholarship. But what did happen at Montreuil? Dysentery, malaria, typhus, and pestilential fevers thrived in the muck of sixteenth-century military camps. Norfolk's dispatches show that Montreuil was no exception, with ninety ill on 19 September alone. The likelihood is that Surrey recovered from one disease and Clere died of another. My

5. Casady, p. 123, n. 49; George F. Nott, *The Works of Henry Howard, Earl of Surrey and Sir Thomas Wyatt the Elder* (London, 1815), p. lxviii. The dispatch to which Nott evidently refers is to be found in *Letters and Papers . . . of the Reign of Henry VIII,* ed. J. Gardiner and R. H. Brodie (London, 1862–1932), vol. 19, pt. 2, p. 133. Other documents may be located by date. A full study of the military situation, too extensive to be included in this paper, appears in "Truth and Mourning," pp. 517–22.

6. Sir Charles Oman, *A History of the Art of War in the Sixteenth Century* (London, 1937), pp. 338–42 concludes that Norfolk had no intention of pursuing the siege of Montreuil with any vigor.

own guesses are dysentery for Surrey and malaria for Clere. Finally, the phrase "At Muttrell gates," which may have set off Nott's legendizing, implies no assault. Norfolk's company, as siege practice dictated, were lodged "half a mile from the Abbevile [sic] gate."

I offer none of this as a reductive interpretation of the third quatrain. The poem's particular ambiguities remain. However, the historical likelihood makes it difficult to read the phrase "half dead" as either Surrey's ungracious self-dramatization at Clere's expense or as Surrey's gracious magnification of any deed of Clere's. In short, we can move the ambiguities of the lines and the decentering of Clere out of the realm of psychological guess and toward the sociological and the aesthetic.

Surrey was, of course, thoroughly capable of exaggerating his accomplishments and minimizing his failures, especially his military failures.[7] But his intensities of feeling seem to have been circumscribed and colored not by egotism but by loyalty to his caste and kinship group. Surrey's love, like his hate, is a sentiment politicized by being made familial. For the Tudors, the house of Howard were endlessly useful—as organizers, tacticians, battlers, and broodqueens. Henry VIII kept the Howard males on leash as Rome kept Coriolanus, ready to loose them as policy required. Indeed, Surrey might have sat as a model for Shakespeare's tragic fighter, anticipating his conventional marriage, his class contempt, his impolitic temper, his military foolhardiness, his intense male friendships. The Dean of Westbury, in conversation with a government agent, described Surrey, then twenty-two, as "the most folish prowde boye that ys in Englande."[8] Surrey's capacity for politicized attachments is demonstrated by his year-long and debilitating grief at the death of the Duke of Richmond, Henry VIII's illegitimate son, whose boyhood companion Surrey had been.

Surrey's attachments and aversions had a common motif. His hatred of the Seymours, his quarrel with Thomas Darcy, his bitterness against his sister for her proposed marriage to a Seymour, his fight with Blage, his detestation of the "new men" at Court and finally of Henry VIII himself are evidence of how thoroughly Surrey had made the early sixteenth-century struggles among kinship factions the substance of his emotional life. So it was with his love of Richmond and of Thomas Clere. Norfolk's letter describing his son's long mourning for

7. Gilbert J. Millar, *Tudor Mercenaries and Auxiliaries, 1485–1547* (Charlottesville, 1980), pp. 157–59.
8. Casady, *Henry Howard*, p. 3.

Richmond, Surrey's poem "So Cruel Prison," and his epitaph for Clere testify to his capacity for an uncalculating intensity of feeling. Nonetheless, the two great friendships are also gestures of familial—hence political—incorporation. The two passages we have been examining in the sonnet are, I think, explicable—though only in part, on this view. In both, there are departures from the concrete narrative precision elsewhere in the poem. These result in a slight decentering of their nominal subject. Yet the very argument of the poem—the Howard claim—centralizes rank as in a family or a military portrait. It would be an error to end here, however. Surrey writes a sonnet and, in any case, to possess is to be possessed.

Surrey's argument for burying the remains of Thomas Clere in Lambeth begins with an echo of the epitaph Virgil was long supposed to have written for his own tomb.[9] That epitaph, given currency by Suetonius and Donatus, was to attract not only Surrey, but Dante and Eliot: "Highbury bore me, Richmond and Kew undid me." The suburban ingenue whose undoing was canoeing figures in *The Waste Land* (ll. 393–94) as a contrast through allusion to Dante's La Pia—made by Siena, undone by the Maremma.[10] In Dante the passage merely recalls a striking locution. In Eliot its use is in his characteristic vein of mordant collage. Only Surrey, I think, captures the epitaph's unique use of place in all its symbolism and possibility.

> Mantua me genuit. Calabri rapuere, tenet nunc
> Parthenope; cecini pascua rura duces.
>
> [Mantua bore me, Calabria killed me; now
> Parthenope holds me, I who sang
> Of shepherds, countryside, and great commanders.]

Virgil died at Brundisium. His remains were brought to his beloved Naples and buried nearby. Naples, literally a "new city," had been founded on the site of the older settlement of Parthenope, also the name of a third Siren, not mentioned in Homer, but in later narratives of the Argonauts. By Surrey's time the locale of the myth had shifted, and the Sirens were thought to have done their fatal singing from three rocks in the waters near Naples, the Siren-cliffs of *Aeneid*

9. Paul F. Distler, *Vergil and Vergiliana* (Chicago, 1966), pp. 244–46 collects several "Virgilian" epitaphs for Virgil. The epitaph used by Surrey is part of a *Life* in the Loeb Library *Suetonius*, ed. J. C. Rolfe (New York, 1914), II, ll. 476–477; the translation is mine.

10. *Purgatorio*, V, 134: "Siena mi fè; disfecemi Maremma."

V, 864. Of many details in the evolution of the Siren motif suggestively linking death and poetry in ways particularly appropriate to a poet's epitaph, Surrey was at least familiar with the epitaph itself, believed it Virgil's, and knew Parthenope as both the Siren and the city name.

The epitaph seems memorable now, in part because of its unique use of place to suggest both the limits and the qualities of a life. The character of the locution and its strategic use in the first line initiate two related trains of significance.

The first of these is Surrey's loading of place names with more than referential import. Place is also family, and great magnates were, like the primitive tutelary gods they sometimes seemed to ape, animations of place, which is here further personified in verb use. Norfolk "springs" Clere, Lambeth "holds" him.

Kelsall, Laundersey, Bullen, and Muttrell make up a second place series. One should read the sonnet in texts that do not modernize the place names into travelogue exoticism. In Surrey they belong to private experience and are possessed by his spelling and pronunciation as the actual places were briefly possessed by the fiction of Henry's political claims. There is an instructive surprise in seeing the gloss turn apparently British locales Lowland and Burgundian. The locales of Surrey's battles are, in any case, unlike those of Chaucer's knight, not meant to seem exotically distant, and one wonders if the manly clangor some critics find in their alliteration counted for more in Surrey's word choices than did habit and the pervasive strategy resulting in the sequential clusters of hard c, l, d, and again hard c, and in the mirroring of initial and final sounds in lines 7 and 8.

In any case, Surrey was not writing Pound's Altaforte Sestina, whatever his enthusiasm for war. The battles are bracketed by sighs: "Ay me, while life did last that league was tender." The public toughness in the formal term for political covenant is undercut before and after: directly by the paradoxical "tender," more subtly by "Ay me," Which offers first the rather conventional "Alas," and on our further consideration the insistence of "Yes, it was Surrey, *me,* you chose as Lord." The last quatrain ends with the too easily pathetic "summers four times seven." But this slackness is retrieved by line thirteen: "Ah, Clere, if love had booted, care or cost," with its scrupulous prozeugma of dwindling thirds: love, care, cost—all bootless. That the least of the three had been expended and is stated last affirms the others. (The Patent Rolls show that Surrey aided Clere financially in the last months.)

The last line of the sonnet is the culmination of its emphasis on place. Simply put, Earth loses. Earth's local places have been given all the weight that specificity, rhetorical force, and the dangerous commitments of which they are the scene and prize can give them. Yet in sum they are only an abstraction, canceled by another abstraction which, because it has no earthly reference whatever, is superior. The danger of anticlimax and patness incurred by the last line is avoided—perhaps only narrowly—precisely by Surrey's courting it openly and making anticlimax the vehicle of transvaluation. A gray disposable abstraction is what Norfolk, Montreuil, and the rest amount to at the final hour. Patness is avoided too by the complexity of the word "timely," with its jostling meanings of "too soon," "at just the right time," and "welcome," suggesting a final attitude more complex than the simple acceptance also resisted by the rest of the poem. Behind all this lies "The Dream of Scipio," for the Renaissance the narrative archetype linking Platonic disillusion and heroic imperative; the mean, spinning pebble and the great cities to be held or captured.

A second train initiated by the Virgilian epitaph will perhaps appear more problematic. Is it only its rhetorical force and its use of place that led Surrey to employ it so strategically in the sonnet? Surrey's translations of the *Aeneid* constitute the bulk of his achievement. They are the foundation of the neo-Latin assurance in rhythm and spareness of diction in his most characteristic verse. For Surrey, Virgil was what he had been for Dante, *il poeta.*

The only poem I know of attributed to Thomas Clere is the lament over unrequited love that Mary Shelton sniffed at in the margins of the Devonshire MS, an attribution I think highly unlikely.[11] Why use Virgil's epitaph for Clere? Although he may well have written some verses—in that circle one did—Surrey has him writing only a will. Indeed, we can make very little of Clere from the sonnet. Contrast it in this respect with Surrey's epitaph for Wyatt beginning, "Wyatt resteth here."[12] Many conventional things about the man are said there, but at least they are *said.* The Clere portrait is all passivity. He chooses Shelton and, Surrey, but that is all. After and before he is the object and patient; born, bred, looking on at a coronation, tracing another's steps, taking another's will, and—in the circumlocution of line 11—undergoing a death "procured" by one or more of these services. There is a remarkable lack of otherness in the portrait of Thomas Clere; he is a shadowy one-who-goes-beside. Attributes of

11. Harrier, *The Canon of Sir Thomas Wyatt's Poetry,* p. 40, mentions the possibility.

12. See Frederic B. Tromly, "Surrey's Fidelity to Wyatt in 'Wyatt Resteth Here,'" *Studies in Philology,* 77 (1980), 376–87.

character, even of the most conventional kind, are nowhere stated in the sonnet, at only a few points concretely implied, and even then it is only the connection with Surrey that defines them. The generating utterance of the poem is possession, and hence, identity. The decentering of Clere, examined earlier, further reflects the underlying motif of self-mourning. A half-dead earl gives a will which "procures" death for the recipient, who dies while the earl recovers: a curious paradigm of vital exchange among similars. The legacy of half-death in one is lingering death in the other. Of almost all literary epitaphs we may say, as we say of bereavement itself, that it is Margaret Margaret mourns for. But the portrait of Thomas Clere is almost all mirror.

Surrey's epitaph comes before the great English laments for poets, all of which incorporate some measure of anticipatory self-mourning. It is the nature of elegizing and the particular historic tinge of certain sentiments that shape both the anomalies and the achievements of the sonnet. Yet all of this—the grudging and ultimate rejection of temporality, the bereavement and the self-bereavement—was implicit at the first stroke of the pen. To make the whole poem an address to the dead Clere in petition of his earthly remains was not to give apostrophe's fictive life to a cloud or a stone, or to marshal apostrophe as a trite figure of resurrection. To claim the remains of Clere was for Surrey not only an act of love and respect, but an assumption of forgiveness in the certainty that what could be claimed was dross and what could be petitioned lived.

Joel Fineman

Shakespeare's Sonnets' Perjured Eye

In the sub-sequence of sonnets addressed to a young man Shakespeare writes a matching pair of sonnets that develop the way his eye and heart initially are enemies but then are subsequently friends. The first sonnet begins "Mine eye and heart are at a mortal war, / How to divide the conquest of thy sight" (46).[1] In contrast, the second sonnet, relying on a "verdict" that "is determined" at the conclusion of the first, begins "Betwixt mine eye and heart a league is took, / And each doth good turns now unto the other" (47). This opposition is conventional, but the sonnets develop its two sides so that each sonnet finally asserts the same conclusion, namely, that "thy picture in my sight / Awakes my heart to heart and eye's delight" (47). In this witty way the two sonnets work to do good turns unto each other, hendiadistically arriving, from different starting points, at a common destination. Even more harmoniously, in both sonnets the relationship of eye and heart, whether initially antipathetic or sympathetic, leads immediately, via antithesis or synthesis, to a recuperative and benign assessment of yet other polar differences that the sonnets oppose one to another. War and peace, outward and inward, presence and absence—such binaries are integrated and combined by virtue of the complementary collation of "The clear eye's moiety and the dear heart's part" (46).

A fuller version of this essay appears as "Shakespeare's Perjured Eye" in *Representations,* 8 (Fall 1984), 59–86.

1. All Shakespeare references are to *The Riverside Shakespeare,* ed. G. B. Evans et al. (Boston, 1974).

This systematic complementarity—whereby opposites either are the same or, as opposites, still somehow go compatibly together—speaks to a formal homogeneity that informs sonnets 46 and 47 more deeply than the thematic heterogeneity they momentarily evoke. In 46 it is the difference between eye and heart that establishes the concord between them whereas in 47 the concord derives from their similarity. But this difference, which is the difference between difference and similarity, turns out not to make much difference. In both sonnets the eye is "clear" and the heart is "dear" by virtue of a governing structure of likeness and contrast, identity and difference, similarity and contrariety, that the two sonnets equally and isomorphically employ. What sonnets 46 and 47 share, therefore, is the sameness of their differences: what joins them together is a structural identity that is yet more fundamental and more powerful than their initial opposition. At the level of theme and poetic psychology this yields the Petrarchan commonplace in accord with which the poet's eye and heart come instantly to complement each other, moving from war to peace, from antipathy to sympathy, in a progress that constitutes a short-hand summary of the amatory assumptions of ideal admiration (e.g., the way Cupid shoots his arrows through the lover's eye into the lover's heart). This is a specifically *visual* desire, for in both sonnets it is as something of the eye that the young man's "fair appearance lies" (46) within the poet's heart.

Such homogenizing visual imagery, applied to the poet's love, to his beloved, and to his poetry, pervades the sequence of sonnets addressed to the young man, and this imagery is regularly employed, as in sonnets 46 and 47, to characterize a material likeness that conjoins two distinctive yet univocally collated terms: not only the poet's eye and heart, but, also, the poet and his young man (e.g., 22, 24, 62), the young man and *his* young man (e.g., 3, 10), as well as the poet's poetry and that of which the poetry speaks (e.g., 18, 55, 63). In general, the poet identifies his first-person "I" with the ideal eye of the young man—"Now see what good turns eyes for eyes have done" (24)—and then proceeds to identify these both with the "wondrous scope" (105) of his visionary verse: "You live in this, and dwell in lovers' eyes" (55).

This visual imagery is again nothing but conventional, so much so that the young man sonnets regularly characterize such imagery as something old-fashioned, even antiquated, as in the literary retrospection of sonnet 59: "O that record could with a backward look, / Even of five hundreth courses of the sun, / Show me your image in some antique book." With regard to the poet's ideal desire, which aims to join poetic subject with poetic object—"thou mine, I thine" (108)—the young man's poet can rely upon a familiar Petrarchan motif, derived from Stoic optics, of eroticized *eidola* or likenesses whose very physics establishes a *special* (from *specere,* "to look at") coincidence of lover and beloved—as, for example, when Astrophil at the beginning of Sidney's sonnet-sequence looks into his heart to write, and finds there pre-engraved or "stell'd" upon it the stylized *imago* of the Stella he loves. In turn, this physics of the *eidolon* presupposes an equally familiar and specifically idealist metaphysics of genus and species whereby individual particulars are but sub-species of a universal form or type, an ideal whose immanent universality is regularly conceived in terms of light, as in Platonic *eidos,* from *idein,* "to see," or as at the end of the *Paradiso,* where Dante sees *La forma universal,* as well as the painted likeness, the *effige,* of himself, in his vision of *luce etterna* and *semplice lume.*[2] Moreover, the poetry of idealization, especially as it develops in the self-consciously literary tradition of the Renaissance sonnet, characteristically assimilates such visual imagery, which is its imagery *of* the ideal, to itself, so as to idealize itself as effective *simulacrum* of that which it admires. As an activity of "stelling," such poetry is *Ideas Mirrour,* as Drayton called his sonnet-sequence, and is so precisely because, being something visual and visionary, it can claim to be not only the reflection but also the objectification of its idea of its ideal.

Speaking very generally, we can say that this is the regular force of visual imagery in the tradition of the poetry of praise. With regard to poetics, this is a tradition of specifically visionary poetic likeness—either mimetic likeness, whereby poetry is the simulating visual representation of that which it presents (*ut pictura poesis,* "speaking picture"), or figural likeness, visual similes, as when Aristotle defines metaphor as the capacity "to see the same" (*theorein homoion,* "theorizing sameness").[3] This is a literary tradition in which the poet is a panegyric *Vates* or Seer who, at least ideally, is the same as that which he sees, just as poetic language, as *eikon, speculum, imago, eidolon,* etc., is the same as that of which it speaks (as when Dante identifies his own "beatitude" with "those words that praise my lady," his *lodano* with *la donna,* or as when Petrarch puns on "Laura," "laud," and "laurel").

These are the visionary themes and motifs by reference to which the poetry of praise characteristically becomes a praise of poetry itself. We get some sense of how familiar, over-familiar, this received literary tradition is to Shakespeare if we register the formulaic way the

2. Dante, *Paradiso,* 33, ll. 91–131.
3. Aristotle, *The Art of Poetry,* 1459, ll. 5–8.

young man's poet in sonnet 105 identifies his "love," his "beloved," and his "songs and praises": "Let not my love be called idolatry, / Nor my beloved as an idol show, / Since all alike my songs and praises be." What joins these three together is the ideality they share, an ideality that establishes a three-term correspondence between the speaking, the spoken, and the speech of praise. "'Fair,' 'kind,' and 'true" is all my argument," says the poet in sonnet 105, and these "Three themes in one, which wondrous scope affords," amount to a phenomenological summary, an eidetic reduction, of a Petrarchan metaphysical, erotic, and poetic Ideal: "Fair" identifies the visibility, the *Sichtigkeit,* of an ideal seeing and sight (*idein,* "to see"); "kind" identifies the homogeneous categoriality, the formal elementality, of an ideal essentializing and essence (Platonic *eidos*); "true" identifies the coincidence of ideal knowing and knowledge (*oida,* also from *idein*). It is by reference to such precisely conceived and conceited ideality that sonnet 105 manages to identify "my love," "my beloved," and "my songs and praises," each one of these being "'Fair,' 'kind,' and 'true,'" and therefore, by commutation, each one of these being the truthful mirror-image of the other two. This is how Shakespeare's poetry of visionary praise, because it is addressed to a "wondrous scope" and because it is itself a "wondrous scope," is always, as sonnet 105 puts it, monotheistically, monogamously, monosyllabically, and monotonously "To one, of one, still such, and ever so." This is an ideological poetry, as sonnet 105 seems almost to complain, whose virtue consists in the way its copiousness always copies the same ideal sameness—"Since all alike my songs and praises be"—a universal and a universing poetic and erotic practice whose very ideality is what renders it incapable of manifesting difference: for, as the poet puts it in sonnet 105, "Kind is my love to-day, to-morrow kind, / Still constant in a wondrous excellence, / Therefore my verse, to constancy confin'd, / One thing expressing, leaves out difference."

However, as the palpable claustrophobia of sonnet 105 suggests, it would be possible to look more closely at the sonnets addressed to the young man so as to see the way they characteristically resist and conflictedly inflect their most ideal expressions of visionary unity, the way that they implicitly "express" the "difference" that they explicitly "leave out." If, as Murray Krieger has suggested, we are supposed to hear the "one" in sonnet 105's "*won*drous scope," then so too do we hear the "two" in its "T(w)o one, of one, still such, and even so."[4] So

4. Murray Krieger, "Poetic Presence and Illusion: Renaissance Theory and the Duplicity of Metaphor," *Critical Inquiry,* 5:4 (1979), 169.

too, the entire sonnet is colored by the ambiguous logic of its opening "Since"—"Since all alike my songs and praises be"—since this concessive particle explains both why the young man is an idol as well as why he is not. Such complications add a reservation or a wrinkle to the poet's otherwise straightforward rhetoric of compliment. In such oblique ways the young man sonnets will regularly situate themselves and their admiration at one affective and temporal remove from the ideality they repeatedly and repetitiously invoke, with the peculiar result that in these sonnets an apparently traditional poetics of ideal light comes regularly to seem what sonnet 123 calls "The dressings of a former sight."

This peculiarity is a consistent aspect of the young man sonnets' imagery of the visual and the visible, imagery that is characteristically presented in the young man sonnets as though it were so tarnished with age that its very reiteration is what interferes with the poet's specular identification of his poetic "I" with the ideal "eye" of the young man: "For as you were when first your eye I ey'd" (104). In general, the young man's poet, *as* a visionary poet, seems capable of expressing only a love at second sight: his identification of his ego with his ego-ideal seems worn out by repetition, as though it were the very practice by the poet of an old-fashioned poetry of visionary praise that effectively differentiates the poet as a panegyricizing subject from what he takes to be his ideal and his praiseworthy object. We can take as an example the mixed-up deictic and epideictic compact of the couplet to sonnet 62: "'Tis thee (myself) that for myself I praise, / Painting my age with beauty of thy days," where the confused identification of the poet's "I" and "thou" effectively identifies the first-person of the poet with the difference that obtains between the youth and age of visionary praise.

In this context, we can recall the fact that Shakespeare writes his sonnet-sequence, for the most part, after the Elizabethan sonnet-sequence vogue has passed, in the literary aftermath of the poetry of praise, when such Petrarchan panegyric has come to seem *passé*. This is the historical context within which the sonnets addressed to the young man—conceived long after what Sidney, at the inaugural moment of the Elizabethan sonnet-sequence, called "Poor Petrarch's long-deceased woes"—make a personal issue out of their self-remarked literary belatedness, regularly associating their own old-fashioned literary matter and manner with their poet's sense of his senescence. In sonnet 76, for example, the poet asks: "Why is my verse so barren of new pride? / So far from variation or quick change? / Why with the time do I not glance aside / To new-found methods and to compounds strange?" As the poet first poses them, these are rhetorical questions, but these questions then will press themselves upon the poet's person. They define for him his sense of superannuated self: "Why write I still all one, ever the same, / And keep invention in a noted weed, / That every word doth almost tell my name, / Showing their birth and where they did proceed?" A good many young man sonnets are concerned with just this kind of literary question, and, as in sonnet 76, in these sonnets it appears as if it is the very posing of the question that empties out the poet's praising self: "So all my best is dressing old words new, / Spending again what is already spent: / For as the sun is daily new and old, / So is my love still telling what is told" (76).

This introduces a new kind of self-consciousness into the already highly self-conscious tradition of the Renaissance sonnet. In familiar ways, the poet in sonnet 76 identifies himself with his own literariness. At the same time, however, it is in an unfamiliar way that the poet's subjectivity here seems worn out by the heavy burden of the literary history that his literariness both examples and extends. For what is novel in a sonnet such as 76 is not so much the way the poet takes the ever-renewed sameness of the sun as a dead metaphor for the animating *energeia* and *enargia* of an ideal metaphoricity. Rather, what is striking, and what is genuinely novel, is the way the visionary poet takes this faded brightness personally, the way he identifies his own poetic person and poetic identity with the after-light of this dead metaphoric sun. Identifying himself with an aged but ideal eternality, "ever the same," the young man's poet is like a bleached Dante: he is a visionary poet, but he is so, as it were, after the visionary fact, a Seer who now sees in a too frequently reiterated *luce etterna* a vivid image, an *effige* or *eidolon,* of the death of both his light and life, as in sonnet 73: "In me thou seest the twilight of such day / As after sunset fadeth in the west, / Which by and by black night doth take away, / Death's second self that seals up all in rest."

There is more to say about this imagery of tired light, or tired imagery of light. The novel coloring that Shakespeare's young man sonnets give to their visual imagery, to their imagery *of* the visual, is responsible, to a considerable degree, for the pathos of poetic persona that these sonnets regularly exhibit. It would be a mistake, however, to overemphasize the darkness that informs these sonnets' literary, visionary light. Whatever reservations or suspicions attach to the young man sonnets' imagery of vision, these reservations, like those that shade the poet's various characterizations of the ideality of the young man, are implicit rather than explicit, something we read between their "eternal lines to time" (18).

It is important to insist upon this indirection because this accounts for the residual idealism with which the young man sonnets always turn, heliotropically, to "that sun, thine eye" (49). At least ideally, the young man sonnets would like to be like the courtly "marigold" of sonnet 25, whose "fair leaves spread . . . at the sun's eye." Like such flowers of fancy, the young man sonnets would like to look exactly like what they look at, just as the poet would like his "I" to be "as you were when first your eye I ey'd" (104). Hence the nostalgia of the poet's introspection: the poet sees his difference from a visionary poetics that would always be the same because, as Aristotle says of metaphor, it always "see(s) the same." But this insight serves only to make the poet's bygone ideal vision seem all the more ideal, an image of poetic presence that is always in the past.

This loyally retrospective visuality, a poetry of belated re-turn rather than of simple turn, accounts for the complex texture of the young man sonnets' imagery of vision, but it also distinguishes the young man sonnets from the dark lady sonnets where such ideal imagery of light is explicitly—Shakespeare's word here is important—"forsworn" (152). What gives this "forswearing" its power and distinguishes it from the implicit visual reservations informing the young man sonnets is precisely the fact that the dark lady's poet puts the unspoken visionary suspicions of the young man sonnets directly into words. In the young man sonnets, the young man, whatever his faults, is an "image" whose idealization effectively can represent an ideal that is lost, as in sonnet 31: "Their images I lov'd I view in thee, / And thou (all they) hast all the all of me." In contrast, in the dark lady sonnets, the dark lady has the "power" "To make me give the lie to my true sight, / And swear that brightness doth not grace the day" (149).

This is related to the so-called anti-Petrarchanism of the dark lady sonnets. When the poet looks at the young man he sees "that sun, thine eye" (49). In contrast, when he looks at the dark lady what he sees is the way she is unlike the ideal brightness of the young man: "My mistress' eyes are nothing like the sun" (130). On the face of it, this amounts to a straightforward difference, for, on the one hand, there is brightness, whereas, on the other, there is darkness. What makes this difference complicated, however, is that when the poet gives explicit expression to it, he presents the darkness of the lady as itself the image of this difference, as an image, precisely, of the difference between the black that it is and the light that it is not.

This is why the difference between the lady's stressedly unconventional darkness and the young man's emphatically conventional brightness produces something that is both more and less than a straightforward black and white antithesis of the kind suggested by the "anti-" of anti-Petrarchanism. As an image of that which she is not, the lady is presented as the likeness of a difference, at once a version and perversion of that to which she is, on the one hand, positively and negatively compared and that to which she is, on the other, positively and negatively opposed. The lady is thus beyond both comparison and opposition. She both is and is not what she is, and because she is, *in* herself, something double, the lady cannot be comprehended by a poetics of "To one, of one, still such, and ever so." As the poet puts it in sonnet 130, the lady is a "love," just as she inspires a "love," that is "as rare, / As any she belied with false compare." The irrational ratio of the formula defines the peculiarity of the lady. She is a "she" who is logically, as well as grammatically, both subject and object of "belied with false compare"—comparable, therefore, only to the way comparison has failed.

From the beginning, this characterization of the lady in terms of difference, defined specifically in terms of a new kind of poetics, is what the poet finds distinctive about her, as in the first sonnet he addresses to her: "In the old age black was not counted fair, / Or if it were it bore not beauty's name; / But now is black beauty's successive heir, / And beauty slander'd with a bastard shame" (127). What is supposed to be surprising here is that the lady's traditional foul is characterized as something that is fair, just as in later sonnets, such as 147, this novel fair will be yet more surprisingly foul. In either case, however, whether fair or foul, it is always as images of that which they are not, as something double, fair *and* foul, as something duplicitous and heterogeneous, that the lady and her darkness acquire their erotic and their literary charge. It is for this reason, because something double, that the lady cannot be comprehended by a poetics of "To one, of one, still such, and ever so."

Thus "black" is now "beauty's successive heir," now that "beauty" is "slander'd with a bastard shame." In the context of the sequence as a whole, the force of this unconventional "succession" is that it repeats, but with a difference, the themes of reiterated and legitimately procreated likeness with reference to which the young man at the opening of his sub-sequence is supposed, as an *imago,* to "prove his beauty by succession thine" (2). Instead of the ideal multiplication of kind with kind, the ongoing reproduction of the visual same, by means of which the young man is supposed to "breed another thee" (6), the novel beauty of the lady instead exemplifies a novelly miscegenating "successivity" whereby black becomes the differential substitute, the unkind "heir," of what is "fair." So too with the blackness of the lady's "raven" eyes, a darkness that in sonnet 127 replaces at the same time as it thus displaces the brightness it sequentially succeeds.

This defines the structural and temporal relationship of the dark lady sonnets to the young man sonnets. The second sub-sequence is a subsequential repetition of the first, but a discordant and disturbing repetition because, stressing itself as a repetition, it represents the themes of visionary presence of the first sub-sequence in such a way that its memorial repetition explicitly calls up the poignant absence of that which it recalls. To the degree that this articulates the unspoken reservations that darken the idealism of the young man sonnets, the "black" of the second sub-sequence becomes continuous with the elegiacally retrospective visuality of the first. Yet there is also an emphatic difference between the two to the extent that the dark lady's poet explicitly expresses what the young man's poet preferred to leave implicit: the death of ideal visionary presence. This is significant because, according to the poet, it is this very vision or *imago* of the loss of vision that now thrusts him into novel speech—the discourse of "black beauty"—making him now no longer a poet of the eye, but, instead, a poet of the tongue: "Yet so they [the lady's eyes] mourn, becoming of their woe, / That every tongue says beauty should look so" (127).

As Ulysses says of wanton Cressida, "There's language in her eye." But what is odd about this language is what is odd about the lady's eye, namely, that it is opposed to vision. The difference between this and the way that language is characterized in the young man sonnets is considerable, and we may say that this difference not only exemplifies but thematically describes the novelty of the way a poet speaks in a post-Petrarchan poetics. In the young man sonnets the poet ideally speaks a visionary speech, and, therefore, when he speaks about this speech he speaks of it as something of the eye: "To hear with eyes belongs to love's fine wit" (23). In contrast, the poet in the dark lady sub-sequence will speak about his speech *as* speech, and as something that, for this very reason, is different from a visual ideal. In this "forswearing" way, the dark lady, with the "pow'r" of her "insufficiency," will "make me give the lie to my true sight, / And swear that brightness doth not grace the day" (150). The double way the lady looks is like the double way that language speaks—for both present an absence—which is why when the poet looks at the lady's far too common "common place" (137), at once erotic and poetic, he says "mine eyes seeing this, say this is not" (137).

Thematized in this way, as the *voice* of "eyes . . . which have no correspondence with true sight" (148), language is regularly presented in the dark lady sonnets as something whose truth consists not only in saying but in *being* something false: "My thoughts and my discourse as madmen's are, / At randon from the truth vainly express'd; / For I have sworn thee fair, and thought thee bright, / Who art as black as hell, as dark as night" (147). Correspondingly, because no longer the iconic *eidolon* of what it speaks about, verbal language now defines itself as its forswearing difference from what is " 'Fair,' 'kind,' and 'true' ": "For I have sworn deep oaths of thy deep kindness, / Oaths of thy love, thy truth, thy constancy, / And to enlighten thee gave eyes to blindness, / Or made them swear against the thing they see" (152). And, as a further and more personal result, the poet now identifies himself with the difference that his language thus bespeaks. He is no longer a visionary poet who identifies his "I" and "eye," but instead the subject of a "perjur'd eye": "For I have sworn thee fair: more perjur'd eye, / To swear against the truth so foul a lie!" (152).

It is fair to say, therefore, that in the dark lady sonnets we encounter a poetics in which true vision is captured by false language, and that the conflict thus engendered between sight and word in turn determines specific mutations of traditional sonneteering claims. For this reason, Shakespeare's sonnet-sequence marks a decisive moment in the history of lyric; for when the dark lady sonnets forswear the ideally visionary poetics of the young man sonnets, when poetic language comes in this way to be characterized as something verbal, not visual, we see what happens to poetry when it gives over a perennial poetics of *ut pictura poesis* for, so to speak, literally *so as* to speak, a poetics of *ut poesis poesis,* a transition that writes itself out in Shakespeare's sonnets as an unhappy progress from a poetry based on visual likeness to a poetry based on verbal difference. In the sequence as a whole, this progress from a homogeneous poetics of vision to a heterogeneous poetics of language is fleshed out as a progress from an ideally homosexual desire for what is " 'Fair,' 'kind,' and 'true' " to a misogynistically heterosexual desire for what is fair *and* unfair, kind *and* unkind, true *and* false—a progress, in other words, from man to woman. Here again, however, it is explicitly and literally as a figure *of* speech that the lady becomes the novel "hetero-" opposed as such to an ideal and a familiar neo-platonic "homo-," as when: "When my love swears that she is made of truth, / I do believe her though I know she lies" (138). In this paradoxical way, as a reduplicate belying of the Cratylism of the poetry of praise, the poet expresses the novel duplicity of a specifically linguistic language of desire: "Therefore I lie with her, and she with me, / And in our faults by lies we flattered be" (138).

For all their difference from that which they succeed, however, it is important to recognize that the novelty of Shakespeare's sonnets is nevertheless constrained by the traditional lyric literariness to which these sonnets stand as epitaph. We get some sense of this if we see the way Shakespeare's invention of a heterogeneous and heterosexual poetics amounts to a *predetermined* mutation of the orthodox homogeneity and homosexuality of the poetics of praise:

> Thine eyes I love, and they as pitying me,
> Knowing my heart torment me with disdain,
> Have put on black, and loving mourners be,
> Looking with pretty ruth upon my pain.
> And truly not the morning sun of heaven
> Better becomes the grey cheeks of th' east,
> Nor that full star that ushers in the even
> Doth half that glory to the sober west,
> As those two mourning eyes become thy face.
> O, let it then as well beseem thy heart
> To mourn for me, since mourning doth thee grace,
> And suit thy pity like in every part.
> Then will I swear beauty herself is black,
> And all they foul that thy complexion lack.

As in sonnets 46 and 47, the general conceit of sonnet 123, with its frustrated lover addressing his pitiless, disdaining beloved, is a Petrarchan commonplace, going back beyond Petrarch to the *rime petrose* of Arnault Daniel. Equally common is the intricate development of the imagery of sympathetically erotic vision. We deal here, therefore, with the same poetics Shakespeare presupposes in the young man sonnets. But sonnet 132 further plays upon these traditional light-sight metaphors when, as a result of comparing the beloved's eyes to the sun, it turns out not that her eyes are lamps, but that the sun to which they are compared is therefore black. This too is, in part, conventional (e.g., Stella's eyes are black), but what is striking is the way in which the sonnet stresses its unconventional citation of what has come before. In the young man sonnets the morning is "sacred," "new-appearing" (7), "golden" and "green" (33). Here, instead, "the morning sun of heaven" is obscuring complement to "the grey cheeks of the east," shining in the morning like the evening star at night, because it is a brightness in an encroaching darkness of which it is itself the cause and sign. Where in the sonnets addressed to the young man the sun is a "gracious light" (7) to the morning, here, instead, the morning is a "mourning" whose inversion is a darkening "grace." This pun on "mo(u)rning" explains why in the dark lady sonnets "brightness doth not grace the day." For the point emphasized by the sonnet is that the pun, which must be noticed as such for it to work its poetic effect, does in little what the poem does rhetorically as a whole: repeating itself *in* itself so as to undo itself with its own echo, discovering and producing its own loss of vision at the very moment of calling to our attention the way language, theme, and image displace themselves by folding over upon themselves in paradox: "Then will I swear beauty herself is black, / And all they foul that thy complexion lack."

All this—morning *and* melancholia—is neither Petrarchan nor anti-Petrarchan. The system of logical oppositions and conventional antitheses into which we might be tempted to organize the sonnet's courtly courtship argument falls to pieces as soon as the sonnet brings antithesis into play. Just as the lady's eyes by turning black express a pity occasioned by her heart's disdain, so too does the poet thematize the fact that he here expresses his heart's desire with a language of disdain. The relationship between the lady's eye and the lady's heart, or of the poet to the lady, is a matter, therefore, neither of similarity and contrast nor of pity and disdain. Pity is a figure of disdain just as morning is a version of the night, each of them the homeopathic mirror of the heteropathy of the other. As a result, with likeness emerging as the instance rather than the antithesis of difference, with pity the *complement* to disdain, the sonnet forces its reader to deal with oddly asymmetrical oppositions whereby each polarized side or half of every opposition that the sonnet adduces already includes, and therefore changes by encapsulating, the larger dichotomy of which it is a part. The lady's "charm" consists precisely of the way two apparently antithetical modalities, empathy and antipathy, turn out to be, within their singular propriety, each the contrary double not only of the other but also of itself. With regard to the poet, this means that he cannot speak of his lady with a simple rhetoric of similarity and contrast, for his language undercuts the unifying logic of its oppositions even as it advances an argument for their complementary contrariety.

The difference between this and what happens when sonnets 46 and 47 develop their eye-heart topos is pointed enough. Where the young man sonnets see eye and heart as figure and occasion of each other, sonnet 132 instead describes a desire at odds with itself because at odds with what it sees. Where the two young man sonnets bring out the identity built into their differences, the dark lady sonnet instead brings out the difference built into its identities. Where the two young man sonnets develop an ideal logic of sympathetic opposition, the dark lady sonnet offers instead the paradoxical opposite to such a logic of sympathetic opposition. These are significant differences, but they derive their significance from the structurally systematic way in which sonnet 132 understands its language, stressed as such, to redouble, with a difference, the orthodox, visual, dual unities with which it beings, i.e., from the way the double doubling of sonnet 132 re-turns, or re-verses, the unifying tropes and verses of an idealizing, homogeneous poetics. "Mourning" its "morning," the sonnet puts into words the duplicity of its speech, and thereby undoes both erotic and rhetorical identification. The content of "mourning" *is* the loss of "morning," and this "[w]hole" (134) built into a double language, this difference sounded in a sameness, is what functions both to blind the poet's eye and to break the poet's heart.

It is language, therefore, the "languageness" of language, now conceived and conceited as something linguistic, as both like and unlike the vision to which it is opposed and on which it is superimposed, that in the dark lady sonnets entails as well as describes the redoubling of unity that leads to division, the mimic likeness of a likeness that leads to difference, the representation of presentation that spells the end of presence. Writing at the conclusion of a tradition of poetic idealism and idealization, when poetic language is no longer tautologically the same as what it speaks about, when poetic metaphor no longer "see(s) the same," Shakespeare in his sonnets thus draws the consequences which follow from the death of visual admiration. The dark lady sonnets explicitly break the amatory metaphorics of "Two distincts, division none" ("The Phoenix and the Turtle") by substituting for such a unitary duality a tropic system of triangular, chiasmic duplicity: "A torment thrice threefold thus to be crossed" (133). In the narrative the sequence tells, this double duplication, which brings out the difference built into binary identities, is thematically embodied in the ambiguously duplicitous dark lady and then projected into the double cuckoldry story itself, where the poet is betrayed by both his objects of desire when they couple with each other, and when the sequence as a whole moves from the unity of *folie à deux* to the duality of *ménage à trois*. In terms of the sonnets' own literary self-consciousness, there is an analogous contrast between the traditional poetry of erotic idealization addressed to the young man and the parodic undoing of that tradition by means of the radically *para-*, not *anti-*, Petrarchanism addressed to the dark lady (the erotic now conceived, as in sonnet 134, as "[w]hole" within and without "[w]hole"). Finally, because the self-conscious tradition of the poetry of praise assumes that the language of poetic desire is itself identical to the object of poetic desire—which is why an orthodox poetry of love characteristically writes itself out as a love of poetry—Shakespeare's paradoxical version of the poetry of praise brings out even the difference built into the identity of literary and sexual admiration, which is how the dark lady sonnets describe a poetic desire whose Eros and Logos are themselves thematically out of joint.

It would be possible, of course, to find literary precedents for what seems novel in the *Sonnets*. Yet it is also important to recognize their genuine novelty. The poetic persona of Shakespeare's sonnets can no longer elaborate his subjectivity in accord with the ideal model of a self composed of the specular identification of poetic ego and poetic ego ideal, of "I" and "you," or of eye and eyed. Instead, identifying himself with the heterogeneous look of the lady, and with the duplicity of her speech, the poet, *because* he speaks, identifies himself with difference. The result is that the poet's identity is defined, by chiasmic triangulation, as the disruption or fracture of identity (133). Such a poetic self identifies himself with a constitutive "insufficiency" (150) that is *spoken for* by the "insufficient" language that he speaks. Built up on or out of the loss of itself, its identity defined as its difference from itself, poetry thus opens up a hole within the whole of poetic first-person self-presence. In this way, by joining the rhetorical form of triangular chiasmus to the thematic heartbreak of a "perjured eye," Shakespeare's sonnets give off the subjectivity effect called for by a post-idealist literariness, the literariness, it might be argued, willed to us by the Renaissance.

It has no doubt been noticed that this reading of Shakespeare's sonnets has affinities with a number of the recent preoccupations of critical theory. What I call the "languageness" of language recalls accounts of literariness in Jakobson, Genette, and Riffaterre; my characterization of cross-coupling chiasmus recalls Greimas's "semantic square," Lacan's "Schema L," and de Man's discussions of figural chiasmus; my discussion of the way an idealist homogeneity is disrupted by a supplementary heterogeneity recalls aspects of Derrida's deconstructive phenomenology; most important, my account of a subjectivity precipitated by the paradoxical relationship of language to vision recalls Lacan's psychoanalytic account of the capture of the "Imaginary" by the "Symbolic."[5] I mention this so as to point up the

5. See Roman Jakobson, "Linguistics and Poetics," in *The Structuralists*, ed. R. T. De

way in which contemporary theory has enacted a development very similar not only to the one it is possible to discern in Shakespeare's sonnets—as they move from young man to dark lady—but also to the larger literary development within which these sonnets can be located. For example, in response to Husserl's Dantesque phenomenology of Ideas, Sartre developed a psychology of imagination whose logic and metaphors very much resemble the paranoiac visionary thematics of a good many of Shakespeare's sonnets to the young man.[6] The subjective optics of this Sartrian "gaze" and its mutually persecutory master-slave relation was subsequently subjected, by Merleau-Ponty, to an ironically comic revision whose chiasmic marriage of subject and object repeats more than a few of Shakespeare's most poignant conceits; it was Merleau-Ponty, after all, who introduced "chiasmus" into contemporary critical discourse as a way to explain the way Cézanne paints the trees watching Cézanne. Reacting against what he saw as the psychological and phenomenological sentimentality of Merleau-Ponty's chiasmus and its fully lived "visibility," Lacan in turn developed an account which situates the birth of subjectivity in precisely the place where chiasmus breaks.[7] Lacan's anamorphic "gaze," very different from *le regard* of Sartre or of Merleau-Ponty—together with his account of the way language both potentiates and inherits this rupture of the imaginary—rather perfectly repeats the formal and thematic logic of Shakespeare's "perjur'd eye."[8] So too,

George and F. M. De George (New York, 1972), pp. 85–122; Gérard Genette, "La littérature comme telle," in *Figures I* (Paris, 1966), pp. 253–65, with "Poetic Language, Poetics of Language," in *Figures of Literary Discourse*, trans. Alan Sheridan (New York, 1982), pp. 75–102; Michael Riffaterre, *Semiotics of Poetry* (Bloomington, 1978); A.-J. Greimas and François Rastier, "The Interaction of Semiotic Constraints," *Yale French Studies*, no. 41 (1968), pp. 86–105; A.-J. Greimas and J. Courtés, *Semiotics and Language: An Analytic Dictionary* (Bloomington, 1982), pp. 308–11; Paul de Man, "Pascal's Allegory of Persuasion," in *Allegory and Representation*, ed. S. Greenblatt (Baltimore, 1981), pp. 1–25; Jacques Lacan, "On a Question Preliminary to any Possible Treatment of Psychosis," *Ecrits*, trans. Alan Sheridan (New York, 1977), pp. 179–225; Jacques Derrida, "White Mythology," in *Margins of Philosophy*, trans. Alan Bass (Chicago, 1982), and *Of Grammatology*, trans. Gayatri C. Spivak (Baltimore, 1976). In the latter context, the most relevant works are those in which Derrida criticizes Lacan, e.g., *Positions*, trans. Alan Bass (Chicago, 1981) and "Le Facteur de la vérité," in *La Carte postale* (Paris, 1980), pp. 439–524. For Lacan, see, for example, "The Freudian Thing," "On a Question Preliminary . . . ," and "The Signification of the Phallus" in *Ecrits*.

6. See Jean-Paul Sartre, *L'Imaginaire, psychologie phénomenologique de l'imagination* (Paris, 1940), trans. Bernard Frechtman, *The Psychology of Imagination* (New York, 1948). See also *Being and Nothingness* (New York, 1956), "The Look" ("Le Regard"), pp. 340–400.

7. See Merleau-Ponty's discussion of "entrelacs" in *Le Visible et l'invisible* (Paris, 1964), chap. 4; and Lacan, *The Four Fundamental Concepts of Psychoanalysis* (New York, 1977), "Of the Gaze as *Objet petit a*," pp. 67–122.

8. I refer here not only to Lacan's explicit formulations, but also to the develop-

Derrida's attempt to rupture this rupture, his putatively post-subjective account of a supplemental *différance,* seems from the point of view of Shakespeare's sonnets, nothing but another "increase" that "From fairest creatures we desire" (1)—assuming that we recognize the wrinkle, literally the crease, that Shakespeare introduces into the perennial poetics of copious "increase."

This is very general and selective history of ideas indeed, but it points to something important. Shakespeare's own response to secondariness introduces, I have suggested, a subjectivity altogether novel in the history of lyric: "If there be nothing new, but that which is / Hath been before, how are our brains beguil'd, / Which laboring for invention bear amiss / The second burthen of a former child" (59). It is as the grotesque "second burthen," an aborting second bearing, a re-naissance, of a former child, that we might characterize the subjectivity fathered by the burden of a belated literariness. It is fair to say that contemporary theory, in an exemplary way, takes up this burden of literary history by once again repeating it. Doing so, repeating Shakespeare's repetition, it perhaps puts an end to the modernist literary subject. If we examine the ways in which it does so, however, what we see is the way theory itself is constrained by a literariness larger even than the Shakespearean. It is not only Shakespeare who looks, "with a backward look," to see "your image in some antique book":

> That I might see what the old world could say
> To this composed wonder of your frame,
> Whether we are mended, or whe'er better they,
> Or whether revolution be the same,
> O, sure I am the wits of former days
> To subjects worse have given admiring praise.
> (59)[9]

---

ment of Lacan's thought, from the early emphasis on visual themes, as in the essay on "The Mirror Stage" in *Ecrits* and accompanying discussions of aggressivity, to the later emphasis on language, anamorphosis, and accompanying discussions of (male) desire, as in "The Function and Field of Speech," in *Ecrits* or *Four Fundamentals,* to, finally, as a third term added to the opposition of the Imaginary and the Symbolic, Lacan's increasing emphasis on the "Real," the limits of representation, and accompanying discussions of (female) *jouissance,* as in *Encore* (Paris, 1975). However, Lacan's sense of the Renaissance is colored by a very Catholic and a very French conception of the Baroque—"Le baroque, c'est la régulation de l'âme par la scopie corporelle" (*Encore,* p. 105)—which is why Lacan's direct comments on Shakespeare are often disappointing.

9. I develop a fuller account of Shakespearean subjectivity in *Shakespeare's Perjured Eye: The Invention of Poetic Subjectivity in Shakespeare's Sonnets* (forthcoming, University of California Press). This contains a fuller account of the way metaphors of vision and language are traditionally employed in the literature of orthodox and paradoxical praise. It also describes the way recent theory of rhetoricity and person historically derives from Shakespeare's rewriting of the epideictic.

Stanley Fish

Authors-Readers: Jonson's Community of the Same

Although Ben Jonson's poetry has been characterized as urbane and polished, much of it is marked by a deliberate and labored awkwardness. This is especially true of the beginning of a Jonson poem, where one often finds a meditation on the difficulty of beginning, a meditation that typically takes the form of a succession of false starts after which the poem stumbles upon its subject, having in the meantime consumed up to one third of its length in a search for its own direction. Thus, for example, the poem in praise of Shakespeare spends its first sixteen lines exploring the kinds of praise it will *not* offer before Jonson declares at line 17, "I therefore will begin," and even then what follows is a list of the poets to whom Shakespeare will *not* be compared.[1] In the "Epistle to Katherine, Lady Aubigny" (*The Forest:* 13) Jonson goes on for twenty lines about the dangers one courts by praising before he draws himself up to announce "I madame, am become your praiser" (l. 21). The opening of the "Epistle to Master John Seldon" (*The Under-wood:* 14) is more abrupt: "I know to whom I write," but although he knows, it is another twenty-nine lines before he hazards a direct address and says to Seldon "Stand forth my object." In the Cary-Morison Ode (*The Under-wood:* 70) the halt and start of the verse is imitated by a character—the

A fuller version of this essay appears in *Representations,* 7 (Summer 1984), 26–58.

1. For perceptive observations on Jonson's use of negative constructions, see Richard C. Newton, "Ben./Jonson: The Poet in the Poems," in *Two Renaissance Mythmakers: Christopher Marlowe and Ben Jonson* (Baltimore and London, 1977), pp. 165–95. Unless otherwise noted, all citations are to *Ben Jonson's Poems,* ed. Ian Donaldson (London, Oxford, and New York, 1975).

"brave infant of Saguntum"—who draws back from entering the world and therefore never manages to enter the poem, although he seems at first to be its addressee. And in what is perhaps the most complicated instance of the pattern, "An Elegy on the Lady Jane Paulet, Marchioness of Winton" (*The Under-wood:* 83), Jonson melodramatically portrays himself as unable to recognize the ghost of the Lady, who then identifies herself and immediately vanishes from the poem, leaving the poet with the task of writing an inscription for her tomb, a task he attempts in several aborted ways before resolving to leave off heraldry and "give her soul a name" (l. 22), a resolution that is immediately repudiated by a declaration of poetic inability—"I durst not aim at that" (l. 25)—so that as we reach line 30 of the poem we are being told that its subject cannot possibly be described.

What I would like to suggest in this essay is that Jonson's habit of beginning awkwardly is not simply a mannerism but is intimately related to the project of his poetry, and indeed represents a questioning of that project, since the issue always seems to be whether or not the poem can do what it sets out to do. The issue is also whether or not the reader can do what he is asked to; for quite often the interrupted or delayed beginning of a poem is part of a double strategy of invitation and exclusion in which the reader is first invited to enter the poem, and then met, even as he lifts his foot above the threshold, with a rehearsal of the qualifications for entry, qualifications which reverse the usual relationship between the poet and a judging audience. Here the salient example is of course "An Epistle Answering to One That Asked to Be Sealed of the Tribe of Ben" (*The Under-wood:* 47), where the reader must stand with his foot poised for seventy-eight lines; but a more manageable though equally instructive example is a small, hitherto unremarked-upon poem in the *Ungathered Verse:*[2]

In Authorem

THou, that wouldst finde the habit of true passion,
  And see a minde attir'd in perfect straines;
Not wearing moodes, as gallants doe a fashion,
  In these pide times, only to shewe their braines,

Looke here on *Bretons* worke, the master print:
  Where, such perfections to the life doe rise.
If they seeme wry, to such as looke asquint,
  The fault's not in the object, but their eyes.

2. Here the text I am using in *The Complete Poetry of Ben Jonson,* ed. with intro. and notes by William B. Hunter, Jr. (New York, 1963).

For, as one comming with a laterall viewe,
Unto a cunning piece wrought perspective,
Wants facultie to make a censure true:
So with this Authors Readers will it thrive:

Which being eyed directly, I divine,
His proofe their praise, will meete, as in this line.
Ben: Johnson.

The tension that finally structures this poem at every level surfaces in the very first line in the word "habit," which means both "characteristic form of" and "outward apparel of." The tension lies in the claims implicitly made by the two meanings; the claim of one is to be presenting the thing itself while the claim of the other is limited to the presentation of a surface; and since that surface is a covering there is a suggestion (borne out by the examples of use listed in the *OED*) that what covers also hides and conceals. The uneasy relationship between the two meanings is brought out by the phrase "true passion." Can we truly see true passion if what we see is its habit? The question is not answered but posed again in line 2. Can a mind perfectly seen also be "attir'd?" Is the perfection we are asked to admire the perfection of the mind or of the dress that adorns it and therefore stands between it and our line of vision? The ambiguity of "habit" reappears in "straines," which in addition to being an obvious reference to Breton's verse carries the secondary meaning of pedigree or lineage. Is the perfect strain a perfect verbal rendering, i.e., a representation, or it is a perfect progeny, the direct offspring of the truth and therefore a piece of the truth itself?

As one proceeds through the first stanza, these questions are not insistent, in part because the poem's syntax has not yet stablized. This syntactical hesitation is, as we shall see, typical of Jonson's poetry and allows him to keep alive options that will later converge in a single but complex sense. Thus, for example, it is unclear whether lines 3 and 4 are in apposition to "minde," and therefore descriptive of what the reader can expect to find, or in apposition to "Thou" (l. 1) and therefore descriptive of the reader who is required to do the finding. What is clear is that the description is negative, characterizing something or someone that does not show itself in modes or colors or even wit ("braines"). It is therefore with a particular sense of challenge that the second stanza issues its imperative "Look here!" Look where, one might ask, or at what, since we know that it cannot be at variegated surfaces or eye-catching fashions. The only instruction we receive is to look at "such perfections," but these perfections, whatever they are, have not been given any palpable or visible form; and almost as if to forestall a complaint that we have been assigned an insufficiently explicit task, Jonson delivers a pronouncement on those who find themselves unable to perform it: "If they seeme wry, to such as looke asquint, / The fault's not in the object, but their eyes."

It is at this point that the relationship between the object (so carefully unspecified) and the reader's eyes becomes the poem's focus and its real subject. In the third stanza the requirements for right vision are forthrightly presented in a simile that is as complicating as it is illuminating. Perspective is a device by which one produces in art the same visual effects as are produced without artifice in nature. It is the manipulation of surface in order to produce the illusion of depth; it is the practice of deception in order to disclose the real, and it therefore, as Ernest Gilman has observed, "bestows a double role" on the artist "as truth-teller and liar, and on the viewer as either ideal perceiver or dupe."[3] The paradox of perspective—its "cunning" is designed to neutralize the dificiencies of its own medium—is the paradox already hinted at in the doubleness of "habit," "straines," and "shewe": is what is shown a revelation or is it an interposition—a "mere shewe"—that puts true revelation at even a further remove? Does Breton's work give its reader a sight of "true passion" or does it stand between that sight and his deceived eye? Are the "perfections" that seemingly "rise to the life" (always the tainted claim of illusionistic art) the perfections only of appearance? Such questions are not answered but given a particularly pointed form by the simile's argument, which contrasts the distortion that attends a "laterall" or sideways view with the view of a spectator who is correctly positioned; but that position has itself been forced upon him by the laws of perspective and by the manipulative strategy of the artist who deploys them. From within those laws and that strategy, the observer's judgment may indeed be "true" (l. 11), but is it true to what really is or true only to the constructed reality imposed on him by artifice?

In imitation of Jonson, I have deliberately withheld the context (or perspective) in which these questions receive an answer, the context of the court masque, a perspectival form at whose center is the figure of the monarch, at once audience and subject. In the theatre presided over by Jonson and Inigo Jones, the king's chair occupies the only point in the hall from which the perspective is true. He is therefore

3. Ernest Gilman, *The Curious Perspective: Literary and Pictorial Wit in the Seventeenth Century* (New Haven, 1978), p. 33.

not only the chief observer; he is what is being observed both by the masquers who direct their actions at him and by the other spectators who must strive to see the presentation from his position if they are to "make a censure true." Moreover, since the masque is itself a celebration of the king's virtue, what he watches is himself; and insofar as his courtiers, in their efforts to align their visions with his, reproduce the relationship courtiers always have to a monarch, they are also at once the observers of an action and the performers of what they observe. One can no longer say then that the spectators are taken in or deceived by a contrived illusion, for they are themselves the cause of what they see, and in order to make a "censure true" they need only recognize themselves. There is no distance between them and a spectacle or representation of which they are the informing idea; the relationship between viewer and presentation is not one of subjection and control, but of identity; they are, in essence, the same, and because they are the same the court saw in the mask "not an imitation of itself, but its true self."[4]

It is here in the notion of an observer who is indistinguishable from and the cause of what he sees that the ethical and epistemological dilemmas of representation are resolved or at least bypassed, and it is that notion which informs the concluding lines of stanza 3; "So with this Authors Readers will it thrive." Of course this line bears a perfectly reasonable sense as the conclusion to the simile's argument: the readers of Breton's work will judge it correctly to the extent that their line of vision is direct rather than oblique; but in the context of the masque experience, to which the entire simile has reference, a truly direct vision is the consequence of having recognized oneself and therefore of having become the reader of one's own actions, having become, in short, an author-reader. The composite noun which appears exactly in the center of Jonson's line is an answer (plainly there for all who have the eyes to see) to all the questions the poem implicitly raises. Insofar as the problem of the poem has been to find a position from which a reader of Breton's work can correctly judge it ("make a censure true"), that problem is solved by the assumption of an author-reader; that is, of a reader whose mind is attired with the same perfections as the mind informing the book. Judgment for such a reader will not even be an issue, since the act of judging implies a distance or a gap that has already been bridged by the identity, the sameness, of the censuring mind and its object. In this felicitous epis-

4. Stephen Orgel and Roy Strong, *Inigo Jones: The Theatre of the Stuart Court* (London and Berkeley, 1973), 1:2.

temology, perception is not mediated or "asquint" because it is *self*-perception; there is no obstruction between the eye and its object because there is literally nothing (no thing) between them. The dilemma of representation—its inability to be transparent, to refrain from clothing or covering—is no longer felt because representation is bypassed in favor of the instantaneous recognition, in another and in the work of another, of what one already is.

To solve the poem's problem in this way, however, is only to make the poem itself a problem, along with Breton's work. What exactly is their status? If what the fit reader would see in Breton's work is already in his mind, while others simply "want facultie," what is there left for the work to do? What *could* it do? And insofar as these questions apply to Breton, so do they apply equally to Jonson, who is as much "this author" as anyone else, and is certainly *this* author in relation to *this* poem. Isn't its work as superfluous as the work it purports to praise? Isn't its reader, its author-reader, directed to look at something he already is? All of these questions are rendered urgent by the first word of the concluding couplet, "Which," a word that is itself a question: "Which"? To what does it refer? The only possible candidate in the third stanza is the "cunning piece wrought perspective" of line 10; but it can hardly be that which is to be "eyed directly," since the noun-phrase is part of a simile, of an indirect or lateral approach, and is therefore by definition at a remove from direct perception. No matter how far back one goes in the poem, a satisfactory referent for "which" will not be found; *which* is just the point. The pronoun that stands in for nothing present or available refers to the perfection the poem cannot name because any name or habit serves only to obscure it. "Which" is a sign within the poem of what it cannot do, and a sign also of what is required of its reader as well as of the reader of Breton's work, to eye directly, that is, without any intervening medium, to find in himself what no poem or habit can represent. A reader who can so "eye" will not take from the poem, but give to it the center that will always escape its representational grasp, and the true act of communication which then follows is described (but not captured) in the sonnet's amazing final line: "His proofe, their praise, will meete, as in this line."

"His proofe, their praise" completes the work of "Authors-Readers" by bonding the two agents together in a reciprocal and mutually defining relationship. His proof, in the sense of "that which makes good" his effort, is their praise; i.e., by praising him they give evidence of his work's merit; but that praise is also *their* proof; that is, by providing his proof, they prove themselves capable of recognizing his merit and thereby attest to its residence within themselves: "his proofe, *their* praise." But of course this immediately turns around to become once again the matter of his praise; by fashioning a book that calls for a praise that reflects on the praisers, Breton "proves out" in the sense of producing good results, and therefore earns still another round of praise; their proofe, *his* praise. This self-replenishing circuit of proof and praise, praise and proof is reflected in still another meaning of proof, "a coin or medal usually struck as the test of a die, one of a limited number" (*OED*). It is in this sense that Breton's work is a "master print," a die that strikes off coins in its own image, something that at once tests and is tested (attested) by the absolute sameness of its progeny; it is an object that confers value and has its value conferred on it by the activities of those it makes. Of course this is equally true of Jonson's poem, which is the progeny of Breton's work, a piece of praise that is both Jonson's and Breton's proof, and a die that potentially extends the circuit to those of its readers who can receive its stamp and so become pieces of producing (proving) currency in tbeir turn.

All of these meanings are concentrated in the problematic assertion that the meeting of proof and praise occurs *in this line*. The problem is that on one level, the level on which the poem finally never performs, nothing meets in this line. To be sure, the words "praise" and "proofe" meet, but they are not filled in or elaborated in any way that would validate the claim of the line to contain the essences for which they stand. But on another level, the level on which the poem acts out an anti-representational epistemology, the absence at the center of the line is what makes the assertion good, provides its proof; for the line in which "praise" and "proofe" meet is not the physical (external) line of print and paper but (1) the line of vision established by the instantaneous self-recognition of eyes similarly clear, eyes that communicate directly and without mediation, and (2) the genealogical line that is continually being extended whenever another author-reader is moved to write or praise (they are one and the same) and so give proof of his membership in the community of the clear-sighted. The members of that community eye directly because they have been "eyed" directly, that is, given eyes, by the inner vision that makes them one. They see the same perfection not because some external form compels them to recognize it, but because it *in*forms their perception so that it is impossible for them to see anything else. They see themselves; they see the same. In that sense they have "eyes divine" and they can even announce themselves, as Jonson does, with the indirection characteristic of this poem, as "I divine."

It is a remarkable little poem, but it is also, I think, altogether typical and points us to a recharacterization of Jonson's poetry in which some of the more familiar terms of description will be called into question. First of all, it will hardly do to label Jonson a poet of the plain style, if his poems continually proclaim their inability to describe or "catch" their objects. That inability is not only proclaimed; it is discoursed upon at length in the very poems that announce it. The poet durst not aim at the soul of Lady Jane Paulet because "it is too near of kin to heaven . . . to be described" (ll. 29–30). The mind of Lady Venetia Digby cannot be captured by the usual metaphors "The sun, a sea, or soundless pit" (*The Under-wood:* 84, iv, l. 11). These, Jonson explains, "are like a mind, not it" (l. 12). "No," he continues, "to express a mind to sense / Would ask a heaven's intelligence; / Since nothing can report that flame / But what's of kin to whence it came" (ll. 13–16). In some poems Jonson seems to claim just that status for his art, as when he declares in the "Epistle to Katherine, Lady Aubigny": "My mirror is more subtle, clear, refined, / And takes and gives the beauties of the mind" (ll. 43–44); but as it turns out, what he means is that his poem is a mirror in the sense of being blank, empty of positive assertions, filled with lists of what Lady Aubigny is not, of the companions she does not have, of the masks she does not wear, of the paths she does not take, of the spectacles and shows from which she turns. The poem does not so much occupy as clear its ground, so that when Jonson says of it that it is a glass in which Lady Aubigny can look and see herself (l. 29), his claim is true because there is nothing in it or on it—no account, no description, no representation—to prevent it from functioning as a reflecting surface. She will see nothing it it but her own "form," which she shall find "still the same" (l. 23).

Jonson's poems of praise (and this means most of his poems) are all like that: they present the praisee to herself or himself; they say in effect Sir or Madam So and So, meet Sir or Madam So and So, whom, of course, you already know. Once this is said the poem is for all intents and purposes over, although the result paradoxically is that it often has a great deal of difficulty getting started since it is, in effect, all dressed up with nowhere to go. Epigram 102 says as much in its first two lines: "I do but name thee Pembroke, and I find / It is an epigram on all mankind." Epigram 43, "To Robert, Earl of Salisbury," is even more explicit: "What need hast thou of me, or of my muse / Whose actions so themselves do celebrate?" In Epigram 76, the process is reversed; the poet spends some sixteen lines imagining a proper object of his praise only to dismiss in line 17 what he has written as something merely "feigned" before declaring in line 18,

"My Muse bade, *Bedford* write, and that was she."[5] Of course if he had hearkened to his muse in the beginning and had written the name Bedford, there would have been no need to write the poem, a crisis that is avoided by making that realization the poem's conclusion. Given an epistemology that renders it at once superfluous and presumptuous (it is "like a mind, not it"), a Jonson poem always has the problem of finding something to say, a problem that is solved characteristically when it becomes itself the subject of the poem, which is then enabled at once to have a mode of being (to get written) and to remain empty of representation.

Representation is the line of work that Jonson's poems are almost never in, except when their intention is to discredit; and indeed it is a discreditable fact about any object that it is available for representation, for that availability measures the degree to which it is not "kin to heaven" and therefore can be described. The clearest statement of this aesthetic of negative availability is Epigram 115, "On the Townes Honest Man"[6] who is not named because, as Jonson explains, "this is one / Suffers no name but a description" (ll. 3–4); that is, he is the exact opposite of those (like Pembroke and Lady Bedford) who can be named, but not described, because description can only "catch" surfaces and coverings, and is itself a covering. The point of course is that the town's honest man is all surface; he has no stable moral identity and therefore there is nothing *in* him to which a name could be consistently attached. He is a creature of momentary desires, whims, interests, and movements, and therefore his non-essence is perfectly captured by the ever changing surface and moment to moment adjustments of verse. The very incapacity of Jonson's poetry even to approach the objects of its praise makes it the perfect medium for the objects of its opprobrium. The chameleonlike actions of the town's honest man (usually thought to be Inigo Jones) are chronicled with a particularity and directness one never encounters in the poems addressed to Jonson's patrons and heroes.[7] When he says at the end of the poem "Described, its thus," he has earned the claim; and when he asks "Defined would you it have?" and answers, "*The townes honest*

5. On this and related points see Harris Friedberg's excellent essay, "Ben Jonson's Poetry: Pastoral, Georgic, Epigram," *English Literary Renaissance*, 4 (1974), 115–16.

6. Here I am again using William B. Hunter, Jr.'s text.

7. For the relationship between Jonson's anti-theatricality and his ideal of the "unmoved personality" see Jonas Barish, "Jonson and the Loathed Stage," in *A Celebration of Ben Jonson*, ed. William Blissett, Julian Patrick, and R. W. Van Fossen (Toronto and Buffalo, 1973), pp. 38, 45, 50. As Barish rightly observes, "worth, in the Jonsonian universe, as in that of his Stoic guides, is virtually defined as an inner and hence an invisible quality" (p. 45).

man's her errant'st knave" (ll. 34–35), the pun on "errant'st," at once greatest and most erring, tells us why a definition of the usual kind will not be forthcoming: by definition a definition fixes an essence, but if an entity is always in motion, is always erring, it has no center to be identified and it cannot be defined; it cannot receive a name.

What we have then in Jonson's aesthetic are two kinds of poetry: one that can take advantage of the full resources of language in all its representative power, although what it represents is evil, and another which must defeat and cancel out the power of representation, because the state it would celebrate is one of epistemological immediacy and ontological self-sufficiency; what one wants is not something "like," but "it," and therefore what one doesn't want is a poem. Depending on how it is read, the sixth stanza of *The Under-wood* 84, iv ("The Mind") is descriptive of both kinds of poetry:

> I call you muse, now make it true:
> Henceforth may every line be you;
> That all may say that see the frame,
> This is no picture, but the same.
> (ll. 21–24)

In a poem like Epigram 115, every line is you in quite a literal sense, since the "you" in question has not one identity, but the succession of identities that fill every line. Every line can also be a reference to the art of painting (the dismissal of which is the subject of *The Under-wood* 84, iv), and in that sense too every stroke of the artist's brush fully captures whatever momentary form the town's honest man has taken. Anyone who looks at this picture—that is, at this portrait of movement and instability—will see the same, that is, will see perfectly represented the endless self-fashioning that makes up the life of the "errant'st knave." The same stanza reads quite differently, however, when we relate it to the "mind" of Lady Digby, the drawing of which Jonson claims to be able to "perform alone" (l. 3), without the aid of the painter. That boast does not survive the third stanza and the realization (which I have already quoted) that "nothing can report that flame / But what's of kin to whence it came" (ll. 15–16). Of course that would be no report at all, since to report is to convey something to another, whereas in this transaction (if that is the word) what is of kin simply recognizes itself, recognizes, that is, the same. At this point the poem is running the familiar Jonsonian danger of asserting itself out of business, and, in what amounts to a rescue mission, the poet moves to save it by turning it over to its subject/object: "Sweet mind, then speak yourself" (l. 17). This injunction or invitation or plea can be read in several ways: (1) "Sweet mind, speak in place of me," a reading that preserves the poem's claim to communicate, although with a borrowed voice; or (2) "Sweet mind, speak yourself," in the tautological sense of declaring yourself as opposed to the mediating sense of speaking *about* yourself; which shades into (3) "Sweet mind, speak without mediation, without aid, without voice, without poem, but simply by being."

It is these latter two readings that finally rule, as the mind that is bid to "say" remains just out of reach of the verse and of the reader's apprehension. Indeed, the poem anticipates its own repeated failure when it asks to know "by what brave way / Our sense you do with knowledge fill / And yet remain our wonder still" (ll. 18–20). How can something that is the cause of all knowledge be itself unknown, remain presentationally silent, be our wonder *still* (always, unmoving, quiet)? The question is not answered, but given a succession of experiential lives as every attempt to make the mind speak, to give it a habit as it were, collapses under the weight of its own inadequacy. Richard Peterson describes these lines as "an evocatively tactile and mobile representation of Lady Digby's mind,"[8] but if anything is represented it is the failure and impiety of representation; and if the verse is mobile, it is because whenever it seeks to rest, it finds that its object has once again escaped. (Again compare "On the Townes Honest Man," where the escaping or dissolving of a non-object is what the poem accurately and repeatedly mimes.)

Our possession of that object is at its firmest (although most abstract) at line 55, where it is described as "polisht, perfect, round, and even," but even that hermetic and closed form is presented as a thing of the past that "slid moulded off from heaven" (l. 56). The sliding continues in the next stanza as the mind is embodied in a succession of forms that are always in the act of disintegrating, a cloud, oil (but as it pours forth), showers, drops of balm; in every case a substance that is passing into a state more rarefied than the one in which it is being "presented." In line 63 the verse toys with us by promising a moment in which the mind "stays," but it stays to become a "nest of odorous spice"; that is, it doesn't stay at all. Neither does it rest, despite the teasing appearance of that word at the beginning of line 65, where it is immediately glossed by the phrase "like spirits," and, moreover,

8. Richard S. Peterson, *Imitation and Praise in the Poems of Ben Jonson* (New Haven and London, 1981), p. 85. This fine study is the best general account we have of Jonson's poetry.

"like spirits left behind"; and even this fleeting image is itself left behind as it is expanded to include the alternatives of "bank or field of flowers," flowers which are said to be begotten by a "wind" (l. 67) that enters the poem as an image of the ever-receding mind: "In action, winged as the wind" (l. 64). (In the impossible but typically Jonsonian logic of the poem, the mind as wind begets itself.)

The mind finally comes to rest inside the person of Lady Digby, where it was before this self-extending and self-defeating search for representation began. "In thee . . . let it rest" (l. 68) is the poem's final admission of defeat; "it" will remain enclosed; it will not come out; it will not be brought out; it will not be represented. Instead it will remain in communion with itself, with what it possesses and informs. When Jonson says, "yet know with what thou art possesst" (l. 70), the circuit of knowledge has been narrowed to the space between Lady Digby and her mind, which is no space at all; there is literally no room for anything else because she entertains only ("but") such a mind. The exclusivity of this community is not breached but made more apparent by its final member, "God thy guest" ("But such a mind, mak'st God thy guest"), who is at once guest and host, possessor and possesst. The circle of this trinity closes out everything, and especially the poem, of which one can now truly say, "this is no picture, but the same." If every line is Lady Digby it is only because every line has emptied itself out in the impossible effort to capture her, leaving her and her guest and those of kin to whence they came in a state of perfect self-recognition, with nothing and no one (including the would-be observer-reader) between them.

To the extent that Lady Digby and her mind and God her guest constitute a social unit, a community, it may be necessary to rethink the sense in which Jonson can be called a poet of society; and since, in the standard accounts, the plain-style Jonson and the social Jonson are interdependent, it is not surprising that they would stand or fall together. As it has usually been presented (by Wesley Trimpi, for example), the plain style represents a deliberate attempt to eschew metaphysical and metaphorical flights of fancy in favor of a close and gritty fidelity to "what actually happens," to the facts of the everyday world;[9] and consequently the contours of that world and the experience of the individuals who inhabit it define the limits and the focus of the plain stylist's art.[10] In Jonson's art, however, the facts of the everyday world are given pride of place only in those poems that

9. Wesley Trimpi, *Ben Jonson's Poems: A Study of the Plain Style* (Stanford, 1962), p. 9.
10. Ibid., p. 41.

portray the debased and debasing activities of men and women infected by moral decay; whereas in those poems addressed to persons Jonson admires, that world is continually being shunned or avoided or sent away, and the focus of attention is on a set of values and relationships it does not contain. But that also means, as we have seen, that the poem cannot contain them either. That is, the appropriateness of the plain style to one kind of society makes it entirely *in*appropriate to the society that finally interests Jonson, a society made of beings whose virtue is inaccessible to representation by the plain or any other style, and whose ties are anything but the false ties of preferment, patronage, flattery, and economic gain. As Jonson puts it in "An Epistle to Master Arthur Squib" (*Underwood:* 45), "Those are poor ties, depend on those false ends. / 'Tis vertue alone, or nothing that knits friends" (ll. 11–12). In fact, in Jonson's vision it is virtue alone and therefore no thing, no thing one could point to, that knits friends; so that the community of friendship can no more be described than can the interior worth of its members.

Like the mind of Lady Digby or the perfection of true passion, the virtuous community has a negative relationship to the terms which one might think characterize it. It has no dimension in space, no geographical or actual boundaries. It is marked by no relationships of hierarchy or rank or dependence. Particular identities, locations, times and places have nothing to do with it and indeed are what it is defined against (although that definition can never take any palpable form); and that is why despite the signs of specificity—names, titles, estates, occupations, dates—that fill Jonson's poetry, everyone in it is interchangeable. The only true relationship between members of a Jonson community is one of identity, and no matter how many persons seem to crowd into a poem, the effect of the argument is always to reduce them to one, to the same. The first five lines of Epigram 91, "To Sir Horace Vere," is almost a parody of the technique:

> Which of thy names I take, not only bears
>   A Roman sound, but Roman virtue wears:
> Illustrious Vere, or Horace, fit to be
>   Sung by a Horace, or a muse as free;
> Which thou art to thyself . . .
>
> (ll. 1–5)

Here the community is formed by dividing its one member into two, and then declaring (in a declaration that would hardly have seemed necessary before the poem began) that the two are the same. When the newly reunited Horace Vere is declared fit to be sung by another Horace or even by a muse of different name but like spirit ("as free"), it would seem that the population of the community is expanding; but it immediately contracts when the "muse as free" is identified (a telling word) as "thou thyself," and the absolute closedness and self-sufficiency of the community is reconfirmed. One is hardly surprised to find that the rest of the poem is concerned with what Jonson, as now superfluous muse, will *not* do. "I leave thy acts," he says, explaining that if he were to "prosecute" in detail Vere's every accomplishment, he would seem guilty of flattery; and if he were to celebrate some and omit others he would seem guilty of envy. It is a nice rationale for furthering the project of this poem, which is to get written and yet say nothing at all. Jonson *does* announce that he will say something about Vere's "Humanitie" and "Pietie," but he says only that they are "rare" (l. 16) and "lesse mark'd" (l. 14), which they certainly are in this poem if by "mark'd" one means set down or described. The poem ends without having taken one step from the circle formed by the two names (really one) in its title, "To Sir Horace Vere."

In an influential essay, Thomas Greene calls our attention to the prominence in Jonson's poetry of the notion of the "gathered self" which is always to itself "the same" (Epigram 98, l. 10), a self whose ends and beginnings "perfect in a circle alwayes meet" (Epigram 138, l. 8), a self which presents such a closed face to the world that it is invulnerable to invasion and remains always "untouch'd," a self which may appear to travel and undergo changes in location and situation, but in fact never moves at all. What I am suggesting is that as objects and as discourses Jonson's poems are themselves gathered and closed in exactly these ways: rather than embracing society they repel it; rather than presenting a positive ethos in a plain style, they labor to present nothing at all and to remain entirely opaque. Greene asserts that "the concept of an inner moral equilibrium . . . informs . . . Jonson's verse";[11] but it would be more accurate to say that the concept of an inner moral equilibrium escapes Jonson's verse, which is always citing the concept as its cause, but never quite managing to display or define it. It remains "inner" in a stronger sense than Greene's argument suggests; it remains *locked* in, forever inaccessible to any public inspection or validation. In its determination never to reveal what moves it, Jonson's poetry repeatedly enacts the teasing career of the

11. Thomas Greene, "Ben Jonson and the Centered Self," *Studies in English Literature, 1500–1900,* 10 (1970), 329.

brave infant of Saguntum, always only "half got out" before it hastily returns and makes of itself its own urn, so that we are left to say of it "How summed a circle didst thou leave mankind / Of deepest lore, could we the centre find" (*The Under-wood:* 70, ll. 9–10).

Of course as an account of a poetic project, this raises more questions than it answers, How does one justify a poetry that refuses to describe, is militantly anti-social, and deliberately excludes its readers from a secret of which it will give only tantalizing and fleeting glimpses? How does one justify a poetry that is committed to not asserting, to not communicating, to not being about anything? Curiously enough, the answer lies right on the surface of the question. A poetry that so withholds itself and closes its face to anything outside its circle puts pressure on those who read it to demonstrate, in the very act of reading, that they are already in. Rather than acting as a challenge or as an exhortation to virtuous activity, these poems provide their intended readers (who are also their addressees) with an occasion for recognizing that whatever informs these poems (and it is never, can never, be specified) informs them too. Although the poems restrict access to the community, at the same time and in the same action they *generate* the community by providing a means of identifying its members, both to themselves and to each other.

That identification of course cannot be explicit. The very nature of the community requires that its "marks" not be visible, and the marks that *are* visible—the marks of position, title, wealth, and public achievement—are invoked only so that they can be dismissed as false indicators of a virtue the poetry celebrates by concealing. The result, as we have seen, is a verse that is at once social and anti-social. It is anti-social because the network of political and economic relationships that provides so much of the detail in a Jonson poem and *seems* to constitute its sociality is in fact the network that the knowing reader must shun, recognizing it as not only irrelevant but inimical to the values he is asked to affirm. And it is social because the affirmation, if it is made, earns the affirmer a place in a fellowship so intimate that there are finally no boundaries between its members, all of whom are, with respect to the essence of their fellowship, the same.

"Intimate fellowship" is precisely what Jonson is declared to be incapable of in Edmund Wilson's characterization of him as an anal erotic who holds himself aloof from the world and fortifies himself with "stored-away knowledge."[12] Wilson goes on to link Jonson's defi-

12. Edmund Wilson, "Morose Ben Jonson," in *The Triple Thinkers: Ten Essays on Literature* (New York, 1938), pp. 220, 219. In an attempt to defend Jonson against

ciencies of personality to his "difficulties as an artist," and he sees those difficulties reflected in characteristic artistic failures, in the absence of development or of "any sense of movement," in the lack of variety despite the appearance of multiplicity, in a tendency everywhere to reproduce his own personality ("Jonson merely splits himself up"), in a disastrous restriction of range and sympathy that contrasts so markedly with the expansiveness of Shakespeare. What I have attempted here is a reading in which observations very much like Wilson's lead to a different conclusion and to an account not of Jonson's "glaring defects"[13] but of the strategy by which he offers an art of determined reticence and self-sufficiency as a means of communion.

Wilson's charges, Jonson's admirers have in large part succeeded only in producing the poet of smooth urbanity that appears in most of our accounts. For an exception, see the stimulating essay by Arthur Marotti, "All About Jonson's Poetry," *ELH*, 39 (1972), 208–237.

13. Wilson, pp. 215–16.

Annabel Patterson

Lyric and Society in Jonson's *Under-wood*

In his 1601 comedy, *The Poetaster,* Ben Jonson dramatized a successful relationship between poetry and the State, with Jonson himself as the Roman poet Horace, saved from his detractors and established in the good will and protection of Augustus. Yet that play on its first appearance caused so much scandal, on account of its thinly veiled insults to contemporary writers,[1] that Jonson appended an "Apologetical Dialogue." Here he appeared again, not as Horace, but simply as "Author," to discuss the problems of a writer's relation to society. At the end of this striking act of defamiliarization, the author exits, promising to write in future only for an audience of one, "so he judicious be." "Leave me," he says:

> . . . There's something come into my thought,
> That must, and shall be sung, high, and aloofe,
> Safe from the wolves black jaw, and the dull asses hoofe.[2]

These lines project a move from comedy to tragedy, and in fact predicted *Sejanus,* a play that enacts a totally destructive relationship between the intellectual and the state. The difference between Augustus and Tiberius, imperial patronage and imperial repression, is

1. The chief victims were Philip Marston and Thomas Dekker. See Ben Jonson, *Works,* ed. C. H. Herford and Percy and Evelyn Simpson (Oxford, 1925–52), 1:432–37; 9:533–35; Roscoe A. Small, *The Stage-Quarrel between Ben Jonson & the So-Called Poetasters* (Breslau, 1899), pp. 25–28, 62–132.

2. Jonson, *Works,* 4:324.

partly to be explained by a shift in Jonson's public attitude to Elizabeth made possible by her death, and a desire to warn her successor of the cultural disadvantages of a repressive regime.[3] Jonson's own experience of censorship in the case of *The Poetaster* may have helped to shape *Sejanus;* for the "Apologetical Dialogue," "only once spoken upon the stage," was itself "suppressed by authority."[4] Conversely, this historical fact helps us to interpret those striking metaphors at the end of the dialogue. The intellectual space, "high and aloofe," in which the writer seeks voluntary isolation is delimited for him by two hostile forces; on the one hand, "the dull asses hoofe," philistinism, the uneducated audiences that preferred Shakespeare's plays to his own; on the other hand, the "wolves black jaw," political power as intimidation.

These lines reappear in a new and significantly altered context in a poem in Jonson's *The Under-wood.* "An Ode: To Himselfe" is inarguably lyric in form and by virtue of the traditions it invokes:

Where do'st thou carelesse lie,
Buried in ease and sloth?
Knowledge, that sleepes, doth die;
And this Securitie,
It is the common Moath,
That eats on wits, and Arts, and (oft) destroyes them both.

Are all th'*Aonian* Springs
Dri'd up? lyes *Thespia* wast?
Doth Clarius Harp want strings,
That not a Nymph now sings?
Or droop they as disgrac't,
To see their Seats and Bowers by chattring Pies defac't?

If hence thy silence be,
As 'tis too just a cause;
Let this thought quicken thee,
Minds that are great and free,
Should not on fortune pause,
'Tis crowne enough to vertue still, her owne applause.

3. See ibid., 1:36–37; Jonson, *Sejanus,* ed. Jonas Barish (New Haven, 1965), pp. 16–17; and Annabel Patterson, "'Romane-cast similitude': Ben Jonson and the English Use of Roman History," in *Rome in the Renaissance: The City and the Myth,* ed. P. A. Ramsey (Binghamton, N.Y., 1982), pp. 381–94.

4. According to the 1616 Folio; Jonson, *Works,* 4:193.

What though the greedie Frie
  Be taken with false Baytes
Of worded Balladrie,
And thinke it Poësie?
  They die with their conceits,
And only pitious scorne, upon their folly waites.

Then take in hand thy Lyre,
  Strike in thy proper straine,
With *Japhets* lyne, aspire
Sols Chariot for new fire,
  To give the world againe:
Who aided him, with thee, the issue of Joves braine.

And since our Daintie age,
  Cannot indure reproofe,
Make not thy selfe a Page,
To that strumpet the Stage,
  But sing high and aloofe,
Safe from the wolves black jaw, and the dull Asses hoofe.[5]

The theme of this poem, like that of the "Apologetical Dialogue," is the author's isolation from his culture, his "silence" in a society overrun by cheap versifiers, poetasters, fashionable hacks; and, as at the conclusion of *The Poetaster,* continued articulateness will depend on a successful shift into a different genre. "Then take in hand thy Lyre," Jonson encourages himself, choosing the most lyric of instruments. The genre of elitist communication is narrowed from comedy, through tragedy, to lyric. The address to a "judicious audience" of one is now an address to himself. Yet, for all its claims to transcendence, the personal space is still defined by default, in response to an apparently frustrate public life; the self is generated conceptually out of loss of self-esteem. The poem's resolution is still governed by the black teeth of fear and the dull thud of humiliation. Marked and shocked, the self gathers itself together, and declares itself an autonomous state.

We ask what has happened to the lyric since what was once called the New Criticism was replaced as the ruling methodology in our discipline; but the question's unanswerability serves mainly to reveal a lacuna in the still newer criticisms, which have not, it seems, been able

5. Jonson, *Works,* 8:174–75.

to disturb the premises of the preceding dynasty with respect to lyric, or even to improve on its work. "Lyric" remains a name for an ill-assorted collection of short(er) poems; but the genre continues to be defined normatively, in ways that exclude dozens of poems that their authors once thought of as lyric. The reason for this is clear. The modernist view of lyric as an intense, imaginative form of self-expression or self-consciousness, the most private of all genres, is, of course, a belief derived from Romanticism. As a belief, it is inevitably inhospitable to poems like Jonson's, which derive from a classical tradition, inchoate but powerful, that sanctioned lyric with a social or political content. Theodor Adorno, lecturing in 1957 ("Lyrik und Gesellschaft"), found that his thesis (to which we shall return) depended on the exclusion of lyric in the classical tradition: "The great poets of the more distant past who might be counted as lyric poets according to literary historical concepts of lyric poetry, Pindar and Alcaeus, for example, . . . are very distant indeed from our primary idea of lyric poetry."[6] To add to the problem, the modernist theory of lyric, with its emphasis on subjectivity, seems to run directly counter to its exegetical methods. The records of self-expression are to be treated as isolated "texts," decontaminated, as far as the critic can manage it, from any author's actual experience or concerns.

The newer criticisms—structuralist, deconstructive, Marxist—have, it seems to me, done little to resolve this modernist impasse. "Intertextuality" may show how lyric poems inform each other; but it does not compare for interpretive rigor with the older concept of a poet's career, as the first context with which any interpretation must engage. A theory of "utterance" may restore vigor to rhetorical tropes like invocation and apostrophe; but it leaves unbridged the gap between writer and poem, between strategies of self-presentation and our secret, guilty knowledge that every lyric voice had an original owner. To speak of "modes of production" will not, either, link the premise of self-expression with its textual product, not, at least, until the general thesis that all literature has a socio-political dynamic can encompass, with historical specificity, the problem of individual motivation. The task of this essay is, therefore, to investigate the connection between history (in the narrowed sense of a series of public events), personal motivation, and lyric theory and practice in Ben

6. Theodor Adorno, "Rede über Lyrik und Gesellschaft," *Akzente*, 4 (1957), 8–26; reprinted in *Noten zur Literatur*, 3 vols. (Frankfurt, 1958–61), 1:79–80. "Die grossen Dichter der früheren Vergangenheit, die nach literargeschichtlichen Begriffen der Lyrik zurechnen, Pindar etwa und Alkaios, . . . sind unserer primären Vorstellung von Lyrik ungemein fern." (Translation by Margaret E. Kennington.)

Jonson's *The Under-wood.* This collection of poems, which Jonson would himself have classified as lyric,[7] was published posthumously in 1640. It was, however, almost certainly arranged by him late in life with intent to publish, not least because it was prefaced by a note "To the Reader" explaining the title and the relationship of "these lesser Poems, of later growth" to his 1616 anthology, *The Forrest.*[8]

My reasons for selecting Jonson as a test case include the fact that his lyrics, and especially those of *The Under-wood,* never achieved any status in the New Criticism, and hence have been largely excluded from the modernist lyric canon. Whereas Andrew Marvell's "Horatian Ode upon Cromwell's Return from Ireland" notably passed the tests for irony and ambiguity,[9] Jonson's "Speach according to Horace," for example, excited no modernist interest at all. Yet the two poems clearly shared the same neoclassical assumptions about why one would choose Horace as a lyric model, a model in which socio-political commentary was taken for granted.[10] Secondly, it is precisely the public content or occasion of many of Jonson's lyrics, as well as his obvious concern with social status, that offer both encouragement and challenge to recent developments in Marxist literary criticism, which have not yet, in my view, developed a sufficiently elastic view of how history affects poetry, especially in the seventeenth century. But thirdly, and most important, Jonson's lyrics are peculiarly accessible to a blend of textualist and contextualist approaches, peculiarly suggestive of a new theoretical bridge that might be built between history and the subjective. On the one hand, Jonson wrote poems, like the "Ode: To Himselfe," that

7. The confused tradition of lyric that Jonson inherited made categorization very difficult. In *Timber: or, Discoveries* Jonson in one breath made poetry and lyric coextensive under the sign "carmina," and in the next listed as separate genres "an Epick, Dramatick, Lyricke, Elegiake, or Epigrammatike Poeme" (*Works,* 8:635). Within *Underwood* poems are designated as songs, elegies, odes, epigrams, epistles, sonnets, even an "execration" and a "fit"; yet if challenged, Jonson probably would have reverted to the broader definition of lyric as poetry or song.

8. Jonson, *Works,* 8:126: "With the same leave, the Ancients call'd that kind of body *Sylva, or* ὕλη, in which there were workes of divers nature, and matter congested, as the multitude call Timber-trees, promiscuously growing, a *Wood,* or *Forrest:* So am I bold to entitle these lesser Poems, of later growth, by this of *Under-wood,* out of the Analogie they hold to the *Forrest,* in my former booke, and no otherwise." Although this self-deprecatory statement may have helped to obscure *The Under-wood* from subsequent critical attention, there are reasons, as we shall see, not to take it at face value.

9. Compare the famous dispute between Cleanth Brooks and Douglas Bush as to New Criticism's rights to the *Ode.* Brooks, "Criticism and Literary History: Marvell's 'Horatian Ode,'" *Sewanee Review,* 55 (1947), 199–222; Bush, "Marvell's 'Horatian Ode,'" *Sewanee Review,* 60 (1952), 362–76; Brooks, "A Note on the Limits of 'History' and the Limits of 'Criticism,'" *Sewanee Review,* 60 (1953), 129–35.

10. See Henry Steele Commager, *The Odes of Horace* (New Haven and London, 1962).

discover a personal identity not merely in defiance of but as a *consequence* of external pressures; on the other, he made even the collecting and organizing of his public poems into a lyric act. In *The Under-wood,* poems written for past occasions were selected and arranged in roughly chronological order. In the process, new relationships developed between them, new meanings emerged in the light of his own later knowledge (and ours). The effect is a retrospective of his career, a retelling of his relations with the state, the stage, friends, patrons, politicians. Inserted between the occasional poems are those intermittent assertions of autonomy, statements of intellectual freedom from all relations. And Jonson's self is also present, as it were, in the ordering, in the meditative spaces *between* the poems, where things can be implied that could not be expressed openly. Lyricism in *The Under-wood,* then, is always a socio-political construct, a product of its relations; especially in its declarations of independence, and especially in its silences.

Let us consider some of the poems Jonson wrote for great men of the Jacobean state. One of the finest of these immediately follows, in *The Under-wood,* Jonson's "Ode: To Himselfe," and is there entitled "The Mind of the Frontispice to a Booke." The enigmatic title, however, would conceal from no one the fact that Jonson had written this poem to accompany Sir Walter Raleigh's *History of the World* into the public in 1614, and that the poem not only explicates Raleigh's emblematic engraved frontispiece, but comments in somber language on a world view peculiarly appropriate to Raleigh's situation. In 1614, Raleigh was in prison, a hostage to James I's negotiations with Spain. The *History* was published anonymously and banned by James a few months after its appearance. Jonson's poem was discreetly unsigned; but its message was simultaneously ambiguous and obvious:

From Death, and darke Oblivion, (neere the same)
The Mistresse of Mans life, grave Historie,
Raising the world to good, or Evill fame,
Doth vindicate it to Æternitie.
High Providence would so; that nor the good
Might be defrauded, nor the Great secur'd,
But both might know their wayes are understood,
And the reward, and punishment assur'd.
(ll. 1–8)[11]

11. For the original text of the poem and the circumstances of the *History*'s publication, see Margaret Corbett and Ronald Lightbown, *The Comely Frontispiece: The Emblematic Title-Page in England, 1550–1660* (London, 1979), pp. 128–35.

The role of history, the poem states in its opening lines, is in "raising" men from those twin dangers, death and other men's forgetfulness; a proposition conventional enough, and confirmed by the classicism of the last two lines, which translate Cicero's *De Oratore* (II.36). History is "Times witnesse, herald of Antiquitie, / The light of Truth, and life of Memorie." Yet the stress on the *need* for vindication and the startling distinction between the "good" and the "Great" suggest a context in which justice is not normally done, nor rewards and punishments fairly allocated. When Jonson saved the poem for *The Under-wood* he altered the eighth line to read, with discreet flaccidity, "When Vice alike in time with vertue dur'd." But to retain the poem in his collection was to claim it as his own, an act less discreet than defiant. In 1618 James had succumbed to pressure from the Spanish ambassador Gondomar, and Raleigh was executed for treason. *After* 1618, then, the poem becomes even darker, its emotional power recharged by history. Death has the last word, as well as the first; and with the author of the *History of the World* "defrauded" of his just fame, it was left to Jonson's poem to privatize the historian's role, to vindicate, as it were, in whispers.

In the third line of the Raleigh epitaph (for that is what the poem became) Jonson used the word "Raising," a term of special significance for him in the world of Jacobean politics. The word reappears at the end of his complimentary poem on Sir Francis Bacon's sixtieth birthday. Celebrating at the same time Bacon's new title of Viscount St. Albans, Jonson invoked the expansive tone of ceremonial lyric:

> 'Tis a brave cause of joy, let it be knowne,
> For't were a narrow gladnesse, *kept thine owne.*
> Give me a deep-crown'd Bowle, that I may sing
> In *Raysing* him the wisdome of my King.
> (p. 225, ll. 16–20; italics added)

Although in its original context the poem's good will must have been transparent, its cheerfulness depends on an optimistic reading of the ways and means of success under James I; but if in the spring of 1621 Jonson had felt he might safely "sing / In raysing him the wisdome of my King," what must he have felt when he copied the poem into his personal collection after Bacon's impeachment? By what wisdom, the *Under-wood* setting must inquire, was Bacon sacrificed later in that very same year, 1621, to the struggle between King and Parliament? Similar conditions control the meaning, the *feeling*, of "An Epigram on Sir Edward Coke, when he was Lord Chiefe Justice of England," the retrospective enforced by the title and the opening lines:

> He that should search all Glories of the Gowne,
> And steps of all rais'd servants of the Crowne,
> He could not find, then thee, of all that store
> Whom Fortune aided lesse, or Vertue more.
> Such, Coke, *were thy beginnings . . .*
> (p. 217; ll. 1–5; italics added)

Again, that word "rais'd" offers a historical perspective on the Jacobean *arrivistes,* among whom, of course, Jonson would have to count himself.[12] In retrospect, the connection with the poem on Bacon is more than textual, since Coke had played a major role in Bacon's impeachment; while Jonson's praise of Coke's "manly Eloquence . . . thy Nations fame, her Crownes defence" must have felt differently to him after 1628, when Coke's leadership of the rebellious House of Commons had wrested from Charles the Petition of Right. These poems interrogate each other. The story told by and between them is the old story of fortune's slippery wheel, updated to fit the new social mobility of the seventeenth century, but no less dangerous to the individual than it used to be.

This point is made explicitly, and in decisively lyric form, by a striking disturbance of the volume's implied chronology. Immediately after his poem on Raleigh's *History,* Jonson inserted into the *Under-wood* a Pindaric ode to James Fitzgerald, Earl of Desmond, "Writ," as its title proclaims, "in Queene Elizabeths Time, since lost, and recovered" (p. 176). The poem is far less well known than the wonderful Pindaric ode on Carey and Morison, but it is no less interesting for its discovery of a Pindaric subject to match the form. Jonson calls on Invention to

> Wake, and put on the wings of *Pindar*'s Muse,
> To towre with my intention
> High, as his mind, that doth advance
> Her upright head, above the reach of Chance,
> Or the times envie:
> *Cynthius,* I applie

12. Jonson's career as a court poet only fully developed, under James, with the production of the *Masque of Blackness* in 1605.

My bolder numbers to thy golden *Lyre:*
O, then inspire
Thy Priest in this strange rapture; heat my braine
With *Delphick* fire:
That I may sing my thoughts, in some unvulgar straine.

Fitzgerald was a notable victim of Elizabethan politics. His father had been executed for treason in 1583. He himself had been sent to Ireland, and kept a prisoner in Dublin Castle from 1579 to 1584. He was then transferred to the Tower of London, where he remained until 1600. To Jonson, he was *therefore* a Stoic hero, his integrity created by default, the elevation of his mind produced by the injustice he had suffered for the sins of the fathers:

Nor think your selfe unfortunate,
If subject to the jealous errors
Of politique pretext, that wryes a State,
Sinke not beneath these terrors:
But whisper, O glad Innocence,
Where only a mans birth is his offence.

But Jonson has his own "politique pretext" or subtext here. The role of lyric is doubly to enlarge the prisoner, to make accessible those stoic qualities of patience and loyalty that will produce his release from the Tower:

Then shall my Verses, like strong Charmes
Breake the knit Circle of her stonie Armes,
That holds your spirit
And keepes your merit
Lock't in her cold embraces, from the view
Of eyes more true,

and the poet predicts forgiveness by Elizabeth, that other imprisoning female.

. . . I auspitiously divine
(As my hope tells) that our fair Phoebe's shine,
Shall light those places
With lustrous Graces,
Where darknesse with her gloomie-sceptred hand,
Doth now command;

The last lines, however, carry the ode's original message:

O then (my-best-best lov'd) let me importune,
That you will stand
As farre from all revolt, as you are now from Fortune.

Let us suppose the poem was written in the late 1590s, perhaps even as Fitzgerald's release in 1600 was being spoken of as imminent. It would then bear comparison with *Cynthia's Revels,* a play for which Jonson clearly assumed Elizabeth as his primary auditor, and in which he interceded obliquely for the Earl of Essex.[13] It is conceivable that the ode, too, was intended to have a double audience, the queen and her political prisoner. Paul Fry, in *The Poet's Calling in the English Ode,* has suggested that Jonson's poem was deliberately enigmatic, both in its syntax and in its overlapping of female forces, some positive, some negative. The prisoner's mind, the Tower, darkness and "our fair Phoebe" (Elizabeth) share a mysterious territory, the Pindaric, in which obscurity and difficult transitions were taken for granted; and Fry's conclusion, though hesitantly advanced, is that the ode is "a code of sorts, a political riddle . . . a seditious coterie poem that resorts to the indirectness of Pindar to mystify prying readers."[14] This fertile notion needs, I believe, more careful exposition. In the 1590s the poem, even to Elizabeth, would have read no more seditiously than *Cynthia's Revels.* The ode, while allowing the possibility of confusion between her reign and the "gloomie-sceptred hand" of darkness, ultimately celebrates her clemency and insists on the loyalty of even those whose punishment she authorized; but when Jonson "recovered" this poem for *The Under-wood* and placed it immediately after the poem on Raleigh's *History,* which in turn followed the "Ode: To Himselfe," its darker side, its potential for alienation, was foregrounded. The Pindaric voice, singing "high and aloofe," aligns itself only with other victims of "the wolves black jaw"; and lines initially addressed to another now speak, in the half-light of *The Under-wood,* to the poet himself:

Nor think your selfe unfortunate,
If subject to the jealous errors
Of politique pretext, that wryes a State,
Sinke not beneath these terrors:
But *whisper* . . .

13. *Cynthia's Revels,* produced in 1601, contains an apparent defense of Essex at V.xi.ll.9 ff.

14. Paul Fry, *The Poet's Calling in the English Ode* (New Haven and London, 1980), p. 29.

A poetic form normally, traditionally, used to legitimate the power structure is deployed first enigmatically, to call its decisions in question, and ultimately, with historical hindsight, becomes subversion.

At this point it should become clear that I am using the language of a certain type of Marxist criticism, though not precisely in the orthodox way. Specifically, Fredric Jameson's suggestion, in *The Political Unconscious,* that all literature has either a legitimating or a subversive function is one of enormous potential for seventeenth-century studies.[15] Yet Jameson, for all his poststructural sophistication, still appears constricted by a too rigid notion of class warfare. Any account of ideology in literature that assumes a sharp divide between ruling class and opposition, between writers who legitimate and writers who subvert, any such system as Jameson seems to promote,[16] will fail to deal with Jonson. To account at all for Jonson, and especially for his lyrics, we need to be able to think in both psychological and sociopolitical terms, while avoiding either psychoanalytic or Marxist excess. We need to be able to understand Jonson as a mass of contradictions: reluctant stepson of a bricklayer, always uncertain of his social status, arriviste, allured by power and privilege yet hypercritical of it; court poet, propagandist, and pensioner, yet with an unbroken record of being in trouble with the authorities. His sympathetic identification with Fitzgerald, both originally and when he "recovered" the ode in the 1630s, makes sense only if we recover the record of Jonson's own experience of repression:

> Imprisoned for his share in *The Isle of Dogs,* 1597; cited before Lord Chief Justice Popham for *Poetaster,* 1601; summoned before the Privy Council . . . for *Sejanus,* 1603; imprisoned for his share in *Eastward Ho,* 1605; "accused" for *The Devil is an Ass,* 1616; examined by the Privy Council for alleged verses of his on Buckingham's death, 1628; and cited before the Court of High Commission for *The Magnetic Lady,* 1632.[17]

15. Fredric Jameson, *The Political Unconscious* (Ithaca, 1981), p. 84: "a ruling class ideology will explore various strategies of the *legitimation* of its own power position, while an oppositional culture or ideology will, often in covert and disguised strategies, seek to contest and to undermine the dominant 'value system.'"

16. I am aware that this is only one, rather extreme, statement of a more complex argument; but it seems fair to argue that for Jameson the principle of class dualism has to be preserved at all costs. Thus the explosive sectarianism of the 1640s, for example, is described in *The Political Unconscious* as what happens when "two opposing discourses fight it out within the general unity of a shared code . . . the shared master code of religion" (p. 84).

17. Jonson, *Works,* 11:253.

Although Jonson complained frequently of being misunderstood or, to cite the Fitzgerald ode, of "the jealous errors / of politique pretext," the evidence of *The Under-wood,* that undercover story of his career, suggests that the authorities had some reason to be suspicious. In one of his epigrams to an unidentified bishop (probably John Williams, Bishop of Lincoln), who is complimented for having been *removed* from court office, Jonson had defined the court as a place where "scarce you heare a publike voyce alive, / But *whisper'd Counsells,* and those only thrive" (p. 234; italics added). It is tempting to see *The Under-wood* as a medium devised to repair the failure of the public voice in Jonson's time; a medium of covert self-expression during the poet's life, but one to be preserved, for history's sake, and published only when he deemed it safe.

But there is, as I have said, another voice in *The Under-wood* poems, one that claims to eschew the public voice, whether legitimating or undermining, a voice that asserts an ideal of poetic and intellectual autonomy. This voice is particularly strong in the "Epistle Answering to One That Asked to Be Sealed of the Tribe of Ben" (pp. 218–20), which is, obviously, all about self-hood, or Ben-hood. The poem follows immediately the epigram on Coke, begins by echoing the ethos of the Fitzgerald ode: "Men that are safe, and sure, in all they doe, / Care not what trials they are put unto," and ends with an echo of classical Stoicism:

> Well, with mine own fraile Pitcher, what to doe
> I have decreed; keep it from waves, and presse;
> Lest it be justled, crack'd, made nought, or lesse:
> Live to that point I will, for which I am man,
> And dwell as in my Center, as I can.

But the center of the poem denies, or pretends to deny, that Ben, the holder of these virtues, is a man of his time. He does not belong to "the Covey of Witts" that "censure all the Towne," "vent their Libels," and exchange political rumors. He has no interest in the German wars or the Spanish marriage question. He does not care that he has not been asked to participate, with Inigo Jones, in the "late Mysterie of reception," the artistic plans for receiving Charles's intended bride, the spanish Infanta. He is neither satirist nor satellite of the court. A likely story!

In fact, the poem undermines itself. We do not need to turn back to the earlier "Epistle to a friend, to Persuade Him to the Warres" to discount Ben's claims to neutrality. The old conviction that had taken him to war in the Netherlands under Elizabeth resurfaces here, albeit conditionally:

> But if, for honour, we must draw the Sword,
> . . . .
> I have a body, yet, that spirit drawes
> To live, or fall a Carkasse in the cause.

And the claim to social disinterestedness cannot survive the rancor of Jonson's gibe at "the animated Porc'lane of the Court," a phrase that reveals his envy of Inigo Jones as fast as he denies it. How could this not be conscious strategy? This must be as complex a definition of self, and hence of the lyric, as the post-modernist mind could wish; the self—deliberately revealed as committed to and complicit in society, and only *therefore* conscious of autonomy.

Such penetration, so knowing a blend of self- and societal consciousness, is not unique in the seventeenth century, though it is more often found in prose—the autobiographical passages of Milton's prose, Pepys's diary, the familiar letters of Donne and Marvell. Jonson's "Epistle Answering" hovers, of course, on the generic threshold between lyric and the familiar letter, though it is closer to the core of his lyricism than are most of his verse epistles. This leaves us in danger of seeing here only an eccentric or unilateral experiment in genre, of no generalizability and hence of no real consequence. Partially to avoid that, let us, in conclusion, test against Jonson two other explanatory models, each of which might place his work in a larger theoretical framework. Each, like Jameson's *Political Unconscious,* assumes that literature has, inevitably, a socio-political dimension, though each considerably predates Jameson's poststructuralist perspective.

Theodor Adorno's "Lyrik und Gesellschaft" has already been mentioned. Given originally as a radio lecture in 1957, at the height of New Criticism's reign, the essay takes as a premise that lyric and society are not already linked in the mind of its audience. On the contrary, Adorno addressed what he took to be a general desire to keep lyric pure, "free from objective weight, able to conjure up a life which is unencumbered by the compulsion of prevailing practise, of utilitarianism, of the pressure of stubborn self-preservation"; and he attempted to counter it by explaining that this demand is itself societal. "It implies the protest against a social condition which every individual experiences as inimical, alien, cold and oppressive."[18] Soci-

18. Adorno, pp. 77–78. "Ihr Affekt hält daran fest, dass es so bleiben soll, dass der

ety then becomes the true, original lyricist, inscribing in the individual the protest necessary to produce the subjective, isolated voice.

At first hearing this may sound remarkably descriptive of Jonson's *Under-wood* lyricism. Yet Adorno's position emerges in a way that must finally exclude Jonson, as, in the passage quoted earlier, it excluded classical lyric. The true societal dimension of a text, for Adorno, is not to be confused with "the level of social concern of the work, and especially not that of its author."[19] And, most revealing of all:

> The historical relationship of subject to object, of the individual to society, must have found its precipitate in the medium of the subjective, self-reflecting spirit. It will be the more perfect, the less the structure has treated the I-society relationship as a theme, the more *spontaneously* it crystallizes out of itself in the structure.[20]

In that crucial "unwillkürlicher" Adorno's thesis revealed its uneasy compromise between the tenets of Marxism and New Criticism, both of which, of course, depreciate conscious, deliberate, authorial intention.

Adorno's approach was clearly a response to developments in Marxist aesthetics, to his friendship with Brecht and his own work in the Institute of Social Research in Frankfurt. Yet his intuitive response to lyric remained, in this lecture, essentially post-Romantic. As he himself admitted, the lecture "Lyrik und Gesellschaft" was open to the charge of having betrayed its Frankfurt School imperatives. "You can accuse me of being so afraid of crude sociology that I have sublimated the relationship between lyric poetry and society so that nothing actually remains of it."[21] Precisely.

Though written earlier, Antonio Gramsci's *Prison Notebooks* have only recently begun to attract attention as a theoretical model for a

---

lyrische Ausdruck, gegenständlicher Schwere entronnen, das Bild eines Lebens beschwöre, das frei sei vom Swang der herrschenden Praxis, der Nützlichkeit, vom Druck der sturen Selbsterhaltung. . . . Sie impliziert den Protest gegen einen gesellschaftlichen Zustand, den jeder Einzelne als sich feindlich, fremd, kalt, bedrückend erfährt." (Trans. Margaret E. Kennington.)

19. Ibid., p. 76.

20. Ibid., pp. 82–83. ". . . das geschichtliche Verhältnis des Subjekts zur Objektivität, des Einzelnen zur Gesellschaft im Medium des subjecktiven, auf sich zurückgeworfenen Geistes seiner Niederschlag muss gefunden haben. Er wird um so volkommener sein, je weniger das Gebilde das Verhältnis von Ich und Gesellschaft thematisch macht, je unwillkürlicher es vielmehr im Gebilde von sich aus sich kristallisiert." (Trans. Margaret K. Kennington.)

21. Ibid., p. 83.

new societal criticism; as a model by which to understand Jonson, they seem to have a special appropriateness. The *Prison Notebooks* were themselves, of course, written out of the experience of political repression, during Gramsci's incarceration by the Fascists. Like *The Under-wood,* they were written elliptically and fragmentarily, in evasion of censorship, and were never published in Gramsci's lifetime. But still more to the point, they define a mode of production for the subject, for subjectivity as expressed in literary form, that not only matches what we have seen in Jonson, but connects Gramsci to a very large tradition indeed. In Gramsci's theory of the intellectual, or rather of the two types of intellectual that history reveals society constantly producing, we can recognize Jonson's divided self: on the one hand, the "organic" intellectual, the brains of a new social class, the voice, not untroubled, of upward mobility; on the other, the "traditional" intellectual, Jonson the neoclassicist. In a telling paragraph, Gramsci defined traditional intellectuals as those who, experiencing:

> through an "esprit de corps" their uninterrupted historical continuity and their special qualification, . . . put themselves forward as autonomous and independent of the dominant social group. This self-assessment is not without consequences in the ideological and political field, consequences of wide-ranging import. The whole of idealist philosophy can easily be connected with this position, . . . defined as the expression of that social utopia by which the intellectuals think of themselves as "independent," autonomous, endowed with a character of their own.[22]

It is implied in Gramsci's system that "organic" intellectuals may attempt to become "traditional," thereby legitimating the new historical class they represent; and Jonson's autodidacticism, his strenuous acquisition of what he regarded as "tradition," namely classical authors, acquires in this context a special poignancy. It is not entirely a coincidence that Gramsci's discussion of the intellectual in society is interrupted by a long note on the development of "imperial intellectuals" in Augustan Rome;[23] nor that this essay began with Jonson's self-location in that very time and place.

Gramsci's theory is not without problems of its own, due in large part to the hazards despite which it was produced, and its fragmentary form. But as an explanatory frame for Jonson it is clearly more helpful than either Jameson's political unconscious, with its stress on

22. Antonio Gramsci, *Selections from the Prison Notebooks of Antonio Gramsci,* ed. and trans. Quintin Hoare and Geoffrey Nowell Smith (New York, 1971), pp. 7–8.

23. *Notebooks,* p. 17.

class warfare, or Adorno's *unwillkürlichkeit,* the involuntary subjectivization of societal pressures. It may even be possible to gain from Gramsci a perspective on Romantic and post-Romantic lyric; for if "traditional" intellectuals have always, as Gramsci claimed, asserted their autonomous condition, what may this not explain about the egotistical sublime and the historical origins of *poésie pure?*

PART THREE

Mary Jacobus

Apostrophe and Lyric Voice in *The Prelude*

I

Looking back to the beginning of *The Prelude,* Book VII starts by recalling the "dithyrambic fervour" with which it had opened. Named here as the "glad preamble," these introductory lines are recollected in terms at once of the natural Sublime and the Sublime of poetry itself:

> Five years are vanished since I first poured out . . .
> . . . .
> A glad preamble to this verse. I sang
> Aloud in dithyrambic fervour, deep
> But short-lived uproar, like a torrent sent
> Out of the bowels of a bursting cloud . . .
> (VII.1–7)[1]

Wordsworth's "torrent sent / Out of the bowels of a bursting cloud" is more than just a means of naturalizing the landscape of poetic inspiration; we recognize the source of a poetic Helicon. Geoffrey Hartman has suggested that *The Prelude* "can almost be said to begin with 'an Ode, in passion utter'd'" (V.97).[2] Though he does not en-

This paper is a shortened version of a forthcoming essay on "dithyrambic fervour" and the lyric voice of *The Prelude.*

1. These lines maintain the fiction that *Prelude* I.1–54—the "glad preamble"—were the first lines to be written. References throughout are to the 1805 text of *The Prelude,* ed. Jonathan Wordsworth, M. H. Abrams, and Stephen Gill (New York, 1979).

2. Geoffrey Hartman, "Words, Wish, Worth: Wordsworth," in *Deconstruction and Criticism,* ed. Harold Bloom (London, 1979), p. 190.

large on this connection between the "glad preamble" and the apocalyptic blast heard in the shell of Book V, his allusion to the ode form is worth pursuing. The torrent of eloquence here has quite specific associations with the Sublime or Pindaric and (by popular misconception) "irregular" ode, certainly the highest form of lyric poetry for the eighteenth century,[3] and the one in which the poet was also thought to speak most directly in his own voice. Translating Horace's praise of Pindar in one of his own *Pindarique Odes,* Cowley had written:

> *Pindars unnavigable Song*
> Like a swoln *Flood* from some steep *Mountain* pours along,
> The *Ocean* meets with such a *Voice*
> From his enlarged *Mouth,* as drowns the *Oceans* noise.
>
> So *Pindar* does new *Words* and *Figures* roul
> Down his impetuous *Dithyrambic Tide* . . .[4]

As Cowley notes, the "*Dithyrambic Tide*" of Pindaric eloquence has its dangers, "for it is able to drown any *Head* that is not strong built and well *ballasted.*"[5] Wordsworth too may have glimpsed these dangers. Voice not only drowns the ocean's noise, but threatens to drown the reader too, and perhaps even the writer himself. Keeping one's head above water may even mean shutting one's ears. One might contrast also the torrent of words in the "glad preamble" with Wordsworth's invocation to the "steady cadence" of the River Derwent in Book I, which at once "composes" the infant's thoughts, and, in another sense, the entire poem. Did Wordsworth, perhaps, finding his own dithyrambic tide unnavigable, prefer to emphasize not the voice of the Sublime but the voice of Nature?

There are good reasons for this retreat from the Sublime. Cowley goes on to observe of Pindar's Dithyrambics that they were "*Hymns* made in honour of *Bacchus* . . . a bold, free, enthusiastical kind of Poetry, as of men inspired by *Bacchus,* that is, *Half-Drunk.*"[6] Remem-

3. See Norman Maclean, "From Action to Image: Theories of the Lyric in the Eighteenth Century," in *Critics and Criticism Ancient and Modern,* ed. R. S. Crane (Chicago, 1952), p. 409. See also, for a sustained discussion of the ode, Paul H. Fry, *The Poet's Calling in the English Ode* (New Haven and London, 1980).

4. *The English Writings of Abraham Cowley,* ed. A. R. Waller, 2 vols. (Cambridge, 1905), 1:178. Cf. also Gray's "Progress of Poesy: A Pindaric Ode," where "the rich stream of music winds along" from Helicon to precipice: "Now rolling down the steep amain, / Headlong, impetuous, see it pour" (11. 7, 10–11).

5. *The English Writings of Abraham Cowley,* 1:180.

6. Ibid.

bering himself as a young poet in the throes of composition, Wordsworth speaks of hushing his voice and "composing" his gait so that passers-by wouldn't suppose him mad ("crazed in brain," IV.116–20); "kindled with the stir, / The fermentation and the vernal heat / Of poesy" (IV.93–95), he too is like one half-drunk. At Cambridge, youthful intoxication took the form of getting drunk in Milton's rooms. Apostrophe and libation blend in a heady brew: "O temperate bard!",

> I to thee
> Poured out libations, to thy memory drank
> Within my private thoughts, till my brain reeled,
> Never so clouded by the fumes of wine
> Before that hour, or since.
> (III.303–7)

Drinking to Milton's memory takes on an aspect at once sublime and bacchic—inebriated with his poetry while disrespectful of Milton's own temperance. Milton himself comes to mind in this context not only as the bard of temperance but as the poet most obsessed with the terror of bacchic orgies, whose own apostrophe to Urania at the start of Book VII of *Paradise Lost*—clearly in Wordsworth's mind as he wrote his opening to Book VII of *The Prelude*—invokes protection against just such a Comus-like crew of drunken revelers.

Wordsworth could praise Milton for "a voice whose sound was like the sea" ("Milton," l. 1)—a voice, presumably, in which all others would be lost; but Milton's own anxiety was that his voice would be drowned by savage clamor and the poet dismembered, Orpheus-like, by hordes of Thracian women under the influence of their bacchic cult. Wordsworth himself had translated this part of the Orpheus and Eurydice story from Virgil's *Georgic* IV in 1788, and it is hard to imagine that the legend can have been absent from his mind either at the time of the original literary orgy in Milton's rooms or later, when recollected in *The Prelude*.[7] The figure used by Cowley of the Pindaric Sublime ("it is able to drown any *Head* that is not strong built and well *ballasted*") coincides with the traditional figure of the poet's voice being drowned by barbarous dissonance, and his severed head borne down the flood. Both appear to be articulations of the dread that

7. See *The Poetical Works of William Wordsworth*, ed. Ernest de Selincourt and Helen Darbishire, 5 vols. (Oxford, 1940–49), 1:285, ll. 71–74. For the date, see Mark L. Reed, *Wordsworth: The Chronology of the Early Years, 1770–1799* (Cambridge, Mass., 1967), p. 21.

poetic individuality might be lost—whether by being subsumed into the Sublime or by being dispersed into the meaningless multiplicity of "clamor." The orphic fantasy might be said to involve for Wordsworth, as for Milton, the threat that discomposing bacchic dithyrambs, or possession by the voices of others, would lead to the poet's dismemberment.

One safeguard against such imaginary dismemberment is provided by the compensating fantasy of fully naturalized orphic song. As Frances Ferguson aptly writes, the dying head gives nature a speaking voice ("Ah! poor Eurydice, it feebly cried; / Eurydice, the moaning banks replied").[8] For her, the echoic structure is that of epitaph; but one might also see in it the Wordsworthian desire to appropriate the speaking voice of Nature in an attempt to render his own imperishable. Drowned neither by the voice of the Sublime—Milton's voice—nor by the clamor of all the other voices by which the poet risks being possessed, the voice of Nature permits a loss of individuality which is at once safe and unifying. In Nature, the poet can take refuge against dismemberment.

If the poet's urgent need to constitute himself as a poet leads him to the dithyrambic fervor of the "glad preamble," self-preservation throws him back on naturalized song. On the one hand, the torrential or oceanic voices of past poets; on the other, the murmurings of the Derwent which assimilate the poet's voice to Nature and so preserve it. The ode-like, inspirational passion of the "glad preamble" ultimately "vex[es] its own creation" (I.47), its redundant energy disrupting the flow of river and memory. By contrast, the fiction of a poetry that originates in Nature, like the voice of the Derwent, ensures continuity while providing a safely trans-subjective voice in which the poet's own can be merged. Wordsworth can claim not simply that Nature speaks through him, but that he speaks with Nature's own voice. The characteristic alternations in *The Prelude*—between the uproarious waterspout and the murmuring stream, inspiration and reflection, invocation and narrative—become a sign of this tension between poetic self-assertion and self-immersion. Wordsworth's final sleight of hand may well be that of divesting himself of the Sublime altogether while investing it in Nature instead. One might argue that his counterpart to Milton's cosmic flight derives from the self-immersing Bard of Gray's "Pindaric Ode," who "spoke, and headlong from the mountain's height / Deep in the roaring tide . . . plunged to end-

8. Lines 77–78. See *Wordsworth: Language as Counter-Spirit* (New Haven, 1977), pp. 163–65.

less night" ("The Bard," ll. 143–44)—an ostensibly suicidal loss of individual identity which at once destroys the poet's voice and vests Nature with those qualities (Voice or voices) dangerous to its survival. As we see in Book XIII, this leaves the poet free to take refuge in pastoral, the address of one poet-shepherd to another. If the ode is the sublime and therefore dangerous form of the lyric, then apostrophe could be said to be the figure which most completely characterizes the sublimity of the ode. *The Prelude* begins apostrophically, but ends by addressing the living—Dorothy and Coleridge—in a way designed to assimilate the poet to a safer pastoral community. It is this formal progression that most clearly marks the concession made by a poet whose lyric voice survives finally at the price of renouncing the Sublime altogether. Paradoxically, only by making the torrential and uproarious voice of inspiration that of Nature itself can Wordsworth sustain a voice of his own.

II

> *Apostrophe!* we thus address
> More things than I should care to guess.
> Apostrophe! I did invoke
> Your figure even as I spoke.[9]

Apostrophe, as Jonathan Culler has observed, is an embarrassment. Regularly ignored by writers on the ode, it might be seen "as the figure of all that is most radical, embarrassing, pretentious, and mystificatory in the lyric."[10] Critics turn away from it as it turns away from the discourse in which it is embedded; *apo-strophe*—literally, a turning away, the abrupt transition which, as Cowley puts it in his 1656 Preface, takes the Pindaric ode out of "the common Roads, and ordinary Tracks of *Poesie*. . . . The digressions are many, and sudden, and sometimes long, according to the fashion of all *Lyriques,* and of *Pindar* above all men living."[11] Regarded as a digressive form, a sort of interruption, excess, or redundance, apostrophe in *The Prelude* becomes the signal instance of the rupture of the temporal scheme of memory by the time of writing. Wordsworth's "two consciousnesses"

9. John Hollander, *Rhyme's Reason: A Guide to English Verse* (New Haven, 1981), p. 48.
10. Jonathan Culler, "Apostrophe," *Diacritics,* 7:4 (1977), 60. See also Culler's *Pursuit of Signs* (Ithaca, 1981), chap. 4.
11. *The English Writings of Abraham Cowley,* 1:11.

(II.32) can then be seen as a division, not simply between me-now and me-then, but between discursive time and narrative time—a radical discontinuity which ruptures the illusion of sequentiality and insists, embarrasingly, on self-presence and voice; insists too that invocation itself may be more important than what is invoked. "Apostrophe! I did invoke / Your figure even as I spoke" is a joke that accurately mimes the bringing into being of the poet's voice by way of what it addresses. If apostrophe's characteristic function is to invoke the Muse, it is also, ultimately, a form of self-constituting self-address: "To my soul I say, 'I recognise thy glory'" (VI.531–32). The question of the poet's vocation, translated into invocation, becomes the question of poetic voice. Like Imagination in Book VI, voice halts the poet in his tracks, privileging self-address over narrating the past. The opening apostrophe of the "glad preamble" may constitute Wordsworth as a poet but, in doing so, it loses hold of his subject; there is always this incompatibility between the lyric voice of *The Prelude* and its much-desired, "distracting" epic progress—an incompatibility which typically presents itself as a problem of redundance. Voice usurps on the ceaselessly-murmuring Derwent, making the poet himself the interrupter of his peom.

The "glad preamble" initiates not only *The Prelude,* but the problem of its composition. The erratic progress to which the opening lines of Book VII allude ("'twas not long / Ere the interrupted strain broke forth once more . . . then stopped for years," VII.9–11) may be nothing other than the symptom of Wordsworth's anxiety about writing a long poem. Only in Book XII, looking back from a completed poem, can Wordsworth retrospectively see the image of a longed-for completeness in the stream that has been traced from darkness (XIII.172–80). But perhaps the "glad preamble" should in the last resort be read, not simply as a dramatization of Wordsworth's anxiety about his poetic undertaking or as a record of the fluctuations of inspiration, but rather as a propitiatory gesture that frees the poet from the "burthen of [his] own unnatural self" and, in doing so, from the burdensome past of poetry. *The Prelude*'s opening apostrophe to the breeze would then become an image of liberation which, though predicated on the novelty of self-presence to one "not used to make / A present joy the matter of [his] song" (I.55–56), is directed ultimately at sloughing off his poetic precursors or consciousness of the past:

> O welcome messenger! O welcome friend!
> A captive greets thee, coming from a house

Of bondage, from yon city's walls set free,
A prison where he hath been long immured.
Now I am free, enfranchised and at large,
May fix my habitation where I will.
. . . .
. . . I breathe again—
Trances of thought and mountings of the mind
Come fast upon me. It is shaken off,
As by a miraculous gift 'tis shaken off,
That burthen of my own unnatural self . . .
(I.5–10, 19–23)

The poet's breathing and the breeze are at once the breath of pure, unconstructed sound ('O' or voice) and a prison-break, an escape from the confines of memory and self-consciousness. In the same way, apostrophe itself breaks off from the demands of narrative as a moment of lyric redundance or inspired escape. The "vital breeze" becomes "A tempest, a redundant energy, / Vexing its own creation" (I.46–47), just as in the opening lines of Book VII the grove "tossing its dark boughs in sun and wind— / Spreads through me a commotion like its own" (VII.51–52). This tempest or commotion is not exactly a "corresponding mild creative breeze" (I.43); it is more a vexation or a kind of uneasiness.[12] The effect is that of voice itself, perceived as an interruption of the past from the present.

Wordsworth comments of the "glad preamble," "My own voice cheered me, and, far more, the mind's / Internal echo of the imperfect sound" (I.64–65). The appeal to voice might usually be thought of as having the function of making the self whole. Whereas writing disperses, voice unifies, providing the illusion of a single origin and temporal unity (no "two consciousnesses" here). Yet in this instance, Wordsworth writes of the doubling effect whereby the sound of his own voice has an internal echo, and one which, unlike echo as usually figured, perfects rather than incompletely repeats "the imperfect sound"; it is voice here that functions like echo, since speech is imagined as secondary in its attempt to represent the silence of self-present meaning in consciousness.[13] At this point it seems worth digressing to consider some of the more problematic aspects of the Romantic conception of voice. A small book by Francis Berry, *Poetry and the Physical*

12. See Wordsworth's apostrophic reaction to the news of Robespierre's death ("'Come now, ye golden times. . .'"), where the traveler is "interrupted by uneasy bursts / Of exultation" (X.541, 557–58).

13. See Jacques Derrida's formulation of this myth of voice, in "The Voice That Keeps Silence," *Speech and Phenomena,* trans. David B. Allison (Evanston, 1973), p. 76.

Voice (1962), brings to light the hidden implications of Wordsworth's position. Like Wordsworth, Berry appears to insist on the primacy of voice over writing (seeing the letter simply as a representation of sound), and his book laments the debasing of language as a mere means of communication, or "instrument." Yet this distinction between language as instrument and the poetic use of language as "agent" proves oddly difficult to sustain.

As Wordsworth had been, Berry too is anxious to restore to poetic voice the musicality which he believes once to have been synonymous with poetry itself. But even Wordsworth no longer insists on "feigning that [his] works were composed to the music of the harp or lyre," happily substituting "nothing more than an animated or impassioned recitation."[14] Berry's terms—pitch, duration, volume, timbre, and so on—emphasize the sound of vocal "music" to a degree never risked by Wordsworth himself. In doing so, however, they uncover the underlying myth of voice of which Wordsworth's is a less extreme version; that is, the myth of the "inner ear" (not a kind of memory but a kind of hearing) which leads us to suppose, according to Berry, that though "modern poets compose silently . . . in composing they record what they are inwardly experiencing as vocal sound, usually their own voices however idealized. . . . we could say they record the double experiences of hearing *and* saying";[15] this is what Wordsworth had called "the mind's internal echo of the imperfect sound," likewise surrendering to an auditory myth of self-presence. But there follows for Berry an altogether less composing notion, that of the poet as "a person obsessed, scored and spoored by vocal linguistic sound"; "or, put another way, he is *possessed* by vocal sound as a man was said to be possessed by devils."[16] What it amounts to is that voice, instead of bringing reassurance ("my own voice cheered me") by guaranteeing the existence of a unified consciousness, can equally take on the daemonic aspect of possession. Whose are the voices the poet hears? Not necessarily his own, after all.

In the light of such daemonic vocalism, Berry's notion of individuated voice breaks down. His insistence that the attentive ("listening") reader can recover or reconstruct the unique and authentic voices of,

14. 1815 "Preface," *The Prose Works of William Wordsworth,* ed. W. J. B. Owen and J. W. Smyser, 3 vols. (Oxford, 1974), 3:29.

15. Francis Berry, *Poetry and the Physical Voice* (London, 1962), p. 34. See Derrida's paraphrase of this position: "When I speak, it belongs to the phenomenological essence of the operation that *I hear myself . . . at the same time* that I speak. The signifier . . . is in absolute proximity to me. The living act . . . which animates the body of the signifier . . . seems not to separate itself from itself, from its own self-presence" (*Speech and Phenomena,* p. 77).

16. Berry, pp. 36, 7.

say Tennyson, Milton, or—presumably—Wordsworth on the evidence of "the printed signs on the page" is revealed as a fiction. Calling the self into being through apostrophe becomes rather a matter of calling another into being; perhaps an "authorial" voice, but equally, the variety of haunting, threatening, nightmarish, or apocalyptic voices heard throughout *The Prelude* in "the voice / Of mountain echoes" (I.389–90), or in "Black drizzling drags that spake . . . As if a voice were in them" (VI.563–64), or the "voice that cried / To the whole city, 'Sleep no more!'" (X.76–77), or in a shell that broadcasts "voices more than all the winds"—the voice of "a god, yea many gods" (V.107–8). The voice is always a doubling of self, and more often a multiplication or alienation. Berry's view of poetic language as agent, then, turns out to be characterized not by the individuality of the writer but by something closer to the supernatural—the gift of tongues or hearing voices ("he is *possessed* by vocal sound"). Conceived as a man more vocal than other men, the poet becomes an echo-chamber for all those voices heard while boat-stealing, descending the Vale of Gondo, unable to sleep in Paris after the September Massacres, or in the Arab Dream. They speak through him, so that far from attesting to unity of origin or a stable identity, voice comes to imply all the destabilizing multiplicity of plural (or ancestral) voices—much as the composing "voice" of the Derwent can become the discomposing voice of inspired poetry, "the voice / Which roars along the bed of Jewish song," or the Miltonic "trumpet-tones of harmony that shake / Our shores in England" (V.203–4, 206–7). Given these transformations, Wordsworth's quest turns out not to be for an individual voice so much as for a transcendental one.

The apostrophic moments in Book I of *The Prelude* are, typically, callings into being of supernatural powers:

> Wisdom and spirit of the universe,
> Thou soul that art the eternity of thought,
> That giv'st to forms and images a breath
> And everlasting motion . . .
>
> (I.427–31)

> Ye presences of Nature, in the sky
> Or on the earth, ye visions of the hills
> And souls of lonely places . . .
>
> (I.490–92)

Wordsworth's invocations to the Muse summon up spirits, presences, souls—the supernatural machinery of an unexorcized Nature, arising in the same breath as winds, hills, solitude. If Shelley demands of the wind. "Be thou me, impetuous one!" Wordsworth could be said to ask of Nature to give his voice whatever haunts and denatures landscape; whatever puts the individual origin of voice most in question. The Eolian fantasy so beloved of Romantic poets, after all, is nothing more or less than the wish for the trans-subjective instrumentality which Berry would repress if he could, but fails ultimately to exorcize. Wordsworth's apostrophes to breezes, brooks, and groves, in which he wishes for himself "a music and a voice harmonious as your own" (XI.20–21), are the equivalent of asking to be played on too. The distinction which Wordsworth himself would have endorsed, between language as instrument (or, as he calls it himself, "counter-spirit") and language as agent,[17] falls away to leave only breezes or breathings through the poet, "obedient as a lute / That waits upon the touches of the wind" (III.137–38). Subsumed into transcendental Nature, the poet's voice becomes orphic rather than bacchic, banishing rough music with the myth of natural harmony. Nature steps in to de-daemonize voice, turning possession into eolianism and sanctifying vocalism as "Eolian visitations" (I.104). Instead of the voice of the poet, we have the voice of poetry—that is, Nature. In order to achieve this status for his poetry, Wordsworth has to eschew the very fiction of individual voice which is central to Romantic conceptions of the poet. The transcendental defends against possession, but it also takes away the poet's most distinctive and sought-after personal property, the voice that differentiates him from his predecessors, and from Milton in particular. That, perhaps, may be the trade-off—since not to be either Milton or unlike Milton is in effect to lose the Miltonic voice as well as one's own in the impersonally oceanic voice of Nature, thereby drowning the potentially ventriloquizing voices of the past in "A waterspout from heaven" (VII.9).

III

What is involved for Wordsworth in sound itself? And what is the relation of voice to writing? The aftermath of the "glad preamble" turns out to be largely one of discouragement: "the harp / Was soon defrauded" (I.104–5) and the hope of fixing "in a visible home . . . those phantoms of conceit, / That had been floating loose about so long" (I.129–31) was not to be fulfilled. The disembodied "phantoms of conceit" remain unrepresented, perhaps unrepresenta-

17. "Essays upon Epitaphs," iii, *The Prose Works of William Wordsworth,* 2:35.

ble. A fragment from the *Peter Bell* MS, possibly an early attempt at an introduction to the two-part *Prelude,* had explored the problem of representation in terms directly relevant to the random vocalizings of the "glad preamble":

> nor had my voice
> Been silent—oftentimes had I burst forth
> In verse which with a strong and random light
> Touching an object in its prominent parts
> Created a memorial which to me
> Was all sufficient, and, to my own mind
> Recalling the whole picture, seemed to speak
> An universal language. Scattering thus
> In passion many a desultory sound,
> I deemed that I had adequately cloathed
> Meanings at which I hardly hinted, thoughts
> And forms of which I scarcely had produced
> A monument and arbitrary sign.[18]

Bursting forth in verse becomes the equivalent of a private mnemonic; "to my *own* mind / Recalling the whole picture," the voice only "*seemed* to speak / An universal language." Writing to Godwin in 1800, Coleridge had asked, "Is *thinking* impossible without arbitrary signs? &—how far is the word 'arbitrary' a misnomer?" If Coleridge seems to want to destroy "the old antithesis of *Words* & *Things,* elevating . . . words into Things, & living Things too,"[19] Wordsworth seems to be suggesting that at best poetry can produce "A monument and arbitrary sign" for thought; and at worst, make only desultory sounds. This is the Eolian fantasy demystified, and along with it there collapses the entire Romantic fallacy of spontaneous lyric utterance, whether heard or overheard. In another fragment, Wordsworth alludes to "slow creation" imparting "to speach / Outline and substance."[20] This sounds like fixing phantoms of conceit in a visible home, or writing poetry. It is as if representation only begins at the point where Eolianism—the fiction of unmediated expression—is eschewed; or perhaps, Wordsworth seems to imply, thinking can begin only where

18. *The Prelude,* ed. Jonathan Wordsworth, M. H. Abrams, and Stephen Gill, p. 495, fragment (*a*), ll. 1–13. The passage is also discussed by Jonathan Wordsworth, "As with the Silence of the Thought," in *High Romantic Argument: Essays for M. H. Abrams,* ed. Lawrence Lipking (Ithaca, 1981), pp. 58–64.

19. *Collected Letters of Samuel Taylor Coleridge,* ed. E. L. Griggs, 6 vols. (Oxford, 1956–71), 1:625–26.

20. *The Prelude,* p. 495, fragment (*b*), ll. 3–4.

the monuments and arbitrary signs of language take over from sound (pure voice or breath) and speech (pure presence). In any event, it is clear that writing, the permanent record of thought, involves both the muting of voice—a kind of deafness—and the death of presence.

No wonder, then, that Eolianism pervades *The Prelude;* it is Wordsworth's defense against that inability to hear oneself think (or speak) involved in writing itself. Going back to the opening of Book VII, we find Wordsworth experiencing "Something that fits me for the poet's task" in the infectious "commotion" of his favorite grove, "Now tossing its dark boughs in sun and wind" (VII.50–53). Presumably both grove and poet make a composing noise much like the one that is wasted on the deaf Dalesman, though not on his peaceful grave, memorialized in Wordsworth's final "Essay on Epitaphs":

> And yon tall Pine-tree, whose composing sound
> Was wasted on the good Man's living ear,
> Hath now its own peculiar sanctity;
> And at the touch of every wandering breeze
> Murmurs not idly o'er his peaceful grave.[21]

The Dalesman's epitaph is "A monument and arbitrary sign" masquerading as the sound of murmuring trees, alias the composing sound of the poet's own voice. Why does the pine-tree murmur "not idly"? Is it because the entire epitaph, though ostensibly commemorating a man for whom the mountain vale was soundless and the storm-tossed landscape "silent as a picture"—for whom all voices save those of books were unheard—actually celebrates the poet's own aural imagination as a means of denying the soundlessness of writing? The poet himself, Wordsworth implies, is not only murmurous but has inward ears that can hear; this is what makes him a poet. Imagined sound becomes a way to repress or deny writing and undo death. If a monument marks the site of a grave, voice—breathings for incommunicable powers" (III.188)—gives evidence of a poet's enduring life. For the poet, Wordsworth argues covertly, there can be no such thing as silence, but only, as in the Dalesman's epitaph, "audible seclusions." The soundless world of the Dalesman's solitude and death is one that speaks to him. So much so that in *The Prelude* a moment of visionary seeing is as likely as not to be one of hearing, an attempt to communicate "what e'er there is of power in sound / To breathe an elevated mood":

21. "Essays upon Epitaphs," iii, *The Prose Works of William Wordsworth,* 2:96 (*Excursion* VII.477–81). See Paul de Man on the Deaf Dalesman's epitaph, "Autobiography as Defacement," *Modern Language Notes,* 94 (Winter 1979), 923 ff., 930.

> I would stand
> Beneath some rock, listening to sounds that are
> The ghostly language of the ancient earth,
> Or make their dim abode in distant winds.
> Thence did I drink the visionary power.
> (II.326–30)

Visionary power—"by form / Or image unprofaned"—is a heightened sense of hearing which makes language into something ghostly, nonreferential, ancient, and without origin, like the homeless voice of waters in the Snowdon episode. Along with Francis Berry, Wordsworth wants to believe that the poet hears voices as well as speaking with tongues; but what he most desires to hear are the unheard sighings or breathings that writing ("arbitrary signs") must repress. This is the other side of babble, or Babel, the nonlinguistic murmur of a composing voice that may be the poet's as he saunters "like a river murmuring" (IV.110) or, equally, invoked as that of the Derwent ("O Derwent, murmuring stream," V.509), but is above all that of a unified poetic presence that has no need of discourse.

Wordsworth's definitive statement of the ear's power occurs in his "musical" ode, "On the Power of sound" (1828). As the preposterous "argument" puts it, "The Ear [is] addressed, as occupied by a spiritual functionary, in communion with sounds, individual, or combined in studied harmony."[22] The ode is all apostrophe, all voice, all ear:

> a Spirit aërial
> Informs the cell of Hearing, dark and blind;
> Intricate labyrinth, more dread for thought
> To enter than oracular cave . . .
> (ll. 3–6)

The ear becomes the prime organ of vision, making audible "Ye Voices, and ye Shadows / And Images of voice" (ll. 33–34). The poem's function is both to invoke Spirit (ear) and Muse (voice); or "the mind's / Internal echo of the imperfect sound." As John Hollander's account of the poem has shown, the ear is a place of echo and reverberation, sounding and re-sounding, a cave, a "strict passage," a maze, a temple, a vault, a hollow place where music is made as well as heard.[23] Like the shell, whether a poeticism for the lute or the Ro-

22. *The Poetical Works of William Wordsworth*, 2:323.

23. See the extended discussion in Hollander's "Wordsworth and the Music of Sound," in *New Perspectives on Coleridge and Wordsworth*, ed. Geoffrey Hartman (New York, 1972) pp. 67–79.

manticized seashell, it is both sounded on and sounds, combining the orphic properties of a stringed instrument and the dionysian properties of a wind instrument.[24] In effect, it is nothing less than the ear of God. Wordsworth's originary myth of voice ("A Voice to Light gave Being," l. 209) is also an apocalyptic one: "A Voice shall . . . sweep away life's visionary stir" (ll. 211–12). Compare the dual functions of music and harmony in *The Prelude,* one to build up, the other to destroy; though "The mind of man is framed even like the breath / And harmony of music" (I.351–52), the shell's "loud prophetic blast of harmony" (V.96) in the Arab dream announces the end of the world, and the sublime of Revolutionary terror is accompanied by "Wild blasts of music" (X.419). Music can both frame and unframe, compose and discompose. Wordsworth's unstated argument in "On the Power of Sound" is to reconcile this dual aspect of harmony, claiming that even after earth is dust and the heavens dissolved, "her stay / Is in the WORD, that shall not pass away" (ll. 223–24). His ode is the optimistic, orthodox Christian sequel to the Arab dream, revised not to foretell "Destruction to the children of the earth" (V.98) but rather to prophesy salvation of and through the Word. As the type of the divine fiat, poetry itself is guaranteed survival—the consolatory message unavailable to the Arab or the dreamer in Book V of *The Prelude*—by means of its transformation into the transcendental, imperishable "WORD." Poetic utterance now promises "to finish doubt and dim foreseeing" (l. 211), dependent no longer on "books" (the materiality of stone or shell), but on the special harmony of Christian assurance or faith in life—and therefore faith in hearing—beyond death. This is a word that can continue to hear itself and be heard even after the apocalypse.

The guaranteeing of poetry as "WORD" (voice transcendentalized as Logos) in "On the power of Sound" reveals one function of sound, and particularly of voice, in *The Prelude* itself. What the deaf Dalesman can "hear" are the immortal voices of the poets, secured against "imperfection and decay":

> Song of the muses, sage historic tale
> Science severe, or word of holy writ
> Announcing immortality and joy
> To the assembled spirits of the just,
> From imperfection and decay secure.[25]

24. See John Hollander, "Images of Voice: Music and Sound in Romantic Poetry," Churchill College Overseas Fellowship Lecture, V (Cambridge, 1970), p. 12.

25. *The Prose Works of William Wordsworth,* 2:95 (*Excursion,* VII.450–54).

After the death of the poet, there still remains immortal verse. In lines like these, Wordsworth uses silent reading to free poetry from the monumentality and arbitrary signs of death. Disembodied sound—"The ghostly language of the ancient earth"—comes to be the archetype of poetry. In this light, the "glad preamble" might be seen not only as a means of calling both poet and voice into being, but also as a way to fantasize their transcendence of material representation. In *The Prelude* Wordsworth had hoped vainly "that with a frame of outward life" he might "fix in a visible home . . . those phantoms of conceit / That had been floating loose about so long" (I.128–31). How are we to read this self-proclaimed failure to fix the insubstantial (and hence imperishable) "phantoms of conceit"? The longing "To brace myself to some determined aim" (I.124) is synonymous in *The Prelude* with the epic enterprise itself, yet the poem finally evades even this enterprise by substituting the "WORD"—lasting, but inaudible except to the mind—for an epic theme. It is left celebrating the spirit or "voice" of poetry instead of the form. Like the cuckoo, "No bird, but an invisible thing, / A voice, a mystery" ("To the cuckoo," ll. 15–16), poet as well as poem becomes unavailable, "dispossesse[d] . . . almost of a corporeal existence."[26] An extended personal lyric, *The Prelude* is redeemed from time and death by the unheard voice of the poet, or, as Wordsworth calls it, the Imagination, its declared subject. The entire poem becomes an apostrophe or "prelude" designed to constitute the poet and to permit Wordsworth himself to join the ranks of Homer, the great thunderer, and the Bible, Milton, and even the ballad, as Voice rather than voice, Poetry rather than individual poet; that is, the Voice of Poetry which re-sounds not only in the ears of the living but in the ears of the deaf.

26. 1815 "Preface," *The Prose Works of William Wordsworth,* 3:32.

John Brenkman

The Concrete Utopia of Poetry: Blake's "A Poison Tree"

Preliminaries

Seldom does the question of lyric and society get beyond "extra-textual" considerations, principally the role of social and political ideas in a poet's biographical and intellectual development or in the poetry's thematic content. Marxist criticism mirrors this deficit by relegating poetry to the margins of its own investigations of social and aesthetic experience. William Blake's poetry encourages us to counter the habits of Marxist and non-Marxist criticism alike by recognizing that society and politics shape the very project of a poet's work and the inner dynamics of poetic language itself, its processes of figuration, its status as a linguistic act, its forms and techniques, its effects within the reading process.

Blake was a poet of the volatile decades of the late eighteenth and early nineteenth centuries, writing at the very point when the democratic revolutions were being institutionalized as the class rule of the bourgeoisie. The claims of freedom and liberation that gave impetus to poets and novelists in this period were rapidly coming up against the necessity of establishing the new economic order of capitalism. Blake's vital contribution to our cultural heritage lies in the response that his poetry made to this changing relation of art to the evolution of bourgeois society. He was also a poet who himself constantly reflected on the political and historical possibilities of the imagination.

This essay is part of a chapter on Blake in my *Culture and Domination*, forthcoming from Cornell University Press.—J. B.

For Blake, poetry is the active imposing of imagination or fantasy in the struggles against dominant values and institutions. Casting the poet in the double role of visionary and voice of condemnation, he attributed both a utopian and a negative power to poetic language.

It is this interplay of the utopian and the negative, of imagination and critique, that makes Blake's poetry resonate with the social and aesthetic theories of thinkers like Ernst Bloch and Herbert Marcuse, Walter Benjamin and T. W. Adorno. In this paper, I will test some broad perspectives on art that have come from this tradition of "critical Marxism" against a reading of a poem from the *Songs of Experience.* The reading owes as much to hermeneutics and poststructuralism as it does to the aesthetic writings of the Frankfurt School.[1]

From Bloch I have taken the phrase "concrete utopia." Bloch meant by this that utopian possibilities are latent in the freedom and self-organization which social groups and classes possess, intermittently and fragmentedly, in their everyday existence, political experiences, myths, and artistic endeavors.[2] These latent tendencies have as their heritage all the unfinished or abortive efforts in history to extend justice and happiness. The heritage of utopia is thus a discontinuous history, one that must be constructed from cultural traditions and the popular struggles and revolts of the past. The question we can draw from Bloch's reflections is this: *In what ways is poetry a bearer of utopian hope, of this historical latency which is at once within and beyond society?*

From Marcuse I will borrow a thesis about art and literature that he advanced in his last published work, *The Aesthetic Dimension:* "The inner logic of the work of art terminates in the emergence of another reason, another sensibility, which defy the rationality and sensibility incorporated in the dominant social institutions."[3] The phrase "terminates in the emergence of" suggests, first, that art is utopian insofar as it anticipates new orders of reason and sensibility that can be secured only through political action and social transformation, and, second, that this utopian anticipation is nonetheless concrete insofar

1. The figures associated with the Frankfurt School have indeed produced the most important criticism of poetry that exists in the Marxist tradition. See, in particular, Walter Benjamin, *Charles Baudelaire: A Lyric Poet in the Era of High Capitalism,* trans. Harry Zohn (London, 1973); and Theodor W. Adorno, "Lyric Poetry and Society," *Telos,* 20 (Summer 1974), 56–71.

2. See Ernst Bloch, "Karl Marx and Humanity: The Material of Hope" and "Upright Carriage, Concrete Utopia," in *On Karl Marx* (New York, 1971), pp. 16–45 and 159–73 respectively.

3. See Herbert Marcuse, *The Aesthetic Dimension: Toward a Critique of Marxist Aesthetics* (Boston, 1978), p. 7.

as it stems from what is realized aesthetically in the artwork. Marcuse's thesis leads to a second question about lyric and society: *How does the "inner logic" of the poem at the same time manifest a counterlogic against the constraining interactions organized by society?*

While Bloch and Marcuse help to establish the aims of interpretation and to frame the questions that a socially critical study of poetry needs to address, their own aesthetic reflections rest on suppositions open to challenge from many directions in the recent theory of interpretation and art. Bloch maintains that great artworks are part ideology, part authentic utopia. The first task of analysis is to dissolve the ideological shell of the work by exposing the ways it serves particular rather than general interests and legitimates the forms of domination prevalent in its own society; once this ideological shell is dissolved, the utopian kernel of the work is supposed to shine through, a radiant core of meanings and images expressing the strivings and hopes of humanity. Bloch's conception of interpretation shares with the hermeneutics of Heidegger and Gadamer the insight that cultural meanings come forward only from historically situated works and are appropriated only in historically situated contexts, but he nevertheless tends to view the *valid* meanings of culture as a semantic storehouse that preserves itself intact across historcial periods and epochs. Hence the questionable notion that interpretation can with assurance separate the valid and true aspect of a work from its ideological and false aspect. Contemporary criticism, in the wake of Heidegger and more recently of poststructuralist and deconstructive criticism, raises an inescapable problem concerning our own reception of the art and literature of the past, namely, that there is no ground of meaning or foothold in truth on the basis of which we can with certainty extract the valid significations of a work.

Marcuse's aesthetic reflections accentuate the unity of form. Throughout his work he transcribes into socially critical terms the aesthetic experience that was the basis of bourgeois aesthetics since Schiller. Marcuse attributes the utopian and negative power of art to the sharp contrast that individuals experience between the unity or harmony they apprehend in the artwork and the disharmony and conflict that characterize the social relations they encounter in everyday life. The notion of the artwork's formal harmony has been contested by an array of contemporary theories of the signifying and formal dynamics of literary texts. The transaction between writing and reading, between the poetic text and its reception, can no longer, I believe, be fruitfully described as the subject's inward appropriation of an outwardly realized harmony of sensuous and symbolic elements.

Without undertaking to solve the problem that hermeneutics and poststructuralism pose for the aesthetic thinking of critical Marxism, I have sketched the relevant problems in order to clarify the background of my reading of Blake. For my concern is to transpose the problem of lyric and society and of the negative-utopian power of poetry into a question of poetic language, of poetry as a language practice, and the interaction of writing and reading.

The reading I will present of Blake's "A Poison Tree" is guided by three sets of propositions intended to sharpen this dialogue between critical social theory and contemporary literary theory:

(1) The social dialectic of art does not come from the conflict beween a divided reality and a unified work, but rather takes the form of a conflict *within* the work. By the same token, the social counterlogic that a poem manifests results from the internal contradictoriness of the poem as *text,* not from the wholeness of the poem as *beautiful appearance.* Literature is a practice that acts upon language. The text enters into a complex but determinate relation with the actual social world because language is the very ground of social interaction. The utopian power of poetry stems from its concrete connections, as a language practice, to the social and political realities of its moment rather than from any capacity to shed those connections or set itself above them.

(2) Poetic language solicits, incites, calls for a reading, a reading which at once lets the effects of poetic condensation erupt across the poem and ties those effects to the situation or act of writing itself. Reading always entails this double movement—receptivity to a language that is multivalent and overdetermined and moments of decision in which the multivalence and overdetermination are reconnected to the place or situation from which the poem has arisen. It will be my position that this site of the poem's genesis is social. An analogy might be made between the reading of poetry and psychoanalytic interpretation. The analyst listens with what Freud called a suspended or floating attention in order to hear what reverberates within the subject's discourse and its silences; on the other side of the dialogue, the subject is pressed toward what Lacan called the "moment to conclude," where he or she feels the pressure of the unconscious and integrates it into his or her actual discourse with the analyst, allowing the unconscious to interrupt the false "conclusions" that up to then have resisted it. The two sides of reading poetry are a dialectic of this kind between floating attention and the moment-to-conclude. The reader, however, is more like the patient than the analyst, in that interpretations, usually in the name of their own co-

herence, tend to resist the effects of the poetic text. This is not to argue for the indefinite postponement of interpretive decisions. Such decisions always take place, even when they are masked as in the rhetoric of deconstructive criticism. Every interpretive moment-to-conclude links the interpretation and the text as the two historically—and socially—situated sites of aesthetic experience.

(3) The transaction between writing and reading is thus an encounter between the social situation of literary production and the social situation of literary reception. The problem of ideology is best focused on this encounter and transaction. Art and literature become enmeshed in the vital ideological struggles of the present through the conflict of interpretations, the contesting efforts to understand the texts of the cultural heritage concretely and reflectively. Aesthetic experience is not a given but is *formed* in the interplay of writing and reading. The cultural heritage is not a given but is *constructed.* This heritage becomes charged with significance for the present through the conflict of interpretations.

"A Poison Tree"

Let us first quote the poem in its entirety:

I was angry with my friend;
I told my wrath, my wrath did end.
I was angry with my foe:
I told it not, my wrath did grow.

And I waterd it in fears,
Night & morning with my tears;
And I sunned it with smiles,
And with soft deceitful wiles.

And it grew both day and night.
Till it bore an apple bright.
And my foe beheld it shine,
And he knew that it was mine.

And into my garden stole,
When the night had veild the pole;
In the morning glad I see
My foe outstretchd beneath the tree.

Much depends on the relation of the first stanza to the rest of the poem as it unfolds what happened to the wrath that was not told to the foe. Every time one reads the poem, I believe, the first stanza has the force of a moral statement. The past tense establishes the twin perspective of Blake's action *then* and his judgment *now*. The danger or unhappiness of a wrath that grows, as against a wrath that ends, establishes a set of values or preferences that virtually goes without saying. And all of this is then confirmed in the account of the ensuing anguish that he experienced and the harm he brought on his foe. The poem reads as a kind of confessional utterance in which Blake the speaker shares with the reader a reflective judgment on the actions of Blake in the past, anchored in the view that telling one's wrath is healthy and not telling it is harmful and even self-destructive.

Another extreme, however, emerges against this reading and contradicts its every detail. The last two lines of the poem, breaking the consistent past tense of the rest, can be taken at face value: "In the morning glad I see / My foe outstretchd beneath the tree." A transcendent joy! He has gotten his satisfaction, and his wrath has finally been expressed, yielding the sheer delight of seeing an enemy destroyed. One might try to avert this reading by arguing that the phrase "glad I see" is not really in the present tense, but rather is an elliptical construction for something like "glad I was to see." But the amoral reading of the poem draws on other aspects of its total structure. First of all, there are two oppositions in the first stanza, not only telling as against not telling one's wrath, but also the difference between friend and foe, suggesting that there is no undestructive means of expressing wrath toward a foe but that it must be enacted. Secondly, the poem's words and syntax are not particularly charged with affective connotations; the tone is flat, and this second reading leaves it so by construing the first stanza not as a moral statement but as a statement of fact: wrath can be expressed and immediately dissipated with a friend, but not with a foe. Indeed, one can take this reading to its logical conclusion and say that the poem as a whole, far from being a confessional utterance, is more like a set of instructions on how to do in an enemy and feel relief, even joy.

Either of these readings can account for itself, bringing the various details of the poem into line. In this sense, the poem generates both readings. However, neither reading can account for the possibility of the other, except to declare that it is the product of misreading; they could only accuse one another of naive moralism and amorality respectively. Nor, on the other hand, is it adequate to leave off with these results and declare that the poem is formally or logically undecidable, a pure oscillation between two mutually exclusive meanings. For this undecidability also represents two contrary experiential situations, remorse and remorselessness, condemnation and coldness, constituting an ethical impasse that the reading of the poem need not yet accept, that is, decide to affirm.

The very flatness of the poem's tone allows each reading to invest the poem with the affects appropriate to it. In the first reading, the poem acquires the solemn awe of witnessing an action that the speaker himself can hardly believe he committed. The second reading, on the other hand, takes the speaker's final joy at face value and, in turn, invests the atonal surface of the poem with the connotation of coldness. But the conjoining of coldness and joy calls into question the joy itself. The tone becomes the symptom of a joy that is derived from an altogether different emotion, namely, the wrath that has had to wend its way through elaborate detours in order to manifest itself in the fatal deception of the foe. The conceit which gives the poem its title is the image of this circuitous transformation of wrath into fear, duplicity, and finally deception:

> And I waterd it in fears,
> Night & morning with my tears;
> And I sunned it with smiles,
> And with soft deceitful wiles.
>
> And it grew both day and night.
> Till it bore an apple bright.

Without making reference to any moral judgment against duplicity and deception, we discover in the image of the watering and sunning of the wrath (tree) that there opened within the subject a split between his inner feeling (fear) and his outward show of fraternity (smiles, soft deceitful wiles), which from that moment on precludes any direct connection between emotion and action. This distortion of experience is not subject to a moral condemnation in the sense of a judgment against the speaker himself, for he had made no choice which could be judged. He has sufferred the effects of an anger that cannot immediately express and resolve itself.

The conceit of the poison tree,[4] its simplicity and completeness extending over the last three stanzas as a whole, nonetheless has at its center an indeterminate element—the "apple bright." All the other single elements of the image equating untold wrath with a tree easily

4. If one were immediately to draw the meaning of the image from its biblical source to supply what is missing in the conceit, the poem could be construed as a satire of the Eden myth. God would become the speaker, humankind the foe ensnared by the temptation of something enviable.

find their appropriate equivalents. Within the logic of the conceit, the image of the apple is only vaguely motivated, as by the idea that it is the "fruit" of his wrath. The meaning of "apple bright" is otherwise unspecifiable from the standpoint of the conceit itself. It could be anything—an object, a situation, a person—so long as it fulfilled one general condition: that it be, in the eyes of the foe, an *enviable possession* of the speaker's. Here indeterminacy is an extreme instance of metaphorical condensation. A thousand and one narratives could be told which revolved around an episode in which a character's enemy, thinking he is about to deprive the protagonist of a valued possession, falls to his own ruin:

> And my foe beheld it shine,
> And he knew that it was mine.
>
> And into my garden stole,
> When the night had veild the pole;

These lines resist the poem's moral reading more than any other passage, for they show that this foe could be counted on to try to rob the subject of his possession. Blake had calculated exactly what his foe's reactions and actions would be, having imputed to the other the same destructive antagonism that he had discovered within himself. This equality between protagonist and antagonist now causes the amoral reading to lose its force. The apparent difference between protagonist and antagonist has been dissolved into their essential identity with each other.

At this point, the indeterminacy of the apple and the prototypical nature of the narrative yield a significance that exceeds the grasp of either the moral or the amoral reading. The poem's story is abstract, but not in the sense that it *is* an abstraction. Rather, it unveils the form of abstraction that is historically specific to capitalist society. The prototype narrative and the image of the "apple bright" are like a vortex that pulls everything into itself. Anything could be the enviable possession around which the deadly struggle between Blake and the foe revolves. Possessiveness is not merely an element of their antagonism but its cause; possessiveness pre-forms, socially, their relation to one another as a relation of equality and envy, their mirroring of one another being so complete that the protagonist need only calculatively impute his own aims and motives to the other in order to make his scheme a success. The conditions of the central image-narrative, in other words, are in fact met only in the social conditions of capitalism, where possessive individualism is but the ideological and characterological manifestation of a practice of exchange in which every, that is, *any* object or situation or person is susceptible to an economic designation of value which is then the same for all individuals and becomes something to be possessed. Only under these conditions does the equality of individuals necessarily take the form of antagonism between individuals. Envy, a term borrowed from the ethics of precapitalist societies, is but a name for the fundamental law of interactions in capitalist society as a whole.

The unusual power of this simple poem derives from the play of the image of the "apple bright," which is at once the poem's most abstractly indeterminate and its most concretely, socially determined image. The figurative movement of the image has three distinct moments. First, as an element in the conceit, the "apple bright" stands for the *effect of unexpressed wrath,* a result arrived at in the course of the narrated events. Second, and to the contrary, as a metaphor of the social process of abstraction that forms the very interrelation and interactions of individuals, the "apple bright" stands for the *cause of the antagonism* from which the narrative originated. The conceit substitutes effect for cause. The "apple bright" is thus, at the third moment of its figuration, the trope called a metalepsis. The metalepsis here takes the form of a contradiction between *what is narrated* and *the narrative* itself, for we have discovered the social cause of the poem's narrative in the image that initially stood for the psychological effect of what was narrated, namely, the speaker's unexpressed wrath. In order to have followed this figurative swerve in the poem's language, we have made a break with the two readings, the moral and the amoral, that the text has engendered.

In "A Poison Tree," the critique of bourgeois society is expressed not thematically but in the very articulation of the text and in the dynamic that it provokes. Linguistic theory has distinguished between a text's *énoncé* ("statement") and it *énonciation* ("utterance"), that is, between what is said and the saying of it. In our context, Roman Jakobson's original terminology suffices, distinguishing the *narrated event* and the *speech event.* At the level of the narrated event of "A Poison Tree," an unexpressed wrath results in the destruction of an antagonist by ensnaring him with an enviable possession. The speech event of the poem, I am urging, should be grasped in social and indeed political terms. The text has generated two conflicting and irreconcilable readings, each of which apprehends the poem's status as speech event in a particular way, as a confession or moral judgment on the one hand, and as a cold statement of fact or scenario for destructive action on the other. Neither of these readings can be a true understanding of the text, because neither can explain or cancel the other. Our interpretation has been forced beyond the moral and the amoral reading. The poem must rather be interpreted in terms of its generation of these two partial, blind readings. It generates these readings because they correspond to the two poles of ethical consciousness through which individuals actually live the social relations of capitalist society. The moral reading corresponds to a false morality of goodwill and honesty—which would have been, by the way, the simple object of a satire had Blake kept the poem's notebook title: "Christian Forebearance"! The amoral reading, on the other hand, corresponds to that form of individualism in which individuals, having been made interchangeable with one another, are deprived of the very individuality in the name of which they act.

The dialectic of the text consists in imposing the moral and the amoral readings, which represent the two poles of ethical experience in bourgeois society, and then forcing these two readings back to the figure of the "apple bright" in order for the reader to understand the poem. Both readings are doomed to fail, since they take the "apple bright" as the effect of wrath rather than as the social cause of the antagonism between individuals. The metalepsis, in breaking our interpretation from the two readings, gives form—or figure—to the difference between this act of poetic speech and the lived ethics of bourgeois society.

Let me explain this formulation on poetic form by contrasting the results of the analysis with the position that Marcuse held. For Marcuse, aesthetic experience marks the difference between the real and the possible by presenting an image or appearance whose completeness separates it from the existing conditions and prevalent experiences of social life. Art is sublimation in the sense that it transforms the real into the beautiful appearance; accompanying this aesthetic sublimation, Marcuse argues, is a process of desublimation that occurs in aesthetic perception: "The transcendence of immediate reality shatters the reified objectivity of established social relations and opens a new dimension of experience: the rebirth of rebellious subjectivity. Thus, on the basis of aesthetic sublimation, a *desublimation* takes place in the perceptions of individuals—in their feelings, judgments, thoughts; an invalidation of dominant norms, needs, and values."[5] Now, Blake's "A Poison Tree" does indeed invalidate dominant forms of experience and of ethical consciousness, those which are

5. Marcuse, *The Aesthetic Dimension,* pp. 7–8.

embedded in the socially organized practices and interactions of bourgeois society. But the poem accomplishes this not by means of the beautiful appearance of aesthetic wholeness but rather in the contradiction within the text between the readings it generates and its genesis of the readings. The "dominant norms, needs, and values" the poem negates are as integral to the inner workings of the text as they are inherent in actual social life. What is felt, thought, judged within the historical forms of ethical consciousness that the bourgeois subject must live are themselves a part of the poem's aesthetic dimension, here as the dynamic of the readings which corresponds to the polarity in that ethical consciousness. It is not the unity but the active division of the text which invalidates these social-ethical forms.

So, too, the utopian power of the poem lies not in its protection of an aesthetic appearance of wholeness but in its concrete act of speaking. The concreteness of utopia does not, however, as Bloch would have it, reside in the semantic storehouse of images of happiness and freedom. The utopian is more thoroughly tied to the negative. The poem announces the necessity of an ethical consciousness that cannot yet be lived or represented, but it does so in the fracture between the énoncé and énonciation. The utopian dimension of the poem is enacted in a poetic speaking which manifests the struggle between the social conditions of the poet's speech and the latent possibilities of speech. The movement of figuration, through the three moments of the trope of the "apple bright," invalidates the two readings capable of giving the narrated event (énoncé) and the conceit (tree=wrath) consistency and in this way negates those forms of ethical experience that can be lived in the social context of the poem. What the poem says is negated in the saying of it. What I have called poetic form or figure is here just this difference between énoncé and énonciation, an enactment of the divergence between the real and the possible, the lived and the utopian. "A Poison Tree" points toward a future in which its own story and its mode of telling would no longer be necessary.

The inner logic of Blake's writing is not that of a cultural monument separated from time and change. By the same token, a historicist reading of Blake, intent only on "placing" him "in his own time," would forget that the future is an indispensable dimension of Blake's poetic dialogue with time and history. The socially critical construction of the cultural heritage eschews both the idea that art is above history and the idea that art is merely bound to its own time. When Marx contrasted the bourgeois revolutions of the eighteenth century with the proletarian revolutions of the nineteenth century, he saw in each a specific disharmony of form and content:

> The social revolution of the nineteenth century cannot draw its poetry from the past, but only from the future. It cannot begin with itself before it has stripped off all superstition in regard to the past. Earlier revolutions required recollections of past world history in order to drug themselves concerning their own content. In order to arrive at its own content, the revolution of the nineteenth century must let the dead bury their dead. There the phrase goes beyond the content; here the content goes beyond the phrase.[6]

Blake stands between the realities of the bourgeois revolutions and the possibilities of socialist revolution. Historically, he is a poet of the American and French Revolutions. Unlike the revolutions that stirred his imagination, his poetic practice does not stop short of the goal, rigidifying the forms of freedom and destroying the contents of freedom. Blake was *not* of his time. His poetry demanded a future which the bourgeois revolutions had to resist. I conclude with this juxtaposition of Blake and Marx, of the politics of poetry and the poetics of history, not in order to place Blake within Marx's frame of reference but to situate Marx within a political and cultural process that includes, as a productive and prophetic moment, the poetry of Blake. This becomes all the more necessary in our own historical moment. What for Blake was a future that promised to free him from his present has disappeared within the fabric of our own political and cultural inheritance. We look back at Blake across a wide gap, in that we live a reality that exists because the proletarian revolutions of the nineteenth century did not succeed. We are more the heirs of Blake's restraining reality than of his imagined future. Put another way, his poetry still speaks to us because we have not yet been freed to hear it.

6. Karl Marx, *The Eighteenth Brumaire of Louis Bonaparte* (New York, 1963), p. 18.

TILOTTAMA RAJAN

Romanticism and the Death of Lyric Consciousness

It may seem unusual to begin a discussion of the Romantic lyric by announcing its demise. From the late nineteenth century onward the Romantic period has been characterized as the age of the lyric, by traditions as different as Victorian criticism and the New Criticism. Swinburne, for instance, argues that Shelley holds the same rank in lyric as Shakespeare in drama, ignoring the fact that Shelley did not publish his lyrics, and that Mary Shelley relegated his shorter verse to the end of the collected works.[1] The influence of Symbolism and Imagism, culminating in the New Critical view of the poem as a well-wrought structure in which every rift is loaded with ore and every gap bridged, has done much to perpetuate this critical concentration on the lyric.[2] While the massive presence of the longer poem has been acknowledged, the tendency has been to argue that the Romantics lyricized received forms such as romance, drama, or epic.[3] Moreover, interpretations of Romantic poetry, even when they are not New Critical in method, have been strongly influenced by an ontology

1. For an account of Shelley's reputation as a lyric poet see Frederick Pottle, "The Case of Shelley," in *Shelley: Modern Judgments*, ed. R. B. Woodings (London, 1968), pp. 40 ff.

2. Cf. the emphasis placed by critics like Gittings on Keats's odes, and the New Critical treatment of the odes and romances by Earl Wasserman in *The Finer Tone* (Baltimore, 1953).

3. A recent instance is E. S. Shaffer, *"Kubla Khan" and the Fall of Jerusalem: The Mythological School in Biblical Criticism and Secular Literature, 1770–1800* (London, 1975), pp. 18 ff.

derived from the New Criticism, which assumes that the poem is a reconciliation of opposites, an essential whole unfractured by the differences it synthesizes.

Criticism has thus centered Romantic discourse in the mode (though not the genre) of lyric, with significant consequences for our view of the period. The common view that Romantic literature saw the lyric "as a paradigm for poetic theory"[4] may indeed express an early goal of Romanticism. But it is also designed to provide historical buttressing for the New Critical view of poetic discourse as the creation of a free, autotelic subjectivity or, as Lentricchia puts it, of "an ideal, integrated consciousness" not situated in the world.[5] In different ways, poststructuralism, reader-response theories, and the new Marxism all assume a model of poetry in which the subjective voice, instead of creating its own world, is inscribed within an intersubjective space (be it that of history, literary history, or communication). As we will see, Romantic poetry itself is in the process of discovering a poetic episteme radically at odds with the New Critical one which it is credited with initiating. Thus, although short poems continue to be written, lyric is increasingly absorbed into larger structures which place it within a world of differences. The interdiscursive nature of the Romantic lyric problematizes the mode by revealing the traces of another voice within the seemingly autonomous lyric voice. For instance, Blake's *Songs* and Wordsworth's *Lyrical Ballads* are collections of short poems spoken by different personae, and the *Lyrical Ballads* are, moreover, written by different authors. The collection inevitably forces us to read the individual poem as part of a network of differences, and to consider it in terms of its paradigmatic and syntagmatic relationships with other poems in the collection. By the same token, poems which are commonly taken to interiorize or lyricize received forms can more appropriately be seen as objectifying and thereby complicating a pure subjective discourse by situating it in the world. To give but one example, Coleridge's conversation poems turn monologic effusion into dialogue. In so doing they expose lyrical meditation to the dissent of another voice already present within the supposedly pure *cogito* of lyric discourse. The dialogizing of language at work in all of these poems is most explicitly seen in "The Eolian Harp," where the lyrical voice comes up against a repudiation of its

4. M. H. Abrams, *The Mirror and the Lamp: Romantic Theory and the Critical Tradition* (New York, 1953), p. 98.

5. Frank Lentricchia, *After the New Criticism* (Chicago, 1980), p. 109.

feelings that makes us recognize the self-presence of meaning in the earlier part of the poem as already an illusion.[6]

My argument is that pure lyric is a monological form, where narrative and drama alike are set in the space of difference.[7] The latter present the self in interaction with other characters and events. But lyric, as a purely subjective form, is marked by the exclusion of the other through which we become aware of the difference of the self from itself. Lyric consciousness, in other words, comes as close as possible to approximating what Sartre calls a "shut imaginary consciousness," a consciousness without the dimension of being-in-the-world.[8] The monological autonomy of lyric is something to which Hegel, in the Romantic period, had already drawn attention. The lyric poet, he argues, asserts himself "as a self-enclosed subject," "a subjectively complete world." Although he does not eschew the external world, what he portrays is not objective fact, but "the echo of the external in the mind."[9] Moreover, since lyric, in Hegel's analysis, is based on a hermeneutics of feeling which allows the author to reproduce his own mood in his hearer,[10] lyric utterance communicates internally to a reader who is an echo within the poem and not a separate voice. A semiotics of genre, to complement the structural study of genre begun by Aristotle and the thematics of genre completed by Frye, would see the pure lyric as using its proximity to song in order to mute the gaps between signifier and signified by conferring on the words the illusory unity of a single voice. By contrast, narrative, which dramatizes the gaps between what is told and the telling of it, is always already within a world of textuality, of interpretation rather than origination. A more complex case is that of drama, which at first sight seems to share the lyric proximity to the order of voice. In fact drama deconstructs that order, and reveals the textuality even of voice. For as we will see, it discloses the unitary voice as an illusion and forces us to question the idea of the speaker as a

6. I have dealt with this aspect of the conversation poems in greater detail in *Dark Interpreter: The Discourse of Romanticism* (Ithaca, 1980), pp. 204 ff.

7. Jonathan Culler singles out as the two fundamental conventions of lyric "the expectation of totality or coherence" and a specialization of language which removes the poem from "the ordinary circuit of communication." As a consequence of the latter, the deictics of lyric do not refer us to an external context (*Structuralist Poetics* [London, 1975], pp. 170, 166).

8. Jean Paul Sartre, *The Psychology of Imagination* (New York, 1968), p. 215.

9. G. W. F. Hegel, *Aesthetics: Lectures on Fine Art,* trans. T. M. Knox, 2 vols. (Oxford, 1975), 2:1132, 1120, 1133. Cf. also pp. 1078, 1115–16.

10. Ibid., p. 1110. Cf. also Northrop Frye's comment that lyric is overheard rather than heard, and that it is characterized by "the concealment of the poet's audience from the poet" (*Anatomy of Criticism: Four Essays* [Princeton, 1957], p. 249).

unified person realizing himself through his language. Individual utterances are shown as enmeshed in a language world beyond them, the world of preexisting meanings and of differing intentions present in the other person in the dialogue. This larger language world, moreover, is already present within the individual utterance, because the latter is oriented toward the complexity of this world even as it seeks to minimize its interference.

The difference between the semiotics of lyric and narrative can be seen if we compare a poem such as Wordsworth's "She dwelt among the untrodden ways" with Shelley's *Alastor*. Both deal with a visionary figure who died young and was appreciated more by nature than by humanity. More crucially, both include a second figure, a speaker whose life is somehow changed by this death, a signifier through whose consciousness we must grasp the signified, which is the essential spirit of the visionary figure. At the end of the Wordsworth poem, the speaker allows that something has happened in the hitherto timeless world of lyric: "But she is in her grave, and, oh, / The difference to me!"[11] Yet this intrusion of difference does not seem to disrupt the identity between visionary, nature, speaker, and reader, but rather seals it in the permanence of shared loss. The signified, the ideality of Lucy, remains simple, protected from dismantling by the very brevity of lyric. This poetic reduction to a transcendental signified is precisely what becomes impossible in *Alastor*. As the Narrator represents for us the life of the Poet-Visionary, differences develop in his sense of whether the Poet is an ideal or a failed being, whether he is honored or ignored by nature, whether his death is a universal or a private and insignificant loss. The emergent dialogism of the poem is repressed by the Narrator, who conceives of himself as a lyrist (ll. 42–44) commemorating another lyrist (l. 667).[12] But the very organization of the text militates against the monological, because it is structured as a series of discrepancies between the Poet, the Narrator, the author of the preface, and finally the reader. These discrepancies invite us to approach reading as the disclosure of difference. They are intrinsic to the narrative form, which at its purest, stands at the opposite extreme from the lyric homogenization of the signifier and the signified.

This is not to suggest that the actual lyric ever is a pure origin from which other forms represent a fall, fortunate or otherwise. The no-

11. All references are to *The Poetical Works of William Wordsworth,* ed. Ernest de Selincourt and Helen Darbishire, 5 vols. Oxford, (1940–49; rpt. Oxford, 1966). The 1850 version of *The Prelude* has been used.

12. All references are to Shelley's *Poetical Words,* ed. Thomas Hutchinson (Oxford, 1964).

tion of lyric as the expression of an autonomous and self-coincident subjectivity which either has not uncovered or has resolved the traces of its difference from itself is no more than a hypothesis which the very process of expression inevitably dismantles. The hypothetical lyric described here is like the discourse described by Husserl as occurring "in a language without communication, in speech as monologue, in the completely muted voice of the 'solitary mental life.'"[13] And as Derrida points out in his deconstruction of Husserl's theory of signs, such discourse is an impossibility: the language of the self, even if it does not have to go through the external detour of communication to an other, must submit to the internal detour of expression to itself.[14] But on the other hand it would be wrong to suggest that the logocentric model of lyric developed here is purely a critical fiction projected back onto Romantic poets by their modern interpreters. It is to some extent a Romantic fiction developed by modern critics with theoretical and even practical support from the Romantics themselves. Such a notion of lyric informs, even if it does not sum up, certain Romantic texts. Correspondingly, the dismantling of lyric autotelism is something which happened in Romantic texts themselves, at certain points when the writers themselves became self-consciously aware of the impossibility of such autotelism.

How the intertextualization of the single lyric with other forms of discourse awakens the traces of its difference from itself can be seen if we look at what happens to Wordsworth's brief lyric on the Boy of Winander (the 1799 version from MS JJ) when it is absorbed into Book V of *The Prelude.* There is a certain appropriateness in looking at this poem, because not only is it a lyric, it is also *about* a lyric poet: a boy whose music is made by using his mouth as an instrument, thus absorbing art into nature, writing into song. Subsequent episodes in Book V—the dredging up of a corpse from the lake, and the dream about an Arab who flees from a drowning world—make us aware that this poem may be a narrative rather than an epiphany: a *story* about the drowning of visionary consciousness rather than a lyrical paean to the boy's sustained communion with nature. But if the poem is read by itself, the conventions of lyric set it at a visionary distance, allowing it to remain a foster-child of silence and slow time, and muting our awareness that something *happens* in it. Only at one point is the union of the child with the natural world, and the absorption of ontological

13. Jacques Derrida, *Speech and Phenomena,* trans. David B. Allison (Evanston, 1973), p. 22.

14. Ibid., p. 78.

difference into identity, threatened. That is when the "mimic hootings" of the boy for a moment are not answered by the "halloos and screams" of the owls, and a "lengthened pause / Of silence" baffles "his best skill" (V.372–80). But almost immediately this hiatus, in which something different has intruded into the boy's experience, is filled. He learns to achieve a union with nature through reflective self-consciousness as well as through spontaneous activity, and he remembers silently "the voice / Of mountain torrents" (V.383–84). The poem seems to show that an imaginative communion between the child and nature is sustained even when nature is not immediately present to his consciousness, and hence that all differences in the fabric of vision are ultimately identities. The final lines of the poem appear to confirm this sense. Silence and solitude, we are told, are not vacancy. For in these moments of silence the sky is reflected in the lake, and the entire "visible scene" is then reflected in the child's mind as sky, lake, and consciousness become identical.

The interior monologue of the poem remains unfractured as long as we read it in isolation; for the conventions of lyric, which among other things ask us to respond to poetry on the level of sound rather than content and as song rather than language, allow the poem to unfold in a timeless and transcendental space. But the incorporation of the poem into Book V of *The Prelude* abruptly changes our perspective. It forces us to question the ontology or identity that is part of lyric, as a form which expresses a single mood or transforms difference into sameness. Not only does the space between the lyric and the next verse paragraph create a silence which the reader must fill, and may fill with what the lines avoid saying. There is also a jarring shift of tone from the visionary to the empirical, as we are told "This Boy was taken from his mates, and died / In childhood, ere he was full twelve years old" (V.389–90). These lines of course come after the lyric, but they force us to re-read what has just been said by shifting our frame of reference from a lyrical one, in which we consent to the suspension of time, to a narrative frame, in which we read the text to discover what has happened, what has changed. In other words, they disturb the closure of a poem which previously had been sealed against afterthoughts.

Where the apparent unity of the poem with itself really begins to be dismantled is in the final lines. These lines, as we have seen, had seemed to create an identity between the boy and nature:

> . . . or the visible scene
> Would enter unawares into his mind,

With all its solemn imagery, its rocks,
Its woods, and that uncertain heaven, received
Into the bosom of the steady lake.
(V.384–88)

But they can also be read in a different way. Perhaps the phrase "uncertain heaven" does not refer literally to the clouds reflected in the water but metaphorically to the tenuousness of the paradise the boy constructs out of a material world in which he sees the alphabet of his own imagination. Perhaps then what these lines mean is that this metaphoric heaven is received into the lake as the boy drowns, and the visionary imagination is engulfed by the world. The boy was accustomed to stand by the lake or more perilously still on the cliffs, and though we are not told how he died we are told that he did die. Narcissus, we recall, drowned for not recognizing solitude was vacancy and seeking to become identical with himself, or more precisely with what Lacan would call his specular image. The point is not that these lines tell us the boy died by drowning, but that they raise that possibility, so that the poem now contains its own double or shadow. In retrospect we can no longer say whether this passage commemorates or deconstructs the figure of the young lyric poet. The placing of this lyric beside narratives about drowning, and more generally the interweaving of lyrical and narrative discourse, transforms lyric from a monological to a dialogical form. There are other curious slippages in the passage. One reason we do not think of the original lyric as being about a dead boy, even though it is written in the past tense, is that it uses the past imperfect, the tense of repeated action, in which there is repetition but no change. This tense is maintained throughout in the 1799 version. But in the later version Wordsworth suddenly uses the past perfect, and tells us that a gentle shock "*has* carried" the voices of torrents into the boy's heart, as though there is a certain engulfing finality to this event. Again we do not know whether to read figuratively or literally, whether to understand the shock that carries the mountain torrents into the boy's heart as referring to an emotional fusion between the boy and nature or a literal engulfment of the boy by the torrent. This passage is particularly convenient to consider because it allows us to single out the pure lyric and the interdiscursive lyric as occurrences in the actual history of the text. But in fact Wordsworth's decision to absorb "There was a boy" into *The Prelude* is a paradigm for what happens throughout the prehistory of the longer poem, as the still unwritten lyrical voice is situated in the prose of the world.

Blake's *Songs* provide a more extensive example of the intertextualization of lyric, as something which actually occurs in the textual history of Romanticism. The *Songs of Innocence* were originally published in a separate edition, and there is no indication at this point that Blake intended to complement them with the *Songs of Experience.* The addition of the latter radically changes our interpretation of the *Songs of Innocence,* yet without altering a single word of the individual texts and purely by changing the interpretive conventions within which we read them. Reading the *Songs of Innocence* lyrically, as we must if we take them in isolation, is quite different from reading them interdiscursively, in such a way that the complementary poems become interlocutors which transform lyrical monologues into conversation poems. The lyrical reading produces pietistic interpretations of the poems like those provided by E. D. Hirsch, who sees them as celebrations of an innocence recoverable through faith, imagination, and dream.[15] The interdiscursive reading potentiates in them traces of an irony toward faith and imagination that must haunt even the more organized versions of these faculties for which the innocent state provides only shadowy types. Moreover, these traces were always, already, in the *Songs of Innocence.* But my point is that we are not dealing simply with different reading practices on the part of a modern reader, but with different readings of the same corpus of material elicited by Blake himself at different stages as he reworked his own material and thus transformed the ontopoetics of Romantic discourse. To put it differently, the movement from lyrical to interdiscursive reading is something which happened in the history of Romantic poetry and its perception of itself, and not just something which is happening now in the history of criticism about Romantic poetry. Anne Mellor has pointed to a parallel movement in Blake's graphic work from closed to open form.[16] As he reworked his earlier poems Blake unsealed the book entitled the *Songs of Innocence* and made it into a text, reinscribing what he had earlier written as a reading. In so doing he also made further monological reading impossible. He complicated any future attempt to bind the *Songs* into a book by centering the collection in single poems such as the Bard's "Introduction" or the "Lyca" poems, read lyrically and thus abstracted from a complicating context.

Perhaps the most interesting example of the problematizing of lyric

15. E. D. Hirsch, Jr., *Innocence and Experience: An Introduction to Blake* (New Haven, 1964).

16. Anne Mellor, *Blake's Human Form Divine* (Berkeley, 1974), pp. 58–64.

is Shelley's *Prometheus Unbound,* which he subtitled a lyrical drama. The yoking together of lyric and drama reveals a paradox at the heart of a text which, philosophically, took shape at the crossroads of idealism and dialectical materialism. As visionary lyric, Shelley's text assumes that the world is an extension of the Promethean *cogito,* and can therefore be imaginatively modified by the mind. But as drama it concedes the material objectivity of space and time and does not allow the visionary poem to be a shut imaginary structure insulated from being-in-the-world. A further point about the difference between lyric and drama is made by Hegel, who raises the question of the reader's response to the two modes. Hegel attributes to the lyrical as opposed to the dramatic self the power to constitute the world according to its own desire. The lyric poet, making use of a specialized and "poetic" language, can select his readers and dismiss as irrelevant those whose assumptions do not accord with his own. The simplification of discourse that this permits is not an option available to the dramatist, who must submit his work to a larger and more diverse audience.[17] Interestingly, Hegel does not argue that lyrical subjectivity *is* autonomous, only that the lyrical mode preserves for this subjectivity the illusion of freedom, where the choice of the dramatic mode as the author's means of self-unfolding corresponds to a recognition that language is difference. Given this radical difference between the two modes in terms of the ideality of lyric and the material actuality and correspondingly greater complexity of drama, critics who have dealt with the problem have tended to treat *Prometheus Unbound* as lyric rather than drama. Bennett Weaver suggests that it moves "towards song," and indeed it has been seen as an opera or symphony and sometimes set to music.[18] When the dramatic elements of the text are acknowledged it is read as a dramatic lyric rather than as a lyrical drama. But *Prometheus* is not so much an interiorizing of the dramatic form as an exteriorizing of the lyrical, a reversal of the movement Lukács traces when he sees in Romanticism the beginning of a lyricization of narrative which culminates in the modern novel.[19]

It is interesting in this regard to see which parts of *Prometheus Unbound* can technically be classified as lyric. The lyrical impulse in the play takes two forms: there are extended odes and paeans which are lyrical in the sense that they do not call for a response, and there are

17. Hegel, pp. 1174–75.
18. Bennett Weaver, "*Prometheus Bound* and *Prometheus Unbound,*" *PMLA,* 64 (1949), 132.
19. Georg Lukács, *The Theory of the Novel* (Cambridge, 1971), pp. 112–31.

brief lyrics and songs spoken by figures who are not characterized and are therefore nondramatic. The former include the long celebratory speech by the Spirit of the Hour, which concludes Act III and points the way toward a new dispensation existing at the far goal of time. The latter are spoken by voices of various kinds, who seem to exist in a world of noumenal identity behind the world of the text and therefore in a realm where language has not yet discovered itself as difference. The speeches of the six spirits at the end of Act I are in lyric form, although the complementary Furies are dramatic as well as lyric characters. In Act II the echoes who speak after Panthea has communicated to Asia her dream about the transformation of Prometheus speak in lyric form, inviting Asia to follow them back to the original matrix of things. Lyrics intervene between the sisters' arrival in the realm of Demogorgon and their subsequent, profoundly antiphenomenological dialogue with him. After the conversation with Demogorgon the Spirit of the Hour in the light chariot supposedly destined to bear Asia to Prometheus speaks in lyric form, but interestingly the corresponding spirit in the dark chariot is not set off from the dramatic text in this way. Act II then concludes with two lyrics, the famous "Life of life" lyric and Asia's response, "My soul is an enchanted boat." Most important, Act IV is almost entirely lyrical, and although minor characters from the dramatic text such as Ione and Panthea participate in it, virtually none of the major characters, and certainly none that are human rather than elemental, are present. The form of drama interspersed with lyric is not of course new, being characteristic of Greek drama. In the case of Shelley, however, it has a particular metaphysical and linguistic significance. For it is clear that the lyrics bear the freight of the play's idealistic vision, and that their insertion into a dramatic context radically decenters this vision, potentiating the traces of its differences from itself. I use the word "insertion" advisedly, as at least one of the lyrics, the "Life of life" lyric, was written separately, two years before it was revised for *Prometheus Unbound.*[20] Lyric, because of its proximity to song, is associated with a logocentrism that mutes the difference between language and what it signifies, whereas drama makes explicit the dialogic nature of language, because the presence of more than one speaker makes the text as a whole and even the individual speeches within it a perpetually shifting intersection of textual surfaces rather than something fixed. To put it differently, the dramatic mode foregrounds the subtext by creating not simply silences on the margin of the text,

20. Walter E. Peck, *Shelley: His Life and Work* (1927; rpt. New York, 1969), 2:136.

which exist even in lyric, but also spaces between the discourses that make up the text, silences which, as Pinter has put it, make us aware that "the speech we hear is an indication of that we do not hear. It is a necessary avoidance."[21] The dialogue within the text, in turn, conditions the discourse we construct through reading. It becomes the model for the interpretive process as a dialogue in which the text mediates a series of differences within and between author and reader: differences between author and reader, differences of "author"and "reader" from themselves.

It is perhaps in Act II that we are most aware of the tension between lyric and drama, which is also the tension between phenomenological and poststructuralist concepts of the identity of the text. I have considered elsewhere the antithetical role played by two reading interludes in this act: Asia's dialogue with Panthea on the expression and communication of her two dreams about the renewal of Prometheus and its consequences for mankind, and Asia's dialogue with Demogorgon on whether the Promethean age is imminent.[22] In both scenes Shelley reflects on the nature of understanding or interpreting, seeing it first as a process which brings about an identity between reader, author, and text, and seeing it later as a process through which both reader and author come to know their difference from themselves through the medium of a text which differs from itself. The dialogue on dreams is an attempt to lyricize drama, to take a text woven from separate discourses and reduce it to the unity of a single voice which proclaims the dawning of a new era. Very briefly, the scene starts with a difference: the difference of Panthea, who has had a dream of the ideal, from Asia, who has not. It is this difference which makes dialogue necessary, and makes it premature for Shelley to withdraw to the monological lyricism of the spirits of hope, whose elusive voices we hear in the preceding scene, or of the echoes, whose voices we hear at the end of the scene. But gradually the dreams are communicated and the two sisters achieve an identity of understanding. In a sense the scene is also an allegory of the dialogue of reading, with Panthea functioning as the author who is the hierophant "of an unapprehended inspiration," and Asia functioning as reader. As such it guides us toward a hermeneutics of sympathy in which we seek to merge with the spirit of the work.

Were the play to end here we would read it as a dramatic lyric, in

21. Harold Pinter, "Between the Lines," *The Sunday Times,* 4 March 1962, p. 25.

22. In "Deconstruction or Reconstruction: Reading *Prometheus Unbound,*" *Studies in Romanticism* (forthcoming).

which the registering of the names of the dramatis personae on the page punctuates the text rather than divides it from itself. The effect of this movement from drama to lyric—culminating in the songs of the echoes and a lyrical interlude between spirits and fauns—is like the transcendental reduction described by Husserl. Derrida speaks of this reduction as a "reduction to monologue," which puts "empirical worldly existence between brackets" so as to achieve a moment of pure consciousness and hence of meaning that is completely self-present.[23] But Shelley does not stop at this juncture, and indeed reverses the reduction of drama to lyric. Not only does Demogorgon in the next major scene fail to reassure Asia about the "meaning" supposedly discovered in the previous scenes. The lyrical voice is now situated among other voices that are not at one with it. It is placed in a dramatic context, and gradually becomes different from itself, as Asia in questioning Demogorgon begins to question herself; or (to adapt Derrida), Asia in this scene finds that the individual subject cannot "hear or speak to himself and be affected by the signifier he produces, without passing through an external detour, the world, the sphere of what is not 'his own.'"[24] This alien sphere is Demogorgon, whose cryptic silences and evasive answers gradually dismantle what Asia is saying, but who is also necessary if Panthea's lyrical prophecy is to have a historical as well as an ideal dimension. By compelling Asia to *read* his replies, at times to analyze their grammar in a manner that only frustrates her positivism, Demogorgon makes us see the reading-process as the discovery of differences within a text that cannot be paraphrased and made to coincide with what it is saying. But in this respect, the interchange with Demogorgon is simply the subtext of the earlier interchange with Panthea, which we must now re-read dialogically rather than monologically. When we do this, we discover gaps in its articulation of a seemingly self-present meaning.[25] The presence of the other, an explicit condition of drama, makes us aware that all utterance is incipiently dramatic: a communication to an other (even if the other person be oneself), which forces the language of the self to pass through an external detour and thus to be decentered.

We may argue that it is the impulse to lyricize drama which finally

23. Derrida, p. 43.

24. Ibid., p. 78.

25. For instance, on re-reading the dialogue between Asia and Panthea we find that Asia uses two contradictory images for the visionary communication that occurs when she looks into Panthea's eyes. Panthea's eyes are both transparent, like "the deep, blue, boundless heaven," and labyrinthine, "dark, far, measureless, / Orb within orb, and line through line inwoven" (II.i.114–17).

triumphs here. The remainder of this act and the entire fourth act are after all insistently lyrical. But the discovery that reading is difference makes it impossible hereafter to read the lyrical scenes monologically. A monological reading of the fourth act remains feasible only if we treat it as a shut imaginary structure, and the effect of such a reading is to seal us too within the world of the imaginary. But if we wish to bring its propositional paeans to life by dramatizing them in the theatre of our own experience, we also make them problematical. That the play seeks this kind of animation, which requires it to pass through the external detour of an audience other than Shelley himself, is evident from the fact that it is subtitled a lyrical drama and not a dramatic lyric. Shelley saw its discourse as revolutionary, and thereby set it in the space of historical and personal difference. This brings us to the positive side of the process we have been tracing. Paradoxically the deconstruction of the lyric moment through its insertion into a narrative or dramatic context actualizes as well as dismantles it, and involves a gain as well as a loss. Pure lyric involves a will to transcendental privacy that the Romantics increasingly see as self-limiting, because it compels literary discourse to remain intentional. Hence they seek to actualize lyrical discourse, but in so doing must situate it within a space that extends beyond it and thereby de-idealizes the lyric moment.

The movement in Shelley's play from lyric to drama is one instance of a larger movement in Romanticism toward making the lyric interdiscursive, by intertextualizing it, narrating, or dramatizing it. Eventually the result is also a change in the ideology of what is more narrowly termed the Romantic lyric. We have not touched upon poems like "Mont Blanc," "A Hymn to Intellectual Beauty," or Keats's odes, but they are quite different from the pure lyric, being openly dialogical. Not only do they invite intertextual reading. Individually they are dialogues of self and soul in which the desire of the soul to seek out reality and achieve a phenomenological reduction of mountain, urn, or beauty is continually complicated. We began by saying that Romantic poetry should be seen as an attempt to delyricize discourse by situating it in a more objective space. Before we conclude, however, we must add that the paradoxical nature of Romantic discourse can also be formulated in another way, in terms of the survival of the lyrical voice within forms that erode its autonomy. Both the dismantling of the traditional equation between Romantic literature and lyric consciousness, and the recognition that the lyric is made interdiscursive—but not eliminated—are constitutive moments in our understanding of the ontopoetics of Romanticism. Something other than a New Critical approach to Romantic literature has seemed appropriate, because Romanticism sees the absorption of the centered self into larger processes that operate through it and thus decenter its own discourse. But equally, the survival of the lyrical voice testifies to an understanding of the self that is not quite that of poststructuralism: an understanding of the self as constituted by and not deconstructed by its differences from itself.

CYNTHIA CHASE

"Viewless Wings": Intertextual Interpretation of Keats's "Ode to a Nightingale"

The difficulty of interpreting Keats's poetry is closely bound up with its loveliness, its power to gratify our wish for beauty. For this is a power to provoke nearly unanimous value judgments together with widely disparate accounts of their occasion. Modern criticism of Keats presents a curious picture: a clear consensus on the harmonious tenor of the development leading from "Sleep and Poetry" to the ode "To Autumn," together with strong disagreement on the meaning of its individual moments. I will begin by sketching one such disagreement—about how to characterize Keats's situation in the exquisite fifth stanza of the Nightingale Ode—to help us ask: what investments can we discern here, important enough to be common to such opposite critical readings? For if critics give incompatible accounts of key passages, and yet end with the same judgments, their conclusions must be motivated by some other kind of constraint than the acts of reading from which they ostensibly arise. The nature of such constraints on critical reading can emerge for us, I suggest, if we attend to the tropes and the rhetorical gestures that Keats's ode cites or repeats—if we carry out a certain kind of intertextual reading.

How does one characterize the gesture of the ode's peculiarly Keatsian fifth stanza—naming flowers in the darkness, guessing each sweet, "White hawthorn, and the pastoral eglantine"? It depends on how one reads the fourth: it depends on that notorious crux where—as typically in Keats—the most lovely *and* the most variously interpreted[1] lines of the poem coincide:

1. Morris Dickstein makes this point in *Keats and His Poetry: A Study in Development* (Chicago, 1971), p. 208.

Already with thee! tender is the night,
And haply the Queen Moon is on her throne,
Clustered around by all her starry Fays;
But here there is no light,
Save what from heaven is with the breezes blown,
Through verdurous glooms and winding mossy ways.

The fifth stanza continues, "I cannot see what flowers are at my feet . . ." The question of how to take this passage is loaded by the lines at the opening of stanza four with the issue of Keats's commitment to poetic flight:

Away! away! for I will fly to thee,
Not charioted by Bacchus and his pards,
But on the viewless wings of Poesy,
Though the dull brain perplexes and retards:

The decision how to read what follows amounts to a judgment upon the speaker's commitment to "the viewless wings of Poesy." And it's here that one finds an incipient consensus—not upon the function of the viewless wings in these lines, but upon the desirability of Keats's ultimately giving them up. Interpretations of the fourth and fifth stanzas converge in a final value judgment—that Keats ought to abandon poetic flight—after diverging widely on just *how* these stanzas mean that. Keats's lines effectively resist attempts to determine the matter more precisely by appealing to them alone, for at this decisive juncture the ode's syntax turns radically ambiguous. To judge the effects of recourse to the viewless wings of poesy we have to decide how to voice the exclamation point after "thee." A mute mark stands at the place which is *either* an exclamation at arrival *or* a statement of distance. The punctuation mark doesn't tell us how to hear it: whether as an expression of passionate satisfaction, or as a mere pause for differentiation, like a heavier comma or displaced italics. To have an *ear* for this can only be to have a stake in a story about the Nightingale and Keats.

Earl Wasserman's cold ear—rigorously attentive to the program by which the ode distances the poet from his addressee—can hear that "thee!" as no more than a stressed difference: with *thee* the night is tender, with me, meanwhile, it's not. For Wasserman the fifth stanza, with the poet's evocation of "The coming musk-rose, full of dewy wine, / The murmurous haunt of flies on summer eves," matters chiefly as a deferred and imagined season that cannot match the summer sung "in full-throated ease" by the nightingale.[2]

More typically this "guessing" of "what flowers are at my feet" is taken as a reward, and as a characteristically Keatsian achievement something like the luxurious surmise of the ode "To Autumn." Leslie Brisman takes this stanza as a reward for "the demystified *rejection* of transcendent flight" he finds in the fourth stanza. Casting off the "viewless wings" of the visionary imagination together with "the dull brain [that] perplexes and retards" brings Keats at once to the resonant resources "at my feet"—to a "poetry of earth," "to the significant earth whence all sign-constructions take their origin."[3]

We find the same conclusion at the end of an entirely different reading by Jack Stillinger, for whom the speaker's situation in stanza five is not a reward but a bereavement: he sees in it "the speaker's vivid realization of what he has lost by crossing the boundary into an imaginary ideal"—"the transient natural world he has *left behind* and now longs for."[4] Rejection of wings, return to the earth, or adoption of wings, loss of the earth; diametrically opposed as they are, both readings feed into essentially the same account of Keats's accomplishment. He is praised for renouncing finally the Romantic vision of poetry as transcendent flight, and so inaugurating the demystifying gesture of modernism. Critical unanimity about Keats reflects an agreement on how to place Romanticism in the literary tradition. It is seen as a predominantly symbolic and recurrently visionary and escapist mode, to be valued insofar as critical moments of its greatest men, Keats and Wordsworth, anticipate the undeceived modernist vision which marks our own historical moment.

Keats is the poet most assertively invoked where the Romantics are judged from the standpoint of their consistency with a certain note sounded in Stevens and Williams: a "poetry of earth," committed to the intensities and truths of perception. I would suggest that Keats gets invoked in this context because his poetry has to be appropriated, since in fact it *questions* the status of perception, makes the nature of sensory evidence a difficulty. But at the same time Keats's poetry richly gratifies that wish for beauty that impels us to ascribe epistemological authority to the aesthetic, to presume the continuity of

2. Earl Wasserman, *The Finer Tone: Keats' Major Poems* (Baltimore, 1953), pp. 192–93.

3. Leslie Brisman, *Romantic Origins* (Ithaca, 1978), p. 83.

4. Jack Stillinger, *The Hoodwinking of Madeline and Other Essays on Keats's Poems* (Urbana, 1971), p. 102.

perception with knowledge. It is this that makes Keats's texts peculiarly hard to read.

The predominant critical account would reassure itself about a quite intractable issue. We find Brisman and Bloom, as well as Stillinger (along with other less strikingly disparate critics), praising what Stillinger describes as Keats's "final opting for the natural world, where all the concrete images of poetry come from and where melodies impinge on 'the sensual ear' or not at all."[5] The resemblance to Brisman's praise of stanza five is striking: Keats returns to "the significant earth whence all sign-constructions take their origin." These very affirmations indicate what constrains such different critical readings to conclude with the same affirmation. It is vital that signs be seen to "take their origin" or find their expression in the phenomenal world, just as it is vital that "melodies"—or language—"impinge on 'the sensual ear.'" The intelligibility of language and the meaningfulness of sensory experience require it. But does Keats's text make this guarantee? The problem is indeed that "melodies impinge on 'the sensual ear' or not at all." At stake is the possibility of *hearing* writing—of hearing a voice in, and putting a face or a name to, linguistic signs. At stake is the assumption on which reading depends, the continuity between perception and cognition—and Keats's poetry treats it as an *issue* rather than an assumption. The Nightingale Ode ends with a question about the status of the intense perception it has evoked. "Was it a vision or a waking dream?"

The question of whether perception is not hallucination surfaces often in Keats's poetry, but it arises with special force through the prominence of that paradigmatic lyric mode, the ode. The ode's distinctive trait is a special kind of prosopopoeia or personification, the gesture of address. Odes generally entail apostrophe, sometimes to the reader, sometimes to a nonhuman or an inanimate object. Now, this trope that usually works to "make the objects of the universe potentially responsive forces"—that characteristic lyric function—tends to be not interrogated, but dismissed as meaningless cliché. Critics as various as George Shuster (in *The English Ode from Milton to Keats*) and Michael Riffaterre (in *La Production du texte*) have tended to dismiss apostrophe as being insignificant because it is simply conventional; they tend, as Jonathan Culler and Paul de Man point out, to try to "transform apostrophe into description."[6] But in the characteristic discourse of the lyric, description of objects' sensory qualities—per-

5. Ibid., p. 100.
6. Jonathan Culler, *The Pursuit of Signs* (Ithaca, 1981), p. 138.

ception—only follows upon the primary apostrophic gesture. "The address frames the description it makes possible" (writes de Man); "the figuration" in the text "occurs by way of address."[7] Apostrophe expresses the lyric presupposition that the object may be addressed as a subject, and it makes that vital presupposition quite "independently of any claims made about the actual properties of the object addressed."[8] The figural logic of the lyric as it appears in its paradigmatic form, the ode, would make us grasp the sense of Vico's assertion that poetry—and specifically the trope that "gives sense and passion to insensate things"—is the origin of language.[9] Why then are critics uncomfortable about making the figure of address conspicuous? For good reason: What we suppress when we ignore apostrophe is the dependence of all discourse, including what we call *perception,* on the figure of address. For what the address does is to claim the existence of an addressee capable of *hearing* it: capable of giving ear, of giving voice, to a text; passing from a sign to a sound and a sense; passing between cognition and perception. The trope of address, a prosopopoeia, institutes the intelligibility of language by engendering the figure of a reader—that is, by letting us conceive of the reading of a text as an intelligible perceptual process like hearing.

Keats's "Ode to a Nightingale" plays on the presupposition that the addressee can *hear* by addressing a being which has a *voice.* The address to a creature that sings enforces the assumption that to be able to sing is to be able to listen, that to have a voice is to be able to hear. This kind of reciprocity does *not* exist between a text and a reader, as the *Phaedrus* pointed out: we hear its assertions, but it doesn't hear our questions. But the nightingale, by implication, can, and at the same time the ode represents its own action as an act of listening. Keats's poem is full of phrases and figures from Milton and Shakespeare (seventeen by one count), and one way they function is as echoes: they enforce the ode's basic trope, persuading us that Keats is "listening" by persuading us that we hear what he hears. What motivates this rhetorical strategy? Continuity between singing and listening is desirable in both senses: if to be able to listen is to be able to sing, then Keats's own position in literary history—listening to older voices—is a favorable one. But an intertextual reading will show us that the power to pass from hearing to singing is one the ode ascribes

7. Paul de Man, "Hypogram and Inscription: Michael Riffaterre's Poetics of Reading," *Diacritics,* 11:4 (Winter 1981), p. 32.

8. Culler, *Pursuit of Signs,* p. 140.

9. Giambattisto Vico, *The New Science,* trans. T. G. Bergin and M. H. Fisch (New York, 1961), p. 87.

not to the poet himself but to Milton, the "immortal bird" to whose phrases Keats's ode "listens," "darkling," more than any other.

The poet's sense of distance from the nightingale can then be read as Keats's sense of the discrepancy between his own and his precursor's power of song. Morris Dickstein, among others, is persuasive in linking Keats's adieu to the nightingale with an adieu to "another music he had left behind," as he puts it, and quotes Keats, "I have but lately stood on my guard against Milton. Life to him would be death to me." "Like his tutelage to Milton," Dickstein writes, "Keats's enchantment with the song of the nightingale had in the end turned into a struggle for survival."[10] But the struggle in the ode is of a different sort. We need an intertextual reading less eager to evoke persons and more attentive to recurrent rhetorical patterns. Such reading suggests that the mixed praise and blame in the ode reflects not a struggle with a deafening precursor, but radical ambivalence about the poem's chosen trope. Critics noting Keats's ambivalence about the nightingale frequently approve the poem's final stanza for marking a stage in his renouncement of the visionary imagination and renewed concern for real life: "Adieu! the fancy cannot cheat so well / As she is famed to do, deceiving elf." But it is not the nightingale as the symbol of the visionary mode that is the "deceiving elf" for Keats. The deceiver is not the addressee of the ode but its "fancy," the address itself. And the deception is rather, we might say, a *déception:* it dismays and deceives us by not deceiving us thoroughly enough. The appeal to voice leaves precariously evident the rhetoricity, the fictitiousness, of the vital supposition it imposes. The gesture of address in the Nightingale Ode functions like the "tongueless nightingale" Keats summons up in "The Eve of St. Agnes." With that trope Keats collapses the narrative of Philomel's *recovery* of voice into an emblem expressing how the *figure* of voice is, precisely, voiceless. The intelligibility of language depends on a figure itself mute, unable to make itself intelligible.

The ode's ambivalences mark Keats's confrontation with the fundamental trope that Milton and Wordsworth, as well as Keats, deployed with notable misgiving. We find the same stance toward listening in a turn in Wordsworth's Immortality Ode: "I hear, I hear, with joy I hear! / *But*—" But, indeed: Keats's ode envisages death in these terms: "*Still* I wouldst thou sing, and I *have ears in vain*"—asserting the futility of the very stance he assumes, and measuring that futility as one outlasting the very difference between life and death. Keats's

10. Dickstein, *Keats and His Poetry,* p. 219.

most grimly apostrophic poem, "This Living Hand," deeply resembles Milton's epitaph "On Shakespeare." Milton's fancy here is that Shakespeare's own writings form the one sufficient monument to his name, a monument that has the fluency of speech. This epitaph, like Keats's ode, credits its addressee with a voice. Wordsworth quotes half the poem in his *Essays upon Epitaphs;* he omits a passage which like Keats's "This Living Hand" conceives a poetry which can induce the wish to die, in these telling lines:

> For whilst to the shame of slow-endeavoring art
> Thy easy numbers flow, and that each heart
> Hath from the leaves of thy unvalued book,
> Those Delphic lines with deep impression took,
> Then thou our fancy of itself bereaving
> Dost make us marble with too much conceaving,
> And so sephulchr'd, in such pomp, dost lie
> That kings for such a tomb would wish to die.

The passage represents the dangerous implication of these texts' chief figure, prosopopoeia, or the figure of address, the "thou" we accord a body of writing: that "thou," "our fancy of itself bereaving / Dost make us marble"—monumentalizes us in turn. To *hear* a monument, to hear its "easy numbers flow," is to take on ourselves the mute fixity of a monument or a text.[11]

In "The Fall of Hyperion" Keats writes, "Poesy alone can tell her dreams, / With the fine spell of words alone can save / Imagination from the sable charm / And dumb enchantment." But "The Fall" goes on to show that poesy's spell, the gesture of address, is also spellbinding: when the narrator of "The Fall" invokes the poets, "pledging all the dead whose names are in our lips," the draught brings on a swoon, and a dream-vision entailing further perils of ultimate stillness. ("Die on that marble where thou art," Moneta tells him, and his chief act is to take up Saturn's immobile posture "in the unchanging gloom.") The first stanza of the Nightingale Ode stresses that the voice he lends the nightingale works on him like the "domineering potion" of "The Fall."

Its effect would seem to culminate in stanza six, with the passage, "Darkling I listen. . . . Now more than ever seems it rich to die." What do we make of the fact that this wish to die follows directly upon the ode's single deliberate allusion to Milton? I would suggest that we

11. Cf. Paul de Man, "Autobiography as De-facement," *Modern Language Notes*, 94:5 (December 1979), 928.

must look to the exact context to tell us more than that. Keats alludes to a passage in which Milton himself is apostrophizing, the invocation of Book III of *Paradise Lost,* where Milton frames a regret for his blindness with an address to heavenly light. "Darkling I listen"—"Nightly I visit": the echo runs from Milton's evocation of *his* pledge:

> Thee Sion and the flowrie Brooks beneath
> That wash thy hallowed feet, and warbling flow,
> Nightly I visit: nor sometimes forget
> Those other two equalled with me in Fate,
> So were I equalled with them in renown,
> Blind Thamyris and blind Maeonides,
> And Tiresias and Phineus, Prophets old.
> Then feed on thoughts, that voluntarie move
> Harmonious numbers; as the wakeful Bird
> Sings darkling, and in shadiest Covert hid
> Tunes her nocturnal Note.

What matters here is not simply that Milton identifies himself with the bird, who *sings* darkling, while Keats distinguishes himself from the bird, and listens darkling. John Hollander puts it: "The word is transformed in the echo, not merely by being applied to the response rather than to the act of eloquence, but by including in its sound somehow an acknowledgment of its source, as if to say . . . 'Darkling, I listen to Milton's *darkling.*'"[12] Keats's allusion tells us that he is hearkening to the Milton whose claim to sing issues directly from an address to the heavenly muse.

Prosopopoeia and apostrophe are in fact the central devices of the poems echoed in the ode's earlier stanzas as well, "L'Allegro" and "Il Penseroso" and "Lycidas." But the Milton invoked with "Darkling I listen" has also mobilized the powerful trope of blindness. Blindness means the invisibility of language become pure voice or inner light; it stabilizes prosopopoeia in a ratio where the perceptual and the cognitive, and the visible and the audible, hold fixed places. In the total absence of literal light the troubled connection between perception and cognition is dissolved, in the single certainty that voice represents illumination. The nightingale singing in darkness, named "immortal bird" in the next stanza, is the "self-begotten bird" of *Samson Agonistes:*

12. John Hollander, *The Figure of Echo: A Mode of Allusion in Milton and After* (Berkeley, 1981), p. 90. I owe to conversation with Margaret Ferguson the connection between this nightingale singing in darkness and the "self-begotten bird" of *Samson Agonistes,* discussed below.

Samson's blindness gets linked in this passage to his being "With inward eyes illuminated . . . into sudden flame," like the phoenix, the "secular bird of ages" whose "*fame* survives" although "her *body* die," a clear-cut compensation in which identity is totally preserved, in a "self-same song" (Keats's phrase) "that no second knows nor third" (Milton's). It is in response to this rhetorical figure, rather than to Milton or to the precursor as such, that Keats recalls his impulse to call *death* "soft names in many a muséd rhyme," and "to cease upon the midnight with no pain."

But it is the lines following these in which the misgivings about prosopopoeia reach their greatest intensity, as the conception of death shifts radically: "Still wouldst thou sing, and I have ears in vain; / To thy high requiem become a sod." What is remarkable about these lines, as I suggested earlier, is that the crucial futility, which is the very condition of the poem, to "have ears in vain," is identified as a condition common to both death *and* life. Devastating in the same way is an expression in the opening lament of *Samson Agonistes:* "The sun to me is dark / *And silent* as the moon." Samson laments as desperate blindness an ordinary condition of perception, the silence of the sun. The sun is silent, literally, not just to Samson; to cite this as a catastrophe is to point to how vital is the identification of light with intelligibility conceived as voice. Thinking of the *light* of the senses as *speaking* meaningfully is our way of conceiving phenomenal, perceptual experience to be continuous and consistent with knowledge. This is what we do in ascribing epistemological authority to aesthetic experience; we credit as natural and as given the figure of speaking light, the identification of light, voice, and intelligibility. Samson's describing the silence of the sun as a catastrophe indicates how fatal is the strictly figurative, rhetorical status of that identification. His sentence makes explicit the assumption that to "have ears" or to *see* the sun is as good as to be dead if one does not also *see* and *speak the sense of* what one hears, if one does not also *hear* in one's own voice the significations of "light." Keats's phrase like Milton's describes the perception of the phenomenal world as a hopeless deprivation and signals the precariousness of the trope required to make it meaningful. As Samson puts it, he is "deprived thy prime decree, 'Let there be light,' and there was light." Perception is a deprivation because it hangs on a decree, the primary positing of a "thee" whose word brings light.

Thus when the notorious crux in stanza four hangs our estimation of "the viewless wings of poesy" on a radically undetermined "thee!" it checks interpretive judgment in an exemplary, revealing way. Still more is revealed by the Miltonic pre-text for the same figure. "Viewless wings" echoes (as we say) the same figure in the last stanza of Milton's unfinished poem "The Passion": it reads,

> Or should I thence hurried on viewless wing,
> Take up a weeping on the mountains wild,
> The gentle neighborhood of grove and spring
> Would soon unbosom all their echoes mild,
> And I (for grief is easily beguiled)
>   Might think the infection of my sorrows loud
> Had got a race of mourners on some pregnant cloud.

The poem breaks off there. Margaret Ferguson defines its pertinence to the Nightingale Ode: "excessive pregnancy lapsing into silence." The lapse after flight on viewless wings, only to arrive "already with thee," but find that "here there is no light"—that lapse has a precedent in the effects of the same figure in Milton's poem.

Moreover, these lines disclose the system of assumptions involved in how we describe them, in our calling such a repetition an "echo." Echo is a nymph, initially, with a story much like Philomel's, the tongueless girl who wove her tale into a tapestry before she turned nightingale. These are stories of the victory of voice over meaningless repetition or over mute textile and mutilated figure. Milton's conceit has "the gentle neighborhood of grove and spring / . . . *unbosom* all their echoes mild": echoes are not simply sounds bounced off surfaces but responses issuing from a "bosom," from an inward state. Echoing is at once natural and human; to speak of a person *echoing* another's feeling is to *naturalize* a discursive and not inevitable response, while to speak of a landscape echoing a speaker is to personify a natural element. To speak of a *text* "echoing" another naturalizes and humanizes at the same time what is essentially a semiotic structure. Reading—our conception of reading on the model of a perceptual process, like hearing or seeing—depends on this prosopopoeia; signs must be actualized by an act of perception in a responsive subject. The "listening" reader functions like "the gentle neighborhood of grove and spring," and is just as figurative an entity. Milton's intricate conceit here images echoes as "a *race* of mourners" begotten by the coupling of a human lament and a natural object. Both metaphors presume the same stable primacies: the same generational hierarchy places a sire at the origin of his "race" and a voice at the origin of its echo. Milton's combination of the two metaphors reveals the investments that underlie discussion of "echoes" as well as allusions to poetic "fathers."

To produce echoes is to engender readers, and vice versa. But just here Milton is cut off. The poem breaks off in imagining its unlimited seminal power. Where the text makes the fullest claims for its fundamental trope is also where its statement and its action split entirely. It seems no accident, then, that Keats's poem attains its greatest unintelligibility at the point at which it repeats this figure.

Keats's flight on viewless wings can be situated in another intertextual dimension as well. Eamon Grennan traces the shift in the conception of death in stanza six to Claudio's shift in attitude in Act III, scene i of *Measure for Measure,* where Claudio first proposes to "embrace the darkness like a bride," and then imagines death with dread:[13]

> Ay, but to die, and go we know not where,
> To lie in cold obstruction and to rot,
> This sensible warm motion to become
> A kneaded clod . . .
> . . . .
> To be imprisoned in the viewless winds,
> And blown with restless violence round about
> The pendent world . . .

What authorizes deducing an "echo" here is not the similar sound of "wings" and "winds" but the similar rhetorical patterns. Leslie Brisman takes up the phrase "viewless winds" to convoke another kind of intertext, a text unread by Keats, a revision for the 1850 *Prelude* that introduces the word "viewless" into the passage in Book V celebrating "the great Nature that exists / In works of mighty poets":

> Visionary power
> Attends the motions of the viewless winds,
> Embodied in the mystery of words:
> There, darkness makes abode, and all the host
> Of shadowy things work endless changes . . .

"Viewless winds" is a curious pleonasm. "Viewless *wings*" calls poetry an invisible means of transport: not by any literal vehicle but by the transport of words from literal to figural significations, from visible to viewless referents. Poetry or figurative language is an invisible mechanism for rendering things invisible and hence meaningful. (Placing

13. Eamon Grennan, "Keats's Contemptus Mundi: A Shakespearian Influence on 'Ode to a Nightingale,'" *Modern Language Quarterly,* 36 (1975), 272–92.

this trope in an ode to a nightingale compounds its circularity or tautology: the poet says in effect that he will fly on viewless wings to viewless wings.) "Viewless *winds*" calls figurative language *breath,* the medium of voice. What both these figures do is spirit away the visible and the material status of language, its existence as writing or signs. For acknowledgment of that material dimension one would have to turn to other texts of Keats's or Wordsworth's—Wordsworth's *Essays upon Epitaphs* and poems that title themselves inscriptions, Keats's "This Living Hand," the opening of "The Fall of Hyperion," perhaps, and even the "Ode on a Grecian Urn." The "Ode to a Nightingale" rather confronts the consequences of the figure of *voice* that is our habitual and essential conception of language.

Brisman cites the passage from *The Prelude* in order to contrast Keats's direction with Wordsworth's. "Wordsworth is pointing us 'there'—in signs, in the space separating signs from significance—while Keats returns us 'here'—to the significant earth whence all sign-constructions take their origin."[14] He quotes Heidegger to credit Keats with what *The Origin of the Work of Art* calls "setting forth the earth" and "setting up a world"—and declines to recall that for another Heidegger Being-in-the-world is a condition of *Dasein,* no such thing as a *hiersein;* but one need not stray farther than "Lycidas," really, to dispute Brisman's sanguine reading of stanza five. What he does achieve, though, in adducing the *Prelude* passage, is to charge the question of Keats's stance toward flight on viewless wings with the loaded issue of Keats's stance toward the visionary imagination. And also, brilliantly, he connects visionary power with death, by showing that the images in which Wordsworth describes imagination resemble those with which Shakespeare describes being dead.

Yet these alignments still make up a surprisingly predictable story. They enable Brisman to tell, about stanzas four and five of the Nightingale Ode, the story critics have mostly wanted to tell about Keats's development. Keats's renouncement of visionary transport can now be identified as an evasion of death as well, and his recourse to the earth and its natural objects be construed as a saving return to the *origins* of imaginative life associated too with *originality,* with independence of the precursor. For this story to stick, the reading has to stop with stanza five, to ignore the turn toward death in the sixth stanza. Yet Brisman cites a text which can make us see the ironic logic of this entire sequence. In the second stanza of Wordsworth's "A Slumber Did My Spirit Seal," he points out, we find again the image of being

14. Brisman, *Romantic Origins,* p. 83.

confined in a placeless place, rolled round the earth rather than embedded in it, that marked Claudio's conception of death:

A slumber did my spirit seal;
  I had no human fears:
She seemed a thing that could not feel
  The touch of earthly years.

No motion has she now, no force;
  She neither hears nor sees;
Rolled round in earth's diurnal course,
  With rocks, and stones, and trees.

In the first stanza, a human being is imagined as like a natural "thing," exempt from change, from "the touch of earthly years." In the next stanza it turns out that she is indeed exempt from touch and shares the state of natural objects—and that this is to be, not safe from death, but dead.[15] Identification with natural objects, in an evasion of temporality and death, rather brings on or constitutes that very death—which is not a state of rest but a state of constant motion, precisely like the endless change and placeless place of words or the imagination.

Though we may not hear anything like Wordsworth's toneless irony in Keats's exquisitely inflected middle stanzas, it is productive to read stanzas four through six in the same way. Thus the movement from precarious flight on the viewless wings of poetic language, to sensing the incense of the palpable objects growing "at my feet"—that shift in fact situates the speaker in an "embalméd darkness" which reappears a stanza later as the state of death, as the equivalent of being a senseless "sod." And the sod is still accompanied by the nightingale's "high requiem"—pursued by "viewless wings"—even as to be a "kneaded clod" in Claudio's vision gives no respite from being blown by "viewless winds," and even as the dead "she" of Wordsworth's poem is "rolled round in earth's diurnal course" rather than at rest from the drive of direction toward meaning. In short, these stanzas share with Shakespeare's and Wordsworth's texts a figurative sequence linking imagination, earth, *and* the appeal to natural objects. The appeal to the natural object—whether by imagining a human being as a perceivable thing or by imagining nonhuman things as expressive beings—is shown to be not an escape from but only an-

15. Cf. Paul de Man, "The Rhetoric of Temporality," in *Interpretation: Theory and Practice,* ed. Charles S. Singleton (Baltimore, 1969), pp. 205–6.

other mode of precisely the commitment to figurative language that it sought to avoid, a commitment to the vital and deadly trope of prosopopoeia.

To read Keats's stanzas according to Wordsworth's in this way, though, is to risk overlooking the utterly distinctive qualities and un-Wordsworthian preoccupations of the Nightingale Ode. Keats is particularly concerned with the status of perception. Compare the end of the "Ode to a Nightingale" with the end of "The Solitary Reaper": "The music in my heart I bore / Long after it was heard no more." For Wordsworth perception is subsumed in the act of recollection. For Keats it is made critical, and tentative, by its dependency on an *Erinnerung* felt not as recollection but as guesswork and anticipation:

> I cannot see what flowers are at my feet,
> Nor what soft incense hangs upon the boughs,
> But, in embalmèd darkness, *guess* each sweet
> Wherewith the seasonable month endows
> The grass, the thicket, and the fruit-tree wild;
> White hawthorn, and the pastoral eglantine;
> Fast-fading violets covered up in leaves;
> And mid-May's eldest child,
> The coming musk-rose, full of dewy wine,
> The murmurous haunt of flies on summer eves.

To name these unseen flowers is to guess them, call them, greet them. This straitened tentative perceiving is an act of reading, reminiscent of the closing address to Melancholy in "Il Penseroso," the request for some "mossy cell,"

> Where I may sit and rightly spell
> Of every star that heaven doth shew,
> And every herb that sips the dew;
> Till old experience do attain
> To something like prophetic strain.

Keats attains "to something like prophetic strain" in naming "the coming musk-rose, full of dewy wine," and his doing so depends, like the Penseroso poet's, on "old experience" of the sweets "*endowed*" by every season—"endowment" resting the natural process on a contractual one, the rhetorical contract whereby the months restore us what we greet as "seasonable." The poet's wishful naming of "sweets" is a willful greeting that recalls the flowers he has "spelled," not just the flowers he has seen. His calling recalls the anthology in "Lycidas," framed by its apostrophe:

> Ye valleys low where the mild whispers use,
> Of shades and wanton winds, and gushing brooks,
> On whose fresh lap the swart star sparely looks,
> Throw hither all your quaint enamelled eyes,
> That on the green turf suck the honied showers,
> . . . .
> Bring the rathe primrose that forsaken dies,
> . . . .
> The musk-rose, and the well-attired woodbine . . .

Keats's stanza only suspends, it does not forget, the question posed from Milton's poem: "false surmise" or true. (The "dewy wine" of the musk-rose is not named "the true, the blushful Hippocrene," like the "beaker full of the warm south"; stanza five holds off from too assertive hints that for a thing to blush, to have a face to lose, is for it to be "true.")[16]

The pastoral of *Paradise Lost* affirms "Hesperian fables true; / If true, here only." The guessing of sweets in the Nightingale Ode, like the calling of flowers in "Lycidas," is a "*false* surmise" in the sense that it diverges from the poem's main act of attention: attention to the unnatural death of Lycidas "under the whelming tide," to the "dread voice(s)" that "touch" the poet's "trembling ears," and to the whelming voice of the nightingale. The "uncouth swain" of "Lycidas" has declared explicitly that his song is a gesture that disrupts seasonal time, that shatters its leaves before their "season due," compelled by the occasion of a poet's death. Hence Lycidas' elegist can renounce as false the surmise that the earth's flowers might gather to provide the poet a seasonable grave. But the elegist and celebrant of the Nightingale Ode can make no such assured distinction between false and true surmises of perception, nor between the guesswork that lends names and face and the surmise that lends its *voice* to viewless things. Keats's text displays the effects of knowing that naming or describing an object implies the primary figure of address: the gesture of conferring intelligibility upon a collection of signs by endowing them with an *outline* having the power to *address* us—a face and a voice.

Wordsworth acclaims the visionary power of words insofar as they *embody* thought—and names this function in words naming the medi-

16. On Keats's identifying the "blushful" with the "true," see Christopher Ricks, *Keats and Embarrassment* (London, 1974), pp. 201–2.

um of voice as the power of death, Shakespeare's "viewless winds." And so "the very word" leaves Keats "forlorn": "Forlorn! the very word is like a bell / To toll me back from *thee* to my sole self!" John Hollander points out that even as Keats echoes his own poem, he also echoes Milton's one more time.[17] He is forlorn in the very impossiblity of being alone in his forlornness. For the self-reflection in the weighing of that word dates from Adam's self-delusion, loving Eve:

> How can I live without thee, how forgo
> Thy sweet Converse and Love so dearly join'd,
> To live again in these wild Woods forlorn?

In applying "forlorn" first to a place ("faery lands") and then to himself, Keats reenacts the effect of Milton's syntax, where the "forlorn" applied by Adam to himself makes the wild woods of paradise forlorn too, fallen with him even as he speaks. This is the ode's question also: how can *I* live without *thee?* This passage also suggests how little it signifies when we impose our own unwarranted personification—when we succumb to the tempting simplification of calling the "I" of the poem "Keats." Here "Keats" is tolled back to the "sole self," but not just to *his* "sole self," for his way of doing it shows us that he cannot say "I" without also saying Adam's "I," the first *I* and all *I*'s. *I* and *thee,* like *here, now, there,* are deictics, terms which designate absolutely general categories even as they point to particulars. This linguistic feature makes naming the self a gesture as problematic as affirming the certainty of perception—as futile as asserting the particularity of what "I hear *this passing night,*" or of any here and now. (So in the chapter of the *Phenomenology* entitled "Sensory Evidence" Hegel invites us to write down a piece of paper, "Now is the night.").[18] In the final stanza of the ode, the emptiness of Keats's "sole self" is matched with the emptiness of sensory evidence: "Was it a vision or a waking dream? . . . Do I wake or sleep?"

Let me conclude by distinguishing very explicitly between two ways of interpreting the prominent presence in the ode of both invocation and the description of perception. The fundamental trope of the figure of echo is prosopopoeia: the persuasion that a text has a voice.

17. Hollander, *The Figure of Echo,* pp. 36–37.

18. On the deictic function and on pointing to examples (*Beispiel*) in Chapter 1 of the *Phenomenology,* see Paul de Man, "Hypogram and Inscription: Michael Riffaterre's Poetics of Reading," *Diacritics,* 11:4 (Winter 1981), 27–30; and Andrzej Warminski, "Reading for Example: 'Sense Certainty' in Hegel's *Phenomenology of Spirit,*" *Diacritics,* 11:2 (Summer 1981), 83–94.

This is the same figure that invests responsiveness in a natural object—which can thereby elicit our perception. Now, one way to take the prominence of this trope in Keats's ode is to point to his double concern for the perceived object and the precursor poet, and conclude that he is nostalgic for the freedom from linguistic contingencies which those two imaginary entities enjoy. Keats's ambivalence toward the visionary mode is not then a realism and wisdom inaugural of modern poetry, as in the critical consensus first described here, but rather a nostalgia for pre-Romantic or non-Romantic conditions. This reading at least has the virtue of contradicting the celebration of Keats as the celebrant of "our perishing earth" and of perceptual reality. But it performs another unnecessary characterization, ascribing to Keats himself a psychological configuration which we simply project as the plausible correlative of certain conflicting rhetorical structures in these texts. This account also charges interpretation with an ethical judgment, contrasting Keats with the "greater" Romantics insofar as his poetry "evades" its temporal or linguistic predicament.

We do better to read the conjunction of perception and echo in Keats in another way, pointing to his highly conspicuous rendering of the figure of address. The "Ode to a Nightingale" does not celebrate perception but displays its dependence on prosopopoeia and plays out the implications of that trope. To infer, as Keats's ode leads us to do, the primacy of the figure of address, is to infer that understanding depends on the possibility of imagining a sign as a voice or an image, and a sound or an image as a sign. And it implies that this is a rhetorical moment, rather than a natural given, and rather than, in the first place, a moment in the *experience* of an individual subject (such as Lacan's "mirror stage").

Many other poems of Keats's bring together the same indeterminacies as those of the ode's last stanza. We might for instance reread the apostrophic sonnet "O Thou Whose Face" as spoken by the Nightingale. Could we ignore what seems to sound like the familiar proposal of a negative capability, or a poetry of sensations rather than of thoughts, we should hear this poem offering something quite other than reassurance:

> O fret not after knowledge—I have none,
>   And yet the evening listens.
> . . . .
> And he's awake who thinks himself asleep.

The equation in the last line oscillates indefinitely. No music, only poetry, so leaves us hanging. Intertextual interpretation too must attend to effects like these. It should serve not just to heighten our characterizations of certain voices (blind bard, belated poet), but to uncover the necessities of those other recurrent figures, those sequences of tropes that recur in more than one text. And perhaps one should also reread Keats's letters, looking not at the familiar thematics of "Negative Capability," or "the Vale of Soul-making," but rather at the fleeting comments on the conditions of writing—the condition of writing poems in *letters,* for instance: "I know you would like what I wrote thereon—so *here* it is—as they say of a Sheep in a Nursery Book."[19]

19. John Keats, *Selected Poems and Letters,* ed. Douglas Bush (Boston, 1959), p. 292.

Herbert F. Tucker

Dramatic Monologue and the Overhearing of Lyric

His muse made increment of anything,
From the high lyric down to the low rational.
(*Don Juan* III.lxxxv.5–6)

I would say, quoting Mill, "Oratory is heard, poetry is overheard." And he would answer, his voice full of contempt, that there was always an audience; and yet, in his moments of lofty speech, he himself was alone no matter what the crowd.
(*The Autobiography of William Butler Yeats*)

I

"Eloquence is *heard,* poetry is *overheard.* Eloquence supposes an audience; the peculiarity of poetry appears to us to lie in the poet's utter unconsciousness of a listener. Poetry is feeling confessing itself to itself, in moments of solitude." "Lyric poetry, as it was the earliest kind, is also, if the view we are now taking of poetry be correct, more eminently and peculiarly poetry than any other."[1] Thus wrote John Stuart Mill in 1833, with the wild surmise of a man who had lately nursed himself through a severe depression, thanks to published poetry and its capacity to excite intimate feeling in forms uncontaminated by rhetorical or dramatic posturing. One listener Mill's characteristically analytic eloquence is likely to have found at once was Robert Browning, who moved in London among liberal circles that

1. John Stuart Mill, *Essays on Poetry,* ed. F. Parvin Sharpless (Columbia, S.C., 1976), pp. 12, 36. The quotations come from two essays of 1833, "What is Poetry?" and "The Two Kinds of Poetry."

touched Mill's and who in the same year published his first work, the problematically dramatic *Pauline: A Fragment of a Confession,* to which Mill drafted a response Browning saw in manuscript. Browning's entire career—most notably the generic innovation for which he is widely remembered today, the dramatic monologue—would affirm his resistance to the ideas about poetry contained in Mill's essays. Indeed, as early as *Pauline* Browning was confessing to the open secret of spontaneous lyricism, but in ways that disowned it. What follows is emphatically the depiction of a bygone state:

> And first I sang as I in dream have seen
> Music wait on a lyrist for some thought,
> Yet singing to herself until it came.
> (ll. 377–79)

In this complex but typical retrospect the poet of *Pauline* figures as an eavesdropper on his own Shelleyan juvenilia, themselves relics of a dream of disengaged and thoughtless youth from which the sadder but wiser poet has on balance done well to awaken. Browning's enfolding of a lyrical interval into a narrative history sets the pattern for the establishment of character throughout his subsequent work, a pattern knowingly at odds with the subjectivist convention that governed the reading of English poetry circa 1830 and to which Mill's essay gave memorable but by no means unique voice.[2]

To the most ambitious and original young poets of the day, Browning and Alfred Tennyson, the sort of lyricism Mill admired must have seemed "overheard" in a sense quite other than Mill intended: heard overmuch, overdone, and thus in need of being done over in fresh forms. Among their other generic experiments in the lyrical drama (*Paracelsus, Pippa Passes*), the idyll ("Dora," "Morte d'Arthur"), and the sui generis historical epic form of *Sordello,* during the 1830s Ten-

2. Ideas like Mill's abound, for example, in Macaulay's 1825 essay "Milton," in *Critical and Historical Essays* (London, 1883): "Analysis is not the business of the poet" (p. 3); "It is the part of the lyric poet to abandon himself, without reserve, to his own emotions" (p. 6); "It is just when Milton escapes from the shackles of the dialogue, when he is discharged from the labour of uniting two incongruous styles, when he is at liberty to indulge his choral raptures without reserve, that he rises even above himself" (p. 8). Comparing Mill's writings with T. S. Eliot's "The Three Voices of Poetry" (1953), Elder Olson, *American Lyric Poems* (New York, 1964), p. 2, concludes that "the study of the question has not advanced much in over a hundred years." Olson's conclusion retains its force after two decades. See Barbara Hardy, *The Advantage of Lyric* (Bloomington and London, 1977), p. 2: "Lyric poetry thrives, then, on exclusions. It is more than usually opaque because it leaves out so much of the accustomed context and consequences of feeling that it can speak in a pure, lucid, and intense voice."

nyson and Browning arrived independently at the first recognizably modern dramatic monologues: "St. Simeon Stylites" (1842; written in 1833) and the paired poems of 1837 that we now know as "Johannes Agricola in Meditation" and "Porphyria's Lover." These early monologues were not only highly accomplished pieces; within the lyrical climate of the day they were implicitly polemical as well. The ascetic St. Simeon atop his pillar, exposed to the merciless assault of the elements, stands for an exalted subjectivity ironically demystified by the historical contextualization that is the generic privilege of the dramatic monologue and, I shall argue, one of its indispensable props in the construction of character. Browning's imagination was less symbolically brooding than Tennyson's and more historically alert, and he launched his dramatic monologues with speakers whose insanities were perversions, but recognizably versions, of the twin wellheads of the lyrical current that had come down to the nineteenth century from the Reformation and the Renaissance. The historical figure Johannes Agricola is an antinomian protestant lying against time as if his soul depended on it; and Porphyria's lover, though fictive, may be regarded as a gruesomely literal-minded Petrarch bent on possessing the object of his desire. Each of Browning's speakers, like St. Simeon Stylites, utters a monomaniacal manifesto that shows subjectivity up by betraying its situation in a history. The utterance of each stands revealed not as poetry, in Mill's terms, but as eloquence, a desperately concentric rhetoric whereby, to adapt Yeats's formulation from "Ego Dominus Tuus," the sentimentalist deceives himself.

What gets "overheard" in these inaugural Victorian monologues is history dramatically replayed. The charmed circle of lyric finds itself included by the kind of historical particularity that lyric genres exclude by design, and in the process readers find themselves unsettlingly historicized and contextualized as well. The extremity of each monologist's authoritative assertion awakens in us with great force the counter-authority of communal norms, through a reductio ad absurdum of the very lyric premises staked out in Mill's essays, most remarkably in a sentence that Mill deleted when republishing "What is Poetry?": "That song has always seemed to us like the lament of a prisoner in a solitary cell, ourselves listening, unseen in the next."[3] ("Ourselves"? How many of us in that next cell? Does one eavesdrop in company? Or is that not called going to the theater, and is Mill's overheard poetry not dramatic eloquence after all?) Tennyson's and Browning's first monologues imply that Mill's position was already its

3. *Essays on Poetry*, p. 14.

own absurd reduction—a reduction not just of the options for poetry but of the prerogatives of the unimprisoned self, which ideas like Mill's have been underwriting, as teachers of undergraduate poetry classes can attest, for the better part of two centuries. Tennyson and Browning wanted to safeguard the self's prerogatives, and to that extent they shared the aims of contemporary lyrical devotees. But both poets' earliest dramatic monologues compassed those aims through a more subtle and eloquent design than the prevailing creed would admit: a design that might preserve the self on the far side of, and as a result of, a contextual dismissal of attenuated Romantic lyricism and its merely soulful claims; a design that might, as Browning was to put it in the peroration to *The Ring and the Book* (1869), "Suffice the eye and save the soul beside" (XII.863). St. Simeon, Johannes, and Porphyria's lover emerge through their monologues as characters: poorer souls than they like to fancy themselves but selves for all that, de- and re-constructed selves strung on the tensions of their texts.

II

Both Tennyson and Browning proceeded at once to refine their generic discoveries, though they proceeded in quite different directions. While Tennyson kept the dramatic monologue in his repertoire, he turned to it relatively seldom; and with such memorable ventures as "Ulysses" and "Tithonus" he in effect relyricized the genre, running its contextualizing devices in reverse and stripping his speakers of personality in order to facilitate a lyric drive. Browning, on the other hand, moved his dramatic monologues in the direction of mimetic particularity, and the poems he went on to write continued to incorporate or "overhear" lyric in the interests of character-formation. "Johannes Agricola" and "Porphyria's Lover" had been blockbusters, comparatively single-minded exercises in the construction of a lurid character through the fissuring of an apparently monolithic ego. The gain in verisimilitude of Browning's later monologues is a function of the nerve with which he learned to reticulate the sort of pattern these strong but simple monologues had first knit. The degree of intricacy varies widely, but the generic design remains the same. Character in the Browningesque dramatic monologue emerges as an interference effect between opposed yet mutually informative discourses: between an historical, narrative, metonymic text and a symbolic, lyrical, metaphoric text that adjoins it and jockeys with it for authority. While each text urges its own priority, the ensemble works according to the paradoxical logic of the originary supplement: the alien voices of history and of feeling come to constitute and direct one another. Typically Browning's monologists tell the story of a yearning after the condition of lyric, a condition that is itself in turn unimaginable except as the object of, or pretext for, the yearning that impels the story plotted against it.[4]

What we acknowledge as the "life" of a dramatic monologue thus emerges through the interdependence of its fictive autobiography and its *élan vital,* each of which stands as the other's reason for being, and neither of which can stand alone without succumbing to one of two deconstructive ordeals that beset character in this genre (and that arguably first beset the self during the century in which this genre arose). The first ordeal lies through history and threatens to resolve the speaking self into its constituent influences, to unravel character by exposing it as merely a tissue of affiliations. At the same time, character in the dramatic monologue runs an equal but opposite risk from what certain Romantic poetics and hermeneutics would assert to be the self's very place of strength and what we have been calling, after Mill, the privacy of lyric. A kind of sublime idiocy, lyric isolation from context distempers character and robs it of contour, as Socrates said long ago in the *Ion* (lyric poets are out of their minds), and as Sharon Cameron, with an eye on Greek and earlier origins of lyric, has said again more recently: "the lyric is a departure not only from temporality but also from the finite constrictions of identity."[5] We

4. Genre theorists have often observed this distinction, though usually in honoring the exclusivity of lyric. For Babette Deutsch, *Potable Gold* (New York, 1929), p. 21, the essential distinction lies between prose and poetry: "The one resembles a man walking toward a definite goal; the other is like a man surrendering himself to contemplation, or to the experience of walking for its own sake. Prose has intention; poetry has intensity." According to Kenneth Burke, *A Grammar of Motives* (1945; Berkeley and Los Angeles, 1969), p. 475, "The *state of arrest* in which we would situate the essence of lyric is not analogous to dramatic action at all, but is the dialectical counterpart of action." Olson, "The Lyric," *PMMLA,* 1 (1969), 65, says of lyrics that "while they may contain within themselves a considerable narrative or dramatic portion, that portion is subordinate to the lyrical whole. . . . Once expression and address and colloquy become subservient to a further end as affecting their form as complete and whole in themselves, we have gone beyond the bounds of the lyric." For a recent view of Browning opposed to that of the present essay see David Bergman, "Browning's Monologues and the Development of the Soul," *ELH,* 47 (1980), 774: "For Browning, historicity only prettifies a work. . . . History, the creation of a concrete setting, has never been a major focus for Browning." I would reply that history is indeed a major focus for Browning—one of the two foci, to speak geometrically, that define his notoriously elliptical procedures.

5. *Ion* 534; Sharon Cameron, *Lyric Time* (Baltimore and London, 1979), p. 208. See also the quirky Victorian theorist E. S. Dallas, *Poetics* (London, 1852), p. 83: "The outpourings of the lyric should spring from the law of unconsciousness. Personality or selfhood triumphs in the drama; the divine and all that is not Me triumphs in the lyric."

find this lyric departure superbly dramatized in the valediction of Tennyson's Ulysses, that most marginal of characters, whose discourse poises itself at "the utmost bound of human thought" (l. 32). Insofar as we find Ulysses transgressing that bound—as for me he does in the final paragraph, with its address to a bewilderingly mythical crew of Ithacan mariners and with the concomitant evanescence of its "I"—we find Tennyson trangressing the generic boundary of dramatic monologue as well.

One good reason why the dramatic monologue is associated with Browning's name rather than with Tennyson's, who technically got to it first, is that in Browning the lyrical flight from narrative, temporality, and identity appears through a characteristic, and characterizing, resistance to its allure. Browning's Ulysses, had he invented one, would speak while bound to the mast of a ship bound elsewhere; his life would take its bearing from what he heard the Sirens sing, and their music would remain an unheard melody suffusing his monologue without rising to the surface of utterance.[6] Such a plot of lyricism resisted would mark his poem as a dramatic monologue, which we should be justified in reading as yet another allegory of the distinctive turn on Romantic lyricism that perennially recreated Browning's poetical character. "R. B. a poem" was the title he gave in advance to this allegorical testament, in the fine letter, virtually an epistolary monologue, that he addressed on the subject to Elizabeth Barrett; and by the time of "One Word More" (1855) he could proudly affirm his wife's lyricism as the privately silencing otherness his public character was to be known by.[7]

Dramatic monologue in the Browning tradition is, in a word, anything but monological. It represents modern character as a quotient, a ratio of history and desire, a function of the division of the modern mind against itself. Our apprehension of character as thus constituted is a Romantic affair; in Jerome Christensen's apt phrase for the processing of the "lyrical drama" in Romanticism, it is a matter of learning to "read the differentials." As a sampling of the dozens of poetry textbooks published in recent decades will confirm, the dramatic monologue is our genre of genres for training in how to read between the lines—a hackneyed but valuable phrase that deserves a fresh

6. Although Browning never wrote such a monologue, he glanced at its possibility in "The Englishman in Italy" (1845), with its vision of "Those isles of the siren" (l. 199) and its audition of a song "that tells us / What life is, so clear"; "The secret they sang to Ulysses / When, ages ago, / He heard and he knew this life's secret / I hear and I know" (ll. 223–27). Life's secret, needless to add, goes untold in Browning's text.

7. Letter of 11 February 1845, in *Letters of Robert Browning and Elizabeth Barrett Barrett, 1845–1846*, ed. Elvan Kintner, 2 vols (Cambridge, Mass., 1969), 1:17.

hearing.[8] In the reading of a dramatic monologue we do not so much scrutinize the ellipses and blank spaces of the text as we people those openings by attending to the overtones of the different discourses that flank them. Between the lines, we read in a no-man's-land the notes whose intervals engender character. Perhaps the poet of the dramatic monologue gave a thought to the generic framing of his own art when he had the musician Abt Vogler (1864) marvel "That out of three sounds he frame, not a fourth sound, but a star" (l. 52). The quantum leap from text to fictive persona (the dramatic "star" of a monologue) is no less miraculous for being, like Abt Vogler's structured improvisation, "framed," defined and sustained as a put-up job. That such a process of character-construction tends to elude our received means of exegesis is a contributing cause for the depression of Browning's stock among the New Critics. But one way to begin explicating a dramatic monologue in the Browning tradition is to identify a discursive shift, a moment at which either of the genre's constitutive modes—historical line or punctual lyric spot—breaks into the other.

III

Since the premier writer of dramatic monologues was, as usual in such matters, the most ingenious, it is difficult to find uncomplicated instances in Browning that are also representative. We might sample first a passage from "Fra Lippo Lippi" (1855), a sizeable blank-verse monologue that happens to contain lyric literally in the form of *stornelli,* lyrical catches Englished in italics that Browning's artist monk emits at odd intervals during the autobiography he is improvising for the night watch. In the following lines Lippo is taking off those critics whom his new painterly realism has disturbed:

8. Jerome Christensen, "'Thoughts That Do Often Lie Too Deep for Tears': Toward a Romantic Concept of Lyrical Drama," *Wordsworth Circle,* 12:1 (1981), 61. For an appropriately genealogical testimonial to the pedagogical virtues of the dramatic monologue see Ina Beth Sessions's postscript to "The Dramatic Monologue," *PMLA,* 62 (1947), 516n.: "One of the most interesting comments concerning the dramatic monologue was made by Dr. J. B. Wharey of the University of Texas in a letter to the writer on January 17, 1935: 'The dramatic monologue is, I think, one of the best forms of disciplinary reading—that is, to use the words of the late Professor Genung, "reading pursued with the express purpose of feeding and stimulating inventive power."'" Among the earliest systematic students of the genre in our century were elocution teachers; their professional pedigree broadly conceived goes back at least to Quintilian, who recommended exercises in impersonation (*prosopopoeia*) as a means of imaginative discipline. See A. Dwight Culler, "Monodrama and the Dramatic Monologue," *PMLA,* 90 (1975), 368.

> "It's art's decline, my son!
> You're not of the true painters, great and old;
> Brother Angelico's the man, you'll find;
> Brother Lorenzo stands his single peer:
> Fag on at flesh, you'll never make the third!"
> *Flower o' the pine,*
> *You keep your mistr . . . manners, and I'll stick to mine!*
> I'm not the third, then: bless us, they must know!
> Don't you think they're the likeliest to know,
> They with their Latin?
>
> (ll. 233–42)

The gap for interpretation to enter is, of course, the middle of the second italicized line, marked typographically by ellipsis and prosodically by the wreckage of the embedded snatch of song. Amid Lippo's tale of the modern artist's oppression by his superiors, by religious and representational traditions, and by the Latin learning that backs up both (poetry as overseen?), the apparently spontaneous individual talent bursts forth in a rebellious chant—which is then itself interrupted by a reminder, also apparently spontaneous, of Lippo's answerability to the authorities right in front of him. Lippo's lyric flower breeds a canker: the poetry we and the police thought we were overhearing turns out to be, through versatile revision or instant overdubbing, a rhetorically canny performance. Or, if we take a larger view, it turns out to have been rhetoric all along, Lippo's premeditated means of affirming solidarity with the unlettered night watch by ruefully policing his own speech in advance and incorporating this police action into the larger speech act that is his monologue.

The passage is intensely artificial yet intensely realistic, and we should note that its success does not rely on our deciding whether the monologist has forecast his occasion or stumbled upon it. The twist of the lyrical line against itself nets a speaking subject who is tethered to circumstances and, for that very reason, is anything but tongue-tied. Here as throughout the Browningesque monologue, character is not unfolded to comprehension but enfolded in a text that draws us in. Even after nearly four hundred lines we do not grasp Lippo's character as an essence and know what he is; but if we have negotiated the text we know how he does. In the terms of the passage in question, we know his *manners,* not least his manner of covering up his *mistr.* . . . Lippo's character arises, in the differentials between vitality and circumstances, as a way of life, a mazing text, a finely realized, idiosyncratic instance of a generic method.

A similarly punctuated digression from story, or transgression into lyric, occurs at the center of Browning's most famous monologue, "My Last Duchess" (1842):

> She had
> A heart—how shall I say?—too soon made glad,
> Too easily impressed; she liked whate'er
> She looked on, and her looks went everywhere.
> Sir, 't was all one! My favour at her breast,
> The dropping of the daylight in the West,
> The bough of cherries some officious fool
> Broke in the orchard for her, the white mule
> She rode with round the terrace—all and each
> Would draw from her alike the approving speech,
> Or blush, at least. She thanked men,—good! but thanked
> Somehow—I know not how—as if she ranked
> My gift of a nine-hundred-years-old name
> With anybody's gift.
>
> (ll. 21–34)

The framing hesitations of "How shall I say?" and "I know not how" may or may not come under the Duke's rhetorical control; but a comparable tic or stammer invades his discourse more subtly with the appositional style of the middle lines, which do here with syntax the work done otherwise in Fra Lippo's *stornelli.* Halfway through the monologue, these lines constitute a lyrical interlude around which the Duke's despotic narrative may be seen to circle, with a predatory envy that escapes his posture of condescension. Anaphora and grammatical suspension, time-honored refuges of lyric, harbor recurrent images of the daily and seasonal cycle, of natural affection, and of sexual generation that not only contradict the Duke's potent affiliation with art, culture, and domination but show these contradictions within the text to be contradictions within the Duke. Or rather, to discard the figuration of inside and outside that dramatic monologue at its best asks us to do without, it is these textual contradictions that constitute the Duke's character. The polymorphous perversity he here attributes to his last Duchess is as much an attribute of his own character as is the different, monomaniacal perversity with which he has put a stop to her egalitarian smiles. Each perversity so turns on the other as to knot the text up into that essential illusion we call character. Hence the Duke's characteristic inconsistency in objecting to the "officious fool" who, in breaking cherries for the Duchess, was not breaking ranks at all but merely executing his proper "office" in the Duke's hierarchical world. Hence, too, the undecidable ambiguity of "My favour at her breast": the phrase oscillates between suggestions of a caress naturally given and of an heirloom possessively bestowed, and its oscillation is what makes the star of dramatic character shine. Such a semantic forking of the ways, like the plotting of spontaneity against calculation in Fra Lippo's "*mistr . . . manners*" revision, blocks reference in one direction, in order to refer us to the textual production of character instead.

Because in grammatical terms it is a paratactic pocket, an insulated deviation from the syntax of narrative line, the Duke's recounting of his Duchess's easy pleasures wanders from the aims of the raconteur and foregrounds the speech impediments that make her story his monologue.[9] Moreover, the Duke's listing is also a listening, a harkening after the kind of spontaneous lyric voice that he, like the writer of dramatic monologues, comes into his own by imperfectly renouncing. Lyric, in the dramatic monologue, is what you cannot have and what you cannot forget—think of the arresting trope Browning invented for his aging poet Cleon (1855), "One lyric woman, in her crocus vest" (l. 15)—and as an organizing principle for the genre, lyric becomes present through a recurrent and partial overruling. This resisted generic nostalgia receives further figuration intertextually, in "My Last Duchess" and many another monologue, with the clustering of allusions at moments of lyric release. Here "The dropping of the daylight in the West" falls into Browning's text from major elegies, or refusals to mourn, by Milton ("Lycidas"), Wordsworth ("Tintern Abbey," "Intimations" ode), and Keats ("To Autumn"); and the Duchess on her white mule so recalls Spenser's lyrically selfless Una from the opening of *The Faerie Queene* as to cast the Duke as an archimage dubiously empowered.

Amid the Duke's eloquence the overhearing of poetry, in this literary-historical sense of allusion to prior poems, underscores the choral dissolution that lurks in lyric voice. Furthermore, it reinstates the checking of such dissolution as the mark of the individual self—of the

9. David I. Masson, "Vowel and Consonant Patterns in Poetry," in *Essays on the Language of Literature,* ed. Seymour Chatman and Samuel R. Levin (Boston, 1967), p. 3, observes that "where lyrical feeling or sensuous description occurs in European poetry, there will usually be found patterns of vowels and consonants." For more general consideration of the linguistics of lyric, see Edward Stankiewicz, "Poetic and Non-poetic Language in Their Interrelation," in *Poetics,* ed. D. Davie et al. (Gravenhage, 1961), p. 17: "Lyrical poetry presents the most interiorized form of poetic language, in which the linguistic elements are most closely related and internally motivated." Note that Stankiewicz, following the Russian Formalists, here refers not to psychological inwardness but to the nonreferential, auto-mimetic interiority of language itself.

dramatic speaker and also of the poet who, in writing him up, defines himself in opposition to lyrical orthodoxy and emerges as a distinct "I," a name to conjure with against the ominous: "This grew; I gave commands" (l. 45). Toward the end of his career, in "House" (1876) Browning would in his own voice make more explicit this engagement with the literary past and would defend literary personality, against Wordsworth on the sonnet, as just the antithesis of unmediated sincerity: "'"*With this same key / Shakespeare unlocked his heart,*" once more!' / Did Shakespeare? If so, the less Shakespeare he!" (ll. 38–40). Poetry of the unlocked heart, far from displaying character in Browning's terms, undoes it: Browning reads his chief precursor in the English dramatic line as a type of the objective poet, the poetical character known through a career-long objection to the sealed intimacies of the poem à clef.

IV

In 1831 Arthur Hallam gave a promising description of the best of Tennyson's *Poems, Chiefly Lyrical* (1830) as "a graft of the lyric on the dramatic." The Victorian dramatic monologue that soon ensued from these beginnings was likewise a hybrid genre, a hardy offshoot of the earlier hybrid genre in which the first Romantics had addressed the problem of how to write the long modern poem by making modern civilization and its discontents, or longing and its impediments, into the conditions for the prolonging and further hearing of poetry: the "greater Romantic lyric." The genre M. H. Abrams thus christened some years ago has by now achieved canonical status, but a reconsideration of its given name from the standpoint of the dramatic monologue may help us save it from assimilation to orthodox lyricism by reminding us that the genre Abrams called "greater" was not more-lyrical-than-lyric but rather more-than-lyrical. Despite a still high tide of assertions to the contrary, the works of the first generations of Romantic poets were on the whole much less lyrical than otherwise.[10] Once we conceive the Romantic tradition accordingly as

10. Arthur Hallam, "On Some of the Characteristics of Modern Poetry, and on the Lyrical Poems of Alfred Tennyson," in *The Writings of Arthur Hallam,* ed. T. Vail Motter (New York, 1943), p. 197; M. H. Abrams, "Structure and Style in the Greater Romantic Lyric," in *From Sensibility to Romanticism,* ed. Frederick W. Hilles and Harold Bloom (New York, 1965), pp. 527–60. On the Romantic mixture of lyric with other genres see Cameron, *Lyric Time,* p. 217; Christensen, "'Thoughts,'" pp. 60–62; Robert Langbaum, "Wordsworth's Lyrical Characterizations," *Studies in Romanticism,* 21 (1982),

a perennial intermarriage, which is to say infighting, of poetic kinds, we can situate the Victorian dramatic monologue as an eminently Romantic form. In correcting the literary-historical picture we can begin, too, to see how fin-de-siècle and modernist reactions to the Browningesque monologue have conditioned the writing, reading, and teaching of poetry, literary theory, and literary history in our own time.

At the beginning of Browning's century Coleridge remarked, "A poem of any length neither can be, nor ought to be, all poetry." By the end of the century Oscar Wilde, looking askance at Browning's achievement, took up Coleridge's distinction, but with a difference: "If he can only get his music by breaking the strings of his lute, he breaks them, and they snap in discord. . . . Meredith is a prose Browning, and so is Browning. He used poetry as a medium for writing in prose."[11] The difference between Coleridge's and Wilde's ideas of what a poem should be is in large part a difference that the dramatic monologue had made in nineteenth-century poetry, a difference Browning inscribed into literary history by inscribing it into the characteristic ratios of his texts. Wilde and others at the threshold of modernism wanted Mill's pure lyricism but wanted it even purer. And through an irony of literary history that has had far-reaching consequences for our century, the Browningesque dramatic monologue gave them what they wanted. Symbolist and imagist writers could extract from such texts as *Pauline* and "Fra Lippo Lippi"—and also, to sketch in the fuller picture, from the Tennysonian idyll and most sophisticated Victorian novels—lyrical gems as finely cut as anything from the allegedly naive eras, Romantic or Elizabethan, upon which they bestowed such sentimental if creative regard. The hybrid dramatic monologue, as a result of its aim to make the world and subjectivity safe for each other in the interests of character, had proved a sturdy grafting stock for flowers of lyricism; and the governing pressures of the genre, just because they governed so firmly, had bred hothouse lyric varieties of unsurpassed intensity. These lyrical implants it was left to a new generation of rhymers, scholars, and

319–39. Langbaum's earlier book *The Poetry of Experience* (1957; rpt. New York, 1963), which places the dramatic monologue within Romantic tradition, should be consulted, as should two responses that appeared, almost concurrently, two decades later: Culler, "Monodrama," and Ralph W. Rader, "The Dramatic Monologue and Related Lyric Forms," *Critical Inquiry,* 3 (1976), 131–51.

11. Coleridge is quoted in Frederick A. Pottle, *The Idiom of Poetry* (Ithaca, 1941), p. 82. Wilde's comments occur in "The Critic as Artist" (1890), in *Literary Criticism of Oscar Wilde,* ed. Stanley Weintraub (Lincoln, Neb., 1968), p. 202.

anthologists to imitate, defend, and excerpt in a newly chastened lyric poetry, a severely purist poetics, and a surprisingly revisionist history of poetry.[12]

The fin-de-siècle purism of Wilde, Yeats, Arthur Symons, and others was polemically canted against the example of Browning; yet it remained curiously, even poignantly, in his debt. Consider, for example, Symons's resumption of a rhetoric very like Mill's, as he praises Verlaine in *The Symbolist Movement* (1899) for "getting back to nature itself": "From the moment when his inner life may be said to have begun, he was occupied with the task of an unceasing confession, in which one seems to overhear him talking to himself."[13] The pivotally wishful "unceasing," which distinguishes Symons's formulation from Mill's, also betrays a kind of elegiac overcompensation. Mill had dissolved audience in order to overhear poetry as if from an adjacent cell; Symons, writing at an appreciable historical remove from the achievements of Verlaine, is by contrast trapped in time. Symons's overhearing of poetry resembles less Mill's eavesdropping than the belated Browningesque audition of a poignant echo, and the symbolist movement he hopes to propel is fed by an overwhelming nostalgia that creates from its own wreck the thing it contemplates. The nostalgia for lyric that throbs through the influential versions of the poetic past Symons and his contemporaries assembled sprang from a range of cultural causes we are only beginning to understand adequately.[14] But we can observe here that the rhetorical pattern into

12. Victorian writers were divided as to the chronological priority of lyric over other genres. For Dallas, as for Mill, "Lyrics are the first-fruits of art" (p. 245), while Walter Bagehot contends that "poetry begins in Impersonality" and that lyric represents a later refinement ("Hartley Coleridge" [1852], in *Collected Works*, ed. Norman St. John-Stevas, I [Cambridge, Mass., 1965], pp. 159–60). As to the normative status of lyric, however, the later nineteenth century had little doubt. Summaries and bibliographical aids may be found in Francis B. Gummere, *The Beginnings of Poetry* (New York, 1901), p. 147; Charles Mill Gayley and Benjamin Putnam Kurtz, *Methods and Materials of Literary Criticism* (Boston, 1920), p. 122; W. K. Wimsatt, Jr., and Cleanth Brooks, *Literary Criticism: A Short History* (New York, 1966), pp. 433, 751–52. For representative belletristic histories of poetry from a nostalgic, fin-de-siècle perspective see John Aldington Symonds, *Essays Speculative and Suggestive* (London, 1893), pp. 393 ff.; Edmund Gosse, "Introduction" to *Victorian Songs: Lyrics of the Affections and Nature*, ed. E. H. Garrett (Boston, 1895); and Arthur Symons, *The Symbolist Movement in Literature* (1899; rpt. New York, 1958) and *The Romantic Movement in English Poetry* (New York, 1909). On the influence of F. T. Palgrave's *Golden Treasury* (1861; rev. 1981), an anthology that "established, retroactively and for the future, the tradition of the English lyric," see Christopher Clausen, *The Place of Poetry* (Lexington, 1981), p. 67.

13. Symons, *The Symbolist Movement*, p. 49.

14. Marxian approaches now offer the most promising and comprehensive explanations of the fortunes of lyric as a product of industrial culture, yet recently published Marxian analyses evaluate the social functions of lyric very differently. For Theodor W. Adorno, "Lyric Poetry and Society" (1957; trans. Bruce Mayo, *Telos*, 20 [Summer

which their lyrically normed historiography fell was precisely that of the poetic genre that had preeminently confronted lyricism with history in their century: the dramatic monologue. It is as if what Symons championed as the "revolt against exteriority, against rhetoric,"[15] having repudiated the "impure" Browning tradition in principle, was condemned to reiterate its designs in writing. The symbolist and imagist schools wanted to read in their French and English antecedents an expurgated lyric that never was on page or lip. It was, rather, a generic back-formation, a textual constituent they isolated from the dramatic monologue and related nineteenth-century forms; and the featureless poems the fin-de-siècle purists produced by factoring out the historical impurities that had ballasted these forms are now fittingly, with rare exceptions, works of little more than historical interest.

Virtually each important modernist poet in English wrote such poems for a time; each became an important poet by learning to write otherwise and to exploit the internal otherness of the dramatic monologue. When the lyrical bubble burst within its bell jar, poetry became modern once again in its return to the historically responsive and dialogical mode that Browning, Tennyson, and others had brought forward from the Romantics.[16] And upon the establishment of Yeats's mask, Pound's personae, Frost's monologues and idylls, and Eliot's impersonal poetry, it became a point of dogma among sophisticated readers that every poem dramatized a speaker who was not the poet. "Once we have dissociated the speaker of the lyric from the personality of the poet, even the tiniest lyric reveals itself as drama."[17]

1974], 56–71), "The subjective being that makes itself heard in lyric poetry is one which defines and expresses itself as something opposed to the collective and the realm of objectivity" (p. 59); in contrast, Hugh N. Grady, "Marxism and the Lyric," *Contemporary Literature,* 22 (1981), 555, argues that "the lyric has become a specialized, though not exclusive, genre of Utopian vision in the modern era."

15. Symons, *The Symbolist Movement,* p. 65.

16. Olson, "The Lyric," p. 65, in distinguishing the "verbal acts" of lyric from those of more elaborated forms, himself acts fatally on the strength of a simile: "The difference, if I may use a somewhat homely comparison, is that between a balloon inflated to its proper shape, nothing affecting it but the internal forces of the gas, and a balloon subjected to the pressure of external forces which counteract the internal." But a balloon affected only by internal forces (i.e., a balloon in a vacuum) would not inflate but explode. That the "proper shape" of a poem, as of a balloon, arises not from sheer afflatus but as a compromise between "internal" and "external" forces is precisely my point about the framing of the dramatic monologue—as it is, I think, the dramatic monologue's (deflationary) point about the lyric.

17. Wimsatt and Brooks, *Literary Criticism,* p. 675; see also Cleanth Brooks and Robert Penn Warren, *Understanding Poetry* (1938; rev. ed. New York, 1950), p. liv. Don Geiger, *The Dramatic Impulse in Modern Poetics* (Baton Rouge, 1967), pp. 85–95, provides a capable overview of the persona poetics of the New Criticism.

We recognize this declaration as dogma by the simple fact that we—at least most of us—had to learn it, and had to trade for it older presuppositions about lyric sincerity that we had picked up in corners to which New Critical light had not yet pierced. The new dogma took (and in my teaching experience it takes still) with such ease that it is worth asking why it did (and does), and whether as professors of poetry we should not have second thoughts about promulgating an approach that requires so painless an adjustment of the subjectivist norms we profess to think outmoded.

The conversion educated readers now routinely undergo from lyrical to dramatic expectations about the poems they study recapitulates the history of Anglo-American literary pedagogy during our century, the middle two decades of which witnessed a great awakening from which we in our turn are trying to awaken again. Until about 1940 teachers promoted poetry appreciation in handbooks and anthologies that exalted lyric as "the supreme expression of strong emotion . . . the very real but inexplicable essence of poetry," and that throned this essential emotion in the equally essential person of the poet: "Lyrical poetry arouses emotion because it expresses the author's feeling."[18] By 1960 the end of instruction had shifted from appreciating to understanding poetry, and to this end a host of experts marched readers past the author of a poem to its dramatic speaker. John Crowe Ransom's dictum that the dramatic situation is "almost the first head under which it is advisable to approach a poem for understanding" had by the 1960s advanced from advice to prescription. In Laurence Perrine's widely adopted *Sound and Sense* the first order of business is "to assume always that the speaker is someone other than the poet himself." For Robert Scholes in *Elements of Poetry* the speaker is the most elementary of assumptions: "In beginning our approach to a poem we must make some sort of tentative decision about who the speaker is, what his situation is, and who he seems to be addressing."[19]

That such forthright declarations conceal inconsistencies appears in the instructions of Robert W. Boynton and Maynard Mack, whose *Introduction to the Poem* promotes the familiar dramatic principle but pursues its issues to the verge of a puzzling conclusion. The authors begin dogmatically enough: "When we start looking closely at the

18. Oswald Doughty, *English Lyric in the Age of Reason* (London, 1922), p. xv; Walter Blair and W. K. Chandler, eds., *Approaches to Poetry* (New York, 1935), p. 250.

19. Ransom is quoted in William Elton, *A Glossary of the New Criticism* (Chicago, 1949), p. 38. *Sound and Sense*, 2nd ed. (New York, 1963), p. 21; *Elements of Poetry* (New York, 1969), pp. 11–12.

dramatic character of poetry, we find that we have to allow for a more immediate speaker than the poet himself, one whom the poet has imagined speaking the poem, as an actor speaks a part written for him by a playwright." But then Boynton and Mack, with a candor unusual in the handbook genre, proceed to a damaging concession that dissolves the insubstantial pageant of the dramatic enterprise into thin air: "In some instances this imagined speaker is in no way definite or distinctive; he is simply a voice." (When is a speaker not a speaker? When he is a "voice," nay, an Arnoldian "lyric cry.") With this last sentence Boynton and Mack offer an all but lyrical intimation of the mystification inherent in the critical fiction of the speaker and suggest its collusion with the mysteries of the subjectivist norm it was designed to supplant.[20] It may well be easier to indicate these mysteries than to solve them; what matters is that with our New Critical guides we seem to have experienced as little difficulty in negotiating the confusions entailed by the fiction of the speaker as we have experienced in converting ourselves and our students from lyrically expressive to dramatically objective norms for reading.

Why should we have made this conversion, and why do we continue to encourage it? Why should our attempts at understanding poetry through a New Criticism rely on a fiction that baffles the understanding? These are related questions, and their answers probably lie in considerations of pedagogical expediency. One such consideration must be the sheer hard work of bringing culturally stranded students into contact with the historical particularities from which a given poem arises. Life (and courses) being short, art being long, and history being longer still, the fiction of the speaker at least brackets the larger problem of context so as to define a manageable classroom task for literary studies. To such institutional considerations as these, which have been attracting needed attention of late, I would add a consideration more metaphysical in kind. The fiction of the speaker, if it removes from the study of poetry the burden, and the dignity, of

20. Robert W. Boynton and Maynard Mack, *Introduction to the Poem* (New York, 1965), p. 24. On p. 45, to complete the circuit, the authors equate the "voice" with "the poet." They thus return us through a backstage exit to Clement Wood's definition of lyric in *The Craft of Poetry* (New York, 1929), p. 189, as "the form in which the poet utters his own dramatic monolog." Compare the dramatic metaphor in Benedetto Croce's 1937 *Encyclopedia Britannica* article on "Aesthetic": "The lyric . . . is an objectification in which the ego sees itself on the stage, narrates itself, and dramatizes itself" (quoted in Wimsatt and Brooks, *Literary Criticism,* p. 510). For Geoffrey Crump, *Speaking Poetry* (London, 1953), p. 59, the reverse seems true: "an element of the dramatic is present in all lyrical poetry, because the speaker is to some extent impersonating the poet."

establishing contact with history, puts us in compensatory contact with the myth of unconditioned subjectivity we have inherited from Mill and Symons in spite of ourselves. Through that late ceremony of critical innocence, the readerly imagination of a self, we modern readers have abolished the poet and set up the fictive speaker; and we have done so in order to boost the higher gains of an intersubjective recognition for which, in an increasingly mechanical age that can make Mill's look positively idyllic, we seem to suffer insatiable cultural thirst. The mastery of New Critical tools may offer in this light a sort of homeopathic salve, the application of a humanistic technology to technologically induced ills.

The thirst for intersubjective confirmation of the self, which has made the overhearing of a persona our principal means of understanding a poem, would I suspect be less strong if it did not involve a kind of bad faith about which Browning's Bishop Blougram (1855) had much to say: "With me, faith means perpetual unbelief / Kept quiet like the snake 'neath Michael's foot / Who stands calm just because he feels it writhe" (ll. 666—68). The New Criticism of lyric poetry introduced into literary study an anxiety of textuality that was its legacy from the Higher Criticism of scripture a century before: anxiety over the tendency of texts to come loose from their origins into an anarchy that the New Critics half acknowledged and half sought to curb under the regime of a now avowedly fictive self, from whom a language on parole from its author might nonetheless issue as speech. What is poetry? Textuality a speaker owns. The old king of self-expressive lyricism is dead: Long live the Speaker King! At a king's ransom we thus secure our reading against the subversive textuality of what we read; or as another handbook from the 1960s puts it with clarity: "So strong is the oral convention in poetry that, in the absence of contrary indications, we infer a voice and, though we know we are reading words on a page, create for and of ourselves an imaginary listener."[21] Imaginative recreation "for and of ourselves" here depends upon our suppressing the play of the signifier beneath the hand of a convention "so strong" as to decree the "contrary indications" of textuality absent most of the time.

Deconstructive theory and practice in the last decade have so directed our attention to the persistence of "contrary indications" that the doctrine espoused in my last citation no longer appears tenable. It seems incumbent upon us now to choose between intersubjective and

21. Jerome Beaty and William H. Matchett, *Poetry: From Statement to Meaning* (New York, 1965), p. 103.

intertextual modes of reading, between vindicating the self and saving the text. Worse, I fear, those of us who are both teachers and critics may have to make different choices according to the different positions in which we find ourselves—becoming by turns intertextual readers in the study and intersubjective readers in the classroom—in ways that not very fruitfully perpetuate a professional divide some latter-day Browning might well monologize upon. I wonder whether it must be so; and I am fortified in my doubts by the stubborn survival of the dramatic monologue, which began as a response to lyric isolationism, and which remains to mediate the rivalry between intersubjective appeal and intertextual rigor by situating the claims of each within the limiting context the other provides.

In its charactered life the dramatic monologue can help us put in their places critical reductions of opposite but complementary and perhaps even cognate kinds: on one hand, the transcendentally face-saving misprisions that poetry has received from Victorian romanticizers, Decadent purists, and New Critical impersonalists alike; on the other hand, the abysmal disfigurements of a deconstruction that would convert poetry's most beautiful illusion—the speaking presence—into a uniform textuality that is quite as "purist," in its own way, as anything the nineteenth century could imagine. An exemplary teaching genre, the dramatic monologue can teach us, among other things, that while texts do not absolutely lack speakers, they do not simply have them either; they invent them instead as they go. Texts do not come from speakers, speakers come from texts. *Persona fit non nascitur.* To assume in advance that a poetic text proceeds from a dramatically situated speaker is to risk missing the play of verbal implication whereby character is engendered in the first place through colliding modes of signification; it is to read so belatedly as to arrive only when the party is over. At the same time, however, the guest the party convenes to honor, the ghost conjured by the textual machine, remains the articulate phenomenon we call character: a literary effect we neglect at our peril. For to insist that textuality is all and that the play of the signifier usurps the recreative illusion of character is to turn back at the threshold of interpretation, stopping our ears to both lyric cries and historical imperatives, and from our studious cells overhearing nothing. Renewed stress upon textuality as the basis for the Western written character is a beginning as important to the study of poetry now as it has been for over a century to the writing of dramatic monologues and to the modern tradition they can illuminate in both backward and forward directions. But textuality is only the beginning.

PART FOUR

FREDRIC JAMESON

Baudelaire as Modernist and Postmodernist: The Dissolution of the Referent and the Artificial "Sublime"

The inaugural, the classical, status of Baudelaire in Western poetry can be argued in a number of different ways: a privileged theory of poetic value as it has been developed and transmitted by the modernist tradition is, however, a historicizing one, in which, for each successive period or moment—each successive new *present*—some new ghostly emanation or afterimage of the poet peels off the inexhaustible text. There are therefore many Baudelaires, of most unequal value indeed. There is, for instance, a second-rate post-Romantic Baudelaire, the Baudelaire of diabolism and of cheap *frisson,* the poet of blasphemy and of a creaking and musty religious machinery which was no more interesting in the mid-nineteenth century than it is today. This is the Baudelaire of Pound and of Henry James, who observed, "Les Fleurs du *Mal?* Non, vous vous faites trop d'honneur. What you call *evil* is nothing more than a bit of rotting cabbage lying on a satin sofa." *This* Baudelaire will no doubt linger on residually into the *fin de siècle.*

Then there is the hardest of all Baudelaires to grasp: the Baudelaire contemporary of himself (and of Flaubert), the Baudelaire of the "break," of 1857, the Baudelaire the eternal freshness of whose language is bought by reification, by its strange transformation into alien speech. Of this Baudelaire we will speak no further here.

Instead, I propose two more Baudelaire-simulacra—each identical with the last, and yet each slightly, oddly, distinct: these are the Baudelaire inaugural poet of high modernism (of a today extinct high modernism, I would want to add), and the Baudelaire of post-modernism, of our own immediate age, of consumer society, the Baudelaire of the society of the spectacle or the image. As my title suggests, I will attempt a reading of this society in our present (and of the Baudelaire it deserves) in terms of the machine and the simulacrum, of the return of something like the "sublime." This will then be a speculative and prophetic exercise. I feel on more solid ground with that older period about which we are gradually reaching some general consensus, namely the long life and destiny of high modernism, about which it is safe to assert that one of its fundamental events concerned what we now call the "referent." It is therefore in terms of the disappearance of this last, its eclipse or abolition—better still, its gradual waning and extinction—that we will make our first approach to the poetic text.

Chant d'automne, part I.

Bientôt nous plongerons dans les froides ténèbres;
Adieu, vive clarté de nos étés trop courts!
J'entends déjà tomber avec des chocs funèbres
Le bois retentissant sur le pavé des cours.

Tout l'hiver va rentrer dans mon être : colère,
Haine, frissons, horreur, labeur dur et forcé,
Et, comme le soleil dans son enfer polaire,
Mon coeur ne sera plus qu'un bloc rouge et glacé.

J'écoute en frémissant chaque bûche qui tombe;
L'échafaud qu'on bâtit n'a pas d'écho plus sourd.
Mon esprit est pareil à la tour qui succombe
Sous les coups du bélier infatigable et lourd.

Il me semble, bercé par ce choc monotone,
Qu'on cloue en grande hâte un cercueil quelque part.
Pour qui?—C'était hier l'été; voici l'automne!
Ce bruit mystérieux sonne comme un départ.

Autumnal

Soon cold shadows will close over us
and summer's transitory gold be gone;
I hear them chopping firewood in our court—
the dreary thud of logs on cobblestone.

Winter will come to repossess my soul
with rage and outrage, horror, drudgery,
and like the sun in its polar holocaust
my heart will be a block of blood-red ice.

I listen trembling to that grim tattoo—
build a gallows, it would sound the same.
My mind becomes a tower giving way
under the impact of a battering-ram.

Stunned by the strokes, I seem to hear, somewhere,
a coffin hurriedly hammered shut—for whom?
Summer was yesterday; autumn is here!
Strange how that sound rings out like a farewell.[1]

Three experiences (to begin modestly, with the common sense language of everyday life)—three experiences come together in this text: one is a feeling of some kind, strong and articulated, yet necessarily nameless (is it to be described as "anxiety" or that very different thing, "sadness," and in that case what do we do with that other curious component of eagerness, anticipation, curiosity, which begins to interfere with those two other affective tones as we reach the so characteristic final motif of the "départ"—voyage and adventure, as well as death?). I will have little to say about this affective content of the poem, since, virtually by definition, the Baudelaire that interests us here is no longer the Baudelaire of an aesthetic of *expression:* an aesthetic in which some pre-given and identifiable psychological event is then, in a second moment, laid out and expressed in poetic language. It seems to me at least conceivable that the poetic producer may have thought of his work here in terms of some residual category of expression and expressiveness. If so, he has triumphantly (if even against his own will) undermined and subverted that now archaic category: I will only observe that as the putative "feeling" or "emotion" becomes slowly laid out in words and phrases, in verses and stanzas, it is transformed beyond all recognition, becomes lost to the older psychological lexicon (full of names for states of mind we *recognize* in advance), or, to put it in our own contemporary jargon, as it

1. Charles Baudelaire, "Chant d'automne" I, in *Les Fleurs du mal* (1857; Paris, 1958), p. 61. All subsequent references will be to this edition. Translation by Richard Howard, "Autumnal I," in *Les Fleurs du Mal: The Complete Text of The Flowers of Evil in a New Translation* (Boston, 1982), pp. 61–62. All subsequent translations will be from this edition.

becomes transmuted into a verbal text, it ceases to be psychological or affective in any sense of the word, and now exists as *something else.*

So with this mention we will now leave psychology behind us. But I have suggested that two more "experiences" lend their raw material to this text, and we must now register their banal, informing presence: these are, evidently, a season—fall, the approach of a dreary winter which is also and even more strongly the death of summer itself; and alongside that, a physical perception, an auditory event or experience, the hollow sound of logs and firewood being delivered in the inner courtyard of the Parisian dwelling. Nature on the one hand, the city, the Urban, on the other, and a moment in the interrelationship of these two great contraries in which the first, the archaic cyclical time of an older agriculture and an older countryside, is still capable of being transmitted through what negates it, namely the social institutions of the City itself, the triumphantly un- or anti-natural.

One is tempted, faced with this supreme antithesis between country and city, with this inner contradiction in the raw material of Baudelaire's text between precapitalist society and the new industrial metropolis of nascent capital, to evoke one of the great aesthetic models of modern times, that of Heidegger, in the "Origins of the Work of Art." Heidegger there describes the effect and function of the "authentic" work of art as the inauguration of a "rift" between what he calls World and Earth: what I will rewrite in terms of the dimensions of History and the social project on the one hand, and of Nature or matter on the other—ranging from geographical or ecological constraint all the way to the individual body. The force of Heidegger's description lies in the way in which the gap between these two incommensurable dimensions is maintained and held open: the implication is that we all live in both dimensions at once, in some irreconcilable simultaneity which subsumes older ideological oppositions like those of body and spirit, or that of private and public. We are at all moments in History and in matter; at one and the same time historical beings and "natural" ones, living in the meaning-endowment of the historical project as well as in the meaninglessness of organic life. No synthesis—either conceptual or experiential, let alone symbolic—is conceivable between these two disjoined realms; or rather, the production of such conceptual synthesis (in which, say, History would be passed off as "natural," or Nature obliterated in the face of History) is very properly the production of ideology, or of "metaphysics" as it is often called. The work of art can therefore never "heal" this rift: nothing can do that. What is misconceived is, however, the idea that it ought to be healed: we have here indeed three positions and not two. It is not a question of tension versus resolution, but rather of repression and forgetfulness, of the sham resolution of metaphysics, and then of that third possibility, a divided consciousness that strongly holds together what it separates, a moment of awareness in which difference relates. This is then, for Heidegger, the vocation of the work of art: to stage this irreconcilable tension between History and Nature in such a way that we live *within* it and affirm its reality *as* tension, gap, rift, distance. Heidegger goes on to assimilate this inaugural "poetic" act with the comparable acts of philosophy (the deconcealment of being) and of political revolution (the inauguration of a new society, the invention of new social relations).

It is an attractive and powerful account, and one can read "Chant d'automne" in this way, as staging the fateful gap between organic death, the natural cycle, and the urban, which here greatly expands beyond the city, to include the repressive institutions of society generally, capital execution, war, ceremonial burial, and finally, most mysterious, the faint suggestion of the nomadic, of the "voyage" which seems to mark the interface between nature and human society. One can read the poem in that way, but at what price?

This is the moment to say that the limits of Heidegger's grand conception are less to be found in its account of the poetic act than in its voluntaristic implications for that other act, the act of reception or of reading. Let us assume that the poet—or the artist generally—is always in a position to open World and Earth in this fashion (it is not a difficult assumption to make, since "real" poetry does this by definition, for Heidegger, and art which does not do so is therefore not "really" art in the first place). The problem arises when the reader's turn comes, and in a fallen, secular or reified society is called upon (not least by Heidegger himself) to reinvent this inaugural and well-nigh ritualistic act. Is this always possible? Or must we take into account specific historical conditions of possibility which open or close such a reading? I pass over Heidegger's own sense of historical possibility in the fateful and unnameable moment in which he elaborated this meditation (1935). What is clear is that even this meditation must now return us to the historical in the drearier humdrum sense of the constraints, the situation, which limits possibility and traces the outer boundary even of that more transcendent vision of History as World.

So we now return to the narrower historical situation of this particular Baudelaire, which is the situation of nascent high modernism. Conventional wisdom already defines this for us in a certain number of ways: it is the moment, the Barthes of *Writing Degree Zero* tells us, of the passage from rhetoric to style, from a shared collective speech to the uniqueness and privacy of the isolated monad and the isolated body. It is also the moment, as we know, of the break-up of the older social groups, and not least those relatively homogeneous reading publics to whom, in the writer's contract, certain relatively stable signals can be sent. Both of these descriptions then underscore a process of social fragmentation, the atomization of groups and neighborhoods, the slow and stealthy dissolution of a host of different and coexisting collective formations by a process unique to the logic of capital which my tradition calls reification: the market equivalency in which little by little units are produced, and in the very act by which they are made equivalent to one another are thereby irrevocably separated as well, like so many identical squares on a spatial grid.

I would like to describe this situation, the situation of the poet—the situation this particular Baudelaire must resolve, in obedience to its constraints and contradictions—in a somewhat different, yet related way, as the simultaneous production and effacement of the referent itself. The latter can only be grasped as what is outside language, what language or a certain configuration of language seems to designate, and yet, in the very moment of indication, to project beyond its own reach, as something transcendental to it.

The referent in "Chant d'automne" is not particularly mysterious or difficult of access: it is simply the body itself, or better still, the bodily sensorium. Better yet, it is the bodily perception—better still, even more neutral a term, the *sensation*—which mobilizes the body as its instrument of perception and brings the latter into being over against it. The referent here is then simply a familiar sound, the hollow reverberation of logs striking the courtyard paving. Yet familiar for whom? Everything, and the very mysteries of modernism itself, turn on this word, about which we must admit, in a first moment, that it no longer applies to any contemporary readership. But in a second moment, I will be less concerned to suggest ways in which, even for Baudelaire's contemporaries, such a reference might have been in the process of becoming exotic or obscure, than rather to pose as a principle of social fragmentation the withdrawal of the private or the individual body from social discourse.

We might sharpen the problem of reference by prolonging positivist psychology itself—rigorously coeval with high modernism—and imagining the visual and graphic registration of this unique sound, whose "real nature"—that is to say, whose *name*—we could never guess from looking at its complex spatial pattern. Such registrations perpetuate the old positivist myth of something like a pure atomic sensation in the then nascent pseudo-science of psychology—a myth which in the present context I prefer to read as a symptom of what is happening to the body itself.

For this once "familiar" sound is now driven back inside the body of Baudelaire: a unique event taking place there and utterly alien to anything whose "experience" we might ourselves remember, something which has lost its name, and which has no equivalents: as anonymous and indescribable as a vague pain, as a peculiar residual taste in the mouth, as a limb falling asleep. The semioticians know well this strange seam between the body and language, as when they study the most proximate naming systems—the terms for wine-tasting, say—or examine the ways in which a physician *translates* his patients' fumbling expressions into the technical code of nosology.

But it is *this* that must now be historicized. I would like to make an outrageous (or at least, as they say, unverifiable) generalization, namely that before Baudelaire and Flaubert there are no physical sensations in literature. This does not quite mean advancing a proposition so sweeping as the one which might be expressed, parodying Lionel Trilling, namely, that on or around 1857 we must presume a fundamental mutation in human nature. It does mean, more modestly, and on the side of the object (or the literary raw material), that free-floating bodily perception was not, until now, felt to be a proper content for literary language (you will get a larger historical sense of this by expanding such data to include experiences like that of anxiety—Kierkegaard is after all the contemporary of these writers). And it means, on the side of the subject, or of literary language itself, that the older rhetoric was somehow fundamentally nonperceptual, and had not yet "produced" the referent in our current sense: this is to say that even where we are confronted with what look like masses of sense data—the most convenient example will be, perhaps, Balzac, with his elaborate descriptions, that include the very smell of his rooms—those apparently perceptual notations, on closer examination, prove to be so many *signs*. In the older rhetorical apparatus, in other words, "physical sensation" does not meet the opacity of the body, but is secretly transparent, and always *means* something else—moral qualities, financial or social status, and so forth. Perceptual language only emerges in the ruins of that older system of signs, that older assimilation of contingent bodily experience to the transparency of meaning. The problem, however, and what complicates the description enormously, is that language never ceases to attempt to reabsorb and recontain contingency; that in spite of itself, it always seeks to transform that scandalous and irreducible content back into something like meaning. Modernism will then be a renewed effort to do just that, but one which, faced with the collapse of the older system of rhetorical language and traditional literary meaning, will set itself a new type of literary meaning, which I will term symbolic reunification.

But now we must observe this process at work in our poetic exhibit. The irreducible, the sonorous vibration, with its peculiar hollowness and muffled impact, is here a pure positivity which must be handled or managed in some fashion. This will first be attempted metonymically, by tracing the association of this positive yet somehow ominous sound with something else, which is defined as absence, loss, death—namely the ending of summer. For reasons I will develop later on, it seems useful to formulate this particular axis—positivity/negativity—as one of the two principal operative grids of the poem, the other being the obvious and well-known movement between metonymy and metaphor. The latter will then be the second option of the poetic process: the pure sensation will now be classed metaphorically, by way of analogies and similarities: it is (like) the building of a scaffold, the sound of the battering ram, the nailing up of a coffin. What must be noted here is that this alternate route, whereby the sensation is processed metaphorically rather than metonymically, also ends up in negativity, as though the poetic imagination met some barrier or loop which fatally prevents it from reaching relief or salvation.

This is of course not altogether true: and a complete reading of the poem (not my purpose here) would want to underscore the wondrous reappearance of the place of the subject in the next line—the naive and miraculous, "Pour qui?" and the utter restructuration of the temporal system, in which the past is now abandoned, the new present—now defined, not negatively as the end of summer, but positively, as autumn—reaffirmed to the point at which the very sense datum of the sound itself becomes a promise rather than a fatality.

Let me now rapidly try to theorize the two principal strands of the argument, the one having to do with the production of the "referent," the other with the emergence of modernism. In "Chant d'automne" at least—and I don't want to generalize the model in any unduly dogmatic way—the high modernist strategy can be detected in the move from the metonymic reading of the sense datum to the attempt to reabsorb it in some new symbolic or metaphorical meaning—a symbolic meaning of a type very different from the older transparencies of the rhetorical sign to which I have already referred. What I have not yet sufficiently stressed is the way in which this high modernist or symbolic move is determined by the crisis of the reading public and by the social fragmentation from which the latter springs. Given that crisis, and the already tendential privatization and monadization of the isolated individuals who used to make up the traditional publics, there can no longer be any confidence in some shared common *recognition* of the mysterious sense datum, the hollow sound, which is the "referent" of the poetic text: the multiplication of metaphorical analogies is therefore a response to such fragmentation, and seeks to throw out a range of scattered frameworks in which the various isolated readers can be expected to find their bearings. Two processes are therefore here at work simultaneously: the sound is being endowed with a multiplicity of possible receptions, but as that new multifaceted attack on a fragmented readership is being projected (something whose ultimate stage will be described in Umberto Eco's *Open Work*), something else is taking place as well, namely the emergence of a new type of symbolic meaning, symbolic recuperation, which will at length substitute itself for an older common language and shared rhetoric of what it might be too complicated to describe as a "realistic" kind.

This crisis in readership then returns us to our other theme, namely the production of the referent: a paradoxical way of putting it, you will say, since my ostensible topic was rather the "eclipse" or the "waning," the "disappearance" of the referent. I don't want to be overly subtle about all this, but it seems to me very important to understand that these two things are the same. The "production" of the referent—that is, the sense of some new unnameable ungeneralizable private bodily sensation—something that must necessarily resist all language but which language lives by designating—is the same as the "bracketing" of that referent, its positioning as the "outside" of the text or the "other" of language. The whole drama of modernism will lie here indeed, in the way in which its own peculiar life and logic depend on the reduction of reference to an absolute minimum and on the elaboration, in the former place of reference, of complex symbolic and often mythical frameworks and scaffolding: yet the latter depend on preserving a final tension between text and referent, on keeping alive one last shrunken point of reference, like a dwarf sun still glowing feebly on the horizon of the modernist text.

When that ultimate final point of reference vanishes altogether, along with the final desperate ideology—existentialism—which will attempt to theorize "reference" and "contingency"—then we are in post-modernism, in a now wholly textual world from which all the pathos of the high modernist experience has vanished away—the world of the image, of textual free-play, the world of consumer society and its simulacra.

To this new aesthetic we must now turn, for as I suggested it also knows remarkable anticipations in the work of Baudelaire. There would of course be many ways of approaching post-modernism, of which we have not even time enough to make a provisional inventory. In the case of Baudelaire, one is rather tempted to proceed as follows, by recalling the great dictum of the Philosopher already mentioned, "Language is the house of being." The problem then posed by post-modernism, or more narrowly by the post-modernist elements in Baudelaire, could then be conveyed by the question of what happens when Language is only the *apartment* of Being; when the great urban fact and anti-nature, spreads and abolishes the "path through the field" and the very space and coordinates of some Heideggerian ontological poetry are radically called into question.

Consider the following lines, for example, from "Alchimie de la douleur":

Et sur les célestes rivages
Je bâtis de grands sarcophages.

to shroud my cherished dead,
and on celestial shores I build
enormous sepulchres.[2]

The entire poem amounts to a staging of or meditation on the curious dialectic of Baudelaire's poetic process, and the way in which its inner logic subverts itself and inverts its own priorities, something these concluding lines suggest rather well. It is as though the imagination, on its way toward opening, or toward the gratifications of some positive and well-nigh infinite wish-fulfillment, encountered something like a reality principle of the imagination or of fantasy itself. Not the transfigured nature of the wish-fulfillments of paradise, but rather the ornate, stubborn, material reality of the coffin: the poetic imagination here explicitly criticizes itself, and systematically, rigorously, undermines its first impulse, then in a second moment substituting a different kind of gratification, that of artisanal or handicraft skill, the pleasures of the construction of material artifacts. The

2. Baudelaire, *Les Fleurs du mal,* p. 82. Translation, p. 78.

role of the essentially nostalgic ideal of handicraft labor in Flaubert and Baudelaire has often been rehearsed; as has Baudelaire's fascination for un- or anti-natural materials, most notably glass, which Sartre has plausibly read as part of a whole nineteenth-century middle-class ideology of "distinction," of the repression of the organic and the constriction of the natural body. But this essentially subjective symbolic act, in which human craft manufacture is mobilized in a repression of the body, the natural, the organic itself, ought not to exclude a more "objective" analysis of the social history of those materials, particularly in nineteenth-century building and furnishings, a perspective which will be appropriate for our second exhibit, "La Mort des amants."

Nous aurons des lits pleins d'odeurs légères,
Des divans profonds comme des tombeaux,
Et d'étranges fleurs sur des étagères,
Écloses pour nous sous des cieux plus beaux.

Usant à l'envi leurs chaleurs dernières,
Nos deux cœurs seront deux vastes flambeaux,
Qui réfléchiront leurs doubles lumières
Dans nos deux esprits, ces miroirs jumeaux.

Un soir fait de rose et de bleu mystique,
Nous échangerons un éclair unique,
Comme un long sanglot, tout chargé d'adieux;

Et plus tard un Ange, entr'ouvrant les portes,
Viendra ranimer, fidèle et joyeux,
Les miroirs ternis et les flammes mortes.

The Death of Lovers

We shall have richly scented beds—
couches deep as graves, and rare
flowers on the shelves will bloom
for us beneath a lovelier sky.

Emulously spending their last
warmth, our hearts will be as two
torches reflecting their double fires
in the twin mirrors of our minds.

One evening, rose and mystic blue,
we shall exchange a single glance,
a long sigh heavy with farewells;

and then an Angel, unlocking doors,
will come, loyal and gay, to bring
the tarnished mirrors back to life.[3]

I am tempted to be brutally anachronistic, and to underscore the affinities between this curious interior scene and the procedures of contemporary photorealism, one of whose privileged subjects is not merely the artificial—in the form of gleaming luxury streets of automobiles (battered or mint)—but above all, interior scenes, furnishings without people, and most notably bathrooms, notoriously of all the rooms in the house the least supplied with anthropomorphic objects.

Baudelaire's sonnet is also void of human beings: the first person plural is explicitly displaced from the entombed chamber by the future tense of the verbs; and even where that displacement weakens, and as the future comes residually to fill up the scene in spite of itself, the twin protagonists are swiftly transformed into furnishings in their own right—candelabra and mirrors, whose complex fourway interplay is worthy of the most complicated visual illustrations of Jacques Lacan.

But I am tempted to go even further than this and to underscore the evident paradox—even more, the formal scandal—of the conclusion of this poem, whose affective euphoria (and its literal meaning) conveys the resurrection of the lovers, while its textual elements in effect produce exactly the opposite, the reawakening of an empty room from which the lovers are henceforth rigorously absent. It is as though the text had profited from the surface or manifest movement of its narrative toward the wishfulfillment of resurrection, to secure a very different unconscious solution, namely extinction, by means of assimilation to the dead (albeit refurbished) boudoir. Here "interior" knows its apotheosis, in very much the spirit of Adorno's pages on Kierkegaard where the passion for Biedermeier furnishings and enclosed space becomes the symbolic enactment of that new realm of the private, the personal, of subjective or inner life.[4]

Yet Baudelaire goes a good deal further than Kierkegaard in this historical respect, and we will not do proper justice to this glorious

3. Baudelaire, *Les Fleurs de mal,* p. 149. Translation, p. 149.
4. Theodor W. Adorno, *Kierkegaard* (Frankfurt am Main, 1974).

poem without registering the properly dreadful nature of its contents: what is tactfully conveyed here is indeed to be identified as the worst Victorian kitsch already on its way to the modulation of fin de siècle decadence, as most notably in the proto-Mallarméan flowers, of which we can at least minimally be sure that "in real life" they are as garish as anything Des Esseintes might have surrounded himself with. Even the "soir fait de rose et de bleu mystique" is mediated by the most doubtful pre-Raphaelite taste, if I may use so moralizing a word.

Now this presents us with an interesting axiological problem, as the philosophers would say: in our engrained Cartesianism, it is always difficult to imagine how a whole might possess value whose individual parts are all worthless; meanwhile, our critical and aesthetic traditions systematically encourage us in a kind of slavish habit of apologia in which, faced with a text of great value, we find ourselves rationalizing all of its more questionable elements and inventing ingenious reasons why these too are of value. But culture is often more complicated and interesting than this; and I must here briefly invoke one of the most brilliant pages in what remains I think Jean-Paul Sartre's greatest single book, *Saint Genet,* whose riches, remarkably, have still been little explored: most notably the section in which he reveals the inner hollowness of Genet's sumptuous style. The principal category of Sartre's analysis is the concept of "le toc"—the phony, the garish, that which is in and of itself and in its very essence in bad taste, all the way from religious emblems and the Opéra of Paris, to the cheapest excesses of horrific popular thrillers, porn ads, and the junk adornments and heavy makeup of drag queens. In Genet, as Sartre shows us, the acquired mental habits of Bossuet's style and classical rhetorical periods reorder and stamp these tawdry materials with the tarnished aura of the sublime, in an operation whose deepest inner logic is that of *ressentiment* and of the imperceptible subversion of the bourgeois reader's most cherished values.

Baudelaire, of course, represents a very different order of elegance; his mastery of the raw material of bad taste will be more tactful and allusive, more refined; nor do I wish to follow Sartre along the lines of an analysis of individual or biographical impulses in this writer. Nonetheless, there are curious analogies between the Sartrean analysis and this extraordinary apotheosis of what should otherwise be an oppressively sumptuous interior, whose very blossoms are as asphyxiating as a funeral parlor, and whose space is as properly funereal as the worst Victorian art photographs. These characterizations are not, clearly, chosen at random: the logic of the image here conveys death and the funereal through its very tawdriness, at the same moment in which the words of the narrative affirm euphoria and the elation of hope.

We have a contemporary equivalent for this kind of stylistic operation, which must be set in place here: and this is the whole properly poststructural language which Susan Sontag was the first to identify as "camp,"[5] the "hysterical sublime," from Cocteau and Hart Crane to Jack Spicer and David Bowie, a kind of peculiar exhilaration of the individual subject unaccountably generated by the trash and junk materials of a fallen and unredeemable commodity culture. Camp is indeed our way of living within the junkyard of consumer society and positively flourishing there: it is to be seen in the very gleam and glitter of the automobile wrecks of photorealist paintings, in the extraordinary capacity of our own cultural language to redeem an object world and a cultural space by holding firmly to their surfaces (in mechanisms which Christopher Lasch and others would no doubt identify as "narcissistic"). Camp, better than anything else, underscores one of the most fateful differences between high modernism and post-modernism, and one which is also, I believe, operative in this strange poem of Baudelaire: namely what I will call the disappearance of *affect*, the utter extinction of that pathos or even tragic spirit with which the high moderns lived their torn and divided condition, the repression even of anxiety itself—supreme psychic experience of high modernism—and its unaccountable reversal and replacement by a new dominant feeling tone: the high, the intensity, exhilaration, euphoria, a final form of the Nietzschean Dionysiac intoxication which has become as banal and institutionalized as your local disco or the thrill with which you buy a new-model car.

This strange new—historically new—feeling or affective tone of late capitalism may now be seen as something like a return of the "sublime" in the sense in which Edmund Burke first perceived and theorized it at the dawn of capital. Like the "sublime" (and the "anxiety"), the exhilaration of which we are speaking is not exactly an emotion or a feeling, not a way of living an object, but rather somehow detached from its contents—something like a disposition of the subject which takes a particular object as a mere occasion: this is the sense in which the Deleuze-Guattari account of the emergence, the momentary and fitful sunburst of the individual psychological subject has always seemed exceedingly relevant:

5. Susan Sontag, "Notes on Camp," in *Against Interpretation and Other Essays* (New York, 1966), pp. 275–92.

> Something on the order of a subject can be discerned on the recording surface: a strange subject, with no fixed identity, wandering about over the body without organs, yet always remaining peripheral to the desiring-machines, being defined by the share of the product it takes for itself, garnering here, there, and everywhere a reward, in the form of a becoming or an avatar, being born of the states that it consumes and being reborn with each new state: "c'est donc moi, c'est donc à moi! . . . The subject is produced as a mere residue alongside the desiring machines: a conjunctive synthesis of consumption in the form of a wonderstruck: "c'était donc ça!"[6]

Such an account has the additional merit of linking up with the great Lacanian theme of "second death,"[7] and of suggesting why death and resurrection should have been so stimulating a fantasy-material for a poet intent on capturing the highs and the "elevations" of an intermittent experience of subjectivity. If the subject exists always and only in the moment of rebirth, then the poetic fantasy or narrative process must necessarily first work its way along the path of death, in order to merit this unique "bonus of pleasure" whose place is carefully prepared in advance for it in the empty, dusted, polished, flower-laden chamber. And the latter is of course, for us, as readers, the poem itself: the chamber of the sonnet, Donne's "pretty room," waiting to be the faithful (and joyous) occasion of our own brief, fitful, punctual exhilaration as subjects: "c'est donc moi, c'est donc à moi!"

Burke's problem, as he confronted an analogous and historically equally new form of affect—the sublime—was to find some explanation—not for our aesthetic pleasure in the pleasurable, in "beauty," in what could plausibly gratify the human organism on its own scale, but rather for our aesthetic delight in spectacles which would seem symbolically to crush human life and to dramatize everything which reduces the individual human being and the individual subject to powerlessness and nothingness. Burke's solution was to detect, within this peculiar aesthetic experience, a relationship to being that might as well have been described as epistemological or even ontological (and incidentally a logic which is rigorously un- or a-symmetrical to that of his other term, "beauty"): astonishment, stupor, terror—these are some of the ways in which the individual glimpses a force which largely transcends human life and which Burke can only identify with

6. Gilles Deleuze and Felix Guattari, *The Anti-Oedipus: Criticism and Schizophrenia*, trans. Robert Hurley, Mark Seem, and Helen R. Lane (New York, 1977), p. 16.
7. Jacques Lacan, "Kant avec Sade," in *Ecrits* (Paris, 1971), 2:119–48.

the Godhead or the divine. The aesthetic reception of the sublime is then something like a pleasure in pain, in the tightening of the muscles and the adrenaline rush of the instinct of self-preservation, with which we greet such frightening and indeed devastating spectacles.

What can be retained from this description is the notion of the sublime as a relationship of the individual subject to some fitfully or only intermittently visible force which, enormous and systematized, reduces the individual to helplessness or to that ontological marginalization which structuralism and poststructuralism have described as a "decentering" where the ego becomes little more than an "effect of structure." But it is no longer necessary to evoke the deity to grasp what such a transindividual system might be.

What has happened to the sublime since the time of Burke—although he judiciously makes a place of a concept which can be most useful to us in the present context, namely the "artificial infinite"—is that it has been transferred from nature to culture, or the urban. The visible expression of the suprapersonal mode of production in which we live is the mechanical, the artificial, the machine; and we have only to remember the "sublime" of yesterday, the exhilaration of the futurists before the machine proper—the motorcar, the steamship liner, the machine gun, the airplane—to find some initial contemporary equivalent of the phenomenon Burke first described. One may take his point about self-preservation, and nonetheless wish to formulate this affective mechanism a little more sharply: I would have said myself that in the face of the horror of what systemically diminishes human life it becomes possible simply to change the valence on one's emotion, to replace the minus sign with a plus sign, by a Nietzschean effort of the will to convert anxiety into that experience physiologically virtually identical with it which is eagerness, anticipation, anxious affirmation. And indeed, in a situation of radical impotence, there is really little else to do than that, to affirm what crushes you and to develop one's capacity for gratification in an environment which increasingly makes gratification impossible.

But futurism was an experiment in what Reyner Banham has called the "first machine age": we now live in another, whose machines are not the glorious and streamlined visible vehicles and silhouettes which so exhilarated Le Corbusier, but rather computers, whose outer shell has no emblematic or visual power. Our own machines are those of reproduction; and an exhilaration which would attach itself to them can no longer be the relatively representational idolatry of the older engines and turbines, but must open some access, beyond representation, to processes themselves, and above all the processes of reproduction—movie cameras, videos, tape recorders, the whole world of the production and reproduction of the image and of the simulacrum, and of which the smeared light and multireflective glass of the most elegant post-contemporary films or buildings is an adequate *analogon.* I cannot, of course, pursue this theory of post-modernism in any more detail here;[8] but returning one last time to "La Mort des amants" it is appropriate to see in the play of mirrors and lights of the funereal chamber some striking and mysterious anticipation of a logic of the future, a logic far more consonant with our own social moment than with that of Baudelaire. In that then, as in so much else, he is, perhaps unfortunately for him, our contemporary.

8. But see, for a more complete discussion, my "Postmodernism, or, The Cultural Logic of Late Capitalism," *New Left Review,* 146 (July–August 1984), 53–92.

Barbara Johnson

Les Fleurs du mal armé: Some Reflections on Intertextuality

> Oui, le suspens de la Danse, crainte contradictoire ou souhait de voir trop et pas assez, exige un prolongement transparent.
>
> Mallarmé

Contemporary discussions of intertextuality can be distinguished from "source" studies in that the latter speak in terms of a transfer of property ("borrowing") while the former tend to speak in terms of misreading or infiltration, that is, of violations of property. Whether such violations occur in the oedipal rivalry between a specific text and its precursor (Bloom's anxieties of influence) or whether they inhere in the immersion of any text in the history of its language and literature (Kristeva's paragrams, Riffaterre's hypograms), "intertextuality" designates the multitude of ways a text has of not being self-contained, of being traversed by otherness. Such a conception of textuality arises out of two main theoretical currents: a) Freud's discovery of the unconscious as an "other scene" that intrudes on conscious life in the form of dreams, slips of the tongue, parapraxes, etc., and b) Saussure's discovery of the haunting presence of proper names ana-

The present essay is a translation, revision, and extension of an essay originally published in French in *Discours et pouvoir,* Michigan Romance Studies, vol. 2, ed. Ross Chambers (Ann Arbor, 1982). All translations from the French are my own.

The title, "Les Fleurs du mal armé," is designed to be read as a paradigm for the questions of intertextuality under discussion here. On the one hand, it appears to posit a linear, developmental, slightly overlapping relation between a precursor text ("Les Fleurs du mal") and a disciple (Mallarmé) engendered out of it. On the other hand, the double function of the word "mal" renders Baudelaire's title and Mallarmé's name both inseparable from each other and different from themselves, creating new dividing lines not *between* the two oeuvres but *within* each of them. The proper names thereby lose their properness, and their free-floating parts can combine into new signifying possibilities.

grammatically dispersed in the writings of certain late Latin poets. These two discoveries have been combined by Jacques Lacan into a conception of the "signifying chain" that "insists" in the human subject in such a way that "the unconscious is structured like a language." One might say by analogy that for modern theorists of intertextuality, the language of poetry is structured like an unconscious. The integrity and intentional self-identity of the individual text are put in question in ways that have nothing to do with the concepts of originality and derivativeness, since the very notion of a self-contained literary "property" is shown to be an illusion. When read in its dynamic intertextuality, the text becomes differently energized, traversed by forces and desires that are invisible or unreadable to those who see it as an independent, homogeneous message unit, a totalizable collection of signifieds.

What happens, though, when a poet decides to transform the seemingly unconscious "anxiety of influence" into an explicit theme in his writing? Can the seepage and rivalry between texts somehow thereby be mastered and reappropriated? In an early piece of poetic prose entitled "Symphonie littéraire," Mallarmé prefaces his homage to his three "masters" (Gautier, Baudelaire, and Banville) with the following invocation:

> Muse moderne de l'Impuissance, qui m'interdis depuis longtemps le trésor familier des Rythmes, et me condamnes (aimable supplice) à ne faire plus que relire,—jusqu'au jour où tu m'auras enveloppé dans ton irrémédiable filet, l'ennui, et tout sera fini alors,—les maîtres inaccessibles dont la beauté me désespère; mon ennemie, et cependant mon enchanteresse aux breuvages perfides et aux melancoliques ivresses, je te dédie, comme une raillerie ou,—le sais-je?—comme un gage d'amour, ces quelques lignes de ma vie où tu ne m'inspiras pas la haine de la création et le stérile amour du néant. Tu y découvriras les jouissances d'une âme purement passive qui n'est que femme encore, et qui demain peut-être sera bête.[1]
>
> [O modern Muse of Impotence, you who have long forbidden me the familiar treasury of Rhythms, and who condemn me (pleasurable torture) to do nothing but reread—until the day you will envelop me in your irremediable net, ennui, and all will then be over—those inaccessible masters whose beauty drives me to despair; my enemy, yet my enchantress, with your perfidious potions and your melancholy intoxica-

1. Stephane Mallarmé, *Oeuvres complètes* (Paris, 1945), p. 261. All in-text page numbers refer to this edition.

tions, I dedicate to you, in jest or—can I know?—as a token of love, these few lines of my life written in the clement hours when you did not inspire in me a hatred of creation and a sterile love of nothingness. You will discover in them the pleasures of a purely passive soul who is yet but a woman and who tomorrow perhaps will be a dumb animal.]

It would seem that this text is quite explicitly describing the castrating effect of poetic fathers upon poetic sons. The precursors' beauty drives the ephebe to despair: he is impotent, passive, feminized, *mal armé*. Yet this state of castration is being invoked as a Muse: the lack of inspiration has become the source of inspiration. Mallarmé, as has often been noted, has transformed the incapacity to write into the very subject of his writing. In the act of thematizing an oedipal defeat, Mallarmé's writing thus maps out the terms of an escape from simple oedipal polarities: it is no longer possible to distinguish easily between defeat and success, impotence and potency, reading and writing, passivity and activity.

Before pursuing further the Mallarméan relation between impotence and writing, let us glance for a moment at the father's side of the story. At a time when Baudelaire would have had ample occasion to read Mallarmé's "Literary Symphony" along with the prose poems Mallarmé had dedicated to him, the older poet wrote the following remarks in a letter to his mother in which he had enclosed an article about himself written by Verlaine:

Il y a du talent chez ces jeunes gens; mais que de folies! quelles exagérations et quelle infatuation de jeunesse! Depuis quelques années je surprenais, ça et là, des imitations et des tendances qui m'alarmaient. Je ne connais rien de plus compromettant que les imitateurs et je n'aime rien tant que d'être seul. Mais ce n'est pas possible; et il paraît que l'*école Baudelaire* existe.[2]

[These young people do have talent, but there is such madness! such exaggeration and such youthful infatuation! For several years now I have here and there come across imitations and tendencies that alarm me. I know of nothing more compromising than imitators and I like nothing so well as being alone. But it is not possible; and it seems that the *Baudelaire school* exists.]

The "father" here is "alarmed" not by the hostility but by the imitative devotion of his "sons," whose writing lacks the measure and maturity that he, Baudelaire, by implication attributes to his own. To

2. Charles Baudelaire, *Correspondance* (Paris, 1973), 2:625.

be imitated is to be repeated, multiplied, distorted, "compromised." To be alone is at least to be unique, to be secure in the boundaries of one's self. And to have the luxury of rejecting one's imitators is both to profit from the compliment and to remain uncontaminated by the distortions. Yet even in Baudelaire's expression of alarm and self-containment, otherness surreptitiously intrudes. For while Baudelaire is ambivalently but emphatically imprinting his own name on the writing of his admirers, another proper name is manifesting itself in the very writing of his letter: in speaking of "des tendances qui M'ALARMAIENT," Baudelaire has unwittingly inscribed the name of one of the sources of his alarm. The almost perfect homophony between "m'alarmaient" and "Mallarmé" reveals a play of intertextuality in which the text, while seeming to decry the dangers of imitation, is actually *acting out,* against the express purposes of its author, the far graver dangers of usurpation. And what is usurped is not only Baudelaire's claims to authority over the work of his disciples, but also and more significantly the claims of his conscious intentions to authority over the workings of his own writing. The suppressed name of Mallarmé shows through.

Both of these thematizations of the oedipal dynamics of intertextuality are thus more complex than they at first appear. In both cases, the ongoingness of literary history is acted out by the text despite an apparent attempt to arrest it. Mallarmé carves new territory for poetry out of what looks like a writing block; Baudelaire's writing, in the act of blocking out the successors, inscribes the inevitability of their usurpation.

But what are the effects of this Muse of Impotence not on Mallarmé's critical prose but on his poetry itself? In a poem entitled "L'Azur," written the same year as the "Symphonie littéraire," Mallarmé dramatizes the predicament of the poet who seeks *forgetfulness* as a cure for impotence (thus implying that what the impotent poet is suffering from is too much memory). The poem begins:

> De l'éternel azur la sereine ironie
> Accable, belle indolemment comme les fleurs,
> Le poëte impuissant qui maudit son génie
> A travers un désert stérile de Douleurs.
>
> [The eternal azure's serene irony
> Staggers, with the indolent grace of flowers,
> The impotent poet who damns his genius
> Across a sterile desert of sorrows.]

The poet tries to flee this oppressive azure, throwing night, smoke, and fog across it, until he reaches a moment of illusory victory, followed by a recognition of defeat:

—Le Ciel est mort.—Vers toi, j'accours! donne, ô matière,
L'oubli de l'Idéal cruel et du Péché
A ce martyr qui vient partager la litière
Où le bétail heureux des hommes est couché,

Car j'y veux, puisque enfin ma cervelle, vidée
Comme le pot de fard gisant au pied du mur,
N'a plus l'art d'attifer la sanglotante idée,
Lugubrement bâiller vers un trépas obscur . . .

En vain! l'Azur triomphe, et je l'entends qui chante
Dans les cloches. Mon âme, il se fait voix pour plus
Nous faire peur avec sa victoire méchante,
Et du métal vivant sort en bleus angélus!

Il roule par la brume, ancien et traverse
Ta native agonie ainsi qu'un glaive sûr;
Où fuir dans la révolte inutile et perverse?
Je suis hanté. L'Azur! l'Azur! l'Azur! l'Azur!

[—The sky is dead.—To you I run! give, o matter,
Forgetfulness of the cruel Ideal and Sin
To this martyr who comes to share the straw
Where the happy herd of men is stabled,

For I wish—since my brain no longer, emptied
Like the grease paint pot that lies against the wall,
Has the art to prettify the sobbing idea—
To yawn lugubriously toward an obscure death . . .

In vain! The Azure triumphs, I can hear it sing
In the bells. My soul, it becomes voice,
The better to scare us with its mean success,
And from the living metal bluely rings the angelus.

It rolls through the mist of old and pierces
Like a skillful sword your native agony;
Where is there to flee, in useless and perverse revolt?
I am haunted. Azure! Azure! Azure! Azure!]

This text has always been read—even by Mallarmé himself—as a description of the struggle between the desire to reach a poetic or metaphysical ideal and the attempt to escape that desire for fear of failing. As Guy Michaud puts it, "Even if the poet is freed neither of his dream nor of his impotence, he has at least affirmed the originality of his poetry. He has achieved the *general effect* he was seeking: the obsessive concern with the eternal, which the azure symbolizes."[3] But should this "azure" be understood only in a *symbolic* sense? The fact that the word is repeated four times at the end of the poem would seem to indicate that what haunts Mallarmé is not simply some ideal symoblized by azure but the very word "azure" itself. Even a casual glance at nineteenth-century French poetry reveals that the word "azure" is par excellence a "poetic" word—a sign that what one is reading is a poem. The repetition of this word can thus be read as the return of stereotyped poetic language as a *reflex,* a moment when initiative is being taken by the words *of others,* which is one of the things Mallarmé will later call "chance." Azure, says Mallarmé, "becomes voice." The text ends: "I am haunted: cliché! cliché! cliché! cliché!"[4]

Impotence is thus not a simple inability to write, but an inability to write *differently.* The agony experienced before the blank page arises out of the fact that the page is in fact never quite blank enough.

To write thus becomes for Mallarmé a constant effort to silence the automatisms of poetry, to "conquer chance word by word" (p. 387), to perceive words "independent of their ordinary sequence" (p. 386). But if the blankness of the page is in a sense the place from which literary history speaks, Mallarmé ends up writing *not* by covering the white page with the blackness of his own originality but rather by including *within* his writing the very *spaces* where poetic echoes and reflexes have been suppressed. "Leaving the initiative to words" (p. 366) is a complex operation in which the linguistic work of poetic calculation must substitute for the banalities of poetic inspiration. And the blanks figure as a major ingredient in that calculation. As Mallarmé puts it in a note on the *Coup de dés,* his symphony in white: "The 'blanks' indeed take on importance. . . . The paper intervenes each time an image, of its own accord, ceases or dies back, accepting the succession of others . . ." (P. 455). And as for prose, Mallarmé explains that his blanks take the place of empty transitions: "The reason for these intervals, or blanks . . . —why not confine the subject

3. Guy Michaud, *Mallarmé* (Paris, 1958), p. 25.

4. Interestingly enough, there is a sentence in a letter from Mallarmé to Cazalis that seems unexpectedly to confirm this reading. In discussing the composition of "L'Azur," Mallarmé writes, "I had a lot of trouble with it because, banishing a thousand lyrical turns and beautiful lines that incessantly *haunted* my brain, I wanted to stick implacably to my subject" (January 1864, in *Correspondance 1862–1871* [Paris, 1959], p. 103; italics mine).

to those fragments in which it shines and then replace, by the ingenuousness of the paper, those ordinary, nondescript transitions?" (p. 1576). The act of reading Mallarmé, of sounding that "transparency of allusions" (p. 317), becomes—in his own words—a "desperate practice" (p. 647) precisely because "to read" means "to rely, depending on the page, on the blank" (p. 387), to take cognizance of the text as a "stilled poem, in the blanks" (p. 367). Through the breaks and the blanks in his texts, Mallarmé internalizes intertextual heterogeneity and puts it to work not as a relation *between* texts but as a play of intervals and interruptions *within* texts. Mallarmé's intertextuality then becomes an explicit version of the ways in which a text is never its own contemporary, cannot constitute a self-contained whole, conveys only its non-coincidence with itself. While the desire to escape banality seemed to situate the challenge of poetry in the impossibility of saying something *different,* Mallarmé here reveals through the text's own self-difference an equal impossibility inherent in the attempt to say something *same.* Indeed, his notion of the Book ("the world is made to end up as a Book") is a correlative to this: if for Mallarmé all poets have unwittingly yet unsuccessfully attempted to write THE Book, and if at the same time "all books contain the fusion of a small number of repeated sayings" (p. 367), then difference can only arise out of the process of repetition, and the "defect of languages" that verse is supposed to make up for resides in the fact that it is just as impossible to say the *same* thing as to say something different.

It is perhaps this paradox of intertextual relations, this "unanimous blank conflict between one garland and the same" (p. 74), that is staged by the famous "Swan" sonnet:

Le vierge, le vivace et le bel aujourd'hui
Va-t-il nous déchirer avec un coup d'aile ivre
Ce lac dur oublié que hante sous le givre
Le transparent glacier des vols qui n'ont pas fui!

Un cygne d'autrefois se souvient que c'est lui
Magnifique mais qui sans espoir se délivre
Pour n'avoir pas chanté la région où vivre
Quand du stérile hiver a resplendi l'ennui.

Tout son col secouera cette blanche agonie
Par l'espace infligé à l'oiseau qui le nie,
Mais non l'horreur du sol où le plumage est pris.

Fantôme qu'à ce lieu son pur éclat assigne,
Il s'immobilise au songe froid de mépris
Que vêt parmi l'exil inutile le Cygne.

[The virgin, vivacious, and lovely today—
Will it rend with a blow of its dizzying wing
This hard lake forgotten yet haunted beneath
By the transparent glacier of unreleased flights!

A bygone day's swan now remembers it's he
Who, magnificent yet in despair struggles free
For not having sung of the regions of life
When the ennui of winter's sterility gleamed.

All his neck will shake off this white agony space
Has inflicted upon the white bird who denied it,
But not the ground's horror, his plumage inside it.

A phantom assigned by his gloss to this place,
Immobile he stands, in the cold dream of scorn
That surrounds, in his profitless exile, the Swan.]

The poetry of "today" would thus constitute the rendering of something that is both forgotten and haunted—haunted by the way in which a "bygone day's swan" *did not sing*. The choice of a swan as a figure for the precursor is both appropriate and paradoxical. On the one hand, if the swan sings only at the moment of death, then the poet who says he is haunted by the precursor-swan's song would in reality be marking the *death* of the father. But on the other hand, to seek to silence the father, to speak of his *not* having sung, is to run the risk of bringing the father back to life, since if he does not sing, there is no proof that he is dead. In other words, the survival of the father is in a sense guaranteed by the way in which the son does *not* hear him.

It is interesting to note that this sonnet about a bygone day's swan actually itself refers to the swan of a bygone day—a poem entitled "The Swan," written by Baudelaire and dedicated to *his* poetic precursor, Victor Hugo. It would seem that the swan comes to designate the precursor as such, and it is doubtless no accident that the predecessor-figure in Proust's *Remembrance of Things Past* should also be called by the name of Swann.

But in each of these cases, what is striking about the precursor figure, what in a sense seals his paternity, is the way in which he himself is already divided, rent, different from himself. In Proust's novel, Swann is the model of a man who is never the contemporary of his own desires. Baudelaire's "Swan" poem tells of being divided between the loss of what can never be recovered and the memory of what can never be forgotten, so that irreparable loss becomes the incapacity to let anything go. To return to Mallarmé's sonnet, we can see that the very division between "aujourd'hui" (today) and "autrefois" (bygone day) names the temporality of intertextuality as such. And this division in itself constitutes a textual allusion—to the division of Hugo's *Contemplations* into two volumes entitled precisely "Autrefois" and "Aujourd'hui." "They are separated by an abyss," writes Hugo: "the tomb."[5]

In his preface to *Contemplations*, Hugo suggests that his book should be read "as one reads the work of the dead." In reflecting on this quotation, one can begin to see a supplementary twist to the traditional oedipal situation. For if the father survives precisely through his way of affirming himself dead, then the son will always arrive too late to kill him. What the son suffers from, then, is not the simple desire to kill the father, but the impotence to kill him whose potency resides in his ability to recount his own death.

It is perhaps for this reason that the so-called "fathers of modern thought"—Mallarmé, Freud, Marx, Nietzsche—maintain such a tremendous authority for contemporary theory. In writing of the subversion of the author, the father, God, privilege, knowledge, property, and consciousness, these thinkers have subverted in advance any grounds on which one might undertake to kill off an authority that theorizes the death of all authority. This is perhaps the way in which contemporary theory in its turn has *lived* the problematics of intertextuality.

From the foregoing it would appear that intertextuality is a struggle between fathers and sons, and that literary history is exclusively a male affair. This has certainly been the presumption of literary historians in the past, for whom gender becomes an issue only when the writer is female. In the remainder of this essay, I would like to glance briefly at the ways in which questions of gender might enrich, complicate, and even subvert the underlying paradigms of intertextual theory. What, for example, does one make of Mallarmé's experience of the "pleasures of a purely passive soul who is yet but a woman"? Is Mallarmé's femininity a mere figure for castration? Or is the Muse of Impotence also a means of access to the experience of femininity? Or, to approach it another way, how might we factor into these intertextual relations the fact that Baudelaire's protestations of solitude and paternity are written to his *mother,* and that the tomb that separates "autrefois" and "aujourd'hui" for Hugo is that of his *daughter?* What,

5. Victor Hugo, *Oeuvres poétiques* (Paris, 1967), 2:482.

in other words, are the poetic uses to which women—both inside and outside the text—have been put by these male poets?

It is interesting that the only text by Mallarmé on which Baudelaire is known to have commented is a prose poem in which a beautiful, naked woman stands as a figure for the poetry of the past. Mallarmé's poem, "Le Phénomène futur," describes a degenerating world in which a "Displayer of Things Past" is touting the beauties of a "woman of Bygone Days." Drooping poets-to-be are suddenly revived, "haunted by rhythm and forgetting that theirs is an era that has outlived beauty" (p. 270). Baudelaire, in his notes on Belgium, has this to say about Mallarmé's vision of the future: "A young writer has recently come up with an ingenious but not entirely accurate conception. The world is about to end. Humanity is decrepit. A future Barnam is showing the degraded men of his day a beautiful woman artificially preserved from ancient times. 'What?' they exclaim, 'could humanity once have been as beautiful as that?' I say that this is not true. Degenerate man would admire himself and call beauty ugliness."[6] This encounter between the two poets is a perfect figuration of the progress of literary history from one generation to another. But the disagreement on which Baudelaire insists is less profound than it appears. While the elder poet fears that people will admire something he no longer recognizes as beautiful and the younger poet fears that beauty may no longer be recognizable in his work, Baudelaire and Mallarmé actually agree on two things: beauty is a function of the past, and beauty is a woman.

Nothing could be more traditional than this conception of Beauty as a female body: naked, immobile, and mute. Indeed, the beauty of female muteness and reification reaches its highest pitch when the woman in question is dead (cf. Poe's statement that the most poetic subject is the death of a beautiful woman) or at least—as here—artificially preserved and statufied. The flawless whiteness of the female body is the very image of the blank page, to be shaped and appropriated by the male creative pen. As Susan Gubar remarks in a recent article entitled "'The Blank Page' and Female Creativity":

> When the metaphors of literary creativity are filtered through a sexual lens, female sexuality is often identified with textuality. . . . This model of the pen-penis writing on the virgin page participates in a long tradition identifying the author as a male who is primary and the female as

6. Baudelaire, *Oeuvres complètes* (Paris, 1976), 2:831.

> his passive creation—a secondary object lacking autonomy, endowed with often contradictory meaning but denied intentionality.[7]

In Mallarmé's work, the correlation between Poetry and Femininity is pervasive from the very beginning. The great unfinished poem, "Hérodiade," begun in 1864 and still lying uncompleted on Mallarmé's desk at the time of his death in 1898, provides a telling record of the shifting importance and complexity of his attempt to make poetry speak as a female Narcissus, self-reflexive and self-contained. The failure of Mallarmé's attempt to *dramatize* his poetics under the guise of female psychology is certainly as instructive as the centrality of that project, and deserves more extensive treatment than is possible here. But in Mallarmé's later writing, the identification of femininity with textuality, which becomes both more explicit and more complex, becomes as well completely de-psychologized:

> A déduire le point philosophique auquel est située l'impersonnalité de la danseuse, entre sa féminine apparence et un objet mimé, pour quel hymen: elle le pique d'une sûre pointe, le pose; puis déroule notre conviction en le chiffre de pirouettes prolongé vers un autre motif, attendu que tout, dans l'évolution par où elle illustre le sens de nos extases et triomphes entonnés à l'orchestre, est, comme le veut l'art même, au théatre, *fictif ou momentané.* (p. 296)

> [To deduce the philosophical point at which the dancer's impersonality is located, between her feminine appearance and a mimed object, for what Hymen: she pricks it with a confident point and poses it; then unrolls our conviction in the cipher of pirouettes prolonged toward another motif, presuming that everything, in the evolution through which she illustrates the sense of our ecstasies and triumphs intoned in the orchestra, is, as art itself requires it, in theatre, *fictive or momentary.*]

> A savoir que la danseuse *n'est pas une femme qui danse,* pour ces motifs juxtaposés qu'elle *n'est pas une femme,* mais une métaphore résumant un des aspects élémentaires de notre forme, glaive, coupe, fleur, etc., et *qu'elle ne danse pas,* suggérant, par le prodige de raccourcis ou d'élans, avec une écriture corporelle ce qu'il faudrait des paragraphes en prose dialoguée autant que descriptive, pour exprimer, dans la rédaction: poëme dégagé de tout appareil du scribe. (p. 304)

> [That is, that the dancer *is not a woman dancing,* for the juxtaposed motives that she *is not a woman,* but a metaphor epitomizing one of the

7. In *Writing and Sexual Difference,* ed. Elizabeth Abel (Chicago, 1982), pp. 75, 77.

elementary aspects of our form, sword, goblet, flower, etc., and that *she is not dancing,* suggesting, through the prodigy of short cuts and leaps, with a corporal writing what it would take paragraphs of dialogue and descriptive prose to express, if written out: a poem freed from all scribal apparatus.]

This would certainly seem to be an example of the denial of female interiority and subjectivity and the transformation of the woman's body into an art object. Textuality becomes woman, but woman becomes poet only unconsciously and corporally. But is it different for a man? The question of autonomy and intentionality becomes sticky indeed when one recalls that for Mallarmé it is precisely the intentionality of the poet as such that must disappear in order for initiative to be left to words: "L'oeuvre pure implique la disparition élocutoire du poëte, qui cède l'initiative aux mots . . ." (p. 366). Therefore, the fact that the dancer here is objectified and denied interiority is not in itself a function of her gender. That state of "scribelessness," of "impersonality," is, rather, the ideal Mallarmé sets up for poetry. But the fact remains that the poet is consistently male and the poem female:

> L'Unique entraînement imaginatif consiste, aux heures ordinaires de fréquentation dans les lieux de Danse sans visée quelconque préalable, patiemment et passivement à se demander devant tout pas, chaque attitude si étranges, ces pointes et taquetés, allongés ou ballons, "Que peut signifier ceci" ou mieux, d'inspiration, le lire. A coup sûr on opérera en pleine rêverie, mais adéquate: vaporeuse, nette et ample, ou restreinte, telle seulement que l'enferme en ses circuits ou la transporte par une fugue la ballerine illettrée se livrant aux jeux de sa profession. Oui, celle-là (serais-tu perdu en une salle, spectator très étranger, Ami) pour peu que tu déposes avec soumission à ses pieds d'inconsciente révélatrice ainsi que les roses qu'enlève et jette en la visibilité de régions supérieures un jeu de ses chaussons de satin pâle vertigineux, la Fleur d'abord *de ton poétique instinct,* n'attendant de rien autre la mise en évidence et sous le vrai jour des mille imaginations latentes: alors, par un commerce dont paraît son sourire verser le secret, sans tarder elle te livre à travers le voile dernier qui toujours reste, la nudité de tes concepts et silencieusement écrira ta vision à la façon d'un Signe, qu'elle est. (p. 307)

[The sole imaginative training consists, in the ordinary hours of frequenting Dance with no preconceived aim, patiently and passively, of wondering at every step, each attitude, so strange, those points and *taquetés, allongés* or *ballons,* "What can this signify?" or, better, by inspiration, of reading it. One will definitely operate in full reverie, but adequate: vaporous, crisp, and ample, or restrained, such only as it is enclosed in circlings or transported in a figure by the illiterate ballerina engaging in the play of her profession. Yes, that one (be you lost in the hall, most foreign spectator, Friend) if you but set at the feet of this unconscious revealer, submissively—like the roses lifted and tossed into the visibility of the upper regions by a flounce of her dizzying pale satin slippers—the Flower at first *of your poetic instinct,* expecting nothing but the evidencing and in the true light of a thousand latent imaginations: then, through a commerce whose secret her smile appears to pour out, without delay she delivers up to you, through the ultimate veil that always remains, the nudity of your concepts, and silently begins to write your vision in the manner of a Sign, which she is.]

What the woman is a sign of, what she *unconsciously* reveals, is the nudity of "your" concepts and the flower of "your" poetic instinct. The woman, dancing, is the necessary but unintentional medium through which something fundamental to the male poetic self can be manifested. But this state of unconsciousness, which would seemingly establish the possibility of a female poet, turns out to be valuable only when reappropriated by the male poet. This becomes clear in Mallarmé's discussion of women and jewels.

Precious stones figure often in Mallarmé's descriptions of poetry:

> L'oeuvre pure implique la disparition élocutoire du poëte, qui cède l'initiative aux mots, par le heurt de leur inégalité mobilisés; *ils s'allument de reflets réciproques comme une virtuelle traînée de feux sur des pierreries,* remplaçant la respiration perceptible en l'ancien souffle lyrique ou la direction personnelle enthousiaste de la phrase. (p. 366; italics mine)
>
> [The pure work implies the elocutionary disappearance of the poet, who leaves the initiative to words, through the shock of their mobilized inequality; *they light up with reciprocal reflections like a virtual trail of fire over precious stones,* replacing the breath perceptible in the old lyric inspiration or the passionate personal direction of the sentence.]

In an interview with Jules Huret, Mallarmé expands upon the image of jewelry in the following terms:

> —*Que pensez-vous de la fin du naturalisme?*
>
> —L'enfantillage de la littérature jusqu'ici a été de croire, par exemple, que de choisir un certain nombre de pierres précieuses et en mettre les noms sur le papier, même très bien, c'était *faire* des pierres précieuses. Eh bien! non! La poésie consistant à *créer,* il faut prendre dans l'âme humaine des états, des lueurs d'une pureté si absolue que, bien chantés et bien mis en lumière, cela constitute en effet les joyaux de l'homme: là,

il y a symbole, il y a création, et le mot poèsie a ici son sens: c'est, en somme, la seule création humaine possible. Et si, véritablement, les pierres précieuses dont on se pare ne manifestent pas un état d'âme, c'est indûment qu'on s'en pare. . . . La femme, par exemple, cette éternelle voleuse . . .

Et tenez, *ajoute mon interlocuteur en riant à moitié,* ce qu'il y a d'admirable dans les magasins de nouveautés, c'est, quelquefois, de nous avoir révélé, par le commissaire de police, que la femme se parait indûment de ce dont elle ne savait pas le sens caché, et qui ne lui appartient par conséquent pas . . . (pp. 870–71)

[—*What do you think of the end of naturalism?*

—The childishness of literature up to now has been to think, for example, that to choose a certain number of precious stones and to put their names down on paper, even superbly well, was to *make* precious stones. Not at all! Since poetry consists of creating, one must take from the human soul certain states, certain glimmerings of such absolute purity that, skillfully sung and brought to light, they constitute indeed the jewels of man: there, there is symbol, there is creation, and the word poetry takes on its meaning: that, in sum, is the only human creation possible. And if, truly, the precious stones one dresses in do not manifest a state of mind or mood, then one has no right to wear them. . . . Woman, for example, that eternal thief . . .

And think, *adds my interlocutor half laughing:* what is admirable about those high fashion stores is that they have sometimes revealed to us, through the chief of police, that women have been illegitimately wearing what they didn't know the hidden meaning of, and which consequently does not belong to them . . .]

Women's unconsciousness of meaning—that which makes them capable of *standing for* the male poetic instinct—is what denies the legitimacy of their ever occupying the role of poetic subject. Men know what they are doing when they leave initiative to words or jewels; women don't. It is interesting to recall that Mallarmé almost singlehandedly produced a fashion journal, *La Dernière Mode,* which dealt in great detail with jewelry, clothing, and other items of female decoration, and which he often signed with a feminine pseudonym. It is as though Mallarmé's interest in writing like a woman about fashion was to steal back for consciousness that women had stolen by unconsciousness, to write *consciously* from out of the female unconscious, which is somehow more intimately but illegitimately connected to the stuff of poetry. Intertextuality here becomes intersexuality.

Mallarmé's instatement of the impersonal or unconscious poetic subject thus somehow exposes rather than conceals a question that haunts him from the very beginning: is writing a gendered act? It is this question that informs a poem entitled "Don du poème," which serves as a dedicatory poem to "Hérodiade." The fact that Hérodiade and Mallarmé's daughter Genevieve were "born" at the same time serves as the background for Mallarmé's reflection on gender differences:

Je t'apporte l'enfant d'une nuit d'Idumée!
Noire, à l'aile saignante et pâle, déplumée,
Par le verre brûlé d'aromates et d'or,
Par les carreaux glacés, hélas! mornes encor,
L'aurore se jeta sur la lampe angélique.
Palmes! et quand elle a montré cette relique
A ce père essayant un sourire ennemi,
La solitude bleue et stérile a frémi.
O la berceuse, avec ta fille et l'innocence
De vos pieds froids, accueille une horrible naissance:
Et ta voix rappelant viole et clavecin,
Avec le doigt fané presseras-tu le sein
Par qui coule en blancheur sibylline la femme
Pour les lèvres que l'air du vierge azur affame?
(p. 40)

[I bring you the child of a night spent in Edom!
Black, with pale and bleeding wing, quilless,
Through the glass burned with spices and gold,
Through the icy panes, alas! mournful still,
The dawn flew down on the angelic lamp.
Palms! and when it had shown this relic
To this father attempting an enemy smile,
The blue and sterile solitude was stirred.
O cradler, with your daughter and the innocence
Of your cold feet, welcome a horrible birth:
And your voice recalling viol and harpsichord,
With faded finger will you press the breast
Through which in sibylline whiteness woman flows
For lips half starved by virgin azure air?]

The question of gender is raised immediately in two very different ways in the first line. The word "enfant" is one of the few words in French that can be either masculine or feminine without modification. And the name "Idumée" refers to ancient Edom, the land of the outcast Esau, or, according to the Kabbalah, the land of pre-Adamic man, where sexless beings reproduced without women, or where sexual difference did not exist. The poem thus begins on a note of denial of sexual difference, only to end with a plea that the woman agree to nurture the fruit of such a denial. The means of such nourishment is "blancheur sibylline": white textuality, the blankness that challenges interpretation. The woman, then, is to provide the nourishing blanks without which the newborn poem might die of "azure," which, as we have seen, represents the weight of poetic history. "Idumée" and "Palmes" can be found in Boileau's Satire IX in a passage in which he lists a string of Malherbian poetic commonplaces.[8]

It would seem at first sight that Mallarmé in this poem draws a contrast between the fecundity of natural reproduction and the sterility of poetic creation, and that this poem stands as a typical example of the male pen expressing its womb envy. Yet the masculine here is equated with sexlessness, while the woman functions not as a womb but as a source of music and sibylline whiteness. The opposition between male and female is an opposition between half-dead language and nourishing non-language. But while many writers have valued the woman as something extra-textual, such non-language is valued in Mallarmé's system not because it is outside, but because it is *within,* the poetic text. Both music and whiteness are extraordinarily privileged in Mallarmé's poetics precisely because they function as articulations *without* content. Mallarmé's insistence that what the word "flower" evokes is what is *absent* from any bouquet, that the text is a structure of relations and not a collection of signifieds, that there is no given commensurability between language and reality, functions polemically in the late nineteenth century debates over realism and naturalism. His emphasis on music as a "system of relations" and on blankness as a structured but "stilled" poem functions precisely as a *critique* of the pretensions to representationalism and realism in the literary text. By thus opposing naive referentiality and privileging blankness and silence, Mallarmé also, however, implicitly shifts the gender values traditionally assigned to such questions. If the figure of woman has been repressed and objectified by being equated with the blank page, then Mallarmé, by *activating* those blanks, comes close to writing from the place of the silenced female voice. In his ways of throwing his voice as a woman, of figuring textuality as a dancing ballerina, and of questioning simplistic pretensions to expressivity,

8. It is curious to note that the word with which "Idumée" rhymes in Boileau is "alarmée," and that "alarmes" is the first rhyme in the overture to "Hérodiade," which follows and imagistically grows out of "Don du Poème." Mallarmé's anagrammatical signature seems to lurk just behind these citations of poetic history.

potency, and (masculine) authority, Mallarmé's critique of logocentrism opens up a space for a critique of phallocentrism as well. Intertextuality can no longer be seen simply as a relation between fathers and sons. But although Mallarmé's many feminine incarnations make it impossible to read him as "simply" masculine, the revaluation of the *figure* of the woman by a male author cannot substitute for the actual participation of women in the critical conversation. Mallarmé may be able to speak from the place of the silenced woman, but as long as *he* is occupying it, the silence that is broken in theory is maintained in reality. And while there is no guarantee that when a "real" woman speaks, she is truly breaking that silence, at least she makes it difficult to avoid facing the fact that literal "women" and figurative "women" do not meet on the same rhetorical level of discourse. Indeed, in this essay we have barely begun to explore the true intertextualities of intersexuality.

JULIAN PATRICK

Going Round versus Going Straight to Meaning: The Puzzles of Auden's "Our Bias"

The words of a dead man
Are modified in the guts of the living.
W. H. Auden, "In Memory of W. B. Yeats"

Cleanth Brooks's *Modern Poetry and the Tradition* (1939) can be considered the first broadly successful use of American New Critical terminology. The poetry of Yeats and Eliot had been rudely and uncomprehendingly rejected by much high-brow criticism (F. L. Lucas and John Sparrow, among others), and Brooks's principled, eloquent defense showed clearly how their poetry could be explicated and taught. Brooks thinks of modernism as the third great revolution in literary taste since the Renaissance (after the rise of science in the seventeenth century and the Romantic revolt), and of New Criticism as the criticism called for by the verbal strategies of modern poetry. By contrast with most poetry since Donne, modern poetry notoriously depends upon figurative implication, and it was for this reason that the theory of relations embedded in the figures needed to be made explicit. From this need arose what are to us the familiar concepts, terms, and practices of the New Criticism: the "organic form" implicit in the way one figure relates to another; the emphasis upon reconciliation, achieved through widely contrasting oppositions; the hierarchy of attitudes arising from such reconciliation; a characteristic analysis of metaphor to bring out its capacity to interpret reality; the use of the concept of analogy as a sophisticated substitute for a theory of reference; and finally and most important as a defense against the charge that modern poetry was shapeless and lacked internal development, Brooks's idealist interpretation of poetic structure as above all a structure of meaning.

The echo of Eliot in Brooks's first sentence, "Every poet that we read alters to some degree our total conception of poetry," suggests the extent to which Eliot's own program for literary history has been taken over by Brooks, with additional ballast coming from I. A. Richards and from Coleridge, whose "Ancient Mariner" is called a Symbolist poem and whose theory of the imagination is interpreted in Symbolist terms. A good portion of Brooks's first four essays is given over to an informal poetics of the figure. Here, the concept of irony is employed to transform characteristic period structures like the metaphysical conceit and the romantic image into modern symbols, with all the latter's depth, body, and ontological weight. Because Brooks is following Eliot, some aspects of his argument are directed "against romanticism," the title of Auden's review of the book;[1] but it can also be shown that Brooks's analysis of the metaphysical conceit has the effect of romanticizing this rhetorical device by thinking of it primarily as an expressive symbol. Brooks is trying to defend the conceit against the still potent eighteenth-century charge of levity, but the effect of his defense is to make the rhetoric of wit into serious symbolic statement and to obscure, fatally in the case of Brooks's later treatment of Donne's "The Canonization," the rhetorical terms and conventions actually being used, as well as much else that could count as the material form of the poem's discourse.[2] For Brooks, the value of a unit of form must be immediately cashed as a unit of meaning; indeed, a unit of form (that is, any unit his analysis distinguishes) is conceptualized by Brooks as a unit of meaning.[3] It is generally true to say that New Criticism, following Croce and expressionist aesthetics, ignores genre and parts of genre, with the result that the complexity of a poem's discourse is seriously underestimated while the interpreted meaning often makes the poem appear more complex, certainly more nuanced and attitudinal, than it is. If New Criticism appears to favor lyric poetry over the other modes, it is certainly not the extensive and detailed world of lyric forms—riddle and emblem,

1. *New Republic,* 102, no. 6 (5 February 1940), 187.

2. In 1956, William J. Rooney published a brilliant, and since neglected, "deconstruction" of Brooks's reading of "The Canonization" in *The Well Wrought Urn* (New York, 1947). Rooney establishes the superiority of a rhetorical and generic understanding of the poem, one that anticipates contemporary discourse analysis; see "'The Canonization'—The Language of Paradox Reconsidered," *ELH,* 23 (1956), 36–47.

3. The terms are Marion Trousdale's in "A Possible Renaissance View of Form," *ELH,* 40 (1973), 179–204. The article contains a very suggestive account of New Critical influence.

charm and song, ballad and ode, lyrics of prayer, lyrics of praise—but rather the meaning-making practice of the lyric poet. Brooks is not unaware of the world of small-scale lyric forms, but the direction of his analysis lies elsewhere, in making the practice of the lyric poet a stable icon of the reconciling imagination at work. What Brooks ignores is the space opened up between form and meaning by the rhetorical complexity of lyric poetry.

In hindsight, it is a bit surprising to find Brooks choosing to discuss as his opening exhibit in *Modern Poetry and the Tradition* Auden's epilogue-like prayer with which *Poems* (1930) concludes ("Sir, no man's enemy, forgiving all / But will his negative inversion, be prodigal"). It is surprising because Brooks's categories are not what Auden's poetry requires and there is some evidence that Brooks is aware of it. In the course of the thirties, Auden had become a strongly political poet in his quest for the "adequate and conscious metaphysics" he felt a writer needed to avoid simply copying the details of life or expressing merely an "individual dementia."[4] But for Brooks writing in America, political poetry meant vulgar Marxism, propaganda, thin and diffuse poetry, ideology, and, worst sin of all for a New Critic, a center for the poetry which was thought to lie outside the poetry itself. In Brooks's opinion, the political poet can avoid the heavy-handedness of ideological commitment, or a fall into mere heterogeneity, only "by assimilating [such] discords into a meaningful pattern" and by emphasizing "connections which lace together the various parts of the poem."[5] It is with phrases such as these that Brooks tries to separate the Auden of the early thirties from his later political commitments and return him to the fold of T. S. Eliot's "tradition." It is perhaps significant that Brooks quotes only from *Poems* (1930) and from *The Orators* (1932) and ignores both *Look, Stranger!* (1936) and the poems already published in accessible periodicals that were to make up Auden's first American publication, *Another Time* (1940).

Auden's development throughout the thirties is exceptionally complicated, especially when it is a question of relations between inside and outside. The rhetorical face of many of the later poems of the thirties is cunningly suspended between an inside center to which the progression of the figures appears to refer and an outside condition, often conceived of in scientific, documentary, satirical, or broadly allegorical terms, to which the poems allude or which they represent.

4. Auden, "Mimesis and Allegory," *English Institute Annual, 1940,* ed. Rudolf Kirk (New York, 1941), pp. 18–19.

5. Brooks, *Modern Poetry and the Tradition,* pp. 131, 129.

It is also noteworthy that many of the later poems of the thirties have an unmistakable voice, or voices, which have the effect of making what they say appear consciously intended. It is with the issue of intention, or conscious design, that Brooks appears most uneasy, most eager to retain Auden within the more "iconic" tradition Brooks is comfortable with. When Brooks says of his analysis of another of Auden's early poems, "least of all do I intend to imply that the sets of contrasts were consciously contrived by the poet . . . ,"[6] we see how essential it is for him to retain the illusion that the critic's job is to overhear the poet doing what, for a Romantic or post-Romantic writer, is supposed to come naturally.

Brooks's short but generous piece on Auden contains a buried "contrast" between ideology and lyric form, and a buried judgment that the two are incompatible. The same judgment is overt and hostile in Randall Jarrell's well-known essay "Changes of Attitude and Rhetoric in Auden's Poetry" (1941), and in his later "Freud to Paul: The Stages of Auden's Ideology" (1945).[7] In the course of a brilliant catalogue of what he so thoroughly dislikes, Jarrell reveals his bewilderment at what we would now call Auden's post-modernist insistence on the *écriture* of lyric—the self-consciously foregrounded use of a wide range of lyric forms and rhetorical effects, in conjunction with different kinds of statement. Jarrell is clearly bothered by Auden's misuse of a pure medium:

> It was *necessary* for Auden to develop and depend upon all this rhetorical machinery, because his poetry, his thought itself, was becoming increasingly abstract, public, and prosaic. These rhetorical devices constitute a quasi-scientific method by which you can make rhetorically effective *any* material, by which even the dead, or half living can be galvanized into a sort of animation. . . . Auden . . . has managed to run through a tremendous series of changes so fast that his lyric poetry has been almost ruined. . . . Many of the early poems seem produced by Auden's whole being, as much unconscious as conscious, necessarily made just as they are; the best of them have shapes (just as driftwood or pebbles do) that seem the direct representation of forces that produced them. Most of the later poems represent just as directly the forces that produced *them:* the head, the head, the top of the head; the correct, reasoning, idealistic, sentimental Intelligence. Nietzsche has this terrible sentence: *Euripides as a poet is essentially an echo of his own conscious knowl-*

6. Ibid., p. 129.

7. Originally published in, respectively, *The Southern Review* (Autumn 1941) and *Partisan Review* (Fall 1945); reprinted in *The Third Book of Criticism* (New York, 1969).

> *edge.* It is hard not to apply the judgment to most of Auden's latest poetry.[8]

The oppositions of Jarrell's judgment—organic form versus rational, or what Coleridge called "superinduced" form, Auden's early, free-standing lyric style in which the voice of the poet is indistinguishable from his performance, as against his later thirties style (talky, contingent), the poem often designed for an occasion and rarely the product of it—are the oppositions of New Criticism.[9] Despite the brilliance of the essay, especially the catalogue of rhetorical devices, Jarrell is as poor a guide to Auden's poetry as Nietzsche is to Euripides, largely because Jarrell is haunted by the residual Romanticism in literary modernism and cannot forgive Auden for abandoning the role of poet-seer. (Nietzsche, then under Wagner's influence, is a parallel case.) Jarrell wants the poet to create an authentic presence for himself through the harmonies of sound. If one is to think in poetry, it must be that kind of thinking that Jarrell approves in Stevens: "as we read the poems we are so continually aware of Stevens observing, meditating, creating, that we feel like saying that the process of creating the poem is the poem."[10] As Stevens put a similar thought in "An Ordinary Evening in New Haven": "The poem is the cry of its occasion, / Part of the res itself and not about it."[11] One purpose of poetry, according to Stevens, Jarrell, and perhaps even Brooks, is to create the strong illusion that, as Stevens puts it, "words of the world are the life of the world."

Stevens may be alluding to the separation, traditional in rhetorical theory, between *verba* and *res,* words and things. Whether he is or not, his use of Romantic and Symbolist doctrines of the desirable identity of words and things brings him very close to the Saussurean and post-

8. Jarrell, *The Third Book of Criticism,* pp. 147–48.

9. Auden, in an essay on D. H. Lawrence, repudiates Lawrence's organicism by quoting from Valéry's dialogue *Eupanilos:* "The tree does not construct its branches and leaves; nor the cock his beak and feathers. But the tree and all its parts, or the cock and all his, are constructed by the principles themselves, which do not exist apart from the constructing. . . . But, in the objects made by man, the principles are separate from the construction, and are, as it were, imposed by a tyrant from without upon the material, to which he imparts them by acts. . . . If a man waves his arm, we distinguish this arm from his gesture, and we conceive between gesture and arm a purely possible relation. But from the point of view of nature, this gesture of the arm and the arm itself cannot be separated" (Auden, *The Dyer's Hand* [New York, 1965], p. 283).

10. Jarrell, in a review of Stevens's *The Collected Poems,* reprinted in *The Third Book of Criticism,* p. 63.

11. Quotations from Stevens are from *The Collected Poems of Wallace Stevens* (New York, 1954).

Saussurean thesis of the autonomy of the language-system. Briefly, if owing to the power of words, things appear to be only what those words have evoked of them, or, if words, through the power of sound, begin to take on the appearance of things (to name just two of many possible relations), the poet is claiming, as Stevens does throughout his later poetry, the Adamite power to create by naming, by using names as forms. This modernist doctrine has recently been restated by J. Hillis Miller in a poststructuralist form, itself anticipated by several of Stevens's dicta,

> . . . the form-making act is the creator rather than the copier of meaning. Meaning arises from the internal relationship of signs to one another, from echoing repetitions of rhythm, syntax, rhyme, alliteration and figurative language, from all the forms of similarity in difference within a text, rather than from the correspondence of signs to some already existing pattern of meaning. . . . There is an incompatibility between any form and its pre-formal sources, the incompatibility between meaning and the meaningless.[12]

Miller's formalism, where what is formalist are the properties of language itself rather than, as in the New Criticism, the relation between form and meaning, is clearly related to the literary practice of high modernism. This agreement between high modernism and contemporary critical theory, as well as all that it leaves out, or distorts, can be strongly felt in Stevens's meditation on the relation between sounds, words, nature, and the function of the poet in "Academic Discourse at Havana":

> Is the function of the poet here mere sound?
> Subtler than ornatest prophecy,
> To stuff the ear? It causes him to make
> His infinite repetition and alloys,
> Of pick of ebon, pick of halcyon.
> It weights him with nice logic for the prim.
> As part of nature he is part of us.
> His rarities are ours: may they be fit
> And reconcile us to ourselves in those
> True reconcilings, dark, pacific words,
> And the adroiter harmonies of their fall.
> Close the cantina. Hood the chandelier.

12. Miller, "The Still Heart: Poetic Form in Wordsworth," *New Literary History*, 2 (1971), 298–99.

The moonlight is not yellow but a white
That silences the ever-faithful town.
How pale and how possessed a night it is,
How full of exhalations of the sea . . .
All this is older than its oldest hymn,
Has no more meaning than tomorrow's bread.
But let the poet on his balcony
Speak and the sleepers in their sleep shall move,
Waken, and watch the moonlight on their floors. . . .

It would be unfair to Stevens to remark that one can think of many contexts in which the question of "tomorrow's bread" has a great deal of meaning, contexts which would make repellent the idea of reconciliation to the self through words. But if we leave those contexts to the side for the moment, what is one to make of Stevens's trust in the high modernist dogma that those ethically neutral forces, nature and language, can be in themselves the warrant and locus for self-reconciliation?[13] For Auden, despite his commitment to lyric *écriture,* the act of writing is too convention-bound, too mired in the rifts of representation to be able to make words, even words considered first as sound, perform the tasks Stevens assigns them. Of course, Stevens is writing in the optative mood and does not mean us to take him literally. Nonetheless, it is interesting to notice how Auden is drawn toward a similar hope and on what different grounds he welcomes it, in "The Composer":

All the others translate: the painter sketches
A visible world to love or reject;
Rummaging into his living, the poet fetches
The images out that hurt and connect,

From Life to Art by painstaking adaption,
Relying on us to cover the rift;
Only your notes are pure contraption,
Only your song is an absolute gift.

Pour out your presence, a delight cascading
The falls of the knee and the weirs of the spine,
Our climate of silence and doubt invading;

13. See, for a similar view, Edward Mendelson, *Early Auden* (New York, 1981), p. 354n. This essay is indebted to Mendelson's work, especially to his essay-like sections on modernism, *Early Auden,* pp. 202–9 and on "contradiction," pp. 316–23.

You alone, alone, imaginary song,
Are unable to say an existence is wrong,
And pour out your forgiveness like a wine.[14]

Arts that remain tied to representation, like painting and poetry, also remain attached to ethical issues, or at least, to wounds and hatred, whereas song alone can provide the grace of forgiveness because it escapes entirely the relation between original and copy, escapes the author and authority. Though Auden, at this point in his life, retained his interest in matching words to song, as the "Letter to Lord Byron" implies, he was far more interested in the painter, the filmmaker, and the novelist, whom he described in a poem called "The Novelist," a companion piece to "The Composer," as having "dully [to] put up with all the wrongs of man." Given the choice between Mallarmé and Thackeray, two names he liked to rhyme, Auden preferred the second.

The contrast I have been sketching is of course much more complicated than this. As I shall argue, Auden's most compelling poems of the late thirties neither are nor are not modernist. Instead they straddle boundaries and embrace contradictions, often combining discursive, figural, and rhythmical aspects of meaning in a way that proves disconcerting to formalist analysis. These poems successfully establish an oblique and inwardly directed rhetorical face, but they are also more accessible to readers because they mostly avoid any reliance on a private symbol-system. The simultaneously closed and open nature of Auden's poetry is precisely described in a later poem called "Words," where he discusses what John Fuller calls "the twofold nature of the relationship between language and truth"—that language is both a closed system and therefore true in itself, and an entirely natural activity, like gossiping:[15]

A sentence uttered makes a world appear
Where all things happen as it says they do;
We doubt the speaker, not the tongue we hear:
Words have no word for words that are not true.

Syntactically though it must be clear:
One cannot change the subject half-way through,
Nor alter tenses to appease the ear:
Arcadian tales are hard-luck stories too.

14. Quotations from Auden's poetry, unless otherwise stated, are from *Collected Poems*, ed. Edward Mendelson (London, 1976).

15. John Fuller, *A Reader's Guide to W. H. Auden* (London, 1970), p. 235.

But should we want to gossip all the time,
Were fact not fiction for us at its best,
Or find a charm in syllables that rhyme,

Were not our fate by verbal chance expressed,
As rustics at a ring-dance pantomime
The Knight at some lone cross-roads of his quest?

Because language is a closed system, individual words have to be interpreted by means of other words, making the system circular in that sense: "words," by themselves, "have no word for words that are not true." The word "lie," for instance, is also a word with other meanings. Yet though language is a closed system, it does have regulating principles that prevent it from being simply a world to be used at will. Auden would agree with Chomsky, as against Saussure, in including syntax within the language-system. Speakers lie, not language; language makes us follow.

Both principles are illustrated by the opening line of Browning's poem "Childe Roland to the Dark Tower Came"—"My first thought was he lied in every word," since the protagonist of the poem does actually follow the direction the speaker gives him, for that's the way the road lies, despite his doubt. What complements the closed nature of the language system is our constant use of it to find truth, making it appear momentarily as the authentic home of the concepts we employ. For instance, language is filled with apparently natural, chance formations, like the rhymes "will" and "kill," and "must" and "dust," rhymes that seem to confirm our sense that, for example, necessity and mortality are linked concepts.[16] The mysterious conclusion of "Words," then, provides an analogy for the expression of our fate in words and sums up the self-reflexive and self-enacting quality of the poem's discourse. The first line of the poem performs what it also describes while the last couplet describes a curiously wordless performance. Here, though the rustics seem English rather than Arcadian, syntax must still be observed—"pantomime" is a verb. The poem turns in on its own linguistic procedures and out toward a world beyond language where our fate is thought to lie. Hence, the images of the closed circle and the open cross-roads suggest both the closed nature of language and the "crossed" or contradictory, pulled-in-both-directions nature of fate.

"Words" invokes the relation between language and fate (or choice), and provides a basis for defending Auden against Jarrell's

16. For a discussion of such rhymes, see Hugh Kenner, "Pope's Reasonable Rhymes," *ELH*, 43 (1976), 36–47.

telling accusation that Auden's many changes had ruined his lyric poetry.[17] One reason for Auden's vast influence on younger American poets during the forties and fifties was the breadth of his knowledge of lyric poetry and his equally remarkable Horatian, or Jonsonian, ability to use many of the forms of lyric poetry self-reflexively, as if they were natural discourse. Another source of his influence lay in his ability to open the conventions of the lyric to the voices of history, to, in effect, historicize the lyric by showing how its conventions and formal values could be placed in dialogue with changing social and psychological conditions. This ability to find a place in lyric for the astonishing changes of that time (his own included) gives to his poetry of the late thirties an unparalleled tangibleness and immediacy, whose only real analogue is Brecht's related challenge to inherited theatrical convention. Auden's famous poem "Lullaby," of which these are the first two stanzas, suggests something of the relation between convention and change in the lyric voice:

> Lay your sleeping head, my love,
> Human on my faithless arm;
> Time and fevers burn away
> Individual beauty from
> Thoughtful children, and the grave
> Proves the child ephemeral:
> But in my arms till break of day
> Let the living creature lie,
> Mortal, guilty, but to me
> The entirely beautiful.
>
> Soul and body have no bounds:
> To lovers as they lie upon
> Her tolerant enchanted slope
> In their ordinary swoon,
> Grave the vision Venus sends
> Of supernatural sympathy,
> Universal love and hope;
> While an abstract insight wakes
> Among the glaciers and the rocks
> The hermit's sensual ecstasy.[18]

17. So changeable were the thirties that Kenneth Burke thought of titling *The Philosophy of Literary Form,* "While Everything Flows"! (*The Philosophy of Literary Form* [1941; 3rd ed., rpt. Berkeley and Los Angeles, 1973], p. xvii.)

18. Auden later changed "sensual ecstasy" to "carnal ecstasy"; this text is from *The English Auden: Poems, Essays and Dramatic Writings, 1927–1939,* ed. Edward Mendelson (London, 1977).

The strength of this powerful lyric lies in its refusal of paradox. The poem is called a lullaby, but the grave proves the child ephemeral; a lullaby is sung to a child as it goes to sleep, or as a charm to keep off evil spirits when the child is asleep, but nothing can prevent "noons of dryness," "nights of insult," from affecting this lover; besides, he is being asked to do what he cannot avoid doing; visions of supernatural sympathy arise, but the poet's wish is that the mortal world prove enough for the lover. These formulations, and others, are not put paradoxically because the effect of such a figure would be to close off and suspend the moment of love from the hardness of the outside world. The use of paradox would also distort the time-bound and vulnerable quality of the erotic moment being celebrated. Such consolation as there is depends on realizing that conventional sources of consolation are unavailable. This love lasts for this night. What *is* in question is the relation between the "human" and the "mortal," the "guilty," the "faithless."

It is for this reason that "human" is so out of place at the head of the second line, risking both the suspicion of redundancy and confusion over what it modifies. Another reason is that "human" conceals and reveals the male sex of the lover. In this way, the word "human" specifies the work the poem must do to redefine the quality of being human so that it will include faithlessness, guilt, and the purely mortal world. This it does by breaking with conventional expectations of heterosexual union—equality between lovers, the power of love to transcend the world, to be of benefit to others, the indivisibility of soul and body, and all the rest. Soul and body are indivisible in this poem, but in the gravely ironic sense that neither has any boundaries from the other.[19] Venus sends a vision of supernatural love to lovers in their ordinary swoon, while, equally irrelevantly, the hermit has Venus's "sensual ecstasy" awakened in him by an abstract insight. This chiastic (not paradoxical) redistribution of love's qualities has the effect of focusing the attention on the moment of love itself, and on nothing else. That this moment can turn naturally into a moment of watching, even into a voyeuristic awareness of difference, is strangely made part of what a human love is. When the facts of the time might seem to assault the very conventions of the love-lyric itself, the lyric can be saved from the self-parody that might result by permitting its conventions to engage in a dialogue-like exchange with the "moral" facts the conventions of the lyric might have excluded—faithlessness,

19. *Early Auden,* p. 232.

punishment, the restriction of the imagination to the mortal world, and the casual invocation of "involuntary powers."[20]

It is at this point that the various strands in this essay—the incapacity of New Critical terminology (or any formalism) to do justice to Auden; the different rhetorical strategies of Stevens and Auden on the relation of *verba* to *res;* Auden's strong attraction toward the social world of the novelist and away from modernist symbols for the poet; the challenges that rapid historical and ideological change can cause for a poet of Auden's classicizing temperament; and his moral concern with the subterfuges of language and the more fundamental evasions of the will—can be illuminated by closely examining one of Auden's most widely anthologized sonnets, "Our Bias," with its cunning replacement of the concerns of "History" by those of "Time":

The hour-glass whispers to the lion's roar,
The clock-towers tell the gardens day and night
How many errors Time has patience for,
How wrong they are in being always right.

Yet Time, however loud its chimes or deep,
However fast its falling torrent flows,
Has never put one lion off his leap
Nor shaken the assurance of a rose.

For they, it seems, care only for success:
While we choose words according to their sound
And judge a problem by its awkwardness;

And Time with us was always popular.
When have we not preferred some going round
To going straight to where we are?

20. Auden bent his almost inexhaustible talent for lyric toward the complications and bad faith of the late thirties because he responded so fully to the new truth of the time for poetry, that "History opposes its grief to our buoyant song" (*In Time of War,* sonnet 13 [*English Auden,* p. 256]). Accordingly, in poem after poem (the most prominent are "Spain 1937," "In Memory of W. B. Yeats," *In Time of War,* and "September 1, 1939"), Auden showed himself urgently aware of the twin truths: that "poetry makes nothing happen" and that "all I have is a voice / To undo the folded lie." To be understood in its historical situation, Auden's writing needs inspiration from a nonorganic poetics, such as is now being developed by much poststructuralist writing and whose nearest, historical precursor is the work of M. M. Bakhtin and his circle. As is well known, Bakhtin's poetics began in response to symbolist poetry, the modernist poetics of the Russian Formalists, and in opposition to Saussurean linguistics. His writing tends to concentrate on the social dimension of speech utterances, on the implicit dialogism of all speech, and especially on the nonorganic poetics made neces-

The poem's opening quatrain contains two ironic echoes of Shakespeare, ironic because they undermine and reverse the confident, Renaissance understanding of the relation between poetry and time. The opening line of Shakespeare's sonnet 19, "Devouring time, blunt thou the lion's paw" is echoed in Auden's original version of the first line of "Our Bias," "The hour-glass whispers to the lion's *paw*."[21] The second echo is of *The Winter's Tale* in which the figure of Time, unchanged since the world began, comes to announce the gap of sixteen years between the first and second halves of the play: "I that please some, try all, both joy and terror / Of good and bad; that makes and unfolds error."

This connection of time with "error" and in sonnet 19 with "wrong"[22] is important because the syntax of the first quatrain appears, at first glance, to link "errors" and "wrong" with the lion and the gardens, and not with time. Thus, from the distorting perspective of human time, the lion's roaring, and the garden's calm assurance, have the appearance of a double error. The lion roars and leaps and the garden grows in response to natural laws, whereas man-made instruments for measuring time furnish an external standard for when to act. By this standard, the actions of the lion and the gardens look "wrong . . . in being always right." In addition, their wrongness looks morally wrong as well, for the lion's leap is, from a human perspective, murder, whereas the rose's assurance is, just as surely,

---

sary, in Bakhtin's view, by the age of the novel. "The great organic poetics of the past," says Bakhtin, "those of Aristotle, Horace, Boileau—are permeated with a deep sense of the wholeness of literature and of the harmonious interaction of all genres contained within this whole. It is as if they literally hear this harmony of the genres. In this is their strength—the inimitable, all-embracing fullness and exhaustiveness of such poetics. And they all, as a consequence, ignore the novel. . . . The novel, however, gets on poorly with other genres. There can be no talk of a harmony deriving from limitation and complementariness. The novel parodies other genres (precisely in their role of genres); it exposes the conventionality of their forms and their language. . . . Thus of particular interest are those years when the novel becomes the dominant genre. All literature is then caught up in the process of becoming, . . .In an era when the novel reigns supreme, almost all remaining genres are to a greater or lesser extent 'novelized.' Those genres that stubbornly preserve their old canonic nature begin to appear stylized" (M. M. Bakhtin, *The Dialogic Imagination: Four Essays,* ed. Michael Holquist, trans. Caryl Emerson and Michael Holquist [Austin and London, 1981), p. 5). This sequence of ideas provides the strongest explanation for Auden's success in using a sonnet sequence, *In Time of War,* as a mask for the traditional narrative energies of the epic. The poem describes an ironic progress from creation to the present (1938) genocidal moment in "Nanking, Dachau."

21. The point is made by Fuller, *A Reader's Guide,* p. 176.

22. The final couplet of sonnet 19 reads: "Yet do thy worst old Time despite thy wrong, / My love shall in my verse ever live young."

pride. Thus, taking the instinctive rightness of the animal and plant world to be wrong, a wrong rightness, so to speak, we take the "they" of line 4 to refer, as the "they" which opens the sonnet's sestet unmistakably does, to the lion and the gardens.

But is this reading not in itself an error, induced by the rhythm, that is, by the time of the lines? This rhythm appears to make the sense flow toward the object of the Canute-like whispering of the hour-glass and the ceaseless and irrelevant telling/tolling of the clock-towers. But perhaps (working now against the "natural" flow of the lines) the errors Time has patience for are its own errors, moral failures induced by a merely mechanical image of correctness, as if knowing the time exactly could solve by itself the problem of human choice and right action. Now the "they" of line 4 appears to refer to the hour-glass and the clock-towers—it is they who are wrong in being always right—so that what first sounded like a sermon delivered by Time to the plants and animals now sounds like a confession, and time's anxiety, the anxiety of being wrong when you're right, has been transferred to the reader.

It is perhaps at this point that the question of indeterminacy arises. "How many errors Time has patience for" is, after all, a general statement and doesn't necessarily refer to any specific errors; nor, in context, does the "they" of line four pick out any specific plural to refer to. To put what is perhaps the same point another way, the contrast between humankind and the vegetable and animal kingdoms, which is such an important part of the second quatrain, is not a structural part of the first, which contains a general message, or reflection, on time and error delivered to the nonhuman world. So the first quatrain actually presents the reader with two different kinds of indeterminacy, each kind enacting a slightly different picture of the relation between time and error. The first kind of indeterminacy arises from the question we have already discussed—whether to link "they" to the nonhuman world or to the human means for measuring time (the problem of reference), and the second, from the question of whether to follow up at all the apparent reference of "they" and of "Time" (the problem of the abstract and the concrete). "Time" after all is not necessarily equivalent to the means by which we measure it.

In the second quatrain, by contrast, everything is clear because the attributes of time have been scattered and transformed. The loud chimes are the opposite of the quiet whispering of the hour-glass and the complement of the sound the clock- towers make, as the speed of Time's falling torrent is the complement of the sands of the hour-glass and the opposite of the monotonous telling/tolling of the clock-towers. More important, by exchanging the vehicle of his expression from "whispering" and "telling" to pure statement, and by bracketing the subject of the first quatrain in the repeated "however" clauses of the second, the poet dismisses the tension between Time and its instruments, making unmistakable the difference between the instinctive action of the animals and the plants and the anxiety-ridden world of human time-consciousness. For, as the sestet goes on to imply, it is we who hear time as slow, dropping grain by grain, or loud, or fast, or monotonously regular, and each of these separable hearings represents an anxiety about Time and its uses.

As the second quatrain sweeps briskly into the certainty of statement, we realize that one of the purposes of the contrast between the nonhuman world and our time-consciousness has been to bring out what our world of anxiety would look like to the animals and plants were they human. We would look to them as if we didn't know what to do, as if we chose words according to their sound and were unable to read their plain sense and reference, as if we had forgotten that it must always be possible to construe the denoted sense of words. If this weren't possible, poetry would cease to be understood as utterance, as intended speech, and would have to be understood solely as *langue*. To ignore the plain sense of words is to go round the delusive, echoing channels of sound; and to judge a problem by its awkwardness is to be attracted to ways of understanding that offer the maximum possible degree of error, "awkwardness" reflecting its etymological origin—turning the wrong way, in the wrong direction.

Hence the conclusion of the poem, which brings us straight up against the relation between indeterminacy and choice, the relation which the first quatrian had dramatized and that the second quatrain had appeared to solve: "When have we not preferred some going round / To going straight to where we are?" There are at least two tones in this concluding question, corresponding to two ways of reading the poem. If we think of the question as rhetorical, that is, as a statement, the tone will be that of a wry, bemused acceptance of the necessity of muddle, evasion, and circumlocution in human life and its capacity to defer the awareness of where we are and what we must do. This judgment would come from outside and would not necessarily take into account the process of arriving at it. But if we inflect the question in a slightly different direction, we can hear the traces left by self-conscious readers, trying to justify their own going round the sound of this poem and having come finally straight to where they are: "*When* have we *not preferred* some going round / To going straight to where we are?"

Where are we? Line 13 of the poem has been made metrically complete by the addition of the word "some" to fill out the line; but the last line of the poem, by contrast, is a whole foot short. The reader's ear (at least, my ear) finds it hard to be sure whether it has actually heard a short line (because the poem's last line conveys the strong illusion of completeness through its virtually identical four syllable phrases, each introduced by "to"), and thus the reader beats out the syllables of the line to make sure. We thus evade the problem of decision—of leaping—by measuring the time of what we have heard—going round instead of going straight. This suggests that part of the poem's uncanniness involves a collapse of the alternatives apparently being set up between going round and going straight, to demonstrate that part of the condition of being human is that we do go round in order to go straight, even when we think we have gone straight, and thus to reinforce the pun, with its shift of accent, in the title Auden later chose for the poem, that "Our Bias" is "Hour Bias," that to be creatures of time is necessarily to be creatures both of measure and of error, "wandering," as Auden put it in *In Time of War,* "lost upon the mountains of our choice."

What then is the relation between the question of indeterminacy in the first quatrain and the conclusion? Indeterminacy can be thought of as a kind of syntactical chiasmus, the figure left on the track of the reader's poem as the mind tries to choose first one reading and then another to satisfy the demands of intelligibility. It has probably not escaped you that the conclusion of the poem uses a chiasmus—"we . . . preferred" is related to "we are" as "going round" is related to "going straight." If the point of the poem is to make a journey out of both the apparent alternatives, to suggest, that is, that going round is related to going straight as poetry is related to meaning, then chiasmus, or the figure of the crossroads, prefigures the fate that lies in wait for us in words.

If this is where we are, where is Auden? "Our Bias" demands the kind of centripetal analysis given it here because its continual turning in on itself generates a self-reflexive dialogue between text and reader best served by such an approach. But the poem also reflects the fact that it was written during the most crucial year of Auden's life, within an historical and biographical context that leads the reader, centrifugally, beyond the poem's horizon, even if nothing "in" the poem (where is that?) specifically demands it. Auden's arrival in America to take up permanent citizenship, in January 1939, led directly to his love for Chester Kallman and to their shared interest in literature and song, one strand of which was a passion for Shakespeare's sonnets. It is not hard to imagine "Our Bias" as a love-sonnet on the long series of unhappy love affairs that preceded Auden's discovery in America of where he was. In the summer of 1939, Auden and Kallman journeyed south by bus to New Mexico, to visit Lawrence's grave and to holiday. It was probably there that Auden wrote the long essay entitled "The Prolific [the creator] and the Devourer [the politician]"[23] which was to serve him as a private common-place book for the writing to come. They returned to New York just days before the declaration of war in Europe. "Our Bias" was written in the month following, alongside one of Auden's ugliest and most powerful poems, "September 1, 1939," with its skewed rhythms and bleak, ironic conclusion. The juxtaposition is startling, for "September 1, 1939" is one of the last of Auden's poems to invoke directly the spectre of the time in which it was composed. If, as enjoined in "Words," we doubt the speaker of "Our Bias," we may find something ominous in the thorough-going replacement of the concerns of "History" with those of "Time" in many of the poems of *Another Time.* What is ominous is not the ruin of Auden's lyric poetry, as the extraordinary lyrics of *The Sea and the Mirror* prove, but the emphasis of many poems in *Another Time* on the feeling that sufficient for the day is the evil thereof:

> For us like any other fugitive,
> Like the numberless flowers that cannot number
> And all the beasts that need not remember,
> It is today in which we live.[24]

This entirely understandable existentialism in the face of public disaster was to lead Auden directly to a study of theology, and into the Christian church, that is, from *kairos* to *logos.* He later repudiated "September 1, 1939," a poem about the consequences of a "low dishonest decade," because he felt that the poem, like most literary responses to the rise of fascism, was itself dishonest.[25] This reminder of the historical context of the poem makes us feel that part of the lovely, haunting quality of "Our Bias" lies in the way it hovers between a world ransomed, as Shakespeare put it in *The Winter's Tale,* and one destroyed. It was, of course, not only the world Auden had left that was in ruins, but his own engagement with history.

23. The complete essay has now been published in *Antaeus,* 42 (1981), 7–65.
24. This is the first quatrain of the poem from which the title *Another Time* was taken.
25. *Early Auden,* p. 330.

Eleanor Cook

Directions in Reading Wallace Stevens: Up, Down, Across

> For discussing words with words is as entangled as interlocking and rubbing the fingers with the fingers, in which case it may scarcely be distinguished, except by the one himself who does it, which fingers itch and which give aid to the itching.
>
> (St. Augustine)

I begin with the problem of reading Professor Eucalyptus of New Haven, that enigmatic figure who appears in three of the thirty-one cantos of Wallace Stevens's "An Ordinary Evening in New Haven." For a reading of this figure suggests a reading of the mode of Stevens's entire poem. The mode in turn suggests a way of reading one lyric in the series, and also suggests a perspective on some lyric poetry and criticism of the last twenty years.

I

In 1917, Stevens wrote a short poem, "In the South" (I), which ends thus:

> . . . effects
> Of magenta blooming in the Judas-tree
> And of purple blooming in the eucalyptus—
> Map of yesterday's earth
> And of tomorrow's heaven.[1]

1. *Opus Posthumous: Poems, Plays, Prose by Wallace Stevens,* ed. Samuel French Morse (New York, 1957), p. 9.

"Eucalyptus" means well-covered, as the flower of the eucalyptus tree is, until its time for uncovering arrives in the ordinary course of things. We need to know this, and we need also to hear the echo from John of Patmos in Stevens's last two lines ("Map of yesterday's earth / And of tomorrow's heaven"—"I saw a new heaven and a new earth") in order to read the implicit wordplay: eucalyptus as against *apokalypsis*, or the sudden, extraordinary uncovering of things. In its implicitness, Stevens's little poem enacts its own subject—a eucalyptic poem, we might say.

The same wordplay and the same echo (now also playing) appear in "An Ordinary Evening in New Haven" (1949), where Stevens divides the eucalyptus into tree and professor, both now being seekers and not mappers. Professor Eucalyptus thereby joins Canon Aspirin as a much-punned quest figure, questing, I assume, after natural revelation, as an eighteenth-century botanical invention should. ("He seeks / God in the object," says Stevens, adding, a little mischievously I think, "without much choice," as indeed he has not, once his creator has given him his name and nature.) One of his functions is to point the reader toward the anti-apocalyptic mode of "An Ordinary Evening in New Haven."

For here no "I" sees a new heaven and a new earth; instead, an eye (no first-person "I" enters the poem) sees or rather tries to see New Haven. We can hear the echoing of the consonantal rhyme in, for instance: "The instinct for heaven had its counterpart: / The instinct for earth, for New Haven . . ." Stevens used Hopkins's compound, "heaven-haven," in 1942 in "Notes toward a Supreme Fiction." The new heaven / New Haven pun perhaps began with Hopkins; I surmise that it gave Stevens his title, one of a long list of possible titles,[2] which in turn gave him his poem. If the Apocalypse is an extraordinary dawning in a new heaven, where else could an ordinary evening be for Stevens but in New Haven? (The founders of New Haven, needless to say, would have heard the echo differently.)

Once we hear this wordplay, other words and phrases take on apocalyptic resonance. Thus, in Revelation 5:5, "behold, the Lion of the tribe of Juda, the Root of David, hath prevailed to open the book." "An Ordinary Evening," canto xi, begins:

2. To the question whether Stevens knew this compound was used by Hopkins, the answer is yes. Stevens copied an extract from a review of *The Young Hopkins* (*New Statesman and Nation*, 23 Jan. 1937, p. 124), which included Hopkins's title (Commonplace book, Huntington Library). For the list of titles, see George S. Lensing, "From Pieces of Paper: *A Wallace Stevens Notebook*," *Southern Review*, 15 (1979), 877–920; and see item 339.

In the metaphysical streets of the physical town
We remember the lion of Juda and we save the
The phrase . . .

No book opens; *we* save the phrase, which grows weak in most unleonine fashion, it being a phrase or *phrasis*. Something else "contrives the self-same evocations / And Juda becomes New Haven or else must."

Thus, also, in the Apocalypse, the Christus Victor, supreme interpreter and final reality of things, repeats three times: "I am Alpha and Omega, the beginning and the end" (Rev. 1:8, 21:6, 22:13). Stevens's well-known canto vi opens:

Reality is the beginning not the end,
Naked Alpha, not the hierophant Omega,
Of dense investiture, with luminous vassals.

Against the teleology of Revelation or of Eliot's statements, "In my beginning is my end" and "In my end is my beginning," Stevens presents Alpha and Omega. They are called "characters . . . in the scene"; they look like characters on the page ("A standing on infant legs . . . twisted, stooping . . . Z"); they behave like characters in a drama, miming their own functions—a prosopopoeia of literal limits. Stevens calls both "immaculate interpreters"—the word "immaculate" prohibiting any doctrine of fallen language, and "interpreters" reminding us that even the smallest unit of language, the letter, has an interpretive function (a wide meaning useful to keep in mind during current discussions of interpretation). Even naked Alpha is an interpreter—what we call reality always coming to us in a version—and Stevens also suggests, as does much current theory, that all language turns or tropes to a greater or lesser degree.[3] Alpha has priority, but Omega has authority; he is the ultimate trope, knowing priestly mysteries ("hieropant"), aged ("twisted, stooping"), learned ("polymathic"), venerated ("vassals"), yet like Alpha no more than one of the interpreters of life. To the apocalyptic sentence, "I am Alpha and Omega," Stevens's characters implicitly retort, "*We* are

3. On the existence of texts as versions, see Gerald L. Bruns, "Intention, Authority, and Meaning," *Critical Inquiry*, 7 (1980), 297–309. On the difficulty of speaking about "ordinary language," and the hazards of giving priority to "ordinary language," see Paul de Man, "Literature and Language: A Commentary," *New Literary History*, 4 (1972), 181–92, and Stanley Fish, "How Ordinary Is Ordinary Language?" *New Literary History*, 5 (1973), 41–54.

Alpha and Omega," overleaping Wordsworth's "characters of the great Apocalypse" and Coleridge's "mighty alphabet."

Other apocalyptic echoes, which I shall not follow, inhabit the poem.[4] (Those mentioned here are all included in the abbreviated version of "An Ordinary Evening.")[5]

Though revelation may be one of *the* logocentric notions par excellence (to quote Barbara Johnson on Derrida),[6] critics of very different persuasions still have in common a desire for the language of revelation. Both logocentrics and deconstructionists demonstrate this, either generally (we "unveil" or "unfold" what is "implicit" in the text) or particularly (we variously revise the word "revelation"). (Perhaps this is a perennial desire: if I said that *Untying the Text* was published in 1657 and *The Mystery of Rhetoricke Unvail'd* in 1981, could you be quite sure that I was wrong?) What Stevens does with the language of revelation I find not only interesting in its own right, but also pertinent to current critical concerns, even—rather, especially—where his anti-apocalyptic strategies depart from ours. In this essay, I want to look closely at the lyric in which Stevens revises the *topos* of the earthly paradise, canto xxix. I am particularly interested in the language of direction, which may shape or place the earthly paradise for us, and also place the "revealed" or the "commonplace." I read "An Ordinary

4. I have retained the word "echo," even for so visual a poem as "An Ordinary Evening in New Haven" and such visualized characters as Alpha and Omega, not simply because "An Ordinary Evening" is also auditory, which it is ("a savage assuagement cries / With a savage voice; and in that cry they hear . . ."; "the syllable of recognition, avowal, impassioned cry, / The cry that contains its converse in itself"; "the poem is the cry of its occasion"); not simply because the Apocalypse is the writing of a vision recorded at the behest of a voice which is itself recorded in writing; but because I cannot tell whether I see or hear a pun. Whatever word I use (seeing, hearing, reading, deciphering, decoding) is of a human act, in any case—my human act upon a text given by another human being. Language may use us (in which case "Stevens" is a metonymy for "Stevens-language"), but, so far at least, it does not transmit itself.

5. Abbreviated, but not original, as assumed by Harold Bloom in his *Wallace Stevens: The Poems of Our Climate* (Ithaca and London, 1976), pp. 305 ff. Cf. Stevens: "Actually, An Ordinary Evening in New Haven consists of thirty-one parts. . . . When I wrote the poem I liked the subject and continued to work with it as long as it interested me even though it became much longer than I could possibly use in New Haven. This made it possible for me to make a choice." (Letter of 17 November 1949, with "A poem by Wallace Stevens, *An Ordinary Evening in New Haven,*" Collection of American Literature, the Beinecke Rare Book and Manuscript Library, Yale University; quoted by permission of Holly Stevens and the Yale University Library.) Cf. also: "The lion of Juda is one of the parts of An Ordinary Evening in New Haven which I read in an abbreviated version at a ceremonial at Yale recently. This short version will be printed in the Transactions of the Connecticut Academy." (Letter of 20 December 1949; quoted by permission of Holly Stevens and the Dartmouth College Library.)

6. Translator's Introduction, Jacques Derrida, *Dissemination,* trans. Barbara Johnson (1972; rpt. Chicago, 1981), p. x.

Evening in New Haven" as a purgatorial poem in the anti-apocalyptic mode, but not, I shall argue, a simple reversal—not a poem using a down-versus-up or outside-versus-inside metaphor. My essay is, in effect, a study in direction.

II

Stevens's remarks about "An Ordinary Evening in New Haven" are well known: "Here my interest is to try to get as close to the ordinary, the commonplace and the ugly as it is possible for a poet to get. It is not a question of grim reality but of plain reality. The object is of course to purge oneself of anything false."[7] The verb "purge" suggests that we try reading "An Ordinary Evening" as a purgatorial poem, as a poem in which Stevens tries to see and to try the places of seeing and reading. (The analogy of seeing and reading is maintained throughout.) In the penultimate canto (xxx), Stevens does come to a purged or cleared—not a beatific—vision, a revision of St. Paul's seeing "face to face," as Helen Vendler notes.[8] In canto xxix, as we might expect at the end of a purgatorial poem, Stevens brings the reader to the earthly paradise, the land of the lemon trees, Goethe's *Land, wo die Zitronen blühn* (*Kennst du das Land . . .* ?). Or rather, not us, but mariners—and mariners not in the present tense of most of "An Ordinary Evening" but in the past. When they leave the land of the elm trees (New Haven, long known as Elm-Tree City),[9] they do not move up to the earthly paradise or down from it, but abruptly arrive; once entered, the earthly paradise proves to be the common place turned inside out, a stark and simple reversal.

Or is it? Here is the fable, preceded by the last line of canto xxviii:

> The heavens, the hells, the worlds, the longed-for lands.
>
> xxix
> In the land of the lemon trees, yellow and yellow were
> Yellow-blue, yellow-green, pungent with citron-sap,
> Dangling and spangling, the mic-mac of mocking birds.

7. Letter of 3 May 1949, in *Letters of Wallace Stevens,* ed. Holly Stevens (New York, 1972), p. 636.

8. *On Extended Wings: Wallace Stevens' Longer Poems* (Cambridge, Mass., 1969), p. 296.

9. *Encyclopaedia Britannica* (1911), "New Haven"; Bloom, *Wallace Stevens,* p. 333.

In the land of the elm trees, wandering mariners
Looked on big women, whose ruddy-ripe images
Wreathed round and round the round wreath of autumn.

They rolled their r's, there, in the land of the citrons.
In the land of big mariners, the words they spoke
Were mere brown clods, mere catching weeds of talk.

When the mariners came to the land of the lemon trees,
At last, in that blond atmosphere, bronzed hard,
They said, "We are back once more in the land of the elm trees,

But folded over, turned round." It was the same,
Except for the adjectives, an alteration
Of words that was a change of nature, more

Than the difference that clouds make over a town.
The countrymen were changed and each constant thing.
Their dark-colored words had redescribed the citrons.

A competent close reading will easily find contrasts of light against dark; Impressionist, Mediterranean painting against Dutch, northerly painting; the flowers and fruit of language against weeds of language; tasting language or "rolling" it on the tongue (Stanley Burnshaw said of Stevens's language that "one rolls [it] on the tongue")[10] against having it catch, like burrs. It might also observe the self-consciousness of the land of the elm trees, which, in a post-Cartesian view, marks it as fallen. (Stevens notes not just color, but the act of looking; not just rolling r's, but the act of speaking.) And it would infer the presence of desire in the land of the elm trees from the biblical verb, "looked on."

To read the mariners' voyage requires some knowledge of paradisal or romance traveling, for it is an anti-romance voyage—no difficulty, no deferral in this journey, no threshold ritual, but a swift translation. Once in the earthly paradise, the mariners speak like the linguist Stevens, "creating several languages within a single language" (to quote Marianne Moore).[11] They say: "We are back once more in

10. Stanley Burnshaw: "words and phrases that one rolls on the tongue . . . [but] can hardly swallow today" (*New Masses,* 17 [1935], cited in *Wallace Stevens: A Critical Anthology,* ed. Irvin Ehrenpreis [Harmondsworth, 1972], p. 101).

11. "Conjuries That Endure," in Marianne Moore, *Predilections* (London, 1956), p. 32.

the land of the elm trees, / But folded over, turned round." "Folded over, turned round"? (1) On a piece of paper, folded over, with the letters turned round, lemon becomes elm becomes lemon becomes elm. (2) Folded over: implicit; turned round: troped. And perhaps, (3) folded over: *in aenigmate* (enigmatical, folded language, says Francis Bacon); turned round: reversed, as in a mirror image, *per speculum. Videmus nunc per speculum in aenigmate,* reads St. Paul's famous text. In the land of the lemon trees, the mariners pass beyond the specular symmetry (to use Paul de Man's phrase)[12] of the first half of their canto, and meet face to face themselves and the land of the elm trees. The land of the lemon trees is no enlightening Eden, no place of revelation.

But the first tercet warns the reader if not the mariners that the earthly paradise is itself a *topos,* not necessarily transforming. Stevens's movement between lemon and citron here and throughout the canto corresponds to the double meaning of Goethe's *Zitronen:* first, lemon trees, pointing in part to actual places, Goethe's paradisal Italy and Stevens's once-loved American South, a home of the New World mocking bird; second, citrons, the *citrus medica* or *malus medica* used generically in Thomson's "Bear me, Pomona! to thy citron groves; / To where the lemon and the piercing lime, / With the deep orange . . ." (*Summer,* ll. 661–63); used specifically in Milton's "mark . . . how blows the Citron Grove" (*Paradise Lost* V. 21–22); and the tree Carlyle had in mind when he translated Goethe's *Zitronen* not as lemon trees but as "citron-apples." This is the tree of Virgil's *Georgics,* whose phrase *tristis sucos tardumque saporem / felicis mali* (II. 126–27) Stevens may be translating and condensing in his "pungent with citron-sap" (*tristis . . . saporem . . . mali*—cf. Thomson's "piercing lime"). And if Stevens's echoes reach this far (and he played with Latin puns elsewhere, even with a multilingual metaleptic echo of Dante's Italian five years earlier),[13] we may also hear in Stevens's compound "citron-sap" an echo of Milton's famous punning on fallen *sapor,* itself perhaps originating in Virgil's wordplay, *saporem / felicis mali.* We shall not miss

12. "Anthropomorphism and Trope in the Lyric," *The Rhetoric of Romanticism* (New York, 1984).

13. See my "Riddles, Charms, and Fictions in Wallace Stevens," in *Centre and Labyrinth: Essays in Honour of Northrop Frye,* ed. Eleanor Cook et al. (Toronto, 1983), pp. 231–32. On metaleptic echo, see John Hollander, *The Figure of Echo: A Mode of Allusion in Milton and After* (Berkeley, Los Angeles, London, 1981), pp. 113–32. I also think it is possible that Stevens is translating and condensing Virgil, because he quotes from the *Georgics* in essays of 1948 (*The Necessary Angel: Essays on Reality and Imagination* [New York, 1951], pp. 116–17) and 1951 (*Opus Posthumous* [New York, 1957], p. 239).

the echo of Stevens's own early earthly paradise, "Sunday Morning," where the word "pungent" is twice associated with citrus fruit, and where birds—Old Testament, Miltonic, Keatsean, Tennysonian—are firmly situated in a terrestrial paradise. In "An Ordinary Evening," the mocking birds are strangely non-singing—but the echoes of the mocking birds go far beyond the range of this essay. I cannot solve the problem of tone here;[14] this *topos* might, for example, be an occasion for a poem of terrible loss. Stevens's echoes open out back into a history of the *topos* of the earthly paradise. It seems to me that Stevens presents it, remembers its beauty, tries it, purges it.

Perhaps it is Long Island in any case. The reader who delights in toponymy and paronomasia will recall that Long Island lies (as we say) not far from New Haven; will remember Stevens's phrases, "the longed-for lands" (xxviii), "the afternoon Sound" (xxvi), "a long, inevitable sound, / A kind of cozening and coaxing sound, / And the goodness of lying in a maternal sound" (xxiii); and, listening to the sound of Long Island Sound, will hear therein an invitation to a literary voyage as beguiling as any in the ample pages of Curtius.

Similarly, and briefly, we should note that dark-colored words are still colored, and that, if "description is revelation,"[15] a dark-colored redescription may still be a revelation, though shaded.

Nearly every canto of "An Ordinary Evening" works with contraries, as does this one, placing them so insistently in the foreground that we realize we are watching kinds and degrees of opposition, in an extraordinary effect of looking at and looking through the same language.

III

My reading of "An Ordinary Evening in New Haven" as a purgatorial poem implies that I see it as different in kind from a poem of deconstructionist play, though some of Stevens's strategies are very like those of deconstructionist writing. (Derrida is Stevens's only rival in anti-apocalyptic wordplay—the only other eucalyptic-apocalyptic punster I know, in his recent essay on apocalyptic tone in *Les fins de l'homme.*)[16]

14. Cf. Bloom, *Wallace Stevens,* p. 334.
15. *Collected Poems,* p. 344.
16. Jacques Derrida, "D'un ton apocalyptique adopté naguère en philosophie," in *Les fins de l'homme: à partir du travail de Jacques Derrida* (Paris, 1981), pp. 445–86. My

But neither do I see the poem's anti-apocalyptic mode as a simple reversal. If Stevens does not journey upward to the earthly paradise and beyond to the "Logos vision"[17] like Dante and Eliot, following what he calls "the poem of the ascent into heaven,"[18] neither does he move downward. In fact, he unobtrusively purges his poem of the prepositions "up" and "down" altogether. "An Ordinary Evening" is overwhelmingly a poem of "in's" and "of's," in such disproportion that I shall give statistics: by my count, "of" appears 217 times in all, and "in" 131 times. "Up" and "down" apear only as adverbs, "down" only once, and "up" only seven times in 558 lines. Versions of the word "outside" are similarly restricted, though not as severely. In its movement, "An Ordinary Evening in New Haven" is a poem of acrossness, as in the beautifully balanced closing tercet:

> It is not in the premise that reality
> Is a solid. It may be a shade that traverses
> A dust, a force that traverses a shade.

I should like from any critic, old or new, a good essay on prepositions and adverbs of place. (I am, of course, thinking of much more than a study of frequency.) Jonathan Culler in 1975 remarked that "the importance of such deictics as technical devices in poetry can scarcely be over-estimated."[19] He included "adverbials of place and time whose reference depends on the situation of utterance (here, there, now, yesterday)," and I would urge the addition of prepositions. Criticism itself has begun to play with the metaphoric possibilities of prepositions. Anyone who has taken in Derrida's "Living on Border Lines" will never think about prepositions in quite the same way again. But there has been no significant literary develop-

---

student, Paul Morrison, has pointed out to me the implicit eucalypti-apocalyptic pun in Borges' story, "Death and the Compass."

New Critical weakness in dealing with apocalyptic language may be seen in John Crowe Ransom's inability to read a passage in Wordsworth that uses the language of the Book of Revelation (1850 *Prelude* V. 599–605; in *The New Criticism* [Norfolk, Conn., 1941], pp. 304–6). It is worth noting that students at Toronto were never entirely taken up with New Criticism, being more interested in comparing the methods of A. S. P. Woodhouse at University College and Northrop Frye at Victoria College. Neither Woodhouse nor Frye would have had the slightest difficulty in reading the language of the above passage from *The Prelude*.

17. Northrop Frye, "The Top of the Tower: A Study of the Imagery of Yeats," in his *The Stubborn Structure: Essays on Criticism and Society* (London, 1970), pp. 257–77.

18. *Opus Posthumous*, p. 193.

19. Jonathan Culler, "Poetics of the Lyric," in his *Structuralist Poetics* (1975), p. 165.

ment of Christine Brooke-Rose's useful and suggestive remarks in 1958 on prepositional metaphors.[20] And Paul de Man noted in 1979 that some of us never seriously question an "inside / outside metaphor."[21] Modern poets, of course, continually question and play with the function of prepositions—Stevens in "An Ordinary Evening," Richard Howard in "Crepuscular" (*The Damages*, 1967), John Ashbery in the title-poem of *Self-Portrait in a Convex Mirror* (1975), A. R. Ammons in "Vehicle" and "Easter Morning" (*A Coast of Trees*, 1981). We might consider whether lyrical poems make use of prepositions in a particular way. If the area of lyrical poetry is marked by a "sense of the discontinuous," as Frye argues (p. 31), then the function of prepositions and adverbs of place ought to be of special interest (prepositions "pre-positioning" something for us). Such study might include the function of deictics in placing or redescribing (Stevens's word) the earthly paradise for us.

To return to Stevens: I think he deliberately purges his poem of the words "up" and "down" in order to make it a poem of acrossness, and a poem of the "common place" or the ordinary. For up is the direction of the U-shape of comedy, divine or other. Down is the direction of the upside-down-U-shape of tragedy.[22] In canto xvii, both comedy and tragedy are subordinated to what Stevens calls the commonplace: "The serious reflection is composed / Neither of comic nor tragic but of commonplace." Interpretation of "An Ordinary Evening" suffers, I think, from an inadequate reading of the word "commonplace." Too often, Stevens's "plain reality" slides over into the critic's "grim reality." That is, while Stevens is wary of simple reversals, we ourselves sometimes are not, in spite of the "new new" criticism. We assume that the common place (say, New Haven) is down. Rather, I think we should read the "commonplace" looking for "every latent double in the word"[23]—not just the most reductive plain and ordinary, but also places of argument, *topoi*, the communal, and so on. Stevens's poem includes a complex of cognate, homonymic and near-

20. Christine Brooke-Rose, *A Grammar of Metaphor* (London, 1958), pp. 256–58 ff.

21. Paul de Man, *Allegories of Reading: Figural Language in Rousseau, Nietzsche, Rilke, and Proust* (New Haven and London, 1979), pp. 4–5: "The polarities of inside and outside have been reversed, but they are still the same polarities that are at play: internal meaning has become outside reference, and the outer form has become the intrinsic structure . . . the . . . inside/outside metaphor . . . is never being seriously questioned."

22. Cf. Northrop Frye, *The Great Code: The Bible and Literature* (Toronto, 1982), pp. 169, 176.

23. *Collected Poems*, p. 387.

homonymic words which suggest such a wide reading: commonplace, communication, composed, coming together, coming on and coming forth, Incominicia.[24] Here I shall suggest one other meaning.

Commonplace as Stevens's "serious reflection" would move neither up like comedy nor down like tragedy, but across in a straight line, in the shape of wisdom literature, the literature of the commonplace or proverbial, and also of the light of common day. (Here I am following Northrop Frye.)[25] Stevens himself loved wisdom literature—the Adages of Erasmus, for example—and made his own collection of commonplaces. In 1947, he speaks of the effect of the symbols in the Book of Ecclesiastes as pleasurable: "they give us the pleasure of 'lentor and solemnity' in respect to the most commonplace objects."[26] In canto xix of "An Ordinary Evening," the Ecclesiast enters his poem:

> A figure like Ecclesiast,
> Rugged and luminous, chants in the dark
> A text that is an answer, although obscure.

If the final tercet of the whole series (quoted earlier) speaks with the balance of the voice of wisdom, and in a wisdom formula (no more but also no less), we may say that Stevens desires to place his anti-apocalyptic poem within the perspective of the straight line of wisdom literature, of the commonplace, rather than containing it within a genesis-to-apocalypse structure. His wordplay with "common," his use of the prepositions of place, his purged re-seeing of the *topos* of the earthly paradise, and his revisionary echoing of the Book of Revelation all support such a reading.

IV

Stevens's late poems, some visionary, are the true culmination of this great poem of vision, which also leads toward meditative and visionary lyrics of the last twenty years, poems whose concern is "what our imagination makes of our ordinariness."[27] For example, two of

24. Obviously, I should like a New Haven Common rather than a New Haven Green.

25. Ibid., p. 128, and generally pp. 121–29.

26. *The Necessary Angel*, p. 78.

27. John Hollander, "A Poetry of Restitution," *Yale Review*, 70 (1981), 179. To trace the use of "An Ordinary Evening in New Haven" in later lyrics by other poets would be

Steven's late bird poems grow out of "An Ordinary Evening in New Haven." The first, which ends his *Collected Poems,* is of an Alpha-bird, "like / A new knowledge of reality." The title, "Not Ideas about the Thing But the Thing Iself," alludes to "An Ordinary Evening" xii.2; the bird is of earliest spring with a "scrawny cry" in "c." Stevens permits himself the word "outside" three times in eighteen lines: it is the triumph of Alpha. In this poem, Stevens show us the possibility of finding the fullness of common experience in language that knows and acknowledges the difficulties of translating what is "outside." The second poem, which ends *Palm at the End of the Mind,* is of an Omega-bird, an ultimate bird "on the edge of space" (to use Omega's phrase in canto vi), a bird using a word from the earthly paradise ("dangle," xxix.3) once again rhymed internally, but a singing bird, even if the song is "foreign." In this poem, Stevens shows us the possibility of finding the fullness of an earthly paradise—that place which Frye connects with lyrical poetry (p. 35)—in language that does not use upwardness but acrossness.

Though "what is invoked cannot be revealed in itself but only in being imagined,"[28] Stevens's late lyrics reveal, as language can, the possibilities of the commonplace—Stevens's Muse now answering the impossible and moving desire of his 1948 essay, written just before "An Ordinary Evening in New Haven":

> One turns with something like ferocity toward a land that one loves, to which one is really and essentially native, to demand that it surrender, reveal, that in itself which one loves. This is a vital affair, not an affair of the heart (as it may be in one's first poems), but an affair of the whole being (as in one's last poems), a fundamental affair of life, or, rather, an affair of fundamental life; so that one's cry of O Jerusalem becomes little by little a cry to something a little nearer and nearer until at last one cries out to a living name, a living place, a living thing, and in crying out confesses openly all the bitter secretions of experience.[29]

---

a considerable task. Two examples are A. R. Ammons's *Sphere: The Form of a Motion* (New York, 1974) and John Hollander's "Looking Ahead," *New Yorker,* 19 January 1981, p. 40.

28. Paul Fry, *The Poet's Calling in the English Ode* (New Haven, 1980), p. 6.

29. *Opus Posthumous,* p. 260.

Mary Nyquist

Musing on Susanna's Music

Quince: He is a very Paramour for a sweet voice.
Flute: You must say paragon. A paramour is, God bless us, a thing of naught.

A Midsummer Night's Dream, IV.ii

One of Stevens's most widely anthologized poems, "Peter Quince at the Clavier" has also occasioned a number of commentaries. To the extent that these articulate New Critical assumptions, they relate the poem's virtuoso use of musical forms to the "Death is the mother of beauty" theme it develops together with its fellow *Harmonium* piece, "Sunday Morning."[1] The opening lines of the poem's fourth section, where this theme is introduced, are often cited to illustrate what Stevens means by insisting he is a poet of reality, a reality which, to use a formulation he approved, "is never familiar to us in the way in which Plato wished the conquests of the mind to be familiar."[2] When commenting specifically on "Peter Quince," critics are likely to find in these lines, which claim that beauty finds its immortality not "in the mind" but "in the flesh," a statement of its thematic meaning. Not

1. Over the years numerous pieces on "Peter Quince at the Clavier" have appeared in *College English, English Language Notes,* and *The Explicator.* Fred Stocking's contribution to *The Explicator* (5 [1947]), "Stevens' 'Peter Quince at the Clavier,'" has been very influential, as has Joseph Riddel's "Stevens' 'Peter Quince at the Clavier': Immortality as Form" (*College English,* 23 [1962], 307–9). A comparatively recent attempt to explicate the poem by means of Renaissance neo-Platonic theories of love and beauty shows the persistence of the New Critical reading initiated by Stocking; see Carol Flake, "Wallace Stevens' 'Peter Quince at the Clavier': Sources and Structure," *English Language Notes,* 12 (1974), 116–20. Harold Bloom alone suggests that "representation" is one of the poem's concerns (*Wallace Stevens: The Poems of Our Climate* [Ithaca and London, 1976], pp. 35–37).

2. H. D. Lewis, "On Poetic Truth," cited by Wallace Stevens in "About One of Marianne Moore's Poems," *The Necessary Angel: Essays on Reality and the Imagination* (New York, 1951), p. 96.

untypically, comments on the fourth section's affirmations are presented as if revealing the meaning of the poem as an organic whole. Michel Benamou, for example, states conclusively of section and poem: "Permanent beauty is not a Mallarméan or neo-platonic Idea, but the revelation of an actual presence among us, on earth. In the teeth of Platonism and docetism, Stevens affirms . . . the mystery of incarnation. The essence of things depends on their perishable existence. Such appears to be the difficult, modern, meaning of Susanna's legend."[3] In what follows, I shall suggest that this can be the modern meaning of Susanna's legend only if the poem is thought to possess the kind of familiar or pseudo- alterity that is attributed to Susanna herself whenever she is regarded as merely an object or symbol of beauty. If, instead, we question "Peter Quince" 's thematic unity, taking up its invitation to phonic play by interrogating the development of its figure for desire, music, we will find that Susanna's legend, far from providing the poem's univocal meaning, generates a plurality of difficult modern meanings, meanings which simple lyric utterance such as we find in the fourth section would, like New Criticism, perhaps rather suppress.

The poem's very title could be said to announce a concern with representation. Shakespeare's Peter Quince both under- and overvalues the reliability and stability of his artistic medium, the stage. "Peter Quince at the Clavier" opens with the speaker of the poem bemusedly trying to figure out, while performing on the clavier, a poetics of desire. By positioning its speaker at the clavier, the poem suggests in a self-consciously clownish manner that he is living testimony to what Pater famously called "the great Anders-streben of all art," whereby it "constantly aspires to the condition of music."[4] The opening tercet of the poem plays a variation on this Symbolist theme when its speaker draws an analogy between the way his fingers "make" music and the way the "selfsame sounds" affect him, an analogy that works so well he feels he can go on to assert a relation of identity between music and the capacity for desire or response: "Music is feeling, then, not sound."[5] What we have here are clearly only the trappings of logical argument. But because the opposition between inner and outer governs so many logical and symbolic opposi-

3. Michel Benamou, *Wallace Stevens and the Symbolist Imagination* (Princeton, 1972), p. 79.

4. Walter Pater, *The Renaissance*, ed. Kenneth Clark (New York, 1961), p. 129.

5. Quotations from "Peter Quince at the Clavier" are from *The Collected Poems of Wallace Stevens* (New York, 1954).

tions, this use of music as a figure for desire or response appears to be, in its own way, eminently reasonable: the nonverbal art can, metaphorically, signify the inward self-presence of feeling. Having got this far, the speaker is then able to apply this figurative identity to the desire he is now, at this very moment, experiencing:

> And thus it is that what I feel,
> Here in this room, desiring you,
>
> Thinking of your blue-shadowed silk,
> Is music.

At this point, however, the problematical nature of the verbal medium actually in use begins to reveal itself. In his essay "Poésie Pure," Valéry contrasts the poet's lot with the musician's by stating that the poet, as a solitary man, must create an artificial and ideal order "au moyen d'une matière d'origine vulgaire" [by means of material of vulgar origin]; language is "l'instrument pratique, l'instrument grossier et créé par n'importe qui, l'instrument de chaque instant, utilisé pour les besoins immédiats et modifié à chaque instant par les vivants" [the practical instrument, the coarse instrument, created by anyone at all, the instrument of the moment, used for immediate needs and modified at every moment by the living].[6] It is on this that Stevens's Peter Quince actually plays, although, like the court audience in *A Midsummer Night's Dream,* we have probably up to this point been trying politely to ignore this common instrument's imperfect performance. Language, the poem seems to acknowledge, as the clavier, represented speaker, and absent interlocutor all fade out, is neither a system of simple notation nor a well-tempered clavier. The strain of striving after another condition becomes evident when the speaker tries verbally to turn his own erotic desire into music, for the poem then suddenly lapses back into analogy, as if forced by its very medium to abandon the logic of the metaphorical oneness of music and desire: "It is like the strain / Waked in the elders by Susanna." This lapse, which marks, to use the phrase Northrop Frye has introduced, the "moment of blockage," is, simultaneously, a lapse into narrative and "thus" into the use of some of the conventional features of literary representation: character, action, temporality, meaning. It also creates a disturbing correspondence between the speaker "think-

6. Paul Valéry, "Calepin d'un poète," *Oeuvres,* ed. Jean Hytier (Paris, 1957), p. 1461. Translation mine.

ing of your blue-shadowed silk" and the elders "watching" Susanna bathe. One of the reasons it is disturbing is because desire, the appropriate figure for which is supposed to be the sound of music, here becomes associated with the mind's as well as the body's eye: it becomes associated with what Jacques Lacan terms the specular gaze, which makes the imagined or visual object the Other.[7]

The moment the speaker falls back on analogy, then, the poem begins to produce, willy-nilly, some of the ambiguities of language's representational dimension. We can see this by looking at "Peter Quince"'s representation of Susanna. Susanna is in part portrayed as if, present only to herself, she were an innocent, sensuous, and unself-regarding subject. As fictive creator, Stevens is able to represent Susanna in section two of the poem as someone who appears to enjoy the fulness and simplicity of a prelapsarian kind of self-originating desire. Positioned "in her still garden," "In the green water, clear and warm," Susanna prophetically fulfills the New Testament injunction "Seek and ye shall find" in her own, emphatically erotic manner:

> She searched
> The touch of springs,
> And found
> Concealed imaginings.

The "witching chords" (the aperiodic "throb" of the chords presumably producing a "witching" or discordant sound that is, acoustically, damped), the "pizzicati" that "pulse" in the blood of the elders, and the "noise like tambourines" made by the attendant Byzantines have no capacity for resonance, for sustained and creative sound. The "accessible bliss" (a phrase from "It Must Change" in "Notes toward a Supreme Fiction") that Susanna experiences in the green water is, in contrast, something that the poem can represent metaphorically as "so much melody." "Peter Quince" makes us feel that the Susanna of this *locus amoenus* has the right to be what we might, following Lévi-Strauss, called a floating signifier.[8] Not that she signifies "nothing";

7. The single most comprehensive discussion of specularity and sexual difference is to be found in Stephen Heath's "Difference," which both uses and critiques Lacanian discourse at the same time as examining the ways in which it has been appropriated by feminist and film theorists (*Screen*, 19:3 [1978], 51–112). See also Shoshana Felman's "Women and Madness: The Critical Phallacy" in *Diacritics*, 5:3 (1975), 2–10.

8. The "signifiant flottant" is a term used by Claude Lévi-Strauss to suggest the signifying potential of symbolic thought; it is associated with the productions of art, poetry, myth, and aesthetics, all of which are in our culture gender-marked "feminine." See his "Introduction à l'oeuvre de Marcel Mauss," in Marcel Mauss's *Sociologie et Anthropologie* (Paris, 1950), p. xlix.

but not meaning anything, not representing anything, she is free simply, erotically, to be. A kindred spirit of pastoral poetry's *genius loci,* her special sympathies with nature are suggested in the third stanza of this section, where the winds, her figurative "maids," serve her obediently in a way her attendant Byzantines miserably fail to do.

The erotically self-sufficing Susanna is not, however, the only Susanna that the poem causes us to see. For although the elders (with whom, we must remember, the speaker has associated himself) are not re-represented in the second section, we cannot help but see Susanna through their "red-eyed" gaze. Like our first sight of Eve and Adam in *Paradise Lost,* our sight of the gardened Susanna is a filtered, not to say furtive, sight. Because we know the elders are watching, we inevitably see the free-floating Susanna of the second section as a Susanna who also represents or signifies their desire, a Susanna who has been arrested and fixed by the specular gaze. We ourselves see her as mirroring their desired potency and power. And fixed by the gaze of the elders, Susanna appears to us not self-sufficing but self-mirroring, narcissistic. It is because we share their gaze that we find ourselves wondering secretly, and rather repressively, about those "concealed imaginings," those "spent emotions" and "old devotions." To use a distinction that Kenneth Clark and, later, John Berger (in *Ways of Seeing*) use, Stevens permits us to see Susanna both as she is as if to herself, which is simply as "naked," and as the elders see her, which is as "nude": nudity being nakedness as it is surveyed by the pornographic and patriarchal eye, the eye that assumes it has a right to possession.[9] Such, in our culture, are some possible ambiguities of the representational mode.

Although "Peter Quince" carefully signifies narrative progression ("She walked"; "She turned"; and in the third section "Soon," "Anon," "And then"), it does not by any means retell the Apocryphal narrative, *Daniel and Susanna,* which gives the story of Susanna and the elders. In that narrative, the elders surprise Susanna in her garden and try to coerce her into having sexual relations with them by threatening to accuse her publicly of having an affair with a young man if she refuses. Devout and faithful wife of the Babylonian

9. John Berger, *Ways of Seeing* (London, 1972), pp. 45–64. In this section of his influential study of spectatorship, Berger discusses briefly two paintings of Susanna and the Elders by Tintoretto, one of which portrays Susanna looking at herself in a mirror while the Elders and, thus, the spectators also gaze on her. For a fuller discussion of pictorial representations of Susanna see Mary D. Garrard, "Artemisia and Susanna," in *Feminism and Art History,* ed. Norma Broude and Mary D. Garrard (New York, 1982), pp. 146–71.

Joakim, Susanna shuns the sin of submission and virtuously chooses to suffer the elders' false accusation. Since the elders themselves preside at her trial, she is found guilty of adultery and is condemned to death. It is just as she is being led off to be executed that the young Daniel, divinely inspired, intervenes, and by setting up a counter-trial cleverly gets the elders to convict themselves, thus successfully and simultaneously vindicating Susanna and restoring justice.

As if seeking to ally itself with yet another sister art, painting, Stevens's poem gives us only faint traces or figural tokens of this narrative. For example, the shouts that both Susanna and the elders raise when she decides to resist are represented exclusively by means of the musical figure, that is, symbolically: "A cymbal crashed, / And roaring horns." The accusation against Susanna is also represented only indirectly. We see the accused Susanna through the eyes of the attendants who, having been taken in by the elders, seem to think they have discovered her guilt when their lamps "Revealed Susanna and her shame." For straightforward narrative progression which would unambiguously assert Susanna's innocence, Stevens substitutes a progression that is purely modal. The abrupt discontinuity between the third and fourth sections of the poem establishes a decisive and significant shift from a narrative to a lyrical, from a representational to a nonrepresentational mode. As we have seen, the representational mode has implicated speaker, reader, elders, and attendants in the guilty desire now (wrongly) associated with Susanna. The lyrical mode that supersedes it seeks to abandon these human figures at the very moment that Susanna has herself been abandoned by her attendants. Yet in doing so it seems ceremonially to offer us both a vindicated Susanna and a purified desire.

But can modal progression in and of itself really accomplish such spiritual feats? New Critical accounts of the poem do not of course even pose this question, for it suggests that a break or gap in the text might be productive of meaning. In an early essay, Joseph Riddel, for example, makes a typical New Critical move when he refers to the fourth section as the "recapitulation with coda" that grows out of the second and third section's "development" and the first section's "exposition." By giving the poem the structure of a well-unified "three-part sonatina," Riddel simply assumes an analogy with organic form, an analogy he extends to the poem's thematic content which, he states, concerns "the need for vital form in the experience of beauty." In Riddel's view, the elders represent an inappropriately unaestheticized response to what he too complacently calls "Susanna's allure." The poem's speaker, also its protagonist (an issue we will turn to in a moment), on the other hand, is from first to last the poem's exemplar of the properly attuned aesthetic spirit; he meets the need for vital form in the experience of beauty when his "controlled tonalities preserve Susanna in the enduring form of art."[10]

Yet in the Apocryphal narrative, Susanna's innocence is established when Daniel represents her legally and publicly in a trial; the elders are punished with death and Susanna is vindicated only because Daniel represents her. By contrast, in the last section of "Peter Quince" the poet wishes to appear to save the abandoned Susanna by turning to a mode that resolutely refuses to represent her. Although the poem alludes to the elders' Apocryphal fate with the phrase "Death's ironic scraping," by not so much as hinting that Susanna was represented by Daniel, it actually twice over refuses to take his role. In spite of this, the concluding lines of the lyrical fourth section would seem to imply that Susanna's innocent subjectivity is being celebrated. The text indirectly affirms the purity of Susanna's music, as we can see by comparing it with Mallarmé's "Sainte," which enacts a Symbolist rewriting of the Saint Cecilia legend. In the closing lines of this poem Mallarmé replaces Saint Cecilia's "viole" with the angelic "plumage instrumental" that makes her into a "Musicienne du silence."[11] Not thus silencing his saint, Stevens, poet of reality, says of her music: "Now in its immortality, it plays / On the clear viol of her memory." Though not going so far as to represent Susanna, Stevens seems here to let her "music" play, thus appearing to restore to her the expressive vitality of her inwardness.

If we stop to interrogate the logic of the poem's central figure, however, we find ourselves wondering if Susanna's "music" is in any real sense hers. We can grant the speaker his introductory "Music is feeling, then, not sound." But the poem's rather devious and disjunctive development compels us to ask, *whose* feeling? Read strictly as a metaphor, the figure as it is used in the last section of the poem signifies what we have just suggested it does, that is, Susanna's subjective experience. Yet the text inscribes "Susanna's music" in a context that makes it act as a metonymy as well:

10. Riddel, "Immortality as Form," pp. 308, 309. For an example of Riddel's more recent deconstructive work on Stevens—within a discussion of this poet's place in New Criticism and after—see his "The Climate of Our Poems," *The Wallace Stevens Journal* (Special Issue: Stevens and Postmodern Criticism), 7:3–4 (Fall 1983), 59–75.

11. Benamou has pointed out that Stevens's "viol" is related to Mallarmé's "viole," *Symbolist Imagination,* p. 39. M. Charles Mauron has observed that ancient instruments such as the viol, clavier, and mandore are associated in Mallarmé with a chaste and often maternal feminity; see the annotations on "Sainte" in *Oeuvres,* ed. Henri Mondor and G. Jean-Aubry (Paris, 1945), p. 1469. It is probably worth mentioning that "Sainte" plays on "viole" and "vol."

Susanna's music touched the bawdy strings
Of those white elders; but, escaping,
Left only Death's ironic scraping.
Now, in its immortality, it plays
On the clear viol of her memory,
And makes a constant sacrament of praise.

Here, Susanna's music is, *inescapably,* a metonymy for the effect her nude body has on the elders' bawdy strings. Her music is not metaphorically hers, but is instead what the first section calls "the strain / Waked in the elders by Susanna." It is, in short, the fourth section's climatic illustration of its ostensibly anti-Platonic thesis that beauty is "in the flesh" immortal, the flesh, like the "body's beauty," being exemplified by Susanna. As A. Walton Litz (who is not at all aware that he suppresses one aspect of the figure for another) paraphrases the poem's concluding statement: "Susanna's beauty is 'immortal' because it is reincarnated in the music of feeling evoked by every beautiful woman, specifically by the one of 'blue-shadowed silk' to whom the poem is addressed."[12] The very elision of the subject in the phrase "but, escaping," suggests that the text would actually encourage the metonymic aspect of the figure to predominate over the metaphoric. Grammatically, like *amor matris,* "Susanna's music" is of course potentially either subjective or objective genitive. This is also true of "her memory" in the penultimate line. Yet as a result of the discursive pressures exerted by the concluding section, it is the objective genitive that dominates to make a "constant" meaning of both "Susanna's music" and "her memory." "Susanna's music" therefore becomes immortal when playing not on her own memory, but rather on our memory of her, or, more accurately, when "it plays" reflexively on the memory of her that the poem, itself a thing of beauty, creates by constituting a "constant sacrament of praise." Capable of such effects, Susanna's metonymic music would thus seem to point the way to one of Stevens's adages: "A poet looks at the world the way a man looks at a woman."[13] But if the "basses" (to use the pun Stevens introduces in the first section) of "Susanna's music" is her bodily beauty, together with the scopic drive it arouses, then in representing her the way it has the poem utterly fails, in spite of itself, to vindicate her. Even if its poetic intentions are in some sense honorable, by memorializing Susanna's beauty at the expense of her virtue, "Peter

12. A. Walton Litz, *Introspective Voyager: The Poetic Development of Wallace Stevens* (New York, 1972), p. 44.

13. Wallace Stevens, "Adagia," *Opus Posthumous,* ed. Samuel French Morse (New York, 1957), p. 165.

Quince" acts in deep complicity with the patently sexist Renaissance and post-Renaissance pictorial tradition that represents Susanna as a Venus whose very resistance to the elders is seductively becoming.[14] And indeed the text seems unconsciously aware that its triumph over appearances rests on a sacrifice; it communicates this awareness in a secondary meaning of "viol," suggested by the French *viol.* What *viol* acknowledges is that Susanna's reality has been violated; by refusing to vindicate her, to represent her, the poem has left her memory stained, not "clear."

Since Litz has recalled it, let us now inquire after the erotic desire experienced by the speaker, which in the first section guilty and ironically compared itself with the "strain" experienced by the elders. What has the poem's progression from a representational to a non-representational mode made of the *speaker's* "music"? As we noticed earlier, the moment the speaker likens his desire to that of the elders is also the moment the poem seems to admit that its medium is, after all, language. It is as if "Peter Quince" associates writing and autoeroticism just as, in Derrida's analysis of his thought in *Of Grammatology,* Rousseau does. Involving a presence that is absent, both writing and autoeroticism are from a logocentric perspective substitutive and therefore degraded activities.[15] The opening three lines of the fourth section of "Peter Quince" seem roundly to repudiate the guilty sterility of this autoeroticism:

> Beauty is momentary in the mind—
> The fitful tracing of a portal;
> But in the flesh it is immortal.

14. Garrard discusses the influence of the Venus archetype on depictions of Susanna in *Feminism and Art History,* pp. 149–55. By failing to make so much as an allusion to the trial, Stevens also perpetuates the tradition's strikingly disproportionate interest in the "erotic" encounter between Susanna and the Elders as against the Judgment of Daniel and the Stoning of the Elders (pp. 153, 168). As my essay indicates, the critical reception of "Peter Quince" itself participates in and perpetuates this tradition. This is further illustrated by an astonishingly brutal critical encounter between "Peter Quince" and Eugene Nassar, who is persuaded that in Stevens's poem Susanna is both raped and killed (*College English,* 26 [1965], 549–51). In a rebuttal, Laurence Perrine claims that Nassar "does violence to the story told in the Apocrypha and also to Stevens' poem," and then goes on to re-tell the Apocryphal story, emphasizing Susanna's chaste and actively virtuous response to the Elders, who die the death Nassar thinks Stevens wishes on Susanna. Perrine claims that "Peter Quince" is "not a *re-telling* of the story but an extended *allusion* to it, a musical version of it." Yet I would argue it is precisely because, as a musical version, it is affiliated with the pictorial tradition that Perrine himself has to resort to *re-telling* in order to vindicate Stevens. For Perrine's rebuttal and Nassar's unconvinced reply see *College English,* 27 (1966), 430–31.

15. Jacques Derrida, *Of Grammatology,* trans. Gayatri C. Spivak (Baltimore, 1976), pp. 144–57.

These lines show the poem deciding to turn in the direction of Yeats's

> God guard me from those thoughts men think
> In the mind alone;
> He that sings a lasting song
> Thinks in a marrow-bone. . . .[16]

But if, as critics are fond of proclaiming, a Platonic or idealizing habit of mind is here repudiated, it is by means of inversion, not negation or subversion. Death is the mother of beauty because the poem finds in mutability not only the flux of becoming but also the stability of recurrence. Although in the line "The body dies; the body's beauty lives," "beauty" remains a property of the body and thus of the world of becoming, it nevertheless becomes associated with the patterned continuities that change gives rise to. The use of anaphora in the lines that follow—the exact parallelism of "So evenings die," "So gardens die," "So maidens die"—musically suggests that flux naturally seeks the form of repetition and sameness. Overtly anti-idealistic, the text's discourse here is thus covertly idealistic, making phenomenal change as familiar to us as the conquests of the mind.

Likewise, the speaker's desire for his absent lover does not, overtly, play any role in the poem's thematic or modal development. But covertly the fourth section clearly dissociates the figure of the poet from "those white elders." Before considering the significance of this dissociation, we must raise, directly, an issue that has so far been skirted, the issue being what is involved in regarding "Peter Quince at the Clavier" as a unified lyric utterance. Is the identity we habitually confer on the speaker of a lyric in this instance as stable as New Critical commentaries would lead us to believe it is? The transparency and self-identity of the consciousness revealed in "Peter Quince" is most often merely assumed by commentators, who without explaining or justifying the procedure designate its speaking subject as Peter Quince or, familiarly, Peter, or Quince. Riddel, for example, relates Stevens's figure to Shakespeare's by comments that clearly apply to the poem as a thematic and aesthetic whole: "Stevens' Peter Quince is an *improvisatore* who constructs out of the raw materials of experience the viable forms which will endure; he turns the beauties of flux into the immortality of art." And Riddel is by no means the only critic to contrast this Peter Quince, successful artist, with the elders whose

16. W. B. Yeats, "A Prayer for Old Age," *The Collected Poems of W. B. Yeats* (London, 1963), p. 326.

death reveals they are "both lustful men and inadequate artists."[17] But one would like to know when Peter Quince became the dignified exemplar of the artist's capacity to transform experience into significant form; and how the author of "The Comedian as the Letter C" and "The Man on the Dump" could have become so desperate in his search for surrogate artist figures as to have lost, entirely, his sense of humor, along with his class consciousness. The absurdity of this view of the speaking subject's unity is matched only by its insensitivity to the difference in tone between the first and the fourth sections of the poem, a difference clearly related to the conspicuous presence in the first section of a represented speaker, whose counterpart in the fourth section is unrepresented, without a local habitation or a name.

To label both represented and unrepresented speakers Peter Quince and to think of this Quince as the poem's artist figure and protagonist is confusingly to use the identity conventionally bestowed on a poem by its title to fix and stabilize the identity of the speaker, whose value to the unity of the work is, in turn, fixed and stabilized by the discursive or thematic revelations of the climatic fourth section. To assume that meaning lies in the difference between the speaking subject Peter Quince and the "red-eyed elders" is also to deny that meaning can be found in the difference between the self-conscious Laforguian posturing of the speaker's opening performance at the clavier and the grave unself-consciousness of the closing lyrical hymn. When Shakespeare's Peter Quince delivers his prologue to the Mechanicals' play, Hippolyta comments, "Indeed he hath played on this prologue like a child on a recorder; a sound, but not in government." The ironic playfulness of the opening lines of "Peter Quince" signals that the speaker's performance on the clavier is just such a prologue; his production of "music is feeling, then, not sound," is to be heard as colloquial sound, but not in government. By contrast, and as a direct effect of this prominently dramatized self-consciousness, the lyrical utterance of the fourth section has consistently been appropriated by its readers as the real thing: a sound, in government. The relation between a self-consciousness dramatized by means of a bumbling surrogate artist figure and an intensification of the illusions produced by the unrepresented, undramatized artist is

17. Flake, "Sources and Structure," p. 119. In his commentary, Litz provides the exception that proves the rule, for he posits a stable, unproblematical contrast between "the bumbling Peter Quince" and "the delicate music of the clavier" (*Introspective Voyager,* p. 43). How this contrast establishes itself, since both the represented speaker and the clavier (which, I guess, Stevens himself plays) fade out together, is not explained.

thus in "Peter Quince at the Clavier" very much what it is in *A Midsummer Night's Dream.*

This suggests that the poem's effacement of its speaker is responsible for some of the effects, including the important thematic-meaning-effect, that the fourth section has had upon its readers. The poem moves from a dramatized present in which the deictic markers ("these keys," "selfsame," "Here," "in this room") point to the here-and-now of a mock-performance on a mock-clavier, a mock-production of words as music, to an undramatized or lyrical present in which the deictic markers absent themselves to make way for the "Now" of the lyrical utterance:

> Now, in its immortality, it plays
> on the clear viol of her memory,
> And makes a constant sacrament of praise.

In uttering this "Now" the poem subtly but firmly associates the present of its own unself-conscious performance with the self-presence of the lyrical subject playing on the "clear viol"—clearly a figurative viol—of Susanna's memory. In one of his *Adagia,* Stevens says "the poet seems to confer his identity on the reader. It is easiest to recognize this when listening to music—I mean this sort of thing: the transference." If Stevens is right about an experience of music providing the easiest access to this sort of thing, then it is not surprising that we find it happening to us while reading, that is, mentally performing, the lyrical fourth section of "Peter Quince." What is perhaps surprising is that this section has conferred the poet's identity on its readers so successfully that they have sought, in the retrospective reach of critical practice, to confer it on the speaker, Peter Quince, as well. Yet in foregoing any analysis or reflection upon the non-coincidence of dramatized speaker and the figure of the poet, of Peter Quince and the lyric voice making a constant sacrament of praise, New Criticism has perhaps merely been practicing a well-tempered complicity with the poem's own deepest lyric intentions. By obliterating so completely and also so inconspicuously all traces of the speaker dramatized in the opening lines of the poem, and by closing, so solemnly and grandly, with the full presence of lyric utterance, an utterance that can confer the poet's identity upon the reader, the poem successfully achieves and thereby vindicates its late Romantic lyric identity. Its closure by means of a "Now" that is the very present of the poet's self-revelation as a maker of music obtains for it the stability and self-identity it needs if it is to become, in its immortality, a lasting song.

The ironic self-consciousness of the poem's opening thus works in somewhat the way a skillfully deployed defense-mechanism does; if undetected, it enhances the sense of mastery it sought to ensure.[18] If we don't consciously register the disappearance of the comical Peter Quince with his ungoverned sound, then all the greater will be the pleasure we get from (co-)producing a sound, in government. But this need not prevent us from thinking about what the poem's successful effacement of its self-consciousness would rather we ignore. The opening section of the poem suggests that the erotic desire that self-consciously and guiltily affixes itself to Susanna is to be the poem's subject. Indeed, "Peter Quince" would seem, initially, to be an occasional poem, the specific occasion being the experience of desire for an absent woman. Conclusively dissociating poet from elders, the fourth section indicates that Stevens has decided to present us, finally, with a pure poem, "pure poetry," as he explains in his essay "The Irrational Element in Poetry," being a term that "has grown to be descriptive of poetry in which not the true subject but the poetry of the subject is paramount."[19] If we go back to Pater's discussion of this topic, we find that it is the highest aspiration of art "to get rid of its responsibilities to its subject or material," and that the very perfection and preeminence of lyric poetry depends on "a certain suppression or vagueness of mere subject."[20] As we have seen, the text invites us to ignore (as New Critics have done) the distance between the guilty and ironic self-consciousness of the first section and the stately rhythms of the last. To refuse this invitation is to surprise Stevens in the act of choosing to get rid of his responsibilities to his subject and therefore to Susanna. Suppressing what would otherwise appear to be the originating impulse of his lyric utterance, Stevens also, simultaneously, refuses to represent Susanna, wishing to associate himself with the psalmist David, the poet-singer, instead of with the judge Daniel. In place of the elders' earlier, rather pathetic "pizzicati of Hosanna," in which the speaker was clearly implicated, the poet now offers us the

18. But before effacing itself, this ironic self-consciousness also suggests that it *is* a defense-mechanism; the posturing and masking of the opening has the curious effect of calling up the figure not of the poet but of an empirical Stevens, defenseless against desire. Bloom testifies to this effect when he says "it is Stevens who speaks directly of his own desire in the opening section of his own touchpiece" (*The Poems of Our Climate,* p. 36).

19. Stevens, *Opus Posthumous,* p. 222. For an interesting but not always persuasive discussion of the ways in which the English bourgeois poetic tradition offers the reader a position as stable, transcendental ego, see Anthony Easthope, *Poetry as Discourse* (London, 1983).

20. Pater, pp. 131, 132.

poetry of the subject in a lyrical, self-immortalizing Hosanna, "a constant sacrament of praise."

And here we come upon yet another aspect of "Susanna's music." As metonymy, "Susanna's music" is, like "your blue-shadowed silk," the material cause of erotic desire. But because Stevens is a pure poet as well as a poet of reality, "Susanna's music" operates metaleptically as well as metonymically.[21] What as metalepsis "Susanna's music" transumes or leaps over or takes after is its etymon, "muse." Indeed, we can now see that in seeking to rid itself of its responsibilities to its subject, "Peter Quince" has got Susanna's music to take the role of Stevens's muse. Stevens's own writings provide the context which makes this reading not only possible but irresistible. In "To the One of Fictive Music" Stevens early and elaborately associates a muse figure with music. In this poem, the muse is actually invoked, as she is in the prose hymns of "The Figure of the Youth as Virile Poet," which concludes with the poet addressing her thus:

> Inexplicable sister of the Minotaur, enigma and mask, although I am part of what is real, hear me and recognize me as part of the unreal. I am the truth of that imagination of life in which with unfamiliar motion and manner you guide me in those exchanges of speech in which your words are mine, mine yours.[22]

This perfect inter-subjectivity is presented as a well-established domestic habit in "The Final Soliloquy of the Interior Paramour," where instead of being invoked the muse herself speaks from the intimate oneness of "we." But of course this oneness is merely the fictive effect of a prior projection of the muse as the Other, as, specifically, the poet's paramour. Whether the object of an invocation, the ventriloquistic subject of a dialogue of one, or, as in "The Idea of Order at Key West" and "The World as Meditation," the projected counterpart or fictive embodiment of the poet's creative imagination, the female muse is, in Stevens's poetry as in the tradition he inherits, always to some degree represented as the Other who makes possible the creative articulateness of the male voice.[23] In Stevens's thought the

21. See John Hollander's discussion of metalepsis in "The Trope of Transumption," which forms the appendix to *The Figure of Echo* (Berkeley, 1981). Hollander uses as an example of modern metalepsis based on phonic resemblance a phrase from Stevens's "Le Monocle de Mon Oncle," "Like the clashed edges of two words that kill," where "swords" is transumed.

22. *The Necessary Angel*, p. 67.

23. See also the "covering" of Nanzia Nunzio in "Notes toward a Supreme Fiction," as well as the uses to which the figure of the bride is put in "Honors and Acts," *Opus*

muse's Otherness is, in addition, integrally a part of the dialectical relations of the imagination and reality. If reality is to remain something not familiar to us in the way the conquests of the mind are, then the muse must guide the poet "with unfamiliar motion and manner." Or, as the closing petition in "To the One of Fictive Music" puts it, she must retain her identity as one

> Yet not too like, yet not so like to be
> Too near, too clear, saving a little to endow
> Our feigning with the strange unlike, whence springs
> The difference that heavenly pity brings.

This saving difference, springing from the "strange unlike," is itself clearly not conceivable without the gendered difference, fixed in representation itself, between the poet and his muse.

It is, then, Susanna's very Otherness that permits her to act the part of Stevens's muse. And if we take the thematic affirmations of the fourth section merely at face value, then as muse Susanna would appear to be playing her part well, for the poet there sings, playing on her memory, in praise of a phenomenal reality that is strange, unlike. Yet if, once again, we interrogate the shift from aprojected to an introjected Susanna, a shift that makes "Peter Quince" unique among Stevens's muse poems, Susanna's relation to reality appears rather more problematical. We have already commented on the way in which Susanna is introduced as a narrative representative of the absent woman in "blue-shadowed silk" who is associated with the "music" of the speaker's desire. But although in his mind's specular eye the speaker may look upon Susanna and the woman in silk she stands for, the opening lines of the poem do more than suggest that it is his own "music" that has generated the interior gaze. As another poem of Stevens, "Desire and the Object," puts it: "The origin could have its origin."[24] Not wishing to represent the speaker's own "music" (not

---

Posthumous, pp. 242, 243. For a superb discussion of the place of alterity and representation in masculinist discourse see Mary Jacobus's recent "Is There a Woman in This Text?" *New Literary History*, 14 (1982), 117–41. It is of course significant that both the juridical and aesthetic senses of "representation" are relevant to our discussion of "Peter Quince at the Clavier." That the Apocryphal Susanna was saved only by Daniel's representation of her and that "Peter Quince"'s Susanna's "music" is immortalized by Stevens's *not* representing her suggests something of the systematic character of women's exclusion as subjects from the symbolic order. Luce Irigaray's *Speculum de l'autre femme* (Paris, 1974), which is concerned, primarily, with the works of Freud and Plato, provides a brilliant deconstructive critique of this exclusion. See, especially, the chapter "Toute théorie du 'sujet' aura toujours été appropriéé au 'masculin,'" pp. 165–82, and the chapter "Pouvoir du discours, subordination du féminin" in *Ce Sexe qui n'en est pas un* (Paris, 1977), pp. 67–82.

24. *Opus Posthumous*, p. 85.

wishing, perhaps, to provoke the subtitle "Five Finger Exercise"), Stevens has thus initially represented Susanna "In the green water, clear and warm" in order to create a mask for the speaker's autoeroticism. If the inexplicable sister of the Minotaur is both "enigma and mask," then Susanna can appear as the subject of her own music while she masks this autoeroticism. Once she has served this function, however, she ceases to be the paramount subject of her own music and becomes, as a legendary character, a heroine or saint, merely an enigma, her innocence in question, her memory stained. This occurs, and Susanna instead plays the part of interior paramour, when in the fourth section the poet sings lyrically, in the mode that most purely incarnates the poem's figure for desire, music. If music is feeling, then, it is, ideally, feeling purified, feeling sublimated until, by means of the writing that is purified along with it, it has been completely transformed into the spiritual matter of sweet lyric song. Susanna's music, like the body's beauty, "lives." It even remains the syntactical subject of the "music" that sounds in the closing lines, because Suasanna continues to mask what might still appear to be autoerotic impulses, though they are this time the sweet impulses of pure lyric song. Yet the masking here reveals Susanna playing a role that is essentially maieutic. Her "music" thus "lives" only because as the material cause of desire it has also been acting, much more productively, as the formal cause of Stevens's lyric. As the poet's interior paramour, his muse, Susanna's "music" now plays in the "clear" (though not "too clear") element of the poet's imagination. In this element, as in the "green water," Susanna is once again, but this time permanently, a floating signifier.

Unlike the desire experienced by the elders, which "Left only Death's ironic scraping," the speaker's guilty desire has thus been transmuted into lyric song. By means of the now introjected Susanna, an unprofessional Peter Quince at the clavier has given way to the figure of the youth as "virile poet," playing on his muse's "clear viol." As Stevens says in his essay "The Figure of the Youth as Virile Poet," the poet "shares the transformation, not to say apotheosis, accomplished by the poem."[25] The stability of the world effected by this double transformation is associated with artistic virility when in another essay, "The Noble Rider and the Sound of Words," Stevens remarks: "what makes the poet the potent figure that he is, or was, or ought to be, is that he gives to life the supreme fictions without which we are unable to conceive it."[26] Because "Susanna's music," which is

25. *The Necessary Angel,* p. 49.
26. Ibid., p. 31.

not truly hers, is metonymically associated with beauty, the music of the closing lines of "Peter Quince" produces both lyric song and, self-reflexively, itself, a paragon of beauty. The "music" that "makes a constant sacrament of praise" produces out of the "constant" poetic act of praise a sacramental object, that is, a lyric poem which is, in the text, immortal. The signifier "viol" thus has another connotation, suggesting the specific nature of the poem's appropriation of Susanna; "viol" acknowledges that Susanna has become the poem's possession, that she is contained by the poem as reproducible verbal artifact, as if it were a vial. The connection between the vial and the literary artifact is made by one of Stevens's literary elders, Milton, when in *Areopagitica* he says of books that they "do contain a potency of life in them to be as active as that soul whose progeny they are; nay, they do preserve as in a vial the purest efficacy of that living intellect that bred them."

Milton, whose poetry echoes throughout Stevens's, is referred to in "The Noble Rider" when, in discussing the infamous "pressure of reality," Stevens cites an unnamed author who claims that those who now write for a living will have difficulty appreciating the superior creative quality, the verbal suggestiveness and music, of Milton's verse. The passage in which the citation appears seems curiously revealing in its unexpressed identification with this noble rider of an earlier age, a poet who, like Stevens, did not write for a living and who, like him, produced writing that "bears the mark of perfection," and which therefore might not now receive its due.[27] That Milton did not have an economic motive in writing *Paradise Lost* is remarked by none other than Marx himself, who uses the example of Milton to illustrate the difference between productive and unproductive labor. Although he received five pounds for *Paradise Lost,* Milton, Marx says, was an unproductive laborer: "Milton produced *Paradise Lost* for the same reason that a silk-worm produces silk. It was an activity of his nature."[28] The remark is wonderfully Romantic, a veritable cousin of Keats's axiom: "That if poetry comes not as naturally as the leaves to a tree it had better not come at all."[29] But I have cited it here in order to juxtapose it with one of Stevens's *Adagia:* "The poet makes silk dresses

27. Ibid., p. 24.

28. Karl Marx, *Theories of Surplus Value* (Moscow and London, 1969), pt. 1, p. 401. This brief and lucid general statement precedes Marx's illustrative use of Milton: "The capitalist production process, therefore, is not merely the production of commodities. It is a process which absorbs unpaid labour, which makes raw materials and means of labour—the means of production—into means for the absorption of unpaid labour."

29. Cited from a letter to John Taylor written in February, 1818, in *Selected Poems and Letters,* ed. Douglas Bush (Boston, 1959), p. 267.

out of worms." Stevens's adage is both fanciful and ambiguous. Read one way, it suggests a kinship with Yeats's "He that sings a lasting song / Thinks in a marrow bone," cited earlier, or the return in "The Circus Animals' Desertion" to "the foul rag-and-bone shop of the heart"; Stevens's "worms" likewise invoke the Romantic and post-Romantic view that phenomenal experience is an origin that must somehow be honored even if it is artistically transformed. The relation of "silk dresses" to "worms" is, though, potentially much more complex than this. For in producing silk dresses out of worms, the poet is not respecting or paying tribute to an origin such as nature or society. He is, precisely, circumventing both. We can see this more clearly if we get the poet to make "silk dresses" out of "silk worms" instead of "worms." The substitution makes no difference, since the poet in either case does not merely hasten or reproduce natural or social processes, he instead appears to manage bypassing them completely. The product, "silk dresses," evoking Mallarmé and the Symbolist aesthetic, is thus a product, ready for consumption, whose relations with the processes of its production are entirely effaced, not to say mystified. It would of course be foolhardy even to appear to initiate a Marxist analysis of Stevens's poetry on the basis of this adage alone. But it is suggestively relevant to a reading of "Peter Quince at the Clavier" that attends to its effacement of the process by means of which it becomes, as if enduringly, a lyric poem. The process whereby the desire the speaker experiences for the woman in "blue-shadowed silk" comes to produce the living poem is a process which, besides testifying to the poet's creative potency, "preserves as in a vial" the violated Susanna whose "music" has mothered the verbal artifact that contains her.

DAVID BROMWICH

Parody, Pastiche, and Allusion

That it can be parodied, most readers would admit, is one good test of an individual style. But this truism suggests another, which, to judge by common usage, we do not admit so readily: when we call a style individual, we mean anything but inimitable. A general recognition of the uses of parody and a careless half-acceptance of what it implies about style sometimes lead us to suppose that parody belongs to a particular stage in the maturing of a writer. This essay will argue on the contrary that parody ceases only with death, that the sort of work it does is integral to all writing, and that, together with its neighbor, pastiche, it has a place in good standing within the larger family of allusion. Of course, as the few who try to define them have found, parody and pastiche are hard to tell apart for any length of time, but they are so for the same reason that parody and writing are hard to tell apart. One might compare pastiche to the game of adaptation and half-echoing that goes on all the time in a conversation, and parody to the act of perfect mimicking that can bring a conversation to a self-conscious halt. Anyway the distinction is helpful to the extent that it is impracticable, and it may serve as a reminder that parody and pastiche are not odd, intimate, or exceptional, as they have commonly been taken to be. Both involve a normal and not a special practice.

Max Beerbohm was in the habit of secreting in footnotes and small print, where other parodists would look carefully, grave remarks concerning the advantages and disadvantages of parody for life. He said, for example, that good parodies were provoked by love of rather than contempt for the subject, and that the publication of a book of them was the writer's hopeful declaration that his own style had crystallized. In a different connection Beerbohm defended his refusal to rewrite his early work by saying how much he disliked the idea of a scold perched beside the young novice, rapping his knuckles every few lines to signal "Revise!" This was an observation on the morality of style; but it too has a curious significance for parody. The fiction that the mature writer credits is that in revising his youthful work he is making it somehow more truly like himself, less like an involuntary imitation of favorite writers, with the result that he steers it in the opposite direction from parody and pastiche. Yet in this case the very act of revising betrays its aim; for to draw a circle around a poem, a novel, or a play is to confess that the work has not been able to do that for itself; a step further lies the recognition that in the nature of writing it cannot be done.

One reason lyric poetry offers rich opportunities for mixed modes like parody is that it delights in gestures of completion. Our familiarity with closure in short poems has a commonplace cause—we remember endings more easily where we can remember beginnings and middles—but it tempts us to invent a more exalted one. So we may suppose that in the nature of the genre, lyric is a pure expression of voice, and our ability to talk about short poems is a result of our knowledge of a perfected voice. In fact, we never get closer to the author of a lyric than we do to the author of a novel or play. The fiction we sometimes credit as readers, that lyric is the home of an expressive style (attainable elsewhere by "prose poetry"), is only a fanciful way of saying that we can recall entire short poems without much effort; and, with some practice at revolving them in the mind, we can make up fairly well-defended stories about the nature of the voice they lead us to imagine. The following examples go some way to show how this sort of readerly self-deception becomes part of the general atmosphere of parody. The judgment in which they all seem to concur is that the lyric poet is tempted, more extravagantly than other writers, to give a naive essentialist account of his personality.

The parodist or pasticheur is someone who recognizes this, and who stands beside the poet as a conscientious skeptic. But poet and parodist, essentialist and skeptic, may both inhabit a single work, even a single sentence. In an essay called "Diminuendo," Beerbohm gives a vivid illustration of their companionship. Since the essay is a partly spurious memoir, he starts off with the prim vanity of the true memoir-adept, by announcing that even before he went to Oxford he had come to admire Walter Pater less as a stylist than as an intellectual curiosity. He expects the reader to see through this piece of one-upmanship—so plainly a case of "Go him one better or you go him one worse"—and yet he contrives to let us see *him* seeing through it without breaking stride. "Even then I was angry that [Pater] should treat English as a dead language, bored by that sedulous ritual wherewith he laid out every sentence as in a shroud—hanging, like a widower, long over its marmoreal beauty or ever he would lay it, at length, in his book, its sepulchre. From that laden air, the so cadaverous murmur of that sanctuary, I would hook it at the beck of any jade."[1] Every writer is a parodist, in love with what he mimics, who fancies he can decide where parody will stop and writing commence, but whose efforts to exhibit the decision taking place only show that it never does. Here the last clause, suddenly sprightly, tugs at our sleeve with its ingenuous appeal: "Look, how different I am!" And the two preceding sentences reply: "Oh, are you? How different?"

Indeed, to be quite satisfying, our maxim about parody has to be strengthened. Every parodist is a writer *madly* in love with the styles that have formed him. Nothing else will explain "*The Flying Tailor:* Further Extract from 'The Recluse,' a Poem," the unsurpassable parody of Wordsworth by James Hogg.

> Ere he was put
> By his mother into breeches, Nature strung
> The muscular part of his economy
> To an unusual strength, and he could leap
> All unimpeded by his petticoats,
> Over the stool on which his mother sat
> When carding wool, or cleansing vegetables,
> Or meek performing other household tasks.
> Cunning he watch'd his opportunity,
> And oft, as house-affairs did call her thence,
> Overleapt Hugh, a perfect whirligig,
> More than six inches o'er th'astonish'd stool.
> What boots it to narrate, how at leap-frog
> Over the breech'd and unbreech'd villagers
> He shone conspicuous. Leap-frog did I say?
> Vainly so named. What though in attitude
> The Flying Tailor aped the croaking race
> When issuing from the weed-entangled pool,
> Tadpoles no more, they seek the new-mown fields—[2]

We cannot afford to hear out the metaphor; there is simply not enough time. But Hogg, who has all the time in the world, goes on

1. Max Beerbohm, *Works* (London, 1922), pp. 129–30.
2. James Hogg, *The Poetic Mirror* (1816; rpt. London, 1929), pp. 100–101.

like this for page after page, minute, observant, a connoisseur of bathos, and the most appallingly subtle anthropologist of the Wordsworthian habitat who was ever put on earth. Even in these lines, how much he makes us notice for the first time, in a kind of double-take: the Miltonic syntax grafted onto a strangely modern vocabulary ("put / By his mother into breeches"); the sanction prudery gives to an inveterate fondness for periphrasis ("The muscular part of his economy"); the pedantry of measurements, remarked by Wordsworth-parodists ever after ("six inches," exactly); the taste for a word like "whirligig," and the way by indulging it steadily a paternal condescension removes us far from the spirit of childhood it tries to capture; finally the queer lapses into poetic diction, by the author of the Preface to *Lyrical Ballads*. Wordsworth's own response to this is not hard to imagine. If he read it in a wise mood, without any flatterer nearby, he knew that he was being paid a rare compliment.

Such responses are in fact always imaginable because a parodist always has the subject in mind as his intended audience. In this, parody differs from burlesque, which is best thought of as mimicry that points and shouts. Burlesque aims, rather unfairly, to please you by "doing" the style in question and at the same time insinuating that it is just a bag of tricks, easy to open the second time because it was easy the first. Thus an early parodist of Robert Lowell was poised on the verge of burlesque when he wrote:

> The man-god and divided glancer came
> To town. He rose to die with maize and fame
> Was howling in the North where cymbals clashed
> Around the flaying whale's bulk-hulk.[3]

Again, as in Hogg's parody, a polemical intent is visible in the step-by-step cataloguing of the subject's rhetorical traits. We are reminded of Lowell's peculiar habit of bringing a line to a dead stop after the first foot; his corresponding readiness to eke out the last foot of a straggling line with "and X"; his poor ear for assonance and alliteration; together with the unassimilated mannerisms of earlier poets (Crane, Hopkins, Empson), and a certain pervasive senselessness. Yet though well-pondered as criticism, all this does not quite succeed as parody. The personal allusion in the third line gives it away. And with a more celebrated example like "Cui Bono?", the send-up of Byron by Horace and James Smith, we have passed beyond parody altogether.

3. "Bad Day in Black Rock," unsigned, *Didact,* Spring 1954, p. 91.

> Sated with home, of wife, of children tired,
> The restless soul is driven abroad to roam;
> Sated abroad, all seen, yet nought admired,
> The restless soul is driven to ramble home.[4]

This tells us what the Smiths thought of Byron; but they need hardly have read him to think it; only the overt personalities and (if we continue) the Spenserian stanza allow us to identify the subject.

If burlesque is a low form of parody tending toward lampoon, pastiche is a less concentrated and therefore less recondite form—not so much higher as wider, and directed ideally to an audience of all-who-would-come. It is understood in advance that few will note the gesture this mode shares with parody, and its appeal is that it can survive anyway in the esteem of the rest. *The Waste Land,* before Ezra Pound got to it, was mainly pastiche with some elements of burlesque. What Pound did in revising was to make the poem more conventional, so that its passing moves kept the decorum of acknowledgment and allusion; Eliot's notes completed the process, or rather fixed the impression that it was part of the author's design. Still, even without the Popean couplets that Pound deleted, and without "Full fathom five your Bleistein lies," the poem contains sections of accomplished pastiche, much of it Tennysonian or Miltonic. The phrase "a handful of dust" comes from *Maud,* the passage ending "Jug jug to dirty ears" is a reminiscence of Proserpine gathering flowers, in *Paradise Lost*—but in the nature of pastiche, one's tact for the resemblance is a matter not of local echoes but of extensive comparison and memory. Direct allusions of a more common sort, as in the passage beginning "Unreal City," or specific burlesques, as of *Antony and Cleopatra* in "A Game of Chess," Eliot knew very well how to attend to in his notes. But he chose to treat these as the all-important feature of his poem's relationship to other poetry. Academic critics took the hint, and saw *The Waste Land* as fitting into a broadly defined formalist routine. One consequence of this view was that a difficult poem achieved a large reputation within two decades after its first appearance. Another consequence, slower to emerge and less happy for Eliot, is that for most readers the poem is now artificially isolated from "Burbank with a Baedeker," the Sweeney poems, and others which rely on parody and pastiche.

The most intelligent English poet of the generation after Eliot's, William Empson, understood the implications of Eliot's practice, and

4. Horace and James Smith, *Rejected Addresses* (1812; 12th ed., London, 1813), p. 14

wrote poems which derive their unsettling emotional power from the questions they make us ask about the history of a style. How many different times has *this* style been new? What links the occasions of the older poet (in this case, Donne) with those of his legatee? Why does a modern poet so committed to a single past voice feel so little like a ventriloquist?

> Tell me again about Europe and her pains,
> Who's tortured by the drought, who by the rains.
> Glut me with floods where only the swine can row
> Who cuts his throat and let him count the gains.
> It seemed the best thing to be up and go.[5]

One can point to lines and stanzas by Donne where in just this way a question shades into an imperative and the imperative has to be heard as a challenge: "I am strong enough; there is nothing I cannot endure." As for the jostle of idioms almost collapsing under the weight of figures they both conceal and support ("where only the swine can row / Who cuts his throat and let him count the gains"), this again recalls Donne. Yet the passage and the poem it comes from, "Aubade," have nothing of the arbitrary or mixed effect one usually associates with pastiche. After all, as other examples could also show—Tate's "Ode to the Confederate Dead" beside Eliot's "Gerontion," Ashbery's "Soonest Mended" beside Auden's "In Praise of Limestone"—pastiche turns into elective affinity as effortlessly as parody turns into pastiche. The only interesting use of these terms is to break down the categories by which one kind of writing is designated more literary than others.

The concern of the New Critics for maintaining such categories has a great deal to do with their lack of interest in parody, pastiche, and allusion in general. That concern, moved in its early days by the heroic wish to protect art against utilitarian demands, became in time a protective gesture of orthodoxy, assuring the reader that everything he required to interpret a poem was already in the poem. The result was an insulation of poetry not only from the exigencies of present-day politics and the clichés of advertising but also from the unlicensed intrusion of history, nationality, local or or personal culture—in short much of the web of circumstance out of which poems get written. To view such contingent references as part of the necessary construction of a poem went against the belief in the crystalline unity of the whole which gave the New Criticism its strongest link to an older Symbolist

5. William Empson, *Collected Poems* (London, 1955), p. 49.

tradition. For the establishment of a distinct class of literary objects had presupposed a limbo of the extra-literary, and here, within reach of scholars but not interpreters, allusive writing had its place. To adapt a concise definition of W. K. Wimsatt's, one might say parody, pastiche, and allusion could not be seen as things "whose only end was to be known." From this point of view they were parasitic modes, hovering uneasily outside the realm of poetry proper. But once we have stopped looking at parody and pastiche as special cases, the course we follow in dealing with them suggests a different end for writing as such: to be known in all its company—what it presses into service and what it cannot shake loose, everything to which it seems to gesture somehow. The poems that will be discussed in the following pages do not feel like parody or pastiche, and yet they are closer to these than many readers suppose poetry can be. Their style is such that one cannot imagine what it would be like to read them without having read certain other poems. But they do not exist for the sake of those poems. Their task is to modify a language, and they do not exemplify a kind of meaning that arises when language goes on holiday.

Jay Macpherson's first volume of poems, *The Boatman,* bears the following epigraph by the author herself.

> Sir, no man's nightingale, your foolish bird,
> I sing and thrive, by angel finger fed,
> And when I turn to rest, an Angel's word
> Exalts an air of trees above my head,
> Shrouds me in secret where no single thing
> May envy no-man's-nightingale her spring.[6]

The allusions one finds at a glance summon back the dedications to verse-making of earlier poets. Auden's "Sir, no man's enemy, forgiving all," itself a notable instance of Elizabethan pastiche, would have been among the anthology pieces this poet could hardly avoid, in the years when she began thinking about poetry. The fact that its virtuosity came to seem hollow to Auden himself—who omitted it from his 1966 *Collected Shorter Poems*—suits her purpose well since it means the poem can be echoed lightly. Herbert's "Jordan (I)" is a graver utterance, and received with a less casual air. As it entered Herbert's poem, the line "I envie no mans nightingale or spring" was a self-

6. Jay Macpherson, *Poems Twice Told* (Toronto, 1981), p. 9.

vindication free of pride in the ordinary sense; rather, it avowed a command of invention and propriety which owed nothing to the common fictions of wit. Macpherson, equally confident but more simply negative in assertion, figures herself as "no-man's-nightingale." And yet, as the hyphens indicate, this negation is also a name: she is the unserviceable creature, strong in anonymity; being hidden supplies her with a distinctive "word." The plainness of the borrowings and the assurance that they will be understood as an intelligible reserve mark *The Boatman* as a whole.

Either the poet herself or an exceptionally accurate blurb-writer described this volume as "an intricate sequence of short epigrammatic poems—in which there are echoes of ballads, carols, nursery rhymes, and hymns—that bear a whole cosmos of the poet's invention, constructed from Biblical and classical allusions." One thing about the plan is Blakean: its recurrence to single characters under different aspects, as a way of joining the reader's intellectual powers with the active concerns of morality. Thus we have two poems about the phoenix, on the one hand a neutral reduction of several versions of the myth, pitched low and clear of passion, and on the other the following strange lines.

> The wicked Phoenix in her baleful fires
> Here on this ground suspires.
> What God has put sunder here combines
> And viperish intertwines.
> Duplicity of head and heart
> Has taught her lust that art.
> Not strength and sweetness in one frame,
> Dying and rising still the same:
> Her charnel and her marriage bed,
> The womb that her own being bred
> —Strains to rise and cannot fly,
> Looks to death and may not die,
> Writhes on griefs beyond recall
> And shall, till doomfire burn all.[7]

The poem, entitled "O Fenix Culpa," might be described as a pessimistic gloss on an optimistic pun by James Joyce. Yet the bird whose fate could make guilt appear fortunate, by marrying a rise to every fall, was also an appropriate emblem of *discordia concors,* above all for Shakespeare.

7. Ibid., p. 25.

Reason in it selfe confounded
Saw Division grow together:
To themselves yet either neither
Simple were so well compounded

That it cried, how true a twaine,
Seemeth this concordant one. . . .

"The Phoenix and the Turtle" required a second bird for the union it imagined to be both complete and paradoxical. But in "O Fenix Culpa" the creature that can hold together disparate meanings in itself comes to represent something monstrously compensatory in human nature. Because this poem takes no pleasure in the contraries traditionally identified with the Phoenix, it impresses us not as an answer in kind to Shakespeare's poem, but as another poem of the same period, to which "The Phoenix and the Turtle" may be read as a reply. "What God has put asunder here combines / And viperish intertwines," writes the later poet. No, she makes the earlier one answer defensively, "Hearts remote, yet not asunder." A whole register of feelings evoked by the myth, and suppressed in earlier tellings, is restored by this sort of juxtaposition. The effect would be inconceivable in a poem less observant than this of the entire lexical and syntactical decorum of a period not its own.

So a conversation we regarded as closed turns out all along to have concealed certain moves which were left for the late joiner to recover. The gathering force of the poem as it issues in prophecy—"Writhes on griefs beyond recall / *And shall*"— is a triumph of polemic. Yet where the style is pastiche we often dismiss the result as if it were an act without an agent. Language did the work, we say, while the poet listened and transcribed. Intelligent criticism need not altogether disclaim this habitual sort of response. But it will want to modify it in the light of everything that is known about the poet in question. To the reader of "O Fenix Culpa" at least two facts will be important: that all Jay Macpherson's more ambitious poems have been elegiac ("The Boatman" and "The Beauty of Job's Daughters" alone excepted); and that what they lament is an alienated or repressed element of the self. Now, the advantage of pastiche for any poet is that it can seem to say something behind your back, and without your connivance; it may for example console a loss by suggesting that it occurred *before* what you took to be an age of innocence—as when the Phoenix is shown to have been never harmonious, always viperish, by a trick of perspective in style. But after comparing "O Fenix Culpa" with other poems in which the need for an answering eloquence is taken for granted, we may decide on reflection that this is no more than allusion commonly does. It helps us to cross the distance between ourselves and our losses; and it does so without giving credence to any fiction of a single voice or a single speaker. The relevant fiction has to do instead with writing: every topic that once moved an author to utterance is presumed to be still topical. In this respect the poet resembles another character in *The Boatman,* whose task is to raise "both Cain and Babel."

Daryl Hine's lyric monologue, "The Double-Goer," belongs to a slightly later phase of the same modern story. The poet, whom we have come to witness in his quest for unity of form and the concord of "the whole man," is overheard praising doubt and duplicity as the very conditions of writing. For him, the failure of words to crystallize a responsible self is the success of expression, provided the "errors pantomimed" by his effort are sufficiently commanding. The poem at first honors the predictable opposition between art and action, but only for convenience. Underlying this is an antagonism which, as the speaker will argue, concerns any artist far more persistently: between two ideas of expression, as rhetoric and as dialectic, and for the verbal artist as writing and as speech. It is in the nature of the printed poem that it should be controlled by the first member of these pairs, to the artist's own advantage even where he most denies it.

All that I do is clumsy and ill timed.
You move quickly when it must be done,
To spare yourself or save your victim pain.
And then like the light of the sun you move away
While I come face to face with complex crime
Far from the moving of the mellifluous sea.
All that I do is clumsy and ill timed.
When you perform, my errors pantomimed
   Will give an example to the sun
   Of flight, and to shadows how to run.
You will in turn discover in my rhyme
Justifications for your simple crime.

Manifold are the disguises of our love.
We change, our transformations turn about,
Our shadowy forms become the doubles for
Affection or hatred. Yet a kind of growth
Is visible, and may be termed the heart,
Confused by the ambiguities of our art.
Manifold are the disguises of our love.

Contradiction of terms is all we have.
  To please the self and then the soul
  Is difficult and terrible;
Impossible to own a single heart
Lost in the double-dealing of our art.[8]

The "I" of "The Double-Goer" is the writer, interpreter, skeptic, and his "You" the conscious agent usually defined as the empirical self: the "simple crime" is the latter's belief that by acting straightforwardly he clears himself of the double-dealing of art, by which all action is mediated. The issues between art and action, however, and between writing and speech, go back to the Platonic bias against shadows; for, to a mind seeking pure forms seen in the light of the sun, nothing more plainly exhibits our commitment to delusion than the letters of the alphabet: instead of a world of shadowless objects, these deliver us into a world of objectless shadows. Samuel Todes's 1975 article "Shadows in Knowledge," which developed the implicit connection of individual shadows wth alphabetical characters in Plato's use of the allegory of the cave, reached a conclusion about our reliance on a language of shadows that are at once radically distinct and radically adequate: "[the mind's] basic entities are completely representative shadows whose completeness of representation is bought at the price of their being nothing but representations. . . . Pure face, with nothing concealed and everything revealed, the platonically ideal character of perfectly knowable things, turns out to be pure figure, with everything represented, and nothing revealed."[9] A poem of Daryl Hine's entitled "Letter to Shadow," written several years after "The Double-Goer," offers a high-spirited paraphrase of those sentences: "Literature is all a letter says. / What alternative to tell a vision? / So doting on the idiotical light / Within's like staring at the sun: one / Sees no more than if he looked at midnight." But the same argument was sketched already in the counter-turn of "The Double Goer": "When you perform, my errors pantomimed / Will give an example to the sun / Of flight, and to shadows how to run." All action is errant, being a process caught in one aspect by writing, which writing in turn may exalt and justify.

In the next two stanzas, the repetition in conduct that Plato feared as a consequence of any surrender to appearance in words is evoked

8. Daryl Hine, *Selected Poems* (New York, 1980), pp. 18–20.

9. Samuel Todes, "Shadows in Knowledge: Plato's Misunderstanding of Shadows, and of Knowledge as Shadow-free," in *Dialogues in Phenomenology*, ed. Don Ihde and Richard M. Zaner (The Hague, 1975), pp. 112–13.

as the central fact about the poet's art (here the same as the rhetorician's).

Two-edged is the double-goer's tongue,
Malice and honey, and the prizes in
His logomachy, what lie near the heart:
Money, honour and success in love.
Harmonious ambiguities in a swarm
Burrow at the fulcrum of his speech.
Two-edged is the double-goer's tongue.
One side says, Right, the other side says, Wrong;
  One, Love is red, the other, Black;
  One, Go on, and one, Turn back.
One hopes for heaven, one for earth, and each
To strike a concord through cross-purposed speech.

So split and halved and twain is every part,
So like two persons severed by a glass
Which darkens the discerning whose is whose
And gives two arms for love and two for hate,
That they cannot discover what they're at,
And sometimes think of killing and embrace.
So split and halved and twain is every part,
Double the loins, the fingers, and the heart,
  Confused in object and in aim,
  That they cannot their pleasure name,
But like two doubles in a darkened place
Make one obscure assault and one embrace.

Not the glamour of the *acte gratuit* but the poet's sense of arriving at the end of a long succession of possible styles occasions the line, "So split the halved and twain is every part," and the three lines that follow. Both the movement and the diction of the poem at this point establish what certain of its earlier features may have suggested, an affinity with Donne, and at the same time a dissatisfaction with the mystery of words ending in marriage. Donne's chosen symbol for such an ending is one we have seen before: "The Phoenix ridle hath more wit / By us, we two being one, are it, / So, to one neutrall thing both sexes fit." The foregoing stanzas remember Donne, but theirs is the different riddle of self and soul, and they seem to prefer a state in which "I, this one, am two by it." The "neutral" sexuality that they do affirm belongs to an untranquil narcissism.

Donne wrote "The Canonization" to celebrate a love thoroughly at odds with this, and yet what "The Double-Goer" teaches us to regard with suspicion is not that poem, or even Donne's style of wit, so much as a critical style of domesticating irony. The mood of reconciliation in which paradoxes are resolved, and the inside and outside perspectives of irony become finally available to each other, has nothing to do with the divided beings "Confused in object and in aim" who make a dead set at each other without ever joining. One cannot speak of them in the vocabulary of the symbol (fusing opposites) but only in the vocabulary of rhetoric (giving weight to one impulse). "For us today," Cleanth Brooks remarked of "The Canonization," "Donne's imagination seems obsessed wit the problem of unity; the sense in which the lovers become one—the sense in which the soul is united to God. . . . It may not be too far-fetched to see both as instances of, and metaphors for, the union which the creative imagination itself effects."[10] But what if the imagination is assertive rather than creative? What if it prefers conquest to reconciliation? The rhetoric of a poem like Donne's might in that case defeat the author's obsession with the problem of unity. Some such reading at any rate is suggested by "The Double-Goer," in which tensions are if anything retensed. We have to take "confused," for example, in the phrase just quoted, to mean permanently entangled and not beautifully fused together. By the charm of pastiche the later poem even borrows something of Donne's own authority for working its changes. As one gets to know it better, it feels increasingly like a companion-poem to "The Canonization," written by an idiot questioner of the metaphysical style, who takes its means for its end and by his persistence converts us to his misunderstanding. The effect of the double stanza—closer to Donne as a rule in the second half than in the first—is to justify this conversion without seeming aware of it.

The fifth and sixth stanzas extend the pattern of doubling to include all desire, and evidently in a way that rules out procreation. No personal confession is offered. But the human motive of the poet has coincided throughout with the rhetorical motive of the "I": a helpless feeling of the completeness of this identification must have led to the mention of blindness, and the allusion to Milton's "Bright effluence of bright essence increate."

For they were to duality born and bred.
From their childhood the powers of evil were
No less their familiar than the mirror,
Source of a comfortable terror now and then,

10. Cleanth Brooks, *The Well Wrought Urn* (New York, 1947), p. 18.

And romantic: What good is a fiend unless
I can think and he, my double, act?
Thus we were to duality born and bred.
If these two eyes could turn in the one head,
  Bright orbs by a brighter sphere enclosed,
  Mutually blind and self-opposed,
The right supplying what the left one lacked,
Then I can think, and you, my body, act.

In singleness there is no heart or soul
And solitude is scarcely possible.
The one-sailed ship, tossed on a divided sea
As lightly as cork is tossed, as blindly as
The partners toss on their oceanic bed
And rise and fall, is wrecked and lost away.
In singleness there is no heart or soul;
Thus he sees wrong who sees in halves a whole,
  Who searches heaven but for one,
  And not a double of the sun,
Forgets that, being light as cork, the day
Can rise and fall, is wrecked and lost away.

The thematic clarity of these lines makes it worthwhile to remark that the poem as originally published was called "The "The Doppelgänger." Both titles in fact have their advantages, the English in reminding us that more than a literary motif is at stake, the German in recalling the pervasiveness of the motif in Romantic literature. But the double in its traditional sense can startle us with the recognition that identity is nothing but a voluntary projection of the mind. It thus implies a psychology which Romanticism has long been supposed to share with the stronger schools of rhetoric; and anti-Romantic critics are fond of pointing out that if carried into practice the theory is sickening. Most readers will agree that the very idea of a double—a figure, as much myself as I am, whose existence proves everything about me to be contingent—is among those from which a healthy spirit recoils in disgust. Yet neither the complex truth of these stanzas ("we were to duality born and bred") nor the facile half-truth with which it is involved ("In singleness there is no heart or soul") affects to instruct us about life as it is necessarily lived. Rather they portray one form of life associated with one form of art.

Within that form a knowledge of limitation may only add to a poet's individual power, and by showing how it does so the final stanza earns its daring variation on the humility of the first.

All that I do is careless and sublime.
You walk head-downwards, now your opened eyes
Take comfort from the beauty of the site.
What if the vision vary in detail?
What are we but sleepers in a cave,
Our dreams the shades of universal doubt?
All that I do is careless and sublime,
You bore with patience to the heart of time;
  Though your resource of art is small
  And my device yields none at all,
Still this two-handed engine will find out
In us the shape and shadow of our doubt.

If, the first time we read this, we heard "All that I do is clumsy and ill timed," it was our own fault. We stood too far away from the poet or, what comes to the same thing, too close to a kind of success he does not care about. What he said was "All that I do is careless and sublime." For the man of action in this scheme had agreed to be governed by the man of art even before the poem began. As for the site of action, we cannot now help seeing that it is Plato's cave, no matter where we stand—"What if the vision vary in detail?" The conscious agent requires the poet after all if he is to awaken from his dream of constancy, and the poem's final lines are his comfort. We ordinarily think of doubt as a merely destructive power of the mind, so that to place "doubt" in the genetive, as if one could speak of assertions of doubt, fruits of doubt, and so forth, is curious in itself. But the personal claim here is very great. The poem's "two handed engine"—this quotation from "Lycidas" referring at once to the double stanza and the allusive style it has perfected—"will find out / In us the shape and shadow of our doubt." *Find out* manages to concentrate the force of the whole declaration, both for the "you" of the poem and for "you" as any reader: it is perhaps only a piece of information; but its discovery will have the power to open up a buried layer of experience. We are warned against expecting much immediate reward: "Though your resource of art is small / And my device yields none at all. . . ." For all that, the mood is optative. When we doubt an author's "singleness" of style our verdict is apt to be peremptory. When we ask what singleness could mean anyway, as this poem asks, and go on to see what the author has made of his duplicity, we have some chance of being generous. Our recoveries like those of the double-goer divide us into what we are, and the fact leaves nothing to regret. Beyond that, what we call unified wholes, or simple inventions, could not be known by us even if we could be sure they existed.

This may seem a polemical reading of a poem that invites other sorts of analysis. It does, or it would not be a poem. But "The Double-Goer" is as thorough a recent instance as can be found of a poem that resists the critical assumptions of the age in which it was produced. Indeed, if one tries to imagine a New Critical abstract of its argument, one will not get very far. Any effort to trace a resolution of the central paradox is rewarded with cross-purposed speech: the "opened eyes" are again surrounded by shades, and the promise nullified; the ship that is to bear self and soul harmoniously out of the poem turns out to be a "one-sailed ship, tossed on a divided sea / As lightly as cork is tossed, as blindly as / The partners toss on their oceanic bed." Why do New Critical habits of reading feel so inadequate here? They look for a poem to move from confusion to certainty, or to a higher synthesis of more edifying confusions. They can hardly begin to deal with a poem in which one paradox is a figure for another, with the second as insoluble as the first. Or, at that point they have to fall back on image-counting. But poems like "The Double-Goer," though rich in persuasive figuration, are often surprisingly bare of imagery, at least in the sense of the word valued by modern pedagogy. When a detail is repeated, like the mirror, the cave, or "the mellifluous sea," it is likely to be used for so many traditional associations that the pretense of intrinsic meaning cannot be maintained. Such poems do not even *seem* to generate their own conventions.

Still, it is wrong to suppose that there is, or for that matter ever has been, a "fit" between poetry and the criticism that explains it convincingly. The New Criticism started with Donne and Eliot, and went on from there. What it had to say was not essentially right for some poets and essentially less so for others. The rhetorical criticism of the past decade started with Wordsworth and Baudelaire, and is going on from there. If what it says is interesting, the application is not limited to a few select followers of Wordsworth and Baudelaire. Tact alone decides the quality of a critical statement, and a reader may be tactless with a theory or without one. It seems possible all the same that a general circumstance has given the two poets discussed here their interest for a larger tendency. Both, as Canadians, grew up without any native idiom as available as those of English poetry; and for both one result has been a style that feels at times oddly synchronic, not only at ease with a past but at ease within it. A conviction of the simultaneity of past and present monuments, which Eliot thought common to every creator of a "really new" work of art, may be less universal than he believed when he wrote "Tradition and the Individual Talent." But it does seem capable of fostering a tacit alliance among writers of a certain time and place, and this generation of postwar Canadians serve as an impressive example. These pages have been concerned with a small part of what any such group can tell us. When we choose to regard the decision to write as an entry into a conversation, then allusive modes like parody and pastiche, as much as the process of allusion itself, belong to the usual give and take. They are not an interruption of the true business of writing any more than a sidelong glance is an interruption of sight.

Jonathan Arac

Afterword: Lyric Poetry and the Bounds of New Criticism

This volume has largely avoided the dangers of enclosure, even within what the editors conceived in proposing the topic and assembling the contributors. The actual, achieved combination has produced something quite other from what anyone might have anticipated. This volume demonstrates the intellectual necessity for criticism to confront what threatens, not merely what explicitly challenges, its presuppositions and results. Thus, to take the case of the dramatic monologue which Herbert Tucker so illuminates, in the quarter century since Robert Langbaum's *The Poetry of Experience* (1957) established this category as fruitful for critical thought, its very possibility has been threatened. A literary type that depends upon the balance between sympathy and judgment, between the pure claim of a self and the rigors of ethics, can neither as a poetic practice nor as a critical artifact ignore the threats to the "self" and to ethics that have marked poststructuralist theory, whether in the deconstruction of Derrida (whose critique of Husserl so many contributors draw upon) or in the Marxist *Political Unconscious* (1981) of Fredric Jameson. These essays demonstrate the importance for critics to read not only other criticism but also "theory"—typically well beyond the "literary." This fundamental commitment to reach beyond disciplinary boundaries may be what most marks our difference from the New Criticism. Yet even within the discipline, Jonathan Culler has admirably suggested discursive "Changes in the Study of Lyric." On the far side of the further changes enacted in these essays, I venture to reshade his preliminary map.

First, however, I want to pose a terminological question. Grant that these essays betray no stale fatigue, none of the derivative belatedness Frank Lentricchia has found *After the New Criticism* (1980), it is still possible that many of them do not so much surpass New Criticism as renovate it through revision: less "Beyond the New Criticism" than a "New New Criticism." From Culler's contrast of Cleanth Brooks and Paul de Man on Yeats's "Among School Children," it emerges clearly that the new new criticism shares with the old New Criticism an emphasis that is textual and technical, more concerned with method than with scholarship, and fundamentally unhistorical, especially in its confidence about the extensive applicability of its operative terms. In a notion that Michel Foucault has developed, both Brooks and de Man are "specific" intellectuals, rather than "general" intellectuals like Voltaire or Matthew Arnold, Sartre or Irving Howe.[1]

Yet even within academic bounds, there are further distinctions. To the extent that they do not proceed by close reading, Northrop Frye, Frank Kermode in *Romantic Image* (1957), and Hillis Miller in *Poets of Reality* (1965) differ from any "new new criticism." (See the animadversions of W. K. Wimsatt against Miller in "Battering the Object," reprinted in *Day of the Leopards*.) Likewise, in confronting the historical variability in the terms of critical understanding, Paul Bové's *Destructive Poetics* (1980) marks more a divergence from than an innovative augmentation to New Criticism. In their concern for the historical specificities that feed upon scholarship, Alastair Fowler (*Triumphal Forms,* 1970), Rosalie Colie ("*My Ecchoing Song,*" 1970), and Lawrence Lipking (*The Life of the Poet,* 1981) are post- but not new-new critical students of lyrics. In crossing the gravity of erudition with an inventive levity, the work of Geoffrey Hartman, especially many of the essays in *Beyond Formalism* (1970) and *The Fate of Reading* (1975), stands on the border-ground, inviting a passage that few of the present contributors have attempted. I find it remarkable that so many essays from such diverse concerns agree to ignore so much important work. This is a fundamental *aporia* of current literary studies, the no-thoroughfare which effectively re-encloses a field of new new criticism.

As we look back through the prism of these essays, Culler's five fundamental changes since New Criticism still seem relevant. Two of them, the shift from symbol to allegory and the change in the status of self-reference, demonstrate that New Criticism and its successor remark exactly the same "places" and "moves" in the poems they are

1. "Truth and Power," in *Power/Knowledge,* ed. Colin Gordon (New York, 1980), pp. 126–30.

reading, but they give different *values* to the features they agree in discerning. If allegory emphasizes distance and difference rather than the intimate reconciliation effected by the symbol, and if self-reference no longer performs a comforting embrace but instead opens up vertiginous abysses, this is all to register an inversion in what we may call the plot of criticism. Interpretation is no longer what Northrop Frye would call a "romance" of unification but the "irony" of dispersal. The new new criticism is a satire on the old, veering between parody and parricide. Yet as each works to turn the poet's song into the critic's prose, to display the poem's charm (a term etymologically related to song), the difference between them may be understood as the difference that works within the word "disenchantment" (by etymology, an un-singing). The disenchanted world may be that which makes Dulcinea a princess, the frog a prince, or it may be the "disenchanted world" that forms our "iron cage" in Max Weber's *Protestant Ethic*.[2]

In setting a new-new-critical concern with "babble and doodle," what some might call the materiality of the signifier, against New Critical concern with "form as meaning," Culler probes an extremely important and vexed area. New Criticism and new new criticism alike worry over the *relation* between the aesthetic and the cognitive. This relation may be posed as union, tension, opposition, difference, and no doubt in other ways. The "aesthetic" and the "cognitive" may be redeployed as the "rhetorical" and "epistemological," as the "perceptible" and the "intelligible," or as many other related pairs. The struggle with this system has energized many of the most notable papers of this collection, including those by Paul de Man and Cynthia Chase. This struggle falls within the post-Kantian problematic that Richard Rorty has tried to banish in going "beyond" analytic philosophy. Work that pursued Rorty into the *Consequences of Pragmatism* (1982) could not, I think, be readily described as "new new criticism."

I find it hard to follow Culler in distinguishing New Critical attention to the language of poetry as "utterance" from new new critical concern with "trope," that is, with figuration as an effect of language itself, rather than as contained within, motivated and naturalized by, a speaking self. For I find that New Criticism and new new criticism *share* emphasis on "literary language." This phrase recurs crucially even in the latest essays of de Man's *Blindness and Insight* (1971), while

2. Against the negative weight of "die entzauberte Welt" in Max Weber, Walter Benjamin posed a utopian, fairy-tale "Entzauberung" in section 17 of "The Storyteller."

Brooks's *The Well Wrought Urn* begins from the nature of literary language. The very opening chapter, which contains the reading of "The Canonization" that Culler rereads, starts by boldly asserting (against imagined opposition) that "the language of poetry is the language of paradox." The second chapter commences its reading of *Macbeth* by situating itself within "the debate about the proper limits of metaphor." New Criticism, moreover, is notorious for having reduced plays from human drama to patterns of language. Although Brooks does write of the "drama" of poems, he means less anything tied to the character of a speaker than the action and conflict within the language itself that make the poem's "structure" a "process" rather than a "statement." Allen Tate contrasts "linguistic analysis" to any critical concern with expression or emotion.[3] To my understanding, the kind of difference Culler aims at could more precisely be described as the impact of semiotics on contemporary criticism. Even here, however, one must recall that the work of Charles Morris on the sign is contemporary with New Criticism and entered its debates. I shall return to the semiotic concern with language as "monument and arbitrary sign" (Wordsworth, cited by Mary Jacobus).

The final area Culler pointed to, that of "intertextuality" as a challenge to the autonomy of the individual poem, has been highly significant in these papers and requires close attention. This change within Anglo-American work begins with Northrop Frye's archetypal critique of New Criticism and thus allows some confluence between "new new criticism" and its usually ignored alternative.

This challenge to the autonomy of the individual poem may be closely connected with institutional and pedagogic urgencies. In the United States, New Criticism so effectively established itself as the dominant critical practice in the postwar years in part because its emphasis on the text alone made it eminently suitable for teaching the new masses of students that the GI Bill allowed to come to college without the elite cultural background upon which traditional belletristic teaching relied. Yet the New Criticism, in presenting the text alone, lived off an invisible cultural capital. To unpack, or proliferate, ambiguities by reference to the *OED* was to build on, or chip away at, decades of conservative, positivist, philological toil, and it was to have access in synoptic form to a vast body of historical reading experience. After the original New Critics, after the curricular transformations that their displacement of scholarship by criticism helped to effect, we have largely regained the guilty innocence Matthew Arnold at-

3. Allen Tate, "Longinus and the 'New Criticism'" (1948), in *The Man of Letters in the Modern World* (Cleveland, 1955), p. 186.

tributed to the Romantics: we do "not know enough." "Intertextual" reading prods into consciousness cultural traces that we wish—in some happier time—could remain unconscious but that we know—now—would not otherwise exist at all. This touches the question of the "canon," which, except for Donne's "Canonization," these essays have largely left aside. Nonetheless, Ernst Robert Curtius in *European Literature and the Latin Middle Ages* (1948) and Claudio Guillén in *Literature as System* (1971) have demonstrated historically that the very notion of the "lyrical" has been greatly determined by the canonization of particular authors within anthologies, textbooks, and histories.

The question of intertextuality in this volume has made visible a crucial methodological concern. In the North American study of lyric, Harold Bloom's attention to the "inter-poet" produced by the "anxiety of influence" has done most to bring intertextual issues to prominence. The struggle that Bloom makes deeply psychological, however, Barbara Johnson here chooses to treat with literal superficiality, as the echo of a name, while David Bromwich turns it to the larger arena of style. Cynthia Chase most specifically argues against Bloom's personalizing insistence and suggests instead that "patterns of rhetoric" are the appropriate intertextual configurations for Keats and other poets. Why then does her paper depend upon quotations attributed by name to the most famous poets in English—Shakespeare, Milton, Wordsworth? Why not just make up appropriate patterns of rhetoric out of the language environment? Why not find the relevant patterns on the street or TV? Why not in poets later than Keats, or lesser known than the holy trinity? These questions—all of which require detailed investigation—testify to the provocative value of Chase's inquiry. The obvious answers, however, (as distinguished from those that may result after investigation) indicate the power of the canon: it limits what we ourselves know well enough to quote and remember, and it limits what our hearers will consider authoritative enough to accept as evidence for our argument. They also indicate the power of the model of genius: only Shakespeare, Milton, and Wordsworth, we believe, stretch language to its limits and make evident its latent capacities and complexities. They also reveal the power of the model of chronology: intertexts, like influences, must, we believe, come earlier. In a word, these answers all testify to the continuing power of the model of "the history of poetry," which is Hegelian and neither new nor new new.[4]

4. Here I agree with Paul de Man: "Whether we know it, or like it, or not, most of us are Hegelians." See "Sign and Symbol in Hegel's Aesthetics," *Critical Inquiry*, 8 (1982), 763.

My special point in elaborating this issue is that "intertextuality," as used in this volume, has moved far from its point of entry into contemporary criticism. As the editors observed in commissioning these papers, there has been much recent emphasis on narrative, and I would note that "intertextuality" as a term comes from the study of narrative, in such early essays of Julia Kristeva as "The Bounded Text" and "Word, Dialogue, Novel," now translated in *Desire in Language* (1980). Kristeva drew her notion from the then almost wholly unknown work of Mikhail Bakhtin, whose "dialogism" has inspired much of Tilottama Rajan's argument. You could hardly learn from these papers that Bakhtin's critical focus was called "novelness"[5] and has much in common with Friedrich Schlegel's claims for "romantic" literature in *Athenaeum*-Fragment 116, meaning both that of the postclassical period and that which pertained to the novel (*Roman*). Kristeva's own *The Revolution of Poetic Language: The Late Nineteenth-Century Avant-Garde: Lautréamont and Mallarmé* (1974) has nothing to say on "lyric" in 650 pages. *Rabelais and His World* and *Problems of Dostoevsky's Poetics* by Bakhtin make clear, as does also Kristeva's use of "intertextuality," that the term was not meant to link author to author, or passage to passage between poems. It suggests less the echoing among highly literary phrases than the kind of effect Robert Penn Warren noted in "Pure and Impure Poetry" in *Romeo and Juliet:* Romeo's hyperbolic protestations must coexist with Mercutio's wit, Juliet's logic, and the Nurse's earthiness. A more precise word for this would be "interdiscursivity."

With this new term, I would like to consider what I will call "the historical study of the orders of language." Such a project is one of the most important possibilities "beyond the New Criticism," but it has little place in "new new criticism" or in most of what happens in these essays. Joel Fineman most fully attempts such study, while the feminism of Mary Nyquist and Barbara Johnson, like the Marxism of Fredric Jameson and John Brenkman, also leads toward it. The history of new new criticism helps to explain the small place of such inquiry here. Like Culler, I take Paul de Man's work as most clearly instantiating and inaugurating the "new new criticism" of the lyric—particularly his three essays from the end of the sixties, "Literary History and Literary Modernity," "Lyric and Modernity," and "The Rhetoric of Temporality" (newly collected in the second edition of *Blindness and Insight*).

5. On "novelness," see Mikhail Bakhtin, *The Dialogic Imagination,* ed. Michael Holquist, trans. Caryl Emerson (Austin, 1981), pp. xxxi, 68, 430.

On the first page of "The Rhetoric of Temporality" de Man records in a footnote those whose work has helped bring into existence the renewal of rhetoric that he is furthering. He cites there among others Foucault's *Order of Things* and Walter Benjamin's work, to which he returns here. What happens if we look at these "sources" for the new new criticism? I find a methodologically powerful pattern of omission. Foucault's work values immensely, and would not have been possible without, Mallarmé's mystique of "language" that has been with avant-garde literature for about a century. Nonetheless, Foucault *places* Mallarmé's position within the episteme of the post-classical period. Only on the basis of historical philology having already been established and having defined language in a certain way, only through its difference from Nietzsche's interrogation of language, does Mallarmé's "word" have any function or being. Yet Foucault's argument claims that we are leaving the space of that episteme. Thus, the overall effect of *The Order of Things* is historically to circumscribe, and thus to reduce, Mallarmé's understanding and practice of language as negativity that in France we associate with Maurice Blanchot and in America with Paul de Man. Foucault likewise responds to the debate between structuralism and hermeneutics in Paris of the 1960s by historically placing "formalization and exegesis" as alternative uses of language. Thus, again, the vexed relation, so important to some of these essays, between the perceptible and the intelligible belongs on the slate that Foucault's gestures wipe clean. Derrida's early essay on Foucault, "Cogito and the History of Madness" (in *Writing and Difference*), challenges the possibility of such historical "placing," but this argument has by no means been satisfactorily worked out, least of all by American new new critics.

Now, what do we find in Benjamin? For one thing, his late essays on Baudelaire exemplify an innovative criticism of the lyric intimately engaged with the question of how poetry relates to socio-cultural codes. Theodor Adorno found the relations Benjamin established too unmediated, and their letters about this are becoming a rich site for study and debate. I would emphasize again that the issue has not been resolved, and has scarcely been addressed by North American new new criticism. It is striking that in his notes for the uncompleted book on Baudelaire, Benjamin, writing in the later thirties, returns to his work of the twenties on baroque allegory—the work that has been decisive for de Man's rehabilitation of allegory. Benjamin is disturbed that he could seem to be saying the same thing about Baudelaire as he had about German poetry of two centuries earlier, and he strives, with what I find major success, to specify differences, both formally and contextually, between seventeenth-century allegory and nineteenth-century allegory.[6] That is, for Benjamin, the "same" rhetorical figure is not the same over history. Theoretical and rhetorical terms do not have trans-historical, typological validity.

Benjamin, Foucault, Bakhtin, all write the language of semiotics; the "sign" is fundamental in their analyses. The question is why the "sign," a human, arbitrary construction, must be understood as murderously negative by so many recent critics. For Vico, what humankind had made—preeminently language—could reliably be known by its maker, and thus it was in the realm of signs, rather than that of nature, that human knowledge was surest and most important. By the nineteenth century, Emerson wrote, "Things are in the saddle and ride mankind": human nature is dominated by its own productions. This is "alienation," but we must further question its status. Marxists, among others, hold that alienation may be historically explained. New new criticism seems to hold to a metaphysical explanation: the terror of the sign is part of the nature of language.[7] So it was for the old New Criticism, only blissfully: the glory of the symbol is part of the nature of poetry. De Man's concluding remarks here on Hegelian pyramidology allow "Egypt" to stand as the end term, the terminus, of inquiry. This "original" position, however, must face further historical and political questions, as Edward Said has shown.[8]

To raise the question of historical semiotics is also to attack the status of "the lyric." I would note that for New Criticism "lyric" was not an object of theoretical concern. Allen Tate locates "structure" not in "genre" but in "language."[9] *The Well Wrought Urn* is about "poetry," not about lyric, and this "critical monism" was attacked in *Critics and Criticism* (1952) by R. S. Crane, a Chicago neo-Aristotelian for whom genre was deeply important. Few of these papers work hard on actually addressing what is at stake in the notion of "lyric poetry." Most notions of lyric offered here are tactical, set up only to be devalued or rejected. The most common sense among those who

6. Benjamin's essays on Baudelaire are translated in *Charles Baudelaire: A Lyric Poet in the Era of High Capitalism* (London, 1973); the exchange with Adorno in *Aesthetics and Politics* (London, 1977), pp. 100–41. The notes on allegory are still untranslated. See fragments 20, 36, 44 in "Zentralpark," first fully published in *Charles Baudelaire*, ed. Rolf Tiedemann (Frankfurt am Main, 1974). For a Marxist appropriation of Benjamin's early work on baroque allegory, see John Beverley, "The Production of Solitude: Góngora and the State," *Ideologies and Literature*, 13 (1980), 23–41.

7. On this argument, see D. Sandy Petrey, "Representing Revolution," *Diacritics*, 9:2 (1979), esp. p. 16.

8. Edward Said, "Egyptian Rites," *Village Voice*, 30 August 1983, pp. 43–46.

9. "Longinus and the 'New Criticism,'" p. 184.

have used the notion is that lyric expresses pure subjectivity. This notion is very recent historically. I find nothing resembling it in Smith's *Elizabethan Critical Essays* and Spingarn's *Critical Essays of the Seventeenth Century*. It does not figure in Rosalie Colie's book on Marvell, whose index lists thirty-three types under "genre." Against positions like those of Annabel Patterson here, Alastair Fowler warns that "lyric" in literary theory from Cicero through Dryden is "not to be confused with the modern term."[10] Norman Maclean's study of eighteenth-century lyric theory confirms René Wellek's *History of Modern Criticism:* this definition of the lyric was only theoretically established in the early nineteenth century.[11] Hegel's *Aesthetics* provides a classic elaboration of the position, and this notion has provoked deconstructive activity in the wake of Derrida. Are the odes of Pindar instances of "pure subjectivity"? Hegel tellingly observes that we remember Pindar's name, not the names of those he praised, yet can such a debater's point stand against all the work of classical scholars? Hegel himself insists of lyric that "a concrete account is possible only if it is historical at the same time."

Hegel's recuperation of an alien culture and sensibility for the framework of his aesthetics—his idealization of Greece—exemplifies what Adorno meant by arguing in "Lyric and Society" for the historically limited validity of our notion of the "lyric." We could usefully go on to define "lyric" as the possibility of a certain kind of reading (this is a version of what de Man has done here and in "Anthropomorphism and Trope in the Lyric"), but even if texts from any period may occasion lyric reading, the question will then be whether that mode of reading is available at all times and places. It once seemed that such inquiry would be part of "structuralist poetics," but little research has been done to qualify one's initial impression: concretely, "lyric reading" has not been widely distributed within Western literature, in contrast to the Chinese and Japanese systems of literature.[12] This whole line of speculation makes clear how important for thinking about the lyric it would be to attend to the questions of translation.

To remain within the bounds set by the editors who asked that each essay work from at least one specific text, let me turn to another

10. Alastair Fowler, *Kinds of Literature* (Cambridge, Mass., 1982), p. 220.

11. Norman Maclean, "From Action to Image: Theories of the Lyric in the Eighteenth Century," in *Critics and Criticism,* ed. R. S. Crane (Chicago, 1952), p. 411. See also Fowler, *Kinds of Literature,* pp. 137, 206.

12. See Earl Miner, "On the Genesis and Development of Literary Systems," *Critical Inquiry,* 5 (1978–79), 339–53, 553–68.

paradigmatic classical instance: the ode of Sappho fragmentarily preserved by Longinus in section ten of *On the Sublime.* (Longinus is our only source for this text fundamental to the history of women's poetry. What would it be like for Western literature if we had of the Hebrew Bible only the opening words that he quotes?) Allen Tate New Critically emphasized Longinus's "transport" (*ekstasis*) in a proto-Coleridgean sense, as reconciling opposites and "making a unity." Rereading might find instead an emphasis that reveals unity as factitious.[13]

Even in Hegel we find this possibility. If the "central point of unity in a lyric" must be "the inner life of the poet," this is no simple matter. For this inner life is only "partly the individual's pure unity with himself"; it is also "partly . . . fragmented and dispersed into the most diversified particularization and most variegated multiplicity." What holds all this together is just that "one and the same self carries them, so to say, as their mere vessel." How then can the poet become "the centre which holds the whole lyric work of art together"? He must first achieve a "*specific* mood" (*Bestimmtheit* der Stimmung) and at the same time "must identify *himself* with this particularization of himself as with himself, so that in it he feels and envisages *himself.*"[14] Through this repetitive babble, one can make out a figurative procedure, basically synecdochal, which Hegel insists is the poet's unique means: "In this way alone does he then become a self-bounded subjective entity" (Totalität).

The procedure Longinus reads in Sappho is comparable. From their separation and dispersal she summons soul and body, ears and tongue, eyes and color: "The result is that we see in her not a single emotion but a [*synodos*] of emotions." *Synodos* is combined from *syn-* (together) and *hodos* (road), but in the compound the aspiration is lost and we hear resonances as well of "ode": the emotions sing together. A synodos is a coming together, a "convention," for as Longinus notes, all that Sappho writes is just the sort of thing that we take as what lovers feel. It is also a "crossroads," where the encounter of erotic passions may provoke violence, as in the Oedipal meeting of father and son at an intersection: a classicist writes of Sappho's "ex-

13. Cf. Neil Hertz, "A Reading of Longinus" (1973), *Critical Inquiry,* 9 (1983), 579–96.

14. *Hegel's Aesthetics,* trans. T. M. Knox (Oxford, 1975) 2:1133. The German reads, "Um den zusammenhaltenden Mittelpunkt des lyrischen Kunstwerks abgeben zu können, muss deshalb das Subjekt einerseits zur konkreten *Bestimmtheit* der Stimmung oder Situation fortgeschritten sein, andererseits sich mit dieser Besonderung seiner als mit sich selber *zusammenschliessen,* so dass es *sich* in derselben empfindet und vorstellt."

plosion" of body and mind.[15] One English translation is especially provocative: a "concourse," which is not, as in French, a competition, but "a large open space for the gathering or passage of crowds, as in a railroad station" (*American Heritage Dictionary*). Fighting one anachronism with another, we might then find Sappho's lyric less the expression of a unique soul than a means of mass access to public transport.[16]

15. W. R. Johnson, *The Idea of Lyric* (Berkeley, 1982), p. 39.
16. I am grateful to Andrew Parker for valuable suggestions regarding an earlier draft of this essay.

NOTES ON CONTRIBUTORS

JONATHAN ARAC is author of *Commissioned Spirits* (Rutgers University Press, 1979) and co-editor of *The Yale Critics* (University of Minnesota Press, 1983). An assistant editor and regular contributor at *Boundary 2*, he has put together a special issue, "Engagements: Postmodernism, Marxism, Politics" (Winter 1983). His essays on fiction, criticism, and poetry of the last two centuries have appeared in such journals as *PMLA, Diacritics, ELH,* and *Salmagundi.* He teaches English at the University of Illinois–Chicago.

JOHN BRENKMAN is an Associate Professor at Northwestern University in the Program in Comparative Literature and Theory and the English Department. An editor of the journal *Social Text,* he has published articles on ancient and modern literature, theory, and contemporary culture. His book, *Culture and Domination,* is forthcoming from Cornell University Press.

DAVID BROMWICH is Associate Professor of English at Princeton University, and the author of *Hazlitt: The Mind of a Critic* (Oxford University Press, 1984).

CYNTHIA CHASE, Assistant Professor of English at Cornell University, has published articles on George Eliot, Wordsworth, Baudelaire and Rousseau, Kleist, and Freud. She is working on a study of intertextual relationships in Romantic writing.

ELEANOR COOK is an Associate Professor of English at Victoria College, University of Toronto. She is the author of *Brownings's Lyrics: An*

Exploration (University of Toronto Press, 1974) and has published essays on nineteenth- and twentieth-century literature in *American Literature*, *ELH*, and elsewhere. She is currently working on a study of the poetry of Wallace Stevens.

JONATHAN CULLER is Class of 1916 Professor of English and Comparative Literature at Cornell University and the author of six books: *Flaubert: The Uses of Uncertainty* (1974), *Structuralist Poetics: Structuralism, Linguistics, and the Study of Literature* (1975), *The Pursuit of Signs: Semiotics, Literature, Deconstruction* (1981), and *On Deconstruction: Literary Theory after Structuralism* (1982), all published by Cornell University Press, and two books in the Modern Masters series: *Ferdinand de Saussure* (Penguin, 1977) and *Roland Barthes* (Oxford University Press, 1983).

PAUL DE MAN was at the time of his death Sterling Professor of the Humanities at Yale University. He is the author of *Blindness and Insight: Essays in the Rhetoric of Contemporary Criticism* (Oxford University Press, 1971), *Allegories of Reading: Figural Language in Rousseau, Nietzsche, Rilke, and Proust* (Yale University Press, 1979), and *The Rhetoric of Romanticism* (Columbia University Press, 1984).

JOEL FINEMAN is the author of various articles on Shakespeare and on literary theory. His book, *Shakespeare's Perjur'd Eye: The Invention of Subjectivity in Shakespeare's Sonnets*, is forthcoming from the University of California Press. He is Associate Professor of English at the University of California at Berkeley.

STANLEY FISH is the William Kenan, Jr., Professor of English and Humanities at Johns Hopkins University. His forthcoming publications include *Milton's Aesthetic of Testimony* and *Change: Studies in Professionalism, Literary Criticism, and the Law.*

NORTHROP FRYE is a University Professor in the University of Toronto, a Professor of English at Victoria College, and Chancellor of Victoria University. His publications include *Fearful Symmetry: A Study of William Blake* (Princeton University Press, 1947), *Anatomy of Criticism* (Princeton University Press, 1957), *Fables of Identity* (Harcourt, Brace & World, 1963), *A Study of English Romanticism* (Random House, 1968), *The Critical Path* (Indiana University Press, 1971), *The Secular Scripture* (Harvard University Press, 1976), and *The Great Code* (Academic Press, 1983).

JOHN HOLLANDER is a poet and a Professor of English at Yale University. His most recent critical studies are *Vision and Resonance: Two Senses of Poetic Form* (Oxford University Press, 1975) and *The Figure of Echo* (University of California Press, 1981); his most recent books of poetry are *Spectral Emanations* (Antheneum, 1978), *Blue Wine* (Johns Hopkins University Press, 1979), and *Powers of Thirteen* (Atheneum, 1983).

CHAVIVA HOŠEK is an Associate Professor of English at Victoria College, University of Toronto. She is the author of essays on Canadian poetry, Canadian fiction, Walt Whitman, and Canadian politics and women. She is currently completing a book called *The Rhetoric of Walt Whitman.*

MARY JACOBUS is Professor of English at Cornell University and the author of *Tradition and Experiment in Wordsworth's Lyrical Ballads* (Oxford University Press, 1976). She is the editor of *Women Writing and Writing about Women* (Croom Helm, 1979) and has written essays on, among others, Wordsworth, Romantic prose, Charlotte Brontë, George Eliot, Thomas Hardy, and feminist literary criticism and theory. At present she is working on a book on *The Prelude,* Romanticism, and writing, and she plans another work on Thomas Hardy.

FREDRIC JAMESON, who teaches at the University of California at Santa Cruz, is the author of *Marxism and Form* (Princeton University Press, 1971), *The Prison-House of Language* (Princeton University Press, 1972), and *The Political Unconscious* (Cornell University Press, 1981).

BARBARA JOHNSON is Professor of Romance Languages and Literatures at Harvard. She is author of *Défigurations: du langage poétique* (Flammarion, 1979), and *The Critical Difference* (Johns Hopkins University Press, 1980), translator of Derrida's *Dissemination* (University of Chicago Press, 1982), and editor of *Yale French Studies,* no. 63, entitled *The Pedagogical Imperative: Teaching as a Literary Genre.*

MARY NYQUIST teaches in the literary studies and women's studies programs at the University of Toronto. The author of articles on Milton and feminist theory, she is currently completing a book on Milton entitled *The Temptation against the Word.* She is also involved in a study of mentors and muses in nineteenth- and early twentieth-century English literature.

Patricia Parker, Professor of English and Comparative Literature at the University of Toronto, is the author of articles on A. R. Ammons, Spenser, Shakespeare, Coleridge, Mallarmé, and others and of *Inescapable Romance: Studies in the Poetics of a Mode* (Princeton University Press, 1979). She is now writing a book on metaphor entitled *The Metaphorical Plot,* and a study of rhetoric in the Renaissance.

Julian Patrick, Associate Professor of English at Victoria College, University of Toronto, teaches courses on the history and theory of literary criticism and on Shakespeare. He has written on Shakespeare and on Aristotle.

Annabel Patterson has taught at the University of Toronto, York University, and the University of Maryland where she currently chairs the English Department. She is the author of *Hermogenes and the Renaissance: Seven Ideas of Style* (Princeton University Press, 1970) and *Marvell and the Civic Crown* (Princeton University Press, 1978) as well as articles on Tasso, Sidney, Donne, Herbert, and Milton. She has just completed a new book, *The Hermeneutics of Censorship and the Politics of Genre.*

Tilottama Rajan teaches at Queen's University. She has published *Dark Interpreter: The Discourse of Romanticism* (Cornell University Press, 1980), as well as articles on Coleridge, Wordsworth, Yeats, and Donne. She is currently at work on a book on hermeneutics and Romanticism, which will involve Romantic theories of the reading process and analyses of how problems of reading, communication, and discourse are thematized in Romantic texts.

Herbert F. Tucker teaches English at the University of Michigan. He has published essays on Spenser, Milton, Goldsmith, Shelley, Browning, and Hopkins, as well as a book, *Browning's Beginnings: The Art of Disclosure* (University of Minnesota Press, 1980). Currently he is writing a book-length study of Tennyson's romanticism.

Eugene Vance, Professor of Comparative Literature at Emory University, is the author of numerous essays about medieval poetics and theories of language, and has recently completed a new book on this subject. His first book, *Reading the Song of Roland* (Prentice-Hall), appeared in 1970, and he has co-edited, with Lucie Brin d'Amour, a volume of essays entitled *Archéologie du signe,* forthcoming from the Pontifical Institute of Mediaeval Studies.

SHELDON ZITNER is a Professor of English at Trinity College, University of Toronto. He teaches courses in Renaissance literature and in criticism and has written on topics in Renaissance poetry and drama. He has edited Beaumont and Fletcher's *The Knight of the Burning Pestle* for the Revels Plays series (University of Manchester and Johns Hopkins University).

SUGGESTIONS FOR FURTHER READING

The following includes a selected bibliography of references cited in the text.

Abel, Elizabeth, ed. *Writing and Sexual Difference.* Chicago: University of Chicago Press, 1982.

Abrams, M. H. "The Deconstructive Angel." *Critical Inquiry,* 3 (1977), 425–38.

———. "How to Do Things with Texts." *Partisan Review,* 46 (1979), 566–88.

———. *The Mirror and the Lamp: Romantic Theory and the Critical Tradition.* New York: Oxford University Press, 1953.

Adorno, Theodor W. "Rede über Lyrik und Gesellschaft." *Akzente,* 4 (1957), 8–26. English translation, Bruce Mayo, "Lyric Poetry and Society." *Telos,* 20 (1974), 56–71.

Althusser, Louis. *For Marx.* Trans. Ben Brewster. London: Allen Lane, 1969.

Altieri, Charles. *Enlarging the Temple: New Directions in American Poetry during the 1960s.* Lewisburg, Pa.: Bucknell University Press, 1979.

———. "Wittgenstein on Consciousness and Language: A Challenge to Derridean Literary Theory." *Modern Language Notes,* 91 (1976), 1397–1423.

Amacher, Richard E., and Victor Lange, eds. *New Perspectives in German Literary Criticism.* Princeton: Princeton University Press, 1979.

Arac, Jonathan. "Bounding Lines: *The Prelude* and Critical Revision." *Boundary 2,* 7:3 (1979), 31–48.

———, et al., eds. *The Yale Critics: Deconstruction in America.* Minneapolis: University of Minnesota Press, 1983.

Arato, Andrew, and Eike Gebhardt, eds. *The Essential Frankfurt School Reader.* New York: Urizen Books, 1978.

Attridge, Derek. *The Rhythms of English Poetry.* London: Longman, 1982.

Bakhtin, Mikhail. *The Dialogic Imagination.* Ed. Michael Holquist. Austin: Univerity of Texas Press, 1981.

Barthes, Roland. *L'Empire des signes.* Geneva: Skira, 1970.

______. *Writing Degree Zero and Elements of Semiology.* Trans. Annette Lavers and Colin Smith. London: Jonathan Cape, 1967.

Benjamin, Walter. *Charles Baudelaire: A Lyric Poet in the Era of High Capitalism.* Trans. Harry Zohn. London: New Left Books, 1973.

______. *Illuminations.* Trans. Harry Zohn. New York: Schocken, 1969.

Bennett, Tony. *Formalism and Marxism.* London: Methuen, 1979.

Benveniste, Emile. *Problems in General Linguistics.* Trans. M. E. Meek. Coral Gables, Fla.: University of Miami Press, 1971.

Blackmur, R. P. *Language as Gesture.* New York: Harcourt, Brace, 1952.

______. *The Lion and the Honeycomb.* New York: Harcourt, Brace, 1952.

Bloom, Harold. *The Anxiety of Influence.* New York: Oxford University Press, 1973.

______. *A Map of Misreading.* New York: Oxford University Press, 1975.

______. *Poetry and Repression.* New Haven: Yale University Press, 1976.

______. *The Visionary Company: A Reading of English Romantic Poetry.* Rev. ed. Ithaca: Cornell University Press, 1971.

______. *Wallace Stevens.* Ithaca: Cornell University Press, 1977.

______, et al., eds. *Deconstruction and Criticism.* New York: Seabury, 1979.

Booth, Stephen. *An Essay on Shakespeare's Sonnets.* New Haven: Yale University Press, 1969.

Booth, Wayne. *Critical Understanding.* Chicago: University of Chicago Press, 1979.

Bové, Paul A. *Destructive Poetics: Heidegger and Modern American Poetry.* New York: Columbia University Press, 1980.

Brisman, Leslie. *Milton's Poetry of Choice and Its Romantic Heirs.* Ithaca: Cornell University Press, 1973.

______. *Romantic Origins.* Ithaca: Cornell University Press, 1978.

Brooks, Cleanth. *Modern Poetry and the Tradition.* Chapel Hill: University of North Carolina Press, 1939.

______. *The Well Wrought Urn.* New York: Harcourt Brace, 1947.

______, and Robert Penn Warren. *Understanding Poetry: An Anthology for College Students.* New York: Holt, 1938.

Brower, Reuben A. *The Fields of Light.* New York: Oxford University Press, 1951.

______, ed. *Forms of Lyric.* New York: Columbia University Press, 1970.

______, and Richard Poirier, eds. *In Defense of Reading.* New York: Dutton, 1962.

Burke, Kenneth. *A Grammar of Motives.* New York: Prentice Hall, 1945.

______. *A Rhetoric of Motives.* Berkeley: University of California Press, 1950.

Cameron, Sharon. *Lyric Time: Dickinson and the Limits of Genre.* Baltimore: Johns Hopkins University Press, 1979.

Chase, Cynthia. "The Accidents of Disfiguration: Limits to Literal and Rhetorical Reading in Book V of *The Prelude*." *Studies in Romanticism,* 18 (1979), 547–55.

______. "Paragon, Parergon: Baudelaire Translates Rousseau." *Diacritics,* 11:2 (1981), 42–51.

Chatman, Seymour. *A Theory of Metre.* The Hague: Mouton, 1965.

______, ed. *Literary Style: A Symposium.* London: Oxford University Press, 1971.

Cixous, Hélène. "Le Rire de la Méduse." *L'Arc,* 61 (1975), 3–54. English translation, "The Laugh of the Medusa," in *New French Feminisms,* ed. Elaine Marks and Isabelle de Courtivron. Amherst: University of Massachusetts Press, 1980.

Colie, Rosalie. *"My echoing song": Andrew Marvell's Poetry of Criticism.* Princeton: Princeton University Press, 1970.

______. *The Resources of Kind: Genre-Theory in the Renaissance.* Ed. Barbara K. Lewalski. Berkeley: University of California Press, 1973.

Cook, Eleanor. "Riddles, Charms and Fictions in Wallace Stevens." In *Centre and Labyrinth: Essays in Honour of Northrop Frye.* Toronto: University of Toronto Press, 1983.

Crane, R. S. "The Critical Monism of Cleanth Brooks." In *Critics and Criticism, Ancient and Modern.* Ed. R. S. Crane et al. Chicago: University of Chicago Press, 1952.

______. *The Languages of Criticism and the Structure of Poetry.* Toronto: University of Toronto Press, 1953.

Culler, Jonathan. *Barthes.* Glasgow: Fontana, 1983.

______. *Ferdinand de Saussure.* Glasgow: Fontana, 1976.

______. *On Deconstruction.* Ithaca: Cornell University Press, 1982.

______. *The Pursuit of Signs.* Ithaca: Cornell University Press, 1981.

______. *Structuralist Poetics.* Ithaca: Cornell University Press, 1975.

de Man, Paul. *Allegories of Reading.* New Haven: Yale University Press, 1979.

______. "Anthropomorphism and Trope in the Lyric." In *The Rhetoric of Romanticism.* New York: Columbia University Press, 1984.

______. "Autobiography as De-facement." *Modern Language Notes,* 94 (1979), 919–30.

______. *Blindness and Insight.* Rev. ed. Minneapolis: University of Minnesota Press, 1983.

______. "Hypogram and Inscription: Michael Riffaterre's Poetics of Reading." *Diacritics,* 11:4 (1981), 17–35.

______. "Intentional Structure of the Romantic Image." In *Romanticism and Consciousness.* Ed. Harold Bloom. New York: Norton, 1970.

______. "Introduction" to Hans Robert Jauss, *Toward an Aesthetic of Reception.* Trans. Timothy Bahti. Minneapolis: University of Minnesota Press, 1982.

______. "The Resistance to Literary Theory." *Yale French Studies,* 63 (1982), 3–20.

______. "Symbolic Landscape in Wordsworth and Yeats." In *Defense of Reading*. Ed. Reuben Brower and Richard Poirier. New York: Dutton, 1962.
Derrida, Jacques. *Dissemination*. Trans. Barbara Johnson. Chicago: University of Chicago Press, 1981.
______. *Margins of Philosophy*. Trans. Alan Bass. Chicago: University of Chicago Press, 1982.
______. *Of Grammatology*. Trans. Gayatri C. Spivak. Baltimore: Johns Hopkins University Press, 1976.
______. *The Post Card*. Chicago: University of Chicago Press, 1984. English translation of *La Carte postale: De Socrate à Freud et au-delà*. Paris: Flammarion, 1980.
______. *Speech and Phenomena*. Trans. David B. Allison. Evanston: Northwestern University Press, 1973.
______. "White Mythology." Trans. F. C. T. Moore. *New Literary History*, 6 (1974), 5–74.
______. *Writing and Difference*. Trans. Alan Bass. Chicago: University of Chicago Press, 1978.
Doggett, Frank, and Robert Buttell, eds. *Wallace Stevens: A Celebration*. Princeton: Princeton University Press, 1980.
Donoghue, Denis. *Ferocious Alphabets*. Boston: Little, Brown, 1981.
Doubrovsky, Serge. *The New Criticism in France*. Trans. D. Coltman. Intro. Edward Wasiolek. Chicago: University of Chicago Press, 1973.

Eagleton, Terry. *Literary Theory: An Introduction*. Oxford: Basil Blackwell, 1983.
______. *Marxism and Literary Criticism*. London: Methuen, 1976.
Easthope, Antony. *Poetry as Discourse*. London: Methuen, 1983.
Eliot, T. S. *On Poetry and Poets*. New York: Farrar, Straus & Cudahy, 1957.
______. *The Sacred Wood* (1920). 3rd ed. London: Methuen, 1932.
______. *Selected Essays, 1917–32*. New York: Harcourt, Brace, 1932.
______. *The Three Voices of Poetry*. London: Cambridge University Press, 1953.
______. *The Use of Poetry and the Use of Criticism*. Cambridge, Mass.: Harvard University Press, 1933.
Ellmann, Maud. "Floating the Pound: The Circulation of the Subject of 'The Cantos.'" *Oxford Literary Review*, 3:3 (1979), 16–27.
______. *Modernist Writing and the Problem of the Subject*. Sussex: Harvester, 1985.
Elton, William. *A Glossary of the New Criticism*. Chicago: Modern Poetry Association, 1949.
Empson, William. *Seven Types of Ambiguity*. London: Chatto & Windus, 1930.
______. *Some Versions of Pastoral*. London: Chatto & Windus, 1935.
______. *The Structure of Complex Words*. London: Chatto & Windus, 1951.

Ferguson, Frances. *Wordsworth: Language as Counter Spirit*. New Haven: Yale University Press, 1977.

Fish, Stanley E. *Is There a Text in This Class? The Authority of Interpretive Communities.* Cambridge, Mass.: Harvard University Press, 1980.

______. *Self-Consuming Artifacts: The Experience of Seventeenth-Century Literature.* Berkeley: University of California Press, 1973.

Forrest-Thomson, Veronica. *Poetic Artifice: A Theory of Twentieth-Century Poetry.* New York: St. Martins Press, 1978.

Foucault, Michel. *The Archaeology of Knowledge.* Trans. A. M. Sheridan Smith. New York: Harper & Row, 1976.

______. *Language, Counter-Memory, Practice: Selected Essays and Interviews.* Trans. Donald F. Bouchard and Sherry Simon. Ithaca: Cornell University Press, 1977.

______. *The Order of Things: An Archaeology of the Human Sciences.* London: Tavistock, 1976. English translation of *Les Mots and les choses: Une archéologie des sciences humaines.* Paris: Gallimard, 1966.

Fowler, Alastair. *Kinds of Literature: An Introduction to the Theory of Genres and Modes.* Cambridge, Mass.: Harvard University Press, 1982.

______. *Triumphal Forms: Structural Patterns in Elizabethan Poetry.* Cambridge: Cambridge University Press, 1970.

Fowler, Roger. *Style and Structure in Literature: Essays in the New Stylistics.* Ithaca: Cornell University Press, 1975.

Freccero, John. "The Fig Tree and the Laurel: Petrarch's Poetics." *Diacritics,* 5:1 (Spring 1975), 34–39.

Fry,Paul. *The Poet's Calling in the English Ode.* New Haven: Yale University Press, 1980.

Frye, Northrop. *Anatomy of Criticism.* Princeton: Princeton University Press, 1957.

______. *Fearful Symmetry: A Study of William Blake.* Princeton: Princeton University Press, 1947.

Genette, Gérard. *Figures of Literary Discourse.* Trans. Alan Sheridan. New York: Columbia University Press, 1982.

Gilbert, Sandra M., and Susan Gubar. *The Madwoman in the Attic: The Woman Writer and the Nineteenth-Century Literary Imagination.* New Haven: Yale University Press, 1979.

______, eds. *Shakespeare's Sisters: Feminist Essays on Women Poets.* Bloomington: Indiana University Press, 1979.

Graff, Gerald. *Literature against Itself.* Chicago: University of Chicago Press, 1977.

______. *Poetic Statement and Critical Dogma.* Chicago: University of Chicago Press, 1970.

Gramsci, Antonio. *Selections from the Prison Notebooks.* Ed. and trans. Quinton Hoare and Geoffrey Nowell Smith. New York: International Publishers, 1971.

Greimas, A.-J. *Sémantique structurale.* Paris: Larousse, 1966.

Guillén, Claudio. *Literature as System: Essays toward the Theory of Literary History.* Princeton: Princeton University Press, 1971.

Guillory, John. "The Ideology of Canon-Formation: T. S. Eliot and Cleanth Brooks." *Critical Inquiry,* 10:1 (1983), 173–98.

Hamlin, Cyrus. "The Hermeneutics of Form: Reading the Romantic Ode." *Boundary 2,* 7:3 (1979), 1–30.

Harth, Phillip. "The New Criticism and Eighteenth-Century Poetry." *Critical Inquiry,* 7:3 (1981), 512–37.

Hartman, Charles O. *Free Verse: An Essay on Prosody.* Princeton: Princeton University Press, 1980.

Hartman, Geoffrey. *Beyond Formalism.* New Haven: Yale University Press, 1971.

———. *Criticism in the Wilderness.* New Haven: Yale University Press, 1980.

———. *The Fate of Reading.* Chicago: University of Chicago Press, 1975.

———. *The Unmediated Vision: An Interpretation of Wordsworth, Hopkins, Rilke, and Valéry.* New Haven: Yale University Press, 1954.

———. "The Use and Abuse of Structural Analysis: Riffaterre's Interpretation of Wordsworth's 'Yew-Trees.'" *New Literary History,* 7:1 (1975), 165–89.

———. *Wordsworth's Poetry.* New Haven: Yale University Press, 1964.

Hawkes, Terence. *Structuralism and Semiotics.* Berkeley: University of California Press, 1977.

Hirsch, E. D., Jr. *Validity in Interpretation.* New Haven: Yale University Press, 1967.

Holland, Norman. *Poems in Persons: An Introduction to the Psychoanalysis of Literature.* New York: Norton, 1973.

Hollander, John. *The Figure of Echo: A Mode of Allusion in Milton and After.* Berkeley: University of California Press, 1981.

———. *Powers of Thirteen.* New York: Atheneum, 1983.

———. *Rhyme's Reason.* New Haven: Yale University Press, 1981.

———. *Vision and Resonance: Two Senses of Poetic Form.* New York: Oxford University Press, 1975.

Homans, Margaret. *Women Writers and Poetic Identity.* Princeton: Princeton University Press, 1980.

Irigaray, Luce. *Ce Sexe qui n'en est pas un.* Paris: Editions de Minuit, 1977. English translation, "This Sex Which Is Not One," in *New French Feminisms,* ed. Elaine Marks and Isabelle de Courtivron. Amherst: University of Massachusetts Press, 1980.

———. *Speculum de l'autre femme.* Paris: Editions de Minuit, 1974. English translation, *Speculum: The Other Woman.* Trans. Gillian Gill. Ithaca: Cornell University Press, 1984.

Jacobs, Carol. *The Dissimulating Harmony.* Baltimore: Johns Hopkins University Press, 1978.

Jacobus, Mary. *Tradition and Experiment in Wordsworth's Lyrical Ballads (1798).* Oxford: Clarendon Press, 1976.

———, ed. *Women Writing and Writing about Women.* New York: Barnes & Noble, 1979.

Jakobson, Roman. "Linguistics and Poetics." *The Structuralists.* Ed. R. T. De George and F. M. De George. New York: Doubleday, 1972.

———. *Questions de poétique.* Paris: Seuil, 1973.

———, and Claude Lévi-Strauss. "Charles Baudelaire's 'Les Chats.'" In *The Structuralists.* R. T. and F. M. De George. New York: Doubleday, 1972.

Jameson, Fredric. *The Political Unconscious.* Ithaca: Cornell University Press, 1981.

———. *The Prison-House of Language: A Critical Account of Structuralism and Russian Formalism.* Princeton: Princeton University Press, 1972.

Jarrell, Randall. *The Third Book of Criticism.* New York: Farrar, Straus & Giroux, 1969.

Jauss, Hans Robert. *Aesthetic Experience and Literary Hermeneutics.* Trans. Michael Shaw. Minneapolis: University of Minnesota Press, 1982.

———. *Toward an Aesthetic of Reception.* Trans. Timothy Bahti. Minneapolis: University of Minnesota Press, 1982.

Johnson, Barbara. *The Critical Difference.* Baltimore: Johns Hopkins University Press, 1980.

———. *Défigurations du langage poétique.* Paris: Flammarion, 1979.

Johnson, W. R. *The Idea of Lyric: Lyric Modes in Ancient and Modern Poetry.* Berkeley: University of California Press, 1982.

Juhasz, Suzanne, ed. *Feminist Critics Read Emily Dickinson.* Bloomington: Indiana University Press, 1983.

Kermode, Frank. *Romantic Image.* London: Routledge & Kegan Paul, 1957.

Krieger, Murray. "Critical Dogma and the New Critical Historians." 1958; reprinted in *The Play and Place of Criticism.* Baltimore: Johns Hopkins University Press, 1967.

———. *The New Apologists for Poetry.* Minneapolis: University of Minnesota Press, 1956.

———. *Theory of Criticism.* Baltimore: Johns Hopkins University Press, 1976.

Kristeva, Julia. *Desire and Language: A Semiotic Approach to Literature and Art.* Ed. Leon S. Roudiez. Trans. Thomas Gora et al. New York: Columbia University Press, 1980.

———. *La Révolution du langage poétique.* Paris: Editions du Seuil, 1974.

Lacan, Jacques. *Ecrits: A Selection.* Trans. Alan Sheridan. London: Tavistock, 1977.

———. *The Four Fundamental Concepts of Psychoanalysis.* London: Tavistock, 1977.

———. *The Language of the Self.* Trans. Anthony Wilden. New York: Dell, 1968.

Lentricchia, Frank. *After the New Criticism.* Chicago: University of Chicago Press, 1980.

Lipking, Lawrence I. *The Life of the Poet: Beginning and Ending Poetic Careers.* Chicago: University of Chicago Press, 1981.

Mack, Maynard. *The Garden and the City: Retirement and Politics in the Later Poetry of Pope, 1731–1743.* Toronto: University of Toronto Press, 1969.

______. "The Muse of Satire." *Yale Review,* 41 (1951), 80–92.

Macksey, Richard, and Eugenio Donato, eds. *The Structuralist Controversy: The Languages of Criticism and the Sciences of Man.* Baltimore: Johns Hopkins University Press, 1972.

Maclean, Norman. "From Action to Image: Theories of the Lyric in the Eighteenth Century." In *Critics and Criticism Ancient and Modern.* Ed. R. S. Crane. Chicago: University of Chicago Press, 1952.

Marcuse, Herbert. *The Aesthetic Dimension: Toward a Critique of Marxist Aesthetics.* Boston: Beacon, 1978.

McCallum, Pamela. *Literature and Method: Towards a Critique of I. A. Richards, T. S. Eliot and F. R. Leavis.* Atlantic Highlands: Humanities Press, 1982.

McGann, Jerome J. *A Critique of Modern Textual Criticism.* Chicago: University of Chicago Press, 1983.

______. *Don Juan in Context.* Chicago: University of Chicago Press, 1976.

______. *The Romantic Ideology.* Chicago: University of Chicago Press, 1983.

Mendelson, Edward. *Early Auden.* New York: Viking, 1981.

Miller, J. Hillis. "Deconstructing the Deconstructors." *Diacritics,* 5:3 (1975), 24–31.

______. "The New Criticism." *The American Scholar,* 20 (1951), 218–31.

______. *Poets of Reality: Six Twentieth-Century Writers.* Cambridge: Belknap, 1965.

______. "Stevens' Rock and Criticism as Cure" [I & II]. *Georgia Review,* 3:1 (1976), 5–31; 2 (1976), 330–48.

______. "The Still Heart: Poetic Form in Wordsworth." *New Literary History,* 2:2 (1971), 297–310.

Norris, Christopher. *Deconstruction: Theory and Practice.* London: Methuen, 1982.

Ogden, C. K., and I. A. Richards. *The Meaning of Meaning.* New York: Harcourt, Brace, 1923.

Parker, Patricia. *Inescapable Romance.* Princeton: Princeton University Press, 1979.

Rader, Ralph. "The Concept of Genre and Eighteenth-Century Studies." In *New Approaches to the Eighteenth Century.* Ed. Phillip Harth. New York: Columbia University Press, 1974.

Rajan, Tilottama. *Dark Interpreter.* Ithaca: Cornell University Press, 1980.

Ransom, John Crowe. *The New Criticism.* Norfolk, Conn.: New Directions, 1941.

———. *Poems and Essays.* New York: Vintage, 1955.
———. *The World's Body.* Port Washington, N.Y.: Kennikat, 1964.
Reed, Arden, ed. *Romanticism and Language.* Ithaca: Cornell University Press, 1984.
Richards, I. A. *The Philosophy of Rhetoric.* London: Oxford University Press, 1936.
———. *Practical Criticism.* New York: Harcourt, Brace, 1929.
———. *Principles of Literary Criticism.* New York: Harcourt, Brace, 1925.
Riddel, Joseph. *The Clairvoyant Eye: The Poetry and Poetics of Wallace Stevens.* Baton Rouge: Louisiana State University Press, 1965.
———. "From Heidegger to Derrida to Chance: Doubling and (Poetic) Language." *Boundary 2,* 4:2 (1976), 571–92.
———. "Interpreting Stevens: An Essay on Poetry and Thinking." *Boundary 2,* 1:1 (1972), 79–97.
———. *The Inverted Bell: Modernism and the Counterpoetics of William Carlos Williams.* Baton Rouge: Louisiana State University Press, 1974.
———. "'Keep Your Pecker Up'—*Paterson Five* and the Question of Metapoetry." *Glyph,* 8 (1981), 203–31.
Riffaterre, Michael. "Describing Poetic Structures: Two Approaches to Baudelaire's 'Les Chats.'" In *Reader-Response Criticism.* Ed. Jane P. Tompkins. Baltimore: Johns Hopkins University Press, 1980.
———. *Essais de stylistique structurale.* Paris: Flammarion, 1971.
———. "Interpretation and Descriptive Poetry: A Reading of Wordsworth's 'Yew-Trees.'" *New Literary History,* 4 (1973), 229–56.
———. *La Production du texte.* Paris: Editions du Seuil, 1979.
———. *Semiotics of Poetry.* Bloomington: Indiana University Press, 1978.
Rogers, William Elford. *The Three Genres and the Interpretation of Lyric.* Princeton: Princeton University Press, 1983.
Ryan, Michael. *Marxism and Deconstruction.* Baltimore: Johns Hopkins University Press, 1982.

Said, Edward. *Beginnings.* New York: Basic Books, 1975.
———. *The World, the Text and the Critic.* Cambridge, Mass.: Harvard University Press, 1983.
Scholes, Robert. *Elements of Poetry.* New York: Oxford University Press, 1969.
Simpson, David. *Irony and Authority in Romantic Poetry.* London: Macmillan, 1979.
Simpson, Lewis P., ed. *The Possibilities of Order: Cleanth Brooks and His Work.* Baton Rouge: Louisiana State University Press, 1976.
Smith, Barbara Herrnstein. *On the Margins of Discourse.* Chicago: University of Chicago Press, 1978.
———. *Poetic Closure: A Study of How Poems End.* Chicago: University of Chicago Press, 1968.
Stallman, Robert W., ed. *Critiques and Essays in Criticism, 1920–1948.* New York: Ronald Press, 1949.

Stierle, Karlheinz. "Position and Negation in Mallarmé's 'Prose pour des Esseintes.'" *Yale French Studies,* no. 54 (1977), 96–117.
Suleiman, Susan R., and Inge Crosman, eds. *The Reader in the Text.* Princeton: Princeton University Press, 1980.

Tate, Allen. *Collected Essays.* Denver: Swallow, 1959.
———. *Essays of Four Decades.* Chicago: Swallow, 1968.
———, ed. *The Language of Poetry.* New York: Russell & Russell, 1942.
———. *The Man of Letters in the Modern World.* New York: Meridian, 1955.
Tompkins, Jane P., ed. *Reader-Response Criticism.* Baltimore: Johns Hopkins University Press, 1980.
Tucker, Herbert F., Jr. *Browning's Beginnings.* Minneapolis: University of Minnesota Press, 1980.

Vendler, Helen. *The Odes of Keats.* Cambridge, Mass.: Harvard University Press, 1983.
Vickers, Nancy J. "Diana Described: Scattered Woman and Scattered Rhyme." *Critical Inquiry,* 8:2 (1981), 265–79.

Warning, Rainer, ed. *Rezeptionsästhetik.* Munich: Fink, 1975.
Warren, Robert Penn. *Selected Essays.* London: Eyre & Spottiswoode, 1964.
Wellek, René, and Austin Warren. *Theory of Literature.* New York: Harcourt, Brace, 1949.
Welsh, Andrew. *Roots of Lyric.* Princeton: Princeton University Press, 1978.
Wesling, Donald. *The Chances of Rhyme.* Berkeley: University of California Press, 1980.
———. *The New Poetries: Poetic Form since Wordsworth and Coleridge.* Lewisburg, Pa.: Bucknell University Press, 1984.
Wimsatt, W. K. *Day of the Leopards: Essays in Defense of Poems.* New Haven: Yale University Press, 1976.
———. "Genesis: An Argument Resumed." In *The Disciplines of Criticism.* Ed. Peter Demetz et al. New Haven: Yale University Press, 1968.
———. *Hateful Contraries: Studies in Literature and Criticism.* Lexington: University of Kentucky Press, 1965.
———. *The Verbal Icon.* Lexington: University of Kentucky Press, 1954.
———, and Cleanth Brooks. *Literary Criticism: A Short History.* New York: Knopf, 1957.

Zumthor, Paul. *Essai de poétique médiévale.* Paris: Seuil, 1972.
———. *Langue, texte, énigme.* Paris: Seuil, 1975.

INDEX